The
Holy Quran
—Verbatim

An Innovative Translation

The
Holy Quran
—Verbatim

An Innovative Translation

Dr. Mary Saad Assel

Northville, Michigan

THE HOLY QURAN–VERBATIM
Copyright © 2025 Dr. Mary Saad Assel

Print ISBN: 979-8993133300
Ebook ISBN: 979-8993133317

All rights reserved. No part of this publication may be reproduced, stored in a retrieval system, or transmitted in any form or by any means, electronic, mechanical, recording, or otherwise, without the prior written permission of the author.

Published by Solace Press, Northville, Michigan

Library of Congress Cataloging in Publication Data
ASSEL, MARY SAAD
THE HOLY QURAN – VERBATIM by DR. MARY SAAD ASSEL
Library of Congress Control Number: 2025920545

Dr. Mary Assel's translation of the Arabic Quran that she has written in contemporary English subtracts nothing from the original revelations of the Archangel Gabriel to the Prophet Muhammad. She makes the Quran accessible to non-Arabic reading audiences from around the world. Every word and verse are written with specificity and clarity.

–Imam Mohammad Mardini
American Muslim Center, Dearborn, Michigan

The Holy Quran, the only Scripture considered to be the explicit word of God, offers Muslim readers the guidance they need to conduct their daily lives according to God's directives. Dr. Mary Assel's yields a translation that has made this Holy Book an impeccable reference to non-Arabic readers as she refrains from the use of archaic language. She helps to lighten the read and preserve the true meaning of the Holy Quran simultaneously. Her translation is written with impeccable style and eloquence.

–Imam Mohammed Ali Elahi
Islamic House of Wisdom, Dearborn, Michigan

Mary Saad Assel earned her doctorate in Curriculum and Instruction with a specialty in brain science, from Wayne State University in Detroit, Michigan. She is a retired professor and former administrator of the English Language Institute at Henry Ford College in Dearborn, Michigan, as well as a retired adjunct instructor of Bilingual Linguistic Studies at Wayne State University. A certified Arabic-to-English translator, Dr. Assel possesses advanced expertise in translating the grammar and syntax of both languages. Her deep understanding of cultural differences between Arabic and English-speaking communities is essential for preventing misinterpretations. Skilled in various techniques like adaptation, transliteration, and terminology management, she ensures her translations are accurate and culturally relevant. With meticulous attention to detail, she checks grammar, spelling, and meaning to maintain the integrity of her work. Her native-like fluency in both languages enables her to convey complex ideas, idiomatic expressions, and grammatical nuances with precision.

Mary's extensive experience, cultural insight, and technical proficiency make her a reliable and skilled translator. Her ability to adapt content to different audiences ensures clarity and preserves the essence of the original Quranic message. As editor of hundreds of articles for *Al-Iman Magazine* and translator of *Structures and Visions: Readings from the Poetry of Ali Abdullah Khalifah*, she has demonstrated her dedication to excellence. Additionally, she has authored numerous articles on Islamic beliefs, culture, and religion, along with three books: *A Sprinkle of Dust* (her memoir), *25 Icons of Peace in the Quran*, and *Building America: Immigrant Stories of Hope and Hardship*, co-edited with Glenn O'Kray. Mary's work continues to enrich cross-cultural understanding and communication.

Contents

Acknowledgments xiii
Foreword xv
Introduction 1
The Story of Prophet Muhammad 373
Timeline 379
Resources 381
Index 383

The Holy Quran — Verbatim
An Innovative Translation

1 The Opening *al-Fātiha* 9	*16* The Bee *al-Nahl* 136
2 The Cow *al-Baqarah* 10	*17* The Night Journey *al-Isrā* 143
3 The House of Imrān *al-Imran* 30	*18* The Cave *al-Kahf* 149
4 Women *al-Nisā* 42	*19* Mary *Maryam* 155
5 The Table Spread *al-Māi'dah* 55	*20* Tā Hā *Tā Hā* 159
6 The Livestock *al-An'ām* 65	*21* The Prophets *al-Anbiyā* 165
7 The Heights *al-A'rāf* 77	*22* The Pilgrimage *al-Hajj* 170
8 The Spoils *al-Anfāl* 90	*23* The Believers *al-Mu'minūn* 175
9 Repentance *al-Tawbah* 95	*24* Light *al-Nūr* 179
10 Jonah *Yŭnus* 104	*25* The Criterion *al-Furqān* 184
11 Hŭd 111	*26* The Poets *al-Shu'ara* 188
12 Joseph *Yŭsuf* 118	*27* The Ants *al-Naml* 194
13 The Thunder *al-Ra'd* 125	*28* The Stories *al-Qasas* 199
14 Abraham *Ibrāhūm* 129	*29* The Spider *al-Ankabūt* 205
15 Hijr *al-Hijr* 133	*30* The Romans *al-Rūm* 209

31 Luqmān 213	*64* Mutual Loss and Gain *al-Taghābun* .305
32 Prostration *al-Sajdah* 216	*65* Divorce *al-Talāq* 307
33 The Parties *al-Ahzāb* 218	*66* Forbiddance *al-Tahrīm* 309
34 Saba 223	*67* Sovereignty *al-Mulk* 311
35 The Originator *Fātir* 227	*68* The Pen *al-Qalam* 313
36 Yā Sīn *Yā Sīn* 230	*69* The Undeniable Reality *al-Hāqqah* ...315
37 Those Who Are in Ranks *al-Saffāt* ... 233	*70* The Ascending Ways *al-Ma'ārij* 317
38 Sād 237	*71* Noah *Nūh* 319
39 The Throngs *al-Zumar* 241	*72* The Jinn *al-Jinn* 321
40 Forgiver *Ghāfir* 246	*73* Folded in Garments *al-Muzzammil* ..323
41 Expounded *Fussilat* 251	*74* The Enwrapped One *al-Mudda'thir* .325
42 Counsel *al-Shūrā* 255	*75* The Resurrection *al-Qiyāmah* 327
43 Gold Ornaments *al-Zukhruf* 259	*76* The Human Being *al-Insān* 328
44 Smoke *al-Dukhān* 263	*77* Those Sent Forth *al-Mursalāt* 330
45 The Kneeling *al-Jāthiyah* 265	*78* The Good News *al-Naba* 332
46 The Sand Dunes *al-Ahqāf* 267	*79* The Wresters *al-Nāzi'āt* 334
47 Muhammad 270	*80* He Frowned *'Abasa* 336
48 Victory *al-Fath* 273	*81* The Enfolding *al-Takwīr* 337
49 The Chambers *al-Hujurāt* 276	*82* The Riven Asunder *al-Infitār* 338
50 Qāf 278	*83* Those Who Defraud *al-Mutaffifīn* 339
51 The Scatterers *al-Dhāriyāt* 280	*84* The Sundering *al-Inshiqāq* 340
52 The Mount *al-Tūr* 282	*85* The Constellations *al-Burūj* 341
53 The Star *al-Najm* 284	*86* The Nightly Star *al-Tāriq* 342
54 The Moon *al-Qamar* 286	*87* The Most High *al-A'lā* 343
55 The Compassionate *al-Rahmān* 288	*88* The Overwhelming Event *al-Ghāshiyah* 344
56 The Inevitable *al-Wāqiah* 290	
57 Iron *al-Hadīd* 292	*89* The Dawn *al-Fajr* 345
58 She Who Disputes *al-Mujādilah* 295	*90* The City *al-Balad* 346
59 The Gathering *al-Hashr* 297	*91* The Sun *al-Shams* 347
60 She Who is Tested *al-Mumtahenah* .. 299	*92* The Night *al-Layl* 348
61 The Rank *al-Saff* 301	*93* The Morning Brightness *al-Duhā* 349
62 Congregational Prayer *al-Jumu'ah* ... 303	*94* The Expansion *al-Sharh* 350
63 The Hypocrites *al-Munāfiqūn* 304	*95* The Fig *al-Tīn* 351

96 The Blood Clot *al-'Alaq* 352
97 Power *al-Qadr* 353
98 The Clear Proof *al-Bayyinah* 354
99 The Earthquake *al-Zalzalah* 355
100 The Chargers *al-'Ādiyāt* 356
101 The Calamity *al-Qāri'ah* 357
102 Vying for More *al-Takāthur* 358
103 Over Time *al-'Asr* 359
104 The Slanderer *al-Humazah* 360
105 The Elephant *al-Fīl* 361
106 Quraysh 362
107 Acts of Kindness *al-Mā'ūn* 363
108 Abundant Good *al-Kawthar* 364
109 The Disbelievers *al-Kāfirūn* 365
110 Help *al-Nasr* 366
111 The Palm-Fiber *al-Masad* 367
112 Sincerity *al-Ikhlās* 368
113 The Daybreak *al-Falaq* 369
114 Mankind *al-Nās* 370

Acknowledgments

This work would not have been possible without the unwavering support, patience, and willingness of my husband, Ernie, who shared me with God through countless days and nights. His engineering and scientific expertise proved invaluable, especially when I encountered challenges with verses related to scientific intricacies, cosmology, and the laws of physics.

I extend my deepest gratitude to my son, Adam, for his invaluable contribution in refining the rhythm and contemporary prose of so many verses. I am equally grateful to my daughters, Rania and Dania, for their unwavering support and constant encouragement, which have been a great source of strength and inspiration throughout this journey. I also owe special thanks to my late son, Mazen, whose spiritual inspiration continues to guide me. Additionally, I am profoundly thankful to Mazen's wife, Mona, for her steadfast support, and thankful also to all my grandchildren for their ongoing encouragement.

My sincere gratitude goes to my sister, Samerah, for her forty years of translation expertise, as well as her last-minute editing, proofreading, and valuable comments.

I extend special thanks to Imams Mohammed Ali Elahi and Mohammed Mardini, the spiritual leaders of two of Michigan's largest mosques, for their generous praise and compliments on this translation. I also deeply appreciate the insightful resources provided by Dr. Hussein Hakim, a graduate of Islamic Studies from Sorbonne, France.

Furthermore, I am profoundly grateful for the guidance and expertise of Dr. Tallal Turfe. His extensive knowledge of the Holy Quran and his work on key topics in Islam provided me with invaluable insights into many of the most challenging and complex Quranic verses.

Lastly, I owe heartfelt thanks to Todd Engel for his superb cover design, and to Kate Robinson at Starstone Editorial for her exceptional editorial skills and meticulous work in preparing this manuscript for publication.

Foreword

The current growth of Muslim communities in English-speaking countries and increasing academic interest in Islam have led to a surge in English translations of the Qur'an. This development is noteworthy, as the Qur'an's original language is Arabic, and accurately conveying its message in another language is a complex task. Nonetheless, numerous English translations are now available, ranging from literal renditions to those employing interpretive language. These translations serve as valuable tools for understanding the Qur'an, particularly for non-Arabic speakers. They also make the text accessible to a broader audience, enabling individuals with little knowledge of Arabic to appreciate its profound meaning and simple elegance.

Dr. Mary Assel brings a fresh perspective to the translation of the Qur'an into English. While the Qur'an has been translated into various languages for centuries, Dr. Assel's work distinguishes itself through her detailed analysis and deep understanding of the Islamic faith — key elements for an accurate translation. Her comprehensive grasp of the Arabic language enables her to interpret the Qur'an's text with precision, capturing its subtleties and depth. Additionally, her knowledge of Arabic culture adds a layer of insight that is often absent in other translations.

The Qur'an holds immense significance in the Islamic faith and translating it from Arabic to English is an immense responsibility. Dr. Assel approached this task with exceptional care, ensuring every word and phrase was rendered accurately and faithfully. She collaborated with Islamic scholars, Arabic linguists, and other experts to verify the correctness of her work. Dr. Assel has made a remarkable contribution to English translations of the Qur'an. Her expertise in Arabic language, culture, and Islamic faith has allowed her to accurately convey the text's meanings and values. Her work brings a thoughtful approach to the Qur'an's translation, bridging the gap between classical text and modern language while maintaining its integrity.

Fluent in both Arabic and English, Dr. Assel embraced the challenge of translating the Qur'an. She recognized the weight of her responsibility and worked tirelessly to ensure her translation was faithful to the original. Her dedication involved extensive research into word meanings, grammar, and syntax to produce a translation that would resonate with English-speaking audiences while retaining the original's essence.

Dr. Assel's deep understanding of Islam allows her to convey the Qur'an's significance and message with respect and reverence. Her efforts have greatly enhanced the Quran's accessibility, contributing to a broader understanding of Islamic teachings. Her commitment to detail and respect for the Qur'an's text ensured that her work stayed true to its original form while being approachable for readers unfamiliar with Arabic.

Acutely aware of the challenges and controversies surrounding Qur'an translation, Dr. Assel worked diligently to remain true to its content and message. Her dedication has opened the Qur'an to a global audience, providing insights and knowledge to those who might not have otherwise encountered its teachings. Her work is both an achievement and a testament to her skill and commitment.

Dr. Assel's translation adopts a verbatim, word-for-word approach by reflecting the original text's meaning without subjective interpretation. This method preserves the text's structure and context while delivering an accurate rendering in English. Each word and phrase were carefully evaluated to ensure clarity, accuracy, and alignment with the original Arabic.

Accurate translation is paramount, particularly when working with a text as significant as the Qur'an. Dr. Assel's work retains the depth and nuance of the original language, balancing fidelity to the source with accessibility for readers. Her approach highlights the artistry of language, offering readers an emotional connection to the text while staying true to its intent.

By consulting renowned commentaries and immersing herself in the Qur'an's context, Dr. Assel ensured her translation preserved the meaning and integrity of the original. Her success in this monumental task has made the Qur'an more accessible to English-speaking readers, fostering greater appreciation for its teachings. Her skillful adaptation of Arabic structures and idioms has achieved a balance between adherence to the text and readability.

Dr. Assel's work exemplifies the care and expertise required to translate a text of this magnitude. Her translation is a bridge between two languages and cultures, allowing a global audience to access the Qur'an's profound message.

— Professor Tallal Alie Turfe

Introduction

The Quran, one of the most sacred books in history, has been glorified by millions of Muslims from around the world for over 1,400 years. It is the only living scripture considered to be the direct word of God. The Arabic word "Quran" means "the recitation." All 114 surahs consist of over 6,236 verses that were revealed in Arabic verbatim and seriatim to the Prophet Muhammad through the medium of Archangel *Jibril* (Gabriel), beginning in the year 610 CE and ending with the Prophet's death in 632 CE.

Often referred to as "the Sacred Word of God," the Quran is considered the faithful replica of a text contained within a preexistent, well-preserved *Lawh Mahfouz* (Heavenly Tablet). It is described as God's *Al-Kitab* (Heavenly Book) throughout its verses and stands as God's final message to humanity. The Quran follows and confirms the teachings of earlier revelations while addressing the misinterpretations of certain parts of those texts.

Revealed to Prophet Muhammad, the Quran serves to correct these mistakes and to urge people to believe in God and prepare for the Last Day. It is God's final, complete, and eternal scripture—a divine revelation that remains unaltered. The Quran reminds believers that God is the Creator and that all will ultimately return to Him. When God created man, His purpose was to give mankind the opportunity to live in peace and harmony. But man interrupted the harmonious nature of life by failing to remember God's request not to approach the forbidden tree: *"We said, "O Adam, live in the Garden with your wife and eat freely in it from whatever you desire, but do not approach this tree, else you will be among the transgressors"* (Quran, 2:35). Ultimately, Adam was cursed and removed from the Garden of Eden. After Adam's removal, God institutionalized prophethood so that prophets may inform people to only worship Him, their originator, and to know that to Him they will return. *"Remember when God made the covenant of the prophets . . . for I am with you among the witnesses"* (Quran, 3:81). Prophets are no more than couriers. Their primary mission was to encourage people to believe in God and to submit their wills and souls to Him: *"Muhammad is no more than a messenger . . . but God will reward the grateful"* (Quran, 3:144). Though the Quran does not state the exact number of God's messengers, it clearly states that the Prophet Muhammad was one of many messengers responsible for spreading His message and the last to represent previous prophets.

The word *Islam* means "submission." Islam is a monotheistic religion that calls for complete submission to the Eternal and Everlasting God. It invites people to submit their will to God, to trust Him, and to believe in Him. The Prophet Muhammad was God's final representative and a warner to humanity. Despite being rejected by many during his lifetime, his revelations endure, overcoming rejection to establish the ascendancy of Islam in the world today.

The significance of religion lies in its ability to provide individuals and groups with a general understanding of the world, the self, and the relationship between them. It offers a framework of ideas that inspires theological reflection in areas such as religion, politics, economics, science, and ethics. To believe in the Quran and the Absolute Reality of God, the Creator of the universe, one must open their heart to spiritual intelligence—a concept that transcends scientific reasoning or intelligence. Simply put, science does not evoke spiritual feeling. Science examines nature as it exists in its evolutionary phases, where nothing is permanent, and everything has a beginning and an end.

Based on this concept, nothing originates from nothing. For example, if every book has an author, then the natural world must also have an Author. God emphasizes this when He repeatedly describes the creation of every living being. Everything He creates is designed in an orderly manner and is impossible to replicate.

This message is repeatedly clarified throughout the Quran: "*It is He Who created night and day, the sun and the moon, each gliding in an orbit*" (Quran, 21:33). "*We indeed created man from dried clay, molded of black mud*" (Quran, 15:26). Much of what He manifests is complex and difficult for even the best of scientists to emulate or understand. No one can create life or prevent death, and neither can the world around us be recreated. "*O People! A parable is set forth, so listen to it! Truly those that you call upon instead of God will never create a fly, even if they all gather to do so*" (Quran, 22:73). The mystery of man and the world's creation can only be explained by the presence of a super-power, namely, God.

The Quran is easy to read, yet complex. At times, it is difficult to understand the exact meaning of certain verses with respect to the certainty of God's intended message. Also, although certain verses may be quite simple and straightforward, it may take repeated readings of the same verse to reveal newer and deeper meanings. Over the years, almost every letter or expression has been broken down into segments, analyzed, and interpreted differently by the various scholars undertaking Quranic exegesis. Muslim scholars have differed in opinion, and their preferences have led to an evolution of various schools of thought and divisions in the religion. Despite all such critical interpretations, God appeals to every believer, young and old. Many read the Quran repeatedly and faithfully to follow its directives and conduct their lives according to the ways of Prophet Muhammad (*sunnaht al rasoul*).

The Quran was revealed over a period of twenty-three years and many verses are somewhat repetitive, but notably, repetition serves as a reinforcer. The more a concept is repeated, the more it adheres to the senses and the more likely we are to remember and understand it: *"We have indeed sent a Book down to you as a Reminder. Do you not understand?"* (Quran, 21:9). God repeats certain verses to reinforce the notion that there will be consequences for our actions and the sooner we understand, the better. God sent the Quran to reveal that He is the Creator of all things and that unto Him we will return. By believing in the revelations of God through His prophets and through submission to Islam, we find that our perception of the world will change, and our lives will become colored by spiritual intensity and harmony. Our acceptance of life and death becomes intertwined in the mystical force of God the Creator, and His presence becomes no longer questionable.

Nonetheless, readers should not despair at the ambiguity or complexity of certain verses without consulting Quranic exegesis when necessary. Not all verses are revealed in complete sentences; therefore, I have used ellipses or dashes to separate incomplete sentences and to establish modest coherence. The careful flow of this translation aims to enhance the readability of the Quran, provide a deeper examination of God's revelations, strengthen readers' faith in God, and bring tranquility to their inner consciousness. This spiritual connection may gradually engage the conscious mind, paving the way for a more focused and profound faith.

This Translation

My primary goal in undertaking this translation was to adhere to God's words, not my personal views, elucidations, or assumptions. This work is the result of my robust familiarity with the Arabic language: forty years of experience in the translation of essays and manuscripts from Arabic to English, and an undergraduate focus in linguistics and vocabulary in context. I completed a dissertation in neuroscience in my pursuit to understand the complexity of the brain and how everything we see, feel, read about, hear, and think of is the result of underlying brain processes.

The Quran is not an ordinary book to read. It requires skill, patience, and a strong desire to understand its message. Learning a new skill changes how our brain is wired on a deep level, a result of real and complex transformations that occur in our neurocircuitry. Different parts of the brain communicate, coordinate, and fire at incredible speeds, sending electrical signals that help neurons reach their destinations. While all brains generally operate in the same way, and all learning happens in the brain, this does not mean everyone needs to become a neuroscientist to enhance their understanding of the Quran. However, it is important to recognize that research in neuroscience, cognitive science, and education has identified effective strategies for motivation, learning, memory, and retention. Understanding how the brain absorbs and retains new information is crucial. Motivation, repetition, practice, and creativity are key to effective learning. The more you practice reading the Quran, the better you will understand and internalize God's message. This translation employs relatively simple sentence structures to make the Quran accessible and to facilitate a lifelong understanding of its teachings. As a non-religious scholar, I dedicated countless hours—and sometimes days—to the translation of a single word, carefully researching and examining to ensure the translation closely aligns with what God intended to convey. Yet, it is important to acknowledge that many translators, whether academic or spiritual scholars, have faced challenges in capturing the exact meaning of God's words, and no one can ever do so with absolute certainty: ". . . *However, no one knows its interpretation except for God and those firmly rooted in knowledge. They say, "We believe in it. All is from our Lord. None will remember except for those endowed with insight."* (Quran, 3:7). Another notable instance is the presence of *Muqatta'at* (disjointed letters) or *Fawātih* (openers) used at the beginning of 29 out of the 114 surahs in the Quran. The exact meaning of these letters remains unknown, and Islamic scholars have not reached a consensus on their interpretation. This emphasizes the existence of elements within the Quran whose meanings are known only to God.

To ensure impartiality in this work, when a term is translated differently across various schools of thought, the translation most commonly accepted is selected, especially if it aligns with a contextual meaning of a verse. This approach aims to provide clarity and consistency, minimizing potential biases that may arise from differing interpretations. By prioritizing widely accepted translations that fit the context, the work seeks to offer a balanced understanding of the text. This method acknowledges the diversity of interpretations while striving for a translation that resonates with the broader audience. It reflects a commitment to presenting the text in a way that is both accurate and accessible, respecting the nuances of the original language and the perspectives of various scholars.

This strategy also helps in maintaining the integrity of the translation, ensuring that it remains faithful to the intended message of the original text. By adopting this approach, the work endeavors to bridge the gap between different schools of thought, fostering a more unified understanding of the text. Ultimately, this method serves to enhance the reader's comprehension, providing a translation that is both contextually appropriate and widely accepted within the scholarly community.

I have taken great care to avoid potential criticism from patriarchal societies or individuals who might question a woman's competence in translating the Quran. This caution is essential, as women translators have historically faced challenges and skepticism in this field. Unfortunately, this underscores the importance of meticulousness and sensitivity in such endeavors.

To address skepticism and avoid the assumption that this translation is biased—whether in favor of a specific sect of Islam, to elevate the position of women by altering God's words, or to align the text with twenty-first-century interpretations—I have dedicated myself to translating God's words with the utmost accuracy. While modern exegetes contribute significantly to understanding the Quran and the role of women, this translation is by no means an evolution of God's verses.

I firmly believe in the progressive development of *fiqh* (Islamic jurisprudence) that has emerged to uphold women's rights, but this translation is not influenced by personal inclinations. My sole mission is to convey God's exact words without imposing interpretations, even if some may perceive certain verses as unfavorable to women. It is unnecessary to emphasize that the Quran explicitly prohibits the abuse of women when God clearly decrees that no human—male, female, or child—should ever be subjected to any form of abuse: *"Among His signs is that He created mates for you from among yourselves to dwell with them in comfort. He established affection and mercy between you. Truly in that are signs for a people who understand"* (Quran, 30:21). In other words, God created man and woman to love and comfort one another by avoiding abuse and violence. In fact, God reveals the verse: *"When the female infant buried alive is asked for what sin she was slain . . ."* in condemnation of the executors of her death. No one has the right to abuse anyone or slay an innocent life (Quran, 81:8-9). Hence, women are the religious equals of men in every aspect: *"Believing men and believing women are protectors of one another by enjoining right and forbidding wrong . . . they are those whom God will have Mercy upon. Truly God is Mighty and Wise"* (Quran, 9:71).

After intensive research and close examination of interpretations by numerous authors, particularly in their use of archaic English, I chose to use modern English to make this translation simple and straightforward. It is important to note that no translation can fully capture the tone, rhythm, and harmony of the Arabic words and verses as conveyed in the Quran. The Quran was written and intended to be read and recited in Arabic, but because many native English speakers cannot read Arabic, it is essential to provide the Quran in a language they can understand.

This translation prioritizes coherence, clear sentence structure, and the faithful rendering of verses in a verbatim manner. Despite these efforts, it must be acknowledged that no translation, regardless of the time and dedication invested, can be deemed flawless. It is impossible for any scholar, religious or otherwise, to claim with absolute certainty that their translation perfectly reflects the original text. My mission was to translate to the best of my knowledge and ability.

The Holy Quran, the ultimate guidebook for all Muslims, is generally straightforward to read. Its wording has remained unchanged over time. However, certain passages can be challenging to comprehend and are often open to interpretation. This translation focuses on rendering every passage verbatim, with little concern for the interpretations of Quranic verses. To avoid bias and controversy, no reference was made to specific schools of thought, theological perspectives, or individual interpretations.

This does not diminish the importance of interpreting the Holy Quran, as many passages may be complex or mysterious to readers seeking clarification. The intricate nature of some Quranic verses encourages readers to reflect and explore analogical reasoning as presented by Muslim scholars. Discrepancies in translations and interpretations are evident among various sects, highlighting differences in the understanding of many verses. Scholars of *tafsir* (Quranic exegesis) around the world often provide pluralistic explanations, meanings, or opinions for a single verse.

Some statements in the *Sunnah* (practices, teachings, and traditions of Prophet Muhammad) are based on the historical or situational context in which a particular verse was revealed. For example, readers may encounter difficult passages and turn to interpretations provided by qualified religious scholars of their own sect for deeper understanding. Most of these scholars rely on *hadith* (accounts detailing the sayings, actions, or approvals by the Prophet Muhammad) while using the Quran as the primary source. They turn to the Quran for its factual nature as the direct Word of God. However, generalizations in legal areas often encourage readers to reflect more deeply on matters to achieve clarity.

Arabic, a stylistically rich and powerful language, demands understanding and training to derive meaningful and satisfactory interpretations: God makes this clear in this verse: *"Whoever is granted wisdom has been granted an abundance of good. Yet no one remembers except for those endowed with insight* (2:269). However, the reliability of any given source can be subjective, making its accuracy challenging to verify. Therefore, this Quran has been translated verbatim, providing readers with the opportunity to explore its meaning independently or, if they wish, to consider the interpretations of knowledgeable religious scholars of their choice.

This translation of the Quran is among the most labor-intensive projects I have ever undertaken, and it is my hope that it will reach and resonate with many non-Arabic readers around the world who are eager to learn about Islam.

I humbly pray that my Lord forgives me and has mercy upon me if I have fallen short or made errors in this translation. I take full responsibility for this work and hope that readers will recognize the years of effort that went into it, trusting the process that began with my desire to make the Quran accessible to as many English readers as possible. I sincerely hope that I have succeeded in providing them with a positive reading experience and a deeper understanding of Islam.

— Dr. Mary Saad Assel

Surah 1

THE OPENING

al-Fātiha

In the Name of God, the Compassionate, the Merciful

1. In the Name of God, the Compassionate, the Merciful. **2.** Praise be to God, Lord of the Worlds, **3.** the Compassionate, the Merciful, **4.** Master of the Day of Judgment. **5.** It is You Whom we worship, and it is from You that we seek help. **6.** Guide us upon the straight path, **7.** the path of those whom You have blessed, not of those who incur wrath, nor of those who are astray.

Surah 2

THE COW

al-Baqarah

In the Name of God, the Compassionate, the Merciful

1. *Alif. Lam. Mim.* **2.** This is the Book in which there is no doubt, a Book of guidance for the pious **3.** who believe in the Unseen, perform prayer, give from what We have provided them, **4.** who believe in what was sent down to you and what was sent down before you, and are convinced of the Hereafter. **5.** It is they who are truly guided by their Lord, and it is they who will prosper. **6.** It is indeed the same for disbelievers whether you warn them or do not warn them; they will not believe. **7.** God has sealed their hearts and their hearing. There is a veil upon their eyes, and they will suffer a great punishment. **8.** Among people are those who say, "We believe in God and the Last Day," though they have no faith. **9.** They seek to deceive God and the believers, but in reality, they only deceive themselves, though they remain unaware. **10.** There is a sickness in their hearts, and God has increased their sickness. They will suffer a painful punishment because of their denial. **11.** When it is said to them, "Do not perform mischief on earth," they say, "We are only doing what is right." **12.** Truly it is they who create mischief, though they are heedless. **13.** When it is said to them, "Believe as the people believe," they say, "Should we believe like the fools believe?" Truly it is they who are fools, though they do not know. **14.** When they meet those who believe they say, "We believe," but when they are alone with their evil ones, they say, "We are with you. We were only mocking." **15.** God mocks them and leaves them to wander confused in their rebellion. **16.** It is they who bartered error at the price of guidance. Their business has not brought them gain, and they are not rightly guided. **17.** Their example is like one who kindled a fire and when it lit up what was around him, God removed their light and left them sightless in the dark. **18.** Deaf, dumb, and blind, they will not return. **19.** Or like a cloudburst from the sky with darkness, thunder, and lightning, they put their fingers in their ears against the thunderclaps in fear of death. But God encompasses the disbelievers. **20.** The lightning all but snatches away their sight. Whenever there is light, they walk in it, and whenever darkness comes over them, they stand still. Had God willed, He could have removed their hearing and their sight. God is indeed powerful over all things. **21.** O mankind! Worship your Lord who created you and those who were before you, that perhaps you will be reverent. **22.** It is He Who made the earth a place of rest for you, and the sky your canopy, and sent water down from the sky by which He brought forth fruits for your sustenance. So do not knowingly set up equals to God. **23.** If you are in doubt of what We have sent down to Our Servant, then produce a similar sūrah and call your witnesses instead of God if you are truthful. **24.** If you do not, and you will not, then be mindful of the Fire whose fuel is men and stones prepared for the disbelievers. **25.** Give good news to those who believe and perform righteous deeds that Gardens with rivers running beneath will be theirs. Whenever they are given fruit from it as sustenance, they say, "This is the sustenance that we were provided before," and they were given what was similar to it. They will have pure spouses and abide there forever. **26.** God is not shy in presenting the example of a gnat or something smaller. As for those who believe, they know it is the truth from God, and as for those who disbelieve, they will say, "What did God mean by this parable?" He misleads many by it and guides many by it, but He only misleads the sinful. **27.** Those who break God's Covenant after it is ratified, break away what God has commanded to be joined, and perform mischief on the earth, will be the losers. **28.** "How can you deny God? When you were lifeless, He gave you life; then He will cause you to die and bring you back to life again, and to Him, you will ultimately return." **29.** It is He who created everything on the earth for you. He then turned to Heaven and shaped it into seven Heavens. He has knowledge of all things. **30.** When your Lord said to the angels, "I am placing a vicegerent on the earth," they said, "Will You place in it one who will create corruption and shed blood while we glorify Your praise and sanctify You?" He said, "Truly I know what you do not." **31.** He taught Adam all the names. He placed them before the angels and said, "Tell me the names of these, if you are sincere." **32.** They said, "Glory be to You. We have no knowledge except for what You have taught us. You are, indeed, the Knowledgeable and the Wise." **33.** He said, "O Adam! Call them by their names." Then, when he informed them, He said, "Did I not say to you, I know the Unseen of the heavens and earth and I know what you disclose and what you conceal." **34.** When We said to the angels, "Prostrate to Adam," they prostrated except for Iblīs. He refused, grew arrogant, and was among the disbelievers. **35.** We said, "O Adam, live in the Garden with your wife and eat freely in it from whatever you desire, but do not approach this tree, else you will be among the transgressors." **36.** Then Satan made them fall from it and expelled them from the state of felicity they were in. We said, "Get down where each of you will be an enemy unto the other! The earth will be yours for dwelling and enjoyment for a while." **37.** Then Adam received words from his Lord, and He relented unto him. He is the Relenting, the Merciful. **38.** We said, "All of you get down from it! If you receive guidance from Me, then whoever follows My guidance will have no fear, nor will they grieve." **39.** But those who disbelieve and deny Our signs will be the inhabitants of the Fire and abide there forever. **40.** O Children of Israel! Remember My Blessing which I bestowed on you; revere Me and I will fulfill your Covenant. **41.** Believe in what I have sent down, confirming what you have with you. Do not be the first to disbelieve in it, do not sell My signs for a trivial price, and revere Me. **42.** Do not confound truth with falsehood, nor knowingly conceal the truth. **43.** Perform prayer and give alms and bow with those who bow. **44.** Will you bid piety upon people and forget yourselves as you recite the Book? Do you not comprehend? **45.** Seek help in patience and prayer. This is certainly difficult except for the humble **46.** who consider they will meet with their Lord, and they will return to Him. **47.** O Children of Israel! Remember My Blessing which I bestowed on you, and that I favored you over all worlds. **48.** Be mindful of a day when no soul will benefit another soul in any form. No intercession will be accepted from it, nor ransom taken from it, nor will they be helped. **49.** Remember when We delivered you from the House of Pharoah, who inflicted a dreadful punishment on you while slaying your sons and sparing your women. In that was a great trial from your Lord. **50.** Remember, We parted the sea and thus delivered you and drowned the House of Pharoah while you watched. **51.** Remember, when We appointed forty nights for Moses, you took up the calf after he was gone, and you were the wrongdoers. **52.** Then We pardoned you afterward, that perhaps you may give thanks. **53.** Remember, We gave Moses the Scripture and the Criterion that perhaps you may be guided. **54.** Remember Moses said to his people, "O my people! You have wronged yourselves by taking up the calf. So repent unto your Maker and defeat your souls. That is better for you from your Maker's perspective." Then He relented unto you. Truly, He is the Relenting, the Merciful. **55.** Remember when you said, "O Moses, we will not believe in you until we see God openly," and the thunderbolt seized you while you were watching. **56.** Then We raised you up after your death that perhaps you may give thanks. **57.** We shaded you with clouds and sent down manna and quail upon you, saying "Eat of the good things We have provided you." They did not wrong Us, they wronged themselves. **58.** When We said, "Enter this town and eat freely from wherever you desire and enter the gate prostrating. Say, 'Lift the burden!' that We may exonerate your sins, and We will increase the goodly." **59.** But the wrongdoer exchanged the Word for other than what had been said to them.

Therefore, We sent a torment from Heaven on those who did wrong for their transgressions. **60.** Remember, when Moses prayed for water for his people, We said, "Strike the rock with your staff," then twelve springs gushed forth from it. Each people knew their drinking place. "Eat and drink of God's sustenance and do not behave wickedly on the earth as corrupters." **61.** Remember, you said, "O Moses! We will not endure one food. So call on your Lord for us that He might bring forth for us some of what the earth grows: its herbs, its cucumbers, its garlic, its lentils, and its onions." He said, "Will you exchange what is lesser for what is better? Go down to a town and you will have what you ask for." As a result, they were struck with humiliation and poverty and earned a burden of wrath from God. That is because they disbelieved in the signs of God and killed the prophets unjustifiably. That is because they disobeyed and were transgressors. **62.** Indeed, those who believe and those who are Jews, the Christians, and the Sabeans, and whoever believes in God and the Last Day, and perform righteousness, will have their reward with their Lord. No fear will come upon them, nor will they grieve. **63.** Remember, We made a Covenant with you and raised the Mount over you, "Take what We have given you with strength and remember what is in it that perhaps you may be reverent." **64.** Then afterward, you turned away and if it were not for God's Bounty upon you, and His Mercy, you would have been among the losers. **65.** You have surely known those among you who transgressed concerning the Sabbath, and so We said to them, "Be outcast, apes!" **66.** Therefore, We made it a model of punishment for their time and times to come and a warning for the reverent. **67.** Remember Moses said to his people, "God commands you to slaughter a cow," they said, "Do you take us in mockery?" He said, "I seek refuge in God from being among the ignorant." **68.** They said, "Call upon your Lord for us that He may clarify for us what she is." He said, "He says, she is a cow, not old, nor young, somewhere in between, so do what you are commanded!" **69.** They said, "Call upon your Lord for us to show us her color." He said, "He says she is a yellow cow. Her color is bright and pleasing to the onlookers." **70.** They said, "Pray to your Lord for us that He may clarify to us what she is. Cows look alike to us and if God wills, we will certainly be guided." **71.** He said, "He says, she is a cow not broken to plow the earth, or to water the tillage, sound and without blemish." They said, "Now, you have brought us the truth." Subsequently, they slaughtered her, but they almost did not. **72.** Remember you slew a soul and blamed each other for it, but God is the discloser of what you were concealing. **73.** We said, "Strike him with part of it." Thus does God revive the dead and show you His Signs that perhaps you may understand. **74.** Thereafter, your hearts hardened like stones or even harder. For indeed among stones there are those from which streams gush forth, and indeed among them are those that split and water springs out of them. Certainly, among them are those who sink from fear of God. God is not heedless of what you do. **75.** Do you still hope they will believe you, when a group among them hears the Word of God and then knowingly distorts it, even after understanding it? **76.** When they met those who believe, they said, "We believe," but when they were alone with each other, they would say, "Do you share with them what God has revealed to you, so they might use it to argue with you before your Lord? Do you not comprehend?" **77.** Do they not know that God knows what they conceal and what they reveal? **78.** Among them are those who are illiterate and who know nothing of the Book but rumor. They do nothing but speculate. **79.** So woe unto those who write the Book with their hands and then say, "This is from God," that they may sell it for a trivial price. So woe unto them for what their hands have written and woe unto them for what they profit. **80.** They say, "The Fire will not touch us except for a few numbered days." Say, "Have you made a covenant with God, for God will not fail to keep his Covenant. Or do you say of God what you do not know?" **81.** Truly, whoever commits evil and is overwhelmed by their sins will be inhabitants of the Fire, where they will remain forever. **82.** Those who believe and perform righteous deeds are the inhabitants of the Garden, abiding there forever. **83.** Remember, We made a Covenant with the Children of Israel, "Worship none but God, be respectful toward parents, kinsfolk, orphans, the indigent; speak to people in a polite manner, perform prayer, and give alms." Then you turned away, except for a few of you, as you recanted. **84.** Remember, We made a Covenant with you, "Do not shed the blood of your own, and do not expel your own from your homes." Then you ratified it, bearing witness. **85.** Then it was you, yourselves, who slay your own and oust a party of you from their homes, conspiring against them in sin and enmity. If they come to you as captives, you ransom them, though their expulsion was forbidden upon you. Do you then, believe in part of the Book and disbelieve in part? What is the reward for those who behave this way but who disgrace this worldly life? On the Day of Resurrection, they will be consigned to the most severe penalty for God is not heedless of what you do. **86.** They are those who buy this worldly life for the price of the Hereafter. Their penalty will not be reduced, nor will they be helped. **87.** Indeed, We gave the Book to Moses and followed up with a succession of messengers. We gave Jesus, the son of Mary clear signs and strengthened him with the Holy Spirit. Is it not that whenever a messenger comes to you with something your souls did not desire, you grew arrogant where some, you denied, and some, you slew? **88.** They say, "Our hearts are enclosures." Rather God has cursed them for their disbelief, for little do they believe. **89.** Then when a Book from God came to them, confirming what they had with them in the past, they asked for victory over those who disbelieve. However, when what they recognized came to them, they disbelieved in it. So may the curse of God be upon the disbelievers. **90.** They traded their souls for something evil by rejecting what God revealed, driven by envy. God will indeed send down His Grace to whomever He wills among His servants. Consequently, they have drawn wrath over wrath upon themselves. For those who disbelieve, is a humiliating punishment. **91.** When they were told, "Believe in what God has sent down." They say, "We believe in what was sent down to us," and they disbelieve in what is beyond though, it is the truth consolidating what they already have. Say, "Then why did you slay God's prophets aforetime, if you were believers?" **92.** Moses truly brought you clear signs, but then, you took-up the calf while he was away, and you were wrongdoers. **93.** Remember We made a covenant with you and raised the Mount over you, "Take what We have given you with strength and listen." They said, "We heard, and we disobeyed." They had to drink the calf into their hearts because of their disbelief. Say, "If you are believers, what your faith orders you to do is evil." **94.** Say, "If the Abode of the Hereafter with God is exclusively for you without other people, then long for death if you are truthful." **95.** But they will never long for it because of what their hands have presented, and God knows the wrongdoers. **96.** You will find them the most desirous of all people for life even more so than idol worshippers. Each one of them would wish to live a thousand years, although they cannot be exempted from His punishment, and God sees whatever they do. **97.** Whoever is an enemy of Gabriel, it is he who brought it down to your heart by God's will, confirming what was before, and as guidance and good news for the believers. **98.** Whoever is the enemy of God and His angels, His messengers, Gabriel and Michael: God is indeed the enemy of disbelievers. **99.** We have indeed sent down to you clear signs, and only the sinful disbelieve in them. **100.** Is it not that, whenever they make a covenant, a group of them would throw it aside? Indeed, most of them do not believe. **101.** When a messenger from God came to them confirming what was with them, a group of those who had been given the Book, threw the Book of God behind their backs as if they did not know. **102.** They followed what the demons recited against the kingdom of Solomon. Solomon did not disbelieve, but the demons disbelieved while teaching people sorcery and what was sent down to the two angels at Babylon, *Hārūt* and *Mārūt.* But they would not teach anyone until they had said, "We are only a trial, so do not disbelieve." Then they learned from them what could cause separation between a man and his wife. But they could not harm anyone with it except by God's permission. They learned of what would harm them and of what would bring them no benefit, knowing that whoever buys into it will have no share in the Hereafter. Vile is that for which they sold their souls if they only knew. **103.** Had they believed and been reverent a reward from God would be better if they only knew. **104.** O you who believe, do not say, "Attend to us," but say, "Look at us and listen!" For the disbelievers will have a painful punishment. **105.** Neither the disbelievers among the People of the Book, nor the pagans wish that anything good should be sent down to you from your Lord, but God singles out for His mercy whomever He wills, and God is Possessed of Grace Abounding. **106.** No sign do We abrogate or cause to be forgotten, but We bring what is better than it or similar to it. Do you not know that God is Powerful over all things? **107.** Do you not know that God has dominion over the heavens and the earth and that you have no protector not helper besides God? **108.** Or do you wish to question your messenger as Moses was formerly questioned? Whoever switches from faith to disbelief has gone astray from the right way. **109.** Many from the People of the Book wish to turn you back into disbelievers after having believed out of selfish envy and after the truth had become clear to them. But forgive and forbear until God comes with His Command. God truly has power over all things. **110.** Perform prayer and give alms. Whatever good you send forth is for your own souls, and you will find it with God. God truly sees whatever you do. **111.** They say, "No one will enter the Garden unless he is a Jew or a Christian." Those are their aspirations. Say, "Produce your proof if you are truthful." **112.** Indeed, whoever submits his face to God while being virtuous will have his reward with his Lord. No fear will come upon them, nor will they grieve. **113.** The Jews say, "The Christians have nothing to stand on," and the Christians say, "The Jews have nothing to stand on" and both recite the Book. In the same manner, those without knowledge spoke words similar to theirs. God will judge between them on the Day of Resurrection about what they differed upon. **114.** Who does greater injustice than those who ban God's mosques to avoid His Name from being mentioned while aiming for their destruction? They are those who should not enter them except in fear. Disgrace will be theirs in this world, and great punishment will be theirs in the Hereafter. **115.** To God belong the East and the West. Wherever you turn, there is the Countenance of God. God is All Encompassing and All-Knowing. **116.** They say, "God has taken a child." Glory be to Him! Rather, to Him belongs whatever is in the heavens and on the earth. All are devoutly obedient to Him **117.** the Originator of the heavens and the earth. When He decrees a matter, He says to it, "Be!" and it is. **118.** Those who do not know say, "Why does God not speak to us, nor a sign come to us?" Those who came before them spoke similar words as did their hearts. Their hearts are similar. We have indeed made the signs clear to a people who are certain. **119.** We have sent you with the truth as the bearer of good news, and warnings, and you will not be questioned about the inhabitants of Hellfire. **120.** Never will the Jews or Christians be pleased with you until you follow their creed. Say, "Surely, the guidance of God is the true guidance. And if you were to follow their desires after the knowledge that has reached you, you would have no protector or helper against God." **121.** Those to whom We have given the Book, and who recite it as it should be recited, are they who believe in it. Whoever does not believe in it, they are the losers. **122.** O Children of Israel! Remember My Blessing which I bestowed upon you and that I favored you above the worlds. **123.** Be mindful of a day when no soul will reward another in anything, nor will ransom be accepted by it, nor will intercession benefit it. They will not be helped. **124.** Remember that the Lord had tried Abraham with 'words' and he fulfilled them. He said, "I am making you an imam for the nations." He said, "And of my offspring?" He said, "My Covenant does not include the wrongdoers." **125.** Remember that We made the House a place of visitation for people and a sanctuary. "Take the station of Abraham as a place of prayer." We made a covenant with Abraham and Ishmael, "Sanctify My House for those who circumambulate, those who make retreat, and those who bow and prostrate." **126.** Remember, Abraham said, "My Lord, make this a secure land, and provide its people with fruits—those among them who believe in God and the Last Day." He said, "For whomever disbelieves, I will grant him temporary satisfaction, but then, I will compel him toward the punishment of the Fire. What a wretched destination!" **127.** Remember when Abraham and Ishmael raised the foundations of the House: "Our Lord, accept from us. You are truly the All-Hearing and the All-Knowing. **128.** O Lord! Make us submissive to You and from our progeny a nation submissive to You. Show us our rites and relent unto us. You are the Relenting and the Merciful. **129.** O Lord! Send a messenger from among the midst of them who will recite Your Signs and will teach them the Book and Wisdom and purify them. You are truly the Mighty and the Wise." **130.** Who shuns the creed of Abraham but a foolish soul? We chose him in the world and in the Hereafter. He will be among the righteous. **131.** Remember when his Lord said to him, "Submit!" He said, "I submit to the Lord of the Worlds." **132.** Abraham commanded the same upon his children as did Jacob, "O my children, God has chosen your religion, so do not die except in submission." **133.** Or were you witnesses when death came to Jacob when he said to his children, "What will you worship after me?" They said, "We will worship your God and the God of your fathers, Abraham, Ishmael, and Isaac—one God and unto Him we *submit*." **134.** That was a nation that had passed away. Theirs is what they earned, and yours is what you have earned. You will not be questioned about what they did. **135.** They say, "Be Jews or Christians and you will be rightly guided." Say, "Rather the creed of Abraham is a *ḥanīf* (an upright Muslim). He was not of the idol worshippers." **136.** Say, "We believe in God and in what was sent down to us; in what was sent down to Abraham, Ishmael, Isaac, Jacob, and the Tribes; in what Moses and Jesus were given; and in what the prophets were given from their Lord. We make no distinction among them and to Him we *submit*." **137.** If they believe in the like of what you believe in, they will be rightly guided. If they turn away, they will be in schism and God will be enough for you against them. He is the Hearing, the Knowing. **138.** "The baptism of God — and who is better than God in baptism? We are worshippers of Him." **139.** Say, "Will you dispute with us about God while He is our Lord and your Lord? Unto us our deeds and unto you, your deeds, and we are sincere toward Him. **140.** Or do you say that Abraham, Ishmael, Isaac, Jacob, and the Tribes were Jews or Christians?" Say, "Do you know better, or does God?" Who does greater wrong than he who hides a testimony he has from God? God is not heedless of what you do. **141.** That is a nation that has passed away. What they earned is on them and what you earned is on you. You will not be questioned about what they did. **142.** The fools among people will say, "What has turned them away from the *qiblah* [direction of the Sacred Mosque in Mecca] they had been following?" Say, "To God belong the East and the West. He guides whom He desires to the straight path." **143.** Therefore, have We made you a middlemost nation that you may be witnesses for people and the Messenger may be a witness for you. We only appointed the *qiblah* that you had been following to know those who follow the Messenger from those who turn back on their heels, and it was indeed a great undertaking except for those whom God guided. But God will not let your faith be in vain, for God is indeed Kind and Merciful unto people. **144.** We have seen the turning of your face toward Heaven, and We will surely turn you toward a qiblah that will please you. So turn your face toward the Sacred Mosque, and wherever you may be, turn your faces toward it. Indeed, those who were given the Book know that it is the truth from their Lord — God is not unaware of what they do. **145.** If you were to bring every sign to those who were given the Book, they would not follow the *qiblah* and you are not a follower of their *qiblah*, nor are they followers of one another's *qiblah*. Were you to pursue their impulses after the knowledge has come to you, you would be one of the wrongdoers. **146.** Those unto whom We have given the Book, recognize it as they recognize their own children, but a group of them knowingly, conceal the truth. **147.** The truth is from your Lord, so do not be among the doubters. **148.** Everyone has a direction toward which he turns. Therefore, race one another in good deeds. Wherever you are, God will bring you all together. God is truly Powerful over all things. **149.** Whenever you go out, turn your face toward the Sacred Mosque. This is the truth from your Lord and God is not heedless of what you do. **150.** Whenever you go out, turn your face toward the Sacred Mosque and wherever you may be, turn your face toward it so people will have no excuse against you, not even the wrongdoers among them. Do not fear them but fear Me, that I may complete My Blessing upon you that perhaps you may be guided **151.** just as We have sent a messenger among you who recites Our signs to you, purifies you, teaches you the Book and Wisdom, and teaches you what you did not know. **152.** So remember Me, and I will remember you. Give thanks unto Me and do not disbelieve in Me. **153.** O you who believe! Seek help in patience and prayer for indeed God is with those who are patient. **154.** Do not say of those who are slain in the way of God, "They are dead." No, they are alive, but you are unaware. **155.** We will indeed test you with some form of fear and hunger, loss of wealth, souls, fruitages, and give good news to the patient, **156.** those who when afflicted with calamity say, "Indeed to God we belong and to Him is our return." **157.** They are those who receive blessings and compassion from their Lord, and they are those who are rightly guided. **158.** The *Safā* and *Marwah* are among the rituals of God. Therefore, whoever performs the *hajj* to the Sacred House or performs the *'umrah* will not be blamed for walking back and forth between them (the *Safā* and *Marwah*). Whomever volunteers good, God is Thankful and Knowing. **159.** Those who conceal the clear signs and guidance We have sent down after We have made it clear to people in the Book—it is they who will be cursed by God and cursed by the cursers, **160.** except for those who repent, make amends, and show clarity. They are those unto whom I relent for I am the Relenting and the Merciful. **161.** Indeed, those who disbelieve and die disbelievers, upon them will be the curse of God, the angels, and all of humanity. **162.** They will remain there, and their punishment will not be lightened, nor will they be granted respite. **163.** Your God is One God, there is no god but He, the Compassionate, and the Merciful. **164.** Indeed, in the creation of the heavens and the earth, and the alternation of night and day, and the ships that sail at sea for people's benefit; in the water God sends down from the sky to rejuvenate the land after its death, scattering all kinds of beasts within it; and the shifting of the winds and the clouds between the sky and the earth, are certainly signs for a people who are wise. **165.** Among people are some who worship others as equals to God, loving them like loving God. But those who believe are more zealous in their love of God. If the wrongdoers could only realize when they see the punishment that all power belongs to God, and God is severe in punishment. **166.** When those who were followers renounce those who they were following and see the retribution, all relations between them will be cut off. **167.** Those who followed will say, "If we had another chance, we would renounce them as they renounced us." As such, does God show them their deeds as a source of remorse for them, and they will not leave the Fire. **168.** O people! Eat of what is lawful and good and do not follow

Satan's footsteps. Indeed, he is your clear enemy. **169.** He only commands you to evil and obscenities, and to speak of God what you do not know. **170.** When it is said to them, "Follow what God has sent down," they say, "Indeed, we follow what our fathers did." What! Even though their fathers did not understand anything, nor were they rightly guided? **171.** Those who reject faith are like someone who hears nothing but calling and yelling. They do not understand, for they are deaf, dumb, and blind. **172.** O you who believe! Eat of the bounties We have provided you and give thanks to God if it is Him whom you worship. **173.** He has only forbidden you carrion, blood, the flesh of swine, and what has been offered to other than God. But whomever is constrained out of necessity, neither coveting nor transgressing, there will be no sin on him. Truly God is Forgiving and Merciful. **174.** Indeed, those who conceal what God sent down of the Book and sell it for a trivial price are those who ingest nothing but fire in their bellies. God will not address them on the Day of Resurrection, nor will He purify them. Their punishment will be painful. **175.** They are the ones who purchase falsehood in lieu of guidance, and punishment at the price of forgiveness. How will they endure the Fire? **176.** That is because God sent the Book down in truth. Truly, those who have disagreements about the Book are in a distant schism. **177.** It is not piety to turn your faces toward the east and west. Rather, pious is he who believes in God and the Last Day, the angels, the Book, the prophets, and whomever gives of wealth despite his love of it to kinsfolk, orphans, the indigent, the wanderer, the folks who ask, and the ransom of slaves, as are those who perform prayer, pays alms, fulfill their oaths when they pledge them, and those who are patient in misfortune, hardship, throughout moments of panic. It is they who are the truthful, and it is they who are the reverent. **178.** O you who believe! Retribution is prescribed for you in cases of murder: free man for free man, slave for slave, and female for female. But for one who receives any pardon from his brother, let it be treated honorably and pursued with kindness. Grant him compensation in good faith. This is a concession from your Lord and a mercy. Whoever transgresses after that shall face a painful punishment. **179.** In retribution, there is life for you, O people of understanding, that perhaps, you may refrain. **180.** It is prescribed that when death approaches one of you and he leaves some goods, to make a bequest for parents and kinsfolk in an honorable fashion — an obligation upon the reverent. **181.** Then if anyone changes it after hearing it, the guilt will be on those who change it. God truly hears and knows all things. **182.** But whomever fears injustice or wrongdoing from the testator and resolves matters aright between them, he commits no sin. God is truly Forgiving and Merciful. **183.** O you who believe! Fasting is prescribed for you as it was prescribed for those before you, that perhaps you may become reverent,

184. for days numbered. Whomever is ill among you or on a journey, it is a number of days, and for those who can afford it, the ransom is feeding an indigent person. But whoever gives more of his own free will, that is better for him. But to fast is best for you, if you only knew. 185. The month of Ramadan is when the Quran was sent down as a guide for people, as a clear sign of guidance, and as the Criterion. For whoever is present (not away from home) during this month, must fast, but whoever is ill or on a journey, the prescribed number of days should be made up later. God wants to make fasting manageable for you. He does not want to make it difficult for you so you may complete the course and celebrate God for having guided you, that perhaps you may give thanks. 186. When My servants ask you about Me, I am truly close. I answer the supplication of the suppliant if he calls upon Me. So let them respond to Me and believe in Me that perhaps they may be steered righteously. 187. You are permitted on the nights of fast to approach your wives for they are a garment for you, and you are a garment for them. God knew you were betraying yourselves, so He relented unto you and pardoned you. So now, have relations with them and seek what God has ordained for you and eat and drink until you see a clear difference between the white thread and the black thread of dawn. Then complete the fast until nightfall. Do not have relations with them while you are in retreat at mosques. Those are the boundaries set by God, so do not approach them. Thus does God make His signs clear to people that perhaps they may be reverent. 188. Do not consume another's wealth by unjust means nor offer it as bribes to judges in order to knowingly consume part of peoples' wealth. 189. They ask you about the new moons. Say, "They are markers of time for people and for the *hajj*." It is not piety if you enter homes from their back doors. Pious is he who is reverent and enters homes through their front doors. So revere God that you may prosper. 190. Fight in the way of God against those who fight against you, but do not commit aggression. Truly, God does not like transgressors. 191. Slay them wherever you come upon them and expel them from where they expelled you, for oppression is worse than slaying. Do not fight them near the Sacred Mosque unless they fight you there. But if they fight you, slay them. Such is the retribution of the disbelievers. 192. But if they cease, then God is Forgiving and Merciful. 193. Fight them until there is no oppression, and religion is for God. But if they cease, then let there be no enmity except against the oppressors. 194. The sacred month for the sacred month and sacrilege calls for retribution. So whomever transgresses against you, retaliate against him in the same way he transgressed against you. But fear God and know that God is with the reverent. 195. Spend in the way of God and do not hurl yourselves with your own hands into ruin. Be good. Truly God loves those who do good. 196. Complete the *hajj* and *'umrah* for God, but

if you are hindered, then give an offering, if possible. Do not shave your heads until the offering reaches its place of sacrifice. But whoever among you is ill or has an ailment over his scalp, then compensate through fasting, charity, or a sacrifice. When you are safe, let those who enjoy *'umrah* ahead of the *hajj* make an offering if they are able. Whoever cannot, let him fast three days during the *hajj* and seven days when you return. That is ten altogether. This applies to those whose families do not live near the Sacred Mosque. Revere God and know that God is severe in retribution. **197.** The *hajj* is during months well known. Whoever undertakes the *hajj*, let there be neither lewdness, nor iniquity, nor quarreling at the *hajj*. God knows of whatever good you do. Take provisions, but the best of provisions is reverence. O possessors of insight! Worship Me! **198.** There is no blame in seeking bounty from your Lord. But when you pour down from Arafat, remember God at the sacred ground. Remember Him as He guided you even though you were astray before this. **199.** Then go onward from where people go onward and ask God for forgiveness. God is most Forgiving and Merciful. **200.** Once you have completed your rites, remember God as you remember your fathers, or with even stronger remembrance. There are those among people who say, "Our Lord, award us in this world," but have no share in the Hereafter. **201.** But among them are those who say, "God award us good in this world and good in the Hereafter and guard us from the punishment of the Fire!" **202.** These will have a portion from what they have earned, and God is quick in reckoning. **203.** Remember God in the designated days, but whoever hurries on after two days commits no wrong and whoever stays on, commits no wrong if he is among the reverent. So fear God and know that you will be gathered unto Him. **204.** Among people, you may be impressed with he whose speech is about life in this world, yet he calls on God to witness what is in his heart, though he is the most contentious of adversaries. **205.** When he turns away, he endeavors to spread corruption on the earth, and to destroy cultivation, and offspring, but God does not like corruption. **206.** When he is told to revere God, he is sinfully overtaken by pride. Hell is enough for him. What an evil resting place! **207.** And among people is one who sells his soul, seeking God's approval, and God is kind to His servants. **208.** O you who believe! Enter all together in peace and do not follow the footsteps of Satan. He is truly an outright enemy. **209.** If you should stumble after clear signs have come to you, then know that God is Mighty and Wise. **210.** Are they waiting for God himself to come in the shadows of clouds, together with the angels, and that this settles the matter? Unto God all things are returned. **211.** Ask the Children of Israel how many clear signs We gave them. Whomever exchanges the Blessing of God after it has come to him, surely God is severe in retribution. **212.** The life of this world is alluring to those who disbelieve, and they mock those who believe, but the reverent will be above them on the Day of Resurrection. God provides for whomever He wills without reckoning. **213.** Humanity was a single nation, then God sent prophets as bearers of good news and to give warnings. He sent down the Book in truth to judge among people concerning their disagreements. The only ones who disagreed about it were those who received it after clear signs had come to them, driven by envy among themselves. Then by His leave, God guided those who believed in the truth and what they differed upon. God guides whomever He wills unto the straight path. **214.** Or did you assume you would enter the Garden without the trials as those who came before you? They encountered suffering and hardship, and they were so shaken in spirit that the Messenger and those who believed with him said, "When will God's Help arrive?" Ah! Indeed, God's Help is near. **215.** They ask you what they should spend in charity. Say, "Whatever you spend in wealth should be for your parents, kinsfolk, orphans, the indigent, and the wayfarers. Truly God knows of whatever good you do." **216.** Fighting is prescribed to you, even though you hate it. It is possible that you hate something though it is good for you, and it is possible that you like something though it is bad for you. God knows, and you do not know. **217.** They ask you about the sacred month and fighting during it. Say, "Fighting during the sacred month is grave, but blocking God's path, and disbelieving in Him and the sacred mosque and expelling its people from it is graver from God's perspective. Contention is greater than slaying." They will continue to fight you until they make you renounce your religion if they can. Whoever among you renounces his religion and dies as a disbeliever, their deeds will plunge in this world and the Hereafter. They will be inhabitants of the Fire, abiding in it forever. **218.** Truly those who believe and those who struggled in exile and strived in the way of God, it is they who implore for the mercy of God. God is Forgiving and Merciful. **219.** They ask you about wine and gambling. Say, "In them is great sin and benefits for people, but their sin is greater than their benefit." They ask you what they should give—say, "The surplus." Thus does God make clear to you the signs that perhaps you may reflect **220.** upon this world and the Hereafter. They ask you about orphans. Say, "What is best for their well-being. If you intermix with them, they are your brothers, and God knows the corrupt from the good. Had God willed, He could have overburdened you. Indeed, God is Mighty and Wise." **221.** Do not marry unbelieving women until they believe. Truly, a believing servant is better than an unbeliever, though she is alluring to you. And do not marry your women to unbelievers until they believe. They are those who call unto the Fire, but God calls unto the Garden and forgiveness, by His Leave. He makes His signs clear to people that perhaps they may remember. **222.** When they ask you about menstruation, say, "It is harmful, so abstain from women during menses and do not approach them until they are purified. When they are purified, engage with them in the manner ordained to you by God." Indeed, God likes those who repent, and He likes those who purify themselves. **223.** Your women are a tilth to you so engage with your tilth if you so desire. Send forth for your souls, revere God, and know that you will meet Him and inform believers of the good news. **224.** Do not make God an excuse through your oaths of piety, reverence, and in making peace between people. God is Hearing and Knowing. **225.** God will not admonish you for what was unintentional in your oaths, but He will admonish you for what your hearts intended. God is Forgiving and Clement. **226.** Those who foreswear their wives must wait four months. If they return, God is Forgiving and Merciful. **227.** But if they proceed with divorce, God is truly Hearing and Knowing. **228.** Divorced women should wait for three menstruation periods. It is not lawful for them to conceal what God has created in their wombs if they believe in God and the Last Day. Their husbands have better right to retake them during that time if they wish to reconcile. Women have rights similar to the rights against them, according to what is equitable, but men have a degree over them. God is Mighty and Wise. **229.** Divorce is permitted only twice (with the same woman); then either retain her honorably or release her honorably. It is not lawful for you to take back anything you have given her, unless both fear that they will not uphold the limits ordained by God. If you fear that they will not uphold the limits set by God, then there is no blame upon either of them if she sacrifices something for her release. These are the limits set by God, so do not transgress them. Those who transgress the limits set by God are the wrongdoers. **230.** Then if he divorces her, she will no longer be lawful to him until she marries a husband besides him. Should he divorce her, then there is no blame on the two if they return to each other. If they believe, they will uphold the limits ordained by God. These are the limits set by God that He has made clear to a people who know. **231.** When you divorce women and they have completed their waiting period, either retain them with kindness or release them with kindness. Do not retain them with the intention of causing harm or acting unjustly, for anyone who does so only brings harm upon himself. Do not make a mockery of God's signs and remember His favor upon you and the Book and wisdom He has sent down to guide you Revere God and know that God has knowledge of all things. **232.** When you have divorced women and they have fulfilled their term, do not prevent them from remarrying their husbands when they have amicably reconciled. This instruction is for those among you who believe in God and the Last Day. That is more righteous and purer for you. God knows and you do not know. **233.** Let mothers nurse their children for two full years for whomever desires to embrace the entire term. The father must provide for them and clothe them in kindness. No soul is tasked beyond its capacity.

Let no mother be harmed on account of her child, nor a father on account of his child, and the same thing applies to the heir. If the couple decide on weaning through mutual consent and discussion, they commit no error. But if you wish to have your child wet-nursed, there is no blame on you if you pay for what you receive, in kindness. Revere God and know that God sees whatever you do. **234.** Those among you who pass away and leave behind wives, they, the widows, must wait for a period of four months and ten days. When they have satisfied their term, there is no blame on you in what they do with themselves, within the realms of honor. God is Aware of whatever you do. **235.** You commit no error by announcing your engagement to women or even keeping it to yourselves. God knows that you intend to seek them in marriage, but do not make a secret promise with them unless you speak to them in an honorable way. Do not confirm the marriage tie until the term prescribed is fulfilled. Know that God knows what is in your souls, thus beware of Him, and know that God is Forgiving and Forbearing. **236.** There is no blame on you if you divorce women whom you have not touched or have not yet set a dowry. But provide for them, the wealthy, according to his means, and the underprivileged, according to his means—an honorable provision—a requirement upon the righteous. **237.** If you divorce them before touching them, but you have set a dowry, then give them half of what you had set unless they relinquish it, or he who holds the marriage tie forgoes it. But to forego is nearer to piety. And do not forget generosity between one another. God sees everything you do. **238.** Guard your prayers, and the Middle Prayer. Stand before God in devout obedience, **239.** but if you are in fear of an enemy, then pray on foot or riding. Then when you feel safe, remember God, as He has taught you what you did not know. **240.** Those among you who pass away and leave behind wives should bequeath to their wives a one-year provision without sending them away. But if they leave, there is no blame on you in what they do with themselves as long as they preserve their honor. God is Mighty and Wise. **241.** Divorced women shall be given maintenance and an honorable provision, a duty upon the righteous. **242.** Thus does God make His signs clear to you so that perhaps you may understand. **243.** Have you not seen those who left their homes by the thousands, fearing death? Whereupon God said to them, "Die," then He restored them to life. Truly God is gracious, but most people are ungrateful. **244.** So fight in the way of God and know that God is Hearing and Knowing. **245.** Who is he who will lend unto God a considerable loan that God will multiply for him many times over? God withholds or amplifies, and unto Him you will be returned. **246.** Have you not seen the assembly of the Children of Israel, after Moses, when they said to a prophet of theirs, "Appoint a king for us that we may fight in the way of God." He said, "Might it be that if fighting were prescribed for you, you would not fight?" They said,

"Why should we not fight in the way of God given we were turned away from our homes and our children?" Then when fighting was prescribed for them, they turned back, except for a few among them. God knows well the wrongdoers. **247.** Their prophet said to them, "God has appointed Saul to be a king over you." They said, "How can he have authority over us when we have more right to authority than he, and he has not been given an abundance of wealth?" He said, "Truly God has raised him over you and has increased him abundantly in knowledge and physique." God gives His Authority to whomever He desires, and God is All-Encompassing and All-Knowing. **248.** Their prophet said to them, "Truly the sign of his sovereignty will be that the Ark of the Covenant will come to you bearing serenity from your Lord, a remnant left from the House of Moses and the House of Aaron, carried by the angels. Truly, in that is a sign for you, if you are believers." **249.** When Saul set out with the forces, he said, "Surely, God will try you with a river. Whomever drinks from it, is not of me, and whomever does not taste of it, is of me, except one who sips a handful." But they drank of it, except for a few among them. So when he crossed it, he and those who believed with him said, "We have no power today against Goliath and his forces." But those who were convinced they would meet God said, "How many of a small group have conquered a large group by God's will?" God is with the patient. **250.** When they advanced against Goliath and his forces they said, "Our Lord, pour patience upon us, make our steps firm, and help us against a disbelieving people." **251.** They overpowered them by God's Leave and David slew Goliath. God gave him sovereignty and wisdom and taught him what He willed. Had God not repelled people, some by means of others, the earth would have been corrupted, but God is Possessed of Bounty for the worlds. **252.** These are the signs of God that We recite to you in truth, and indeed, you are among the messengers. **253.** We favored these messengers, some above others. God spoke to some while He raised up others in ranks. We gave Jesus, son of Mary, clear signs and strengthened him with the Holy Spirit. Had God so willed, those who succeeded him would not have fought one another after clear signs had come to them. But they contended. Some among them believed while others among them disbelieved. Had God so willed, they would have not fought one another, but God does as He wills. **254.** O you who believe! Spend from what We have afforded you before the day comes wherein there will be neither bargaining, nor friendship, nor intercession. As for the disbelievers, they are the wrongdoers. **255.** God, there is no god but He, the Living, the Superb Upright Sustainer. Neither slumber, nor sleep overtake Him. Unto Him belong whatever is in the heavens and whatever is on the earth. Who is there that can intercede with Him except with His permission? He Knows of what is before them and of what is behind them. They grasp nothing of His Knowledge, save if He wills. His Throne embraces the heavens and the earth. He does not become tired of protecting them. He is the Exalted, and the Magnificent. **256.** There is no coercion in religion and truth has been clearly distinguished from falsehood. Whoever rejects idols and believes in God, will have grasped the most trustworthy and unbreakable handhold. God is Hearing and Knowing. **257.** God is the Protector of those who believe. He takes them out of darkness into the light. As for those who disbelieve, their protectors are the idols who take them out of light into darkness. They are the inhabitants of the Fire who will abide in it forever. **258.** Have you not observed he who disputed with Abraham about his Lord because God granted him sovereignty? Abraham said, "It is my Lord Who provides life and death." He said, "I provide life and cause death." Abraham said, "Truly God brings the sun from the east, so bring it from the west." So was the disbeliever confounded. God does not guide wrongdoing people. **259.** Or like he who passed through a village as it lay collapsed upon its foundations. He said, "How will God ever bring this back to life after its demise?" So God took his life for a hundred years, then resurrected him. He said, "How long have you lingered?" He said, "I lingered for a day or part of a day." He said, "No, you have lingered a hundred years. Look at your food and your drink. They show no signs of aging. Look at your donkey. We have made you a sign for people. Look at the bones, how We arranged them, and then dressed them with flesh." Once it became clear to him, he said, "I know that God is Powerful over all things." **260.** When Abraham said, "O Lord, show me how You revive the dead," He said, "Do you not believe?" Abraham said, "Of course, but I want to put my heart at ease." He said, "Take four birds, and let them be drawn to you. Then place a piece of them on every mountain, then call them and they will rush back to you. Know that God is Mighty and Wise." **261.** The parable of those who spend their wealth in the way of God is like a single seed that sprouts seven ears, each ear containing a hundred grains. God multiplies for whomever He wills. God is All-Encompassing and All-Knowing. **262.** Those who spend their wealth in the way of God and then do not follow up with their gifts with reminders of generosity or with injury will have their reward with their Lord. No fear will overcome them, nor will they grieve. **263.** A kind word and forgiveness is better than an act of charity followed by injury. God is Self-Sufficient and Clement. **264.** O you who believe! Do not strike down your acts of charity through pretention and injury like he who spends his wealth to be seen by people yet does not believe in God or the Last Day. His likeness is that of a smooth, dusty stone where a rainstorm cleanses it and leaves it barren. They will have no power over anything they earned. God does not guide a disbelieving people. **265.** The simile of those who spend their wealth seeking God's Good Pleasure and out of conviction in their souls is like that of a garden upon a hill. A heavy rain strikes it and brings forth its yield twofold. If a heavy rain does not strike it, then a light rain suffices, for God sees whatever you do. **266.** Would any one of you wish to have a garden of date palms and grapevines with rivers running below, where he will have of every kind of fruit therein—then is stricken by old age, has weak children, and is struck and burnt down by a whirlwind of fire? Thus does God make clear to you His signs that perhaps you may reflect. **267.** O you who believe! Give of the good things you have earned and from what We have produced for you from the earth. Do not seek the inferior things to give away or what you would not take for yourselves unless your eyes were closed. Know that God is Self-Sufficient and Praised. **268.** Satan threatens you with poverty and commands you to indecency. God promises you forgiveness and bounty from Him. God is All-Encompassing and All-Knowing. **269.** He Grants wisdom to whomever He wills. Whoever is granted wisdom has been granted an abundance of good. Yet no one remembers except for those endowed with insight. **270.** What you expend from the expendable or from the vow you vow, God certainly knows of it, and the wrongdoers will have no helpers. **271.** It is fine if you disclose your acts of charity, but it is better if you give to the poor in private. This will exonerate you from some of your misdeeds. God is Aware of whatever you do. **272.** Their guidance is not your responsibility since God guides whom He wills. Whatever charity you give is for your own good but must be spent while seeking the Countenance of God. Whatever charity you give will be repaid to you in full, and you will not be wronged. **273.** It is for the poor who are inhibited from traveling the earth in the way of God. They are perceived by the ignorant as wealthy because of their dignity. You know them by their modesty. They do not ask of people importunately. Whatever charity you give, surely God knows of it. **274.** Those who spend their wealth by night and by day, secretly or publicly, will have their reward with their Lord. They will have no fear, nor will they grieve. **275.** Those who devour usury will not rise except as someone confounded by the touch of Satan. That is because they say, "Oh trade is like usury," though God has permitted trade and forbidden usury. One who desists after receiving warnings from his Lord may keep his past earnings and his case rests with God. Those who repeat the offense, will inhabit the Fire and abide in it forever. **276.** God wipes out usury but nurtures all acts of charity. God does not love sinful self-seekers. **277.** Those who believe, perform righteous deeds, maintain prayer, and give alms will have their reward with God. They will have no fear, nor will they grieve. **278.** O you who believe! Revere God and leave what remains of usury if you are believers. **279.** If you do not, then be alerted of a war from God and His Messenger. If you repent, you will have the capital sum of your wealth, and you will neither wrong nor be wronged. **280.** If one is in difficulty, allow for relief and it would be better for you to consider it charity, if you only knew. **281.** Be mindful of a day when you will be returned to God. Then every soul will be paid in full for what it earned, and they will not be wronged. **282.** O you who believe! When you contract a debt with one another for a certain time, write it down. Let a scribe write between you justly. Do not let the scribe refuse to write as God has taught him. So let him write and let the debtor dictate, and let him revere God, his Lord, and not eliminate anything from it. If the debtor is feeble-minded, weak, or unable to dictate himself, then let his guardian dictate justly. Call to witness two men among you, and if there are not two men, then a man and two women whom you approve as witnesses, that if one of the two errs, the other can remind her. Do not let witnesses refuse when they are called, and do not be opposed to writing it down, whether small, or large, including the time of repayment. That is more equitable with God, more suitable as evidence, and more likely to keep you from doubt. But if it is a trade transaction of current goods operating among yourselves, there is no blame on you if you do not write it down. Take witnesses when you trade between yourselves and do not let a scribe or witness be harmed. If you do this, it would be wicked of you. Revere God. God teaches you and God has knowledge of all things. **283.** If you are on a journey and cannot find a scribe, then let there be a pledge in hand. If one of you trusts the other, let him who is trusted deliver his trust, and let him revere God his Lord. Do not conceal the testimony. Whoever conceals it, his heart is indeed sinful. God knows of whatever you do. **284.** To God belongs whatever is in the heavens and whatever is on the earth. Whether you disclose what is in your souls or conceal it, God will hold you accountable for it. He forgives whomever He wills and punishes whomever He wills, and God is Powerful over all things. **285.** The Messenger believes in what was sent down to him from his Lord as do the believers. Each believes in God, His angels, His Scriptures, and His messengers. "We make no distinction between any of His messengers." They say, "We hear and obey. Your forgiveness, our Lord! Unto You is the final destination." **286.** God does not place a burden on a soul beyond what it can bear. It will have what it has earned and be liable for what it has perpetrated. "Our Lord! Pardon us if we forget or err. Our Lord! Do not lay a burden upon us as You laid on those before us. Our Lord! Do not impose on us what we do not have the strength to bear. Pardon us, forgive us, and have mercy upon us. You are our Master, so help us against the disbelieving people."

Surah 3

The House of Imrān

al-Imran

In the Name of God, the Compassionate, the Merciful

1. *Alif. Lām. Mim.* **2.** God, there is no god, but He, the living, the Self-Subsisting. **3.** He sent the Book down to you in truth, confirming what was before it. He sent down the Torah and the Gospel **4.** earlier as a guide to mankind, and He sent down the Criterion. Truly those who disbelieve in the signs of God will have a severe punishment. God is Mighty, the Possessor of Vengeance. **5.** Truly nothing is hidden from God on earth or in Heaven. **6.** It is He Who shapes you in the wombs as He wills. There is no god, but He, the Almighty and the Wise. **7.** He is the One who revealed the Book to you. Within it are verses of foundational wisdom, while other signs are allegorical. But those who have perversity in their hearts will follow the allegorical, seeking enticement and an interpretation. However, no one knows its interpretation except for God and those firmly rooted in knowledge. They say, "We believe in it. All is from our Lord." None will remember except those endowed with insight. **8.** "Our Lord! Do not make our hearts deviate after having guided us and grant us Mercy from Your Presence. You are, indeed, the Giver." **9.** "Our Lord! You will gather the people for a Day where there is no doubt." God will not fail the encounter. **10.** As for those who disbelieve, neither their wealth nor their children will benefit them in any way against God. They will be fuel for the Fire. **11.** It is like the affair of the House of Pharoah and those before him. They denied Our signs and God took them for their sins. God is severe in retribution. **12.** Say to the disbelievers, "You will be overcome and gathered unto Hell, an evil resting place!" **13.** There is a sign for you in the two parties that met. One party fighting in the way of God and the other, disbelieving. From what their eyes could see, they appeared to be a double of themselves. God strengthens through His help whomever He wills. In that is truly an example for those with insight. **14.** Embellished in the eyes of humans is the love of passion. Among them: women, children, hoarded heaps of gold and silver, branded horses, livestock, and tillage. These are the worldly pleasures in life, but to God belongs the best return. 15. Say, "Should I tell you of what is better than that for those who are reverent? God reserves Gardens with rivers running beneath them. They will abide therein, with pure spouses, and satisfaction from God." God is observant of His servants 16. who say, "O Lord! We truly believe, so forgive us for our sins and shield us from the punishment of the Fire—" 17. the patient, the truthful, the devoutly obedient, the spenders, and the those who seek forgiveness before dawn. 18. God bears witness that there is no god but He, as do the angels and those endowed with insight, while upholding justice. There is no god but He, the Mighty, the Wise. 19. Religion before God, is indeed, Islām. Those who were given the Book did not differ except out of envy among themselves and after they had received knowledge. For whomever disbelieves in God's signs, God is truly swift in calling to account. 20. So if they argue with you, say, "I submit my face to God as do those who follow me." Say to People of the Book and to those who are unlettered: "Do you submit?" Then if they submit, they will be rightly guided, but if they turn away, it is solely your duty to convey the message, and God is observant of His servants. 21. Truly, those who disbelieve in God's signs, and slay the prophets unjustifiably, and slay those who bid justice among people— inform them of a painful punishment. 22. They are the ones whose deeds will have come to nothing in this world and the Hereafter. They will have no helpers. 23. Have you not considered those who were given a portion of the Book, calling upon God to judge between them; then a group of them turns away in protest? 24. This is because they said, "The Fire will not touch us except for a limited number of days." What they invented has deceived them in their religion. 25. How will it be when We gather them unto a Day in which there is no doubt, and every soul will be compensated for what it earned? They will not be wronged. 26. Say, "O God, Master of Sovereignty. You give sovereignty to whomever You desire and seize sovereignty from whomever You desire. You honor whomever You desire, and You disgrace whomever You desire. All good is in Your Hand. You truly have power over all things. 27. You cause the night to merge into the day and the day to merge into the night. You bring out the living from the dead and You bring out the dead from the living; and You give sustenance to whomever You please without measure." 28. Do not let the believers take the disbelievers as protectors in preference over the believers. Anyone who does this has no connection with God, except to protect yourselves cautiously from them. God Himself warns you, and to Him is your ultimate return. 29. Say, "Whether you conceal what is in your hearts or disclose it, God knows of it, and He knows whatever is in the heavens and whatever is on the earth." God is Powerful over all things. 30. On the Day each soul finds itself presented with the good deeds it has performed and the evil it has performed, it would wish for a great distance between the two. God Himself is warning you, and to His servants, He is Kind. 31. Say, "If you love God, follow me and God will love you and forgive you your sins. God is Forgiving and Merciful." 32. Say, "Obey God and obey the Messenger." If they turn away, then surely God does not love the disbelievers. 33. Verily God chose Adam, Noah, the House of Abraham, and the House of Imrān above the worlds 34. as progeny, one from another. God is All-Hearing and All-Knowing. 35. Remember the wife of Imrān said, "My Lord! Truly I vow to You what is in my womb in dedication. Therefore, accept it from me. Truly, You are All-Hearing and All-Knowing." 36. When she bore her, she said, "My Lord! I have borne a female." God Knows best what she bore, and the male is not like the female. "I have named her Mary, and I am placing her and her progeny under your protection from the outcast Satan." 37. Her Lord accepted her with gracious acceptance and nurtured with a beautiful nurturing. He placed her under the care of Zachariah. Each time Zachariah entered upon her in the sanctuary, he found sustenance with her. He said, "O Mary, where did you get this from?" She replied, "It is from God. Truly God provides for whomever He pleases without measure." 38. At this point, Zachariah called upon his Lord, "My Lord, grant me from Your presence a good progeny. You are truly the Hearer of supplications." 39. Then, while he was standing in prayer in the sanctuary, the angels called to him: "Truly God gives you good news of John, testifying a word from God, noble and chaste, a prophet from among the righteous." 40. He said, "My Lord, how will I have a boy when age has overcome me, and my wife is barren?" He said, "Thus God does whatever He wills." 41. He said, "My Lord, engage a sign for me." He said, "Your sign is to not speak to people for three days except through signals. Remember your Lord abundantly and glorify [Him] in the evening and at dawn." 42. The angels said, "O Mary, Truly God has chosen you and purified you. He raised you above the women of the world. 43. O Mary! Be devoutly obedient to your Lord. Prostrate and bow as do those who bow." 44. What We reveal to you is from the news of the Unseen. You were not among them when they cast their lots as to who among them would care for Mary and you were not among them when they quarreled. 45. The angels said, "O Mary, truly God gives you good news of a Word from Him. His name is the Messiah, Jesus, son of Mary, highly honored in this world and the Hereafter and from those in close proximity. 46. He will speak to people from the crib and in maturity and will be among the righteous." 47. She said, "My Lord, how will I have a child when no human has touched me?" He said, "Thus does God create whatever He wills." When He decrees a matter, He but says to it, "Be!" and it is. **48.** He will teach him the Book, Wisdom, the Torah, and the Gospel, **49.** a messenger to the Children of Israel. "Truly I have brought you a sign from your Lord. I will create for you the semblance of a bird out of clay. I will breathe into it and by God's Leave, it will become a bird. I will heal the blind and the leper and give life to the dead by God's Leave. I will inform you of what you eat and what you store in your homes. Truly there is a sign for you if you are believers. **50.** I have come confirming what was before me of the Torah, and to make lawful for you part of what was forbidden to you. I have come to you with a sign from your Lord. So fear God and obey me. **51.** Truly God is my Lord and your Lord, so worship Him. This is a straight path." **52.** When Jesus sensed disbelief in them, he said, "Who are my helpers unto God?" The disciples said, "We are God's helpers. We believe in God and bear witness that we are Muslim. **53.** Our Lord, we believe in what You have sent down, and we follow the messenger, so count us among the witnesses." **54.** They planned and planned, and God planned. God is the best of planners. **55.** Remember when God said, "O Jesus, I will take you back, raise you to Myself, and purify you from those who disbelieved. I will make those who follow you superior to the disbelievers until the Day of Resurrection. Then, to Me you will all return, and I will judge between you concerning what you used to dispute. **56.** As for those who disbelieved, I will punish them severely in this world and the Hereafter, and they will have no helpers. **57.** But those who believe and do righteous deeds will receive their full reward, for God does not love the wrongdoers." **58.** These are the signs and the Wise Reminder We recite to you. **59.** Truly, in God's sight, the example of Jesus is like that of Adam. He created him from dust, then said to him, "Be!" and he was. **60.** The truth is from your Lord, therefore, do not be among the doubters. **61.** So whomever disputes with you after knowledge has come to you, say, "Come! Let us call upon our sons and your sons, our women, and your women, and ourselves and yourselves, then, let us pray earnestly and invoke the curse of God on those who lie." **62.** This is indeed the true account. There is no god but God, and Truly God is the Mighty, the Wise. **63.** If they turn away, then God knows well the corrupt. **64.** Say, "O People of the Book! Come to common terms between us and you: that we will worship none but God and will not associate anything with Him and will not take one another as lords in place of God." If they turn away, then say, "Bear witness that we are Muslim." **65.** O People of the Book! Why do you argue about Abraham as neither the Torah nor the Gospel was sent down until after him? Do you not understand? **66.** Behold! You are the very ones who dispute about matters you understand, so why do you argue about things beyond your knowledge? God knows, while you do not. **67.** Abraham was neither a Jew nor a Christian. He was a *hanīf* and was not among the idolaters. **68.** Indeed, the people most deserving of Abraham are those who followed him, this prophet, and those who believe. God is the Protector of the believers. **69.** A group among the People of the Book wishes to mislead you, but they only lead themselves astray, though they fail to realize it. **70.** O People of the Book! Why do you deny God's signs while you are witnesses to the truth? **71.** O People of the Book! Why do you clothe truth with falsehood and knowingly conceal the truth? **72.** A group of disbelievers from the People of the Book say, "Believe in what was sent down unto those who believe at the peak of daylight and disbelieve at the end of the day that perhaps they may return. **73.** Do not believe anyone except he who follows your religion." Say, "Indeed, guidance is God's Guidance in case anyone is granted what is comparable to what you were granted or argues with you before your Lord." Say, "Truly Bounty is in God's Hand. He grants it to whomever He wills, and God is All-Encompassing and All-Knowing." **74.** He selects for His Mercy whomever He wills, and God is Possessed of Great Bounty. **75.** Among the People of the Book is one whom were you to entrust with a quintal, he would give it back to you. Yet among them is one, whom were you to entrust with a dinar, he would not give it back to you unless you persistently stood over him. That is because they say, "There is nothing to stop us when it comes to the non-Jews." They knowingly tell a lie against God. **76.** But indeed, whomever fulfills his covenant and is reverent, God truly loves the reverent. **77.** Indeed those who sell God's covenant and their faith for a trivial price, will have no portion in the Hereafter. God will not speak to them on the Day of Resurrection, nor will He purify them. They will have a painful punishment. **78.** Indeed, there is a portion among them who twist the Book with their tongues, and you would assume it was from the Book, but it is not from the Book. They say, "This is from God," though it is not from God. They knowingly tell a lie against God. **79.** It is not for any human being — to whom God has given the Book, judgment, and prophethood — to then say to the people, "Be servants of me instead of God." Rather, he would say, "Be sages by virtue of your teaching of the Book and your study of it." **80.** He would not direct you to take the angels and the prophets as lords. Would he direct you to disbelief after you had submitted? **81.** Remember when God made the covenant of the prophets— "From what I have given you of a Book and Wisdom, should a messenger then come to you confirming what is with you, you will certainly believe in him, and you will help him." He said, "Do you agree to affirm My Covenant as binding on you?" They said, "We agree." He said, "Bear witness, for I am with you among the witnesses." **82.** Then whoever turns away after that, they are the deceitful. **83.** Are they seeking other than God's religion when whoever is in the heavens and on the earth has submitted to Him willingly or unwillingly? To Him they will be returned. **84.** Say, "We believe in God and what has been sent down to us and what has been sent down to Abraham, Ishmael, Isaac, Jacob, and the Tribes, and in what was given Moses, Jesus, and the prophets from their Lord. We make no distinction among any of them, and unto Him we submit." **85.** Whoever seeks a religion other than Islām, it will not be accepted of him. In the Hereafter, he will be among the losers. **86.** How will God guide a people who have disbelieved after having believed, having borne witness that the messenger was true, and clear signs had come to them? God does not guide people who are wrongdoers. **87.** For them, their penalty is the curse of God, the angels, and all people. **88.** They will dwell there forever, and their punishment will not be lightened, nor will they be granted respite, **89.** except for those who repent afterward and make amends. God is truly Forgiving and Merciful. **90.** Indeed, those who disbelieve after having believed, then increase their disbelief, their repentance will not be accepted, for they have gone astray. **91.** Truly those who disbelieve and die as disbelievers, were they to offer all the gold on earth, it will not be accepted from any of them. There will be a painful punishment for them, and they will have no helpers. **92.** You will never obtain piety until you give of what you love. God is Aware of whatever you give. **93.** All food was lawful unto the Children of Israel except for what Israel forbade upon itself before the Torah was sent down. Say, "Bring the Torah and recite it if you are truthful." **94.** Whoever invents a lie against God after that—they are the transgressors. **95.** Say, "God has spoken the truth. So follow the creed of Abraham, a *hanīf*. He was not of the idolaters." **96.** The first house established for people was indeed, *Al Masjid Al Haram*, the blessed Ka'ba, full of blessing, and guidance for the worlds. **97.** In it are clear signs, 'the Station of Abraham.' Whoever enters it will be secure. For those who can find a way, pilgrimage to the House is a duty to God. For truly, whoever disbelieves, God is beyond need of the worlds. **98.** Say, "O People of the Book! Why do you disbelieve in God's signs when God witnesses what you do?" **99.** Say, "O People of the Book! Why do you obstruct those who believe from the path of God? Are you trying to make it crooked when you were witnesses? God is not heedless of what you do." **100.** O you who believe! If you obey a group among those who were given the Book, they will turn you into disbelievers after you were believers. **101.** How can you disbelieve while God's signs are recited to you and His Messenger is among you? Whoever holds fast to God will indeed be guided to a straight path. **102.** O you who believe! Revere God with due reverence and die only in submission. **103.** Hold fast to the rope of God, altogether, and do not be divided. Remember the Blessing of God upon you when you were enemies, and He joined your hearts. You have since become brothers through His Blessings. You were on the brink of a pit of fire, and He delivered you from it. Thus does God clarify his revelations to you that perhaps you may be rightly guided. **104.** Let there be among you a nation calling to the good, affirming right, and forbidding wrong. It is they who will prosper. **105.** Do not be like those who divided themselves and disputed the clear signs after these had come to them. It is they who will be severely punished **106.** on the Day when some faces will be whitened, and some faces will be blackened. As for those whose faces blacken, "Did you disbelieve after you had believed? Then taste the punishment after having disbelieved." **107.** As for those whose faces whiten, they will be in God's Mercy, abiding forever. **108.** These are God's signs which We recite to you in truth, and God does not desire wrong for the worlds. **109.** To God belongs whatever is in the heavens and whatever is on the earth. Unto God all matters are returned. **110.** You were the best of evolved nations among mankind, affirming righteousness, forbidding wrongdoing, and believing in God. If the People of the Book had believed, it would have been better for them. There are believers among them, but most are sinners. **111.** They will not harm you, save through annoyance. If they fight against you, they will retreat in defeat and receive no support. **112.** They will be struck with shame wherever they stand, save by means of a lifeline from God and a lifeline from the people. They drew the wrath of God upon themselves and will be struck with destitution because they disbelieved in God's signs and killed prophets unjustly. That is for disobeying and transgressing. **113.** They are not all the same. Among People of the Book is an upright people who recite God's revelations throughout the night while they prostrate. **114.** They believe in God and the Last Day, advocate right, and forbid wrong. They are quick to do good deeds. They are among the righteous. **115.** They will not be denied whatever good they do. God knows the reverent. **116.** Indeed, among those who disbelieve, neither their wealth nor their children will benefit them at all against God. They are the inhabitants of the Fire, abiding there forever. **117.** What they spend in this worldly life is similar to a frosty wind that strikes and destroys the tilth of a people who wronged themselves. God did not wrong them — they wronged themselves. **118.** O you who believe! Do not take intimates outside of yourselves. They will not fail to corrupt you. They want you to suffer. Hatred has emerged from their mouths and what is concealed in their hearts is even greater. We have clarified Our signs for you, were you to understand. **119.** So here! You are among those who love them, but they do not love you though you believe in the entire Book. When they meet you, they say, "We believe," but when they are alone, they bite their fingers in rage at you. Say, "Die in your rage!" God truly knows what lies within their hearts. **120.** If you are touched by good, it upsets them, but if evil overtakes you, they rejoice in it. However, if you are patient and reverent, their cunningness will not harm you. God truly grasps what they do. **121.** Remember when you left your household at daybreak to assign battle positions for the believers. God is Hearing and Knowing. **122.** Remember when two parties among you almost lost courage though God was their Protector — in God believers must trust. **123.** God has helped you at Badr when you were down. So revere God that perhaps you may show gratitude. **124.** Remember when you said to the believers, "Is it not enough for you that your Lord should reinforce you by sending down three thousand angels?" **125.** Surely, if you are patient and reverent, even if they come rushing at you, your Lord will reinforce you with five thousand distinctively marked angels. **126.** God only made glad tidings for you that your hearts may be reassured by it. There is no help but from God the Mighty, the Wise, **127.** that He may cut off a party of those who disbelieve or subdues them, so they retreat, disappointed. **128.** It is not your decision whether He relents to them or punishes them, for indeed, they are the wrongdoers. **129.** To God belongs all that is in the heavens and all that is on the earth. He forgives whomever He pleases, and He punishes whomever He pleases. God is Most Forgiving and Most Merciful. **130.** O you who believe! Do not devour usury, doubling and multiplying. Revere God that perhaps you may prosper. **131.** Be mindful of the Fire that has been prepared for the disbelievers. **132.** Obey God and the Messenger that perhaps you may receive mercy. **133.** Rush unto forgiveness from your Lord and for a widespread Garden that embraces the heavens and the earth. It is prepared for the reverent **134.** who give with ease or hardship, contain their rage, and forgive others. God loves the righteous **135.** and those who, when they commit an indecency or wrong themselves, remember God and seek forgiveness for their sins — for who can forgive sins except God? — and they do not persist knowingly in their wrongdoing. **136.** For these, their reward is forgiveness from their Lord, and Gardens with rivers running below, abiding there forever. The reward of the industrious is indeed blessed. **137.** Different traditions have passed before you, so travel the earth and observe the fate of the deniers. **138.** This is a display for humanity, and guidance and warning for the reverent. **139.** Do not weaken and do not grieve, and you will gain mastery if you are believers. **140.** If a wound afflicts you, a similar wound has afflicted others. Such days are given to people in turn that God may know those who believe and take witnesses among you, for God does not love the wrongdoers. **141.** Thus does God purify the believers and annihilate the disbelievers. **142.** Or did you assume you would enter the Garden without God knowing those among you who strived and without knowing those who were patient? **143.** You had indeed longed for death before you met him. You have now seen him while looking on. **144.** Muhammad is no more than a messenger. Messengers have indeed, passed away before him. So if he dies or is slain, will you turn back on your heels? Whoever turns back on his heels will not harm God at all, but God will reward the grateful. **145.** It is not for any soul to die save by God's Leave, a fixed term. Whoever desires the reward of this world, We will give him of it and whoever desires the reward of the Hereafter, We will give him of it. We will reward the grateful. **146.** How many a prophet had God's numerous reverent fighters alongside him? They did not waver in face of what afflicted them in the cause of God, nor did they weaken, nor did they demean themselves. God loves the patient. **147.** All they said was, "Our Lord! Forgive us for our sins and our extravagance in our affairs. Strengthen our steps and help us against the disbelieving people." **148.** God gave them the reward of this world and the best of rewards in the Hereafter. God loves the righteous. **149.** O you who believe! If you obey those who disbelieve, they will turn you back on your heels to your resulting in your own loss. **150.** Rather, God is your Guardian, and He is the best of helpers. **151.** We will cast terror into the hearts of the disbelievers because they attribute to God partners for which He has not sent given any authority. Their refuge will be the Fire, and evil is the abode of the wrongdoers. **152.** God was certainly true to His Promise to you when you eliminated them by His Leave, until you flinched, disputed the command with one another, and disobeyed after He had shown you what you loved. Among you are those who desire this world and among you are those who desire the Hereafter. He then turned you from them to test you, and then, truly, He pardoned you. God is Possessed of Bounty for the believers. **153.** Remember you were climbing up high ground without glancing at anyone while the Messenger was calling at you from your rear. Then He rewarded you with sorrow upon sorrow that you may not grieve over what you missed or what happened to you. God is Aware of whatever you do. **154.** Then after sorrow, He sent security down upon you, a sleepiness that overcame a group among you while another group was stirred to anxiety, thinking unjustly about God—thoughts from the Age of Ignorance—asking, "Do we have any choice in the decision?" Say, "The decision belongs entirely to God." They conceal in their souls what they do not disclose to you, saying, "If we made a decision, we would not have been slain here." Say, "Had you stayed in your houses, those who were destined to be slain would have gone forth to their places of rest." For God tests what is in your breasts that He may purify what is in your hearts. God knows what lies within your breasts. **155.** Those among you who turned back on the day the two armies met were made to stumble by Satan due to the sins they had committed. But God certainly pardoned them, for truly God is Forgiving and Clement. **156.** O you who believe! Do not be like those who disbelieve and say of their brethren, when they travel the earth or engage in fighting, "Had they stayed with us, they would not have died and been slain." God may make this a source of regret in their hearts. God gives life and death, and God sees whatever you do. **157.** Indeed, if you are slain and die in the way of God, forgiveness and mercy from God are certainly better than what they accumulate. **158.** If you are slain or die, you will surely be gathered unto God. **159.** It was through mercy from God that you were lenient with them. Had you been harsh or hard-hearted, they would have scattered about you. Therefore, pardon them, ask forgiveness for them and consult them in matters. Once you are ready, put your trust in God, for God loves those who trust. **160.** If God helps you, no one can overcome you. If He forsakes you, then who can help you thereafter? Let the believers trust in God. **161.** It is not for any prophet to act dishonestly. Whoever defrauds will bring what he gained through dishonesty on the Day of Resurrection. Then each soul will be paid it's due, and they will not be wronged. **162.** Is he who pursues God's satisfaction like he who draws on God's wrath and his refuge is Hell? A wretched final destination! **163.** From God's perspective, they are ranked by degree, and God sees whatever they do. **164.** God certainly favored the believers when He sent a Messenger among them who recites His revelations unto them, and purifies them, and teaches them the Book and Wisdom, though previously, they were in obvious error. **165.** Or when an affliction befell you, even though you wrought an affliction twice as great, did you say, "Where did this come from?" Say, "It is from yourselves." Truly God is Powerful over all things. **166.** What happened to you on the day the two forces met was by God's Leave, that He may know the believers **167.** and that He may know the hypocrites. It was said to them, "Come fight in the way of God or defend yourselves." They said, "Had we known there would be fighting, we would have followed you." They were closer to disbelief than to belief on that day, saying with their mouths what was not in their hearts, but God knows best what they conceal. **168.** Those who said of their brethren while they were sitting in ease, "Had they obeyed us, they would not have been slain." Say, "Then avert death from yourselves if you are truthful." **169.** Do not consider those slain in the way of God to be dead. Rather, they are alive with their Lord, and provided for, **170.** exulting in what God has given them from His Bounty and rejoicing in those who have not yet joined them from among those left behind. No fear will come upon them, nor will they grieve **171.** as they rejoice in God's Blessing and Bounty. God does not allow for the reward of believers to be vain. **172.** There will be a great reward for those who were virtuous and reverent, and who responded to the call of God and the Messenger even after they had been afflicted with wounds. **173.** Those unto whom people said, "Truly the people have gathered against you, so fear them" — it only increased their faith. They said, "God is enough for us. He is an excellent Guardian!" **174.** Therefore, they returned untouched by harm through the Blessing and Bounty of God. They pursued the Satisfaction of God, and God is Possessed of Tremendous Bounty. **175.** It is only Satan who instills fear of his followers in you. Do not fear them but fear Me if you are believers. **176.** Do not let those who rush unto disbelief grieve you. Truly they will not harm God at all. God does not desire to give them a share in the Hereafter, and they will be greatly punished. **177.** Truly those who have purchased disbelief over belief will not harm God at all. They will have a painful punishment. **178.** Do not let those who disbelieve assume that the respite We grant them is good for them. We only grant them respite that they may increase in sin. They will have a humiliating punishment. **179.** God will not leave the believers in their current state until He separates the bad from the good. God will not inform you of the Unseen, however, God selects whomever He wills from among His messengers. Therefore, believe in God and His messengers and if you believe and are reverent, you will have a great reward. **180.** Do not let those who are miserly with what God has given them from His Bounty assume that it is good for them; rather, it is evil for them. On the Day of Resurrection, they will be collared by what they were miserly with. Unto God belongs the inheritance of the heavens and the earth. God is Aware of whatever you do. **181.** God has certainly heard the words of those who said, "God is poor, and we are rich." We will record what they said, and their unjust slaying of the prophets and We will say, "Taste the punishment of the burning." **182.** That is because of what your hands sent forth and God will certainly not oppress His servants. **183.** Those who said, "Truly God promised us not to believe in a prophet until he brings us a sacrifice consumed by fire." Say, "Worthy messengers had certainly, come to you with clear signs before me and with what you are speaking of, so why did you slay them if you are truthful?" **184.** If they denied you, they had certainly denied messengers before you who went to them with clear signs, scriptures, and the Book of Enlightenment. **185.** Every soul will taste death, and you will indeed be paid your reward in full on the Day of Resurrection. Whoever is distanced from the Fire and admitted to the Garden has certainly triumphed. The life of this world is no more than the enjoyment of delusion. **186.** You will certainly be tried in your wealth and your souls. You will hear much to offend you from those who received the Book before you and from those who are idolators. But if you are patient and reverent, that will indeed be a worthy determination. **187.** Remember, God took a covenant from those given the Book: "You will make it clear to the people and not conceal it." They threw it behind their backs and sold it for a trivial price. What a sinful exchange they made! **188.** Do not assume that those who revel in what they have procured, and love to be praised for what they have not done – do not assume they will escape punishment – there is a painful punishment for them. **189.** Unto God belongs sovereignty over the heavens and the earth, and God is Powerful over all things. **190.** Truly, in the creation of the heavens and the earth, and the reversal of night and day, are signs for those endowed with insight **191.** who remember God while standing, sitting, and lying on their sides, and contemplating the creation of the heavens and the earth— "Our Lord! You have not created this in vain! Glory be to You! Guard us from the punishment of the Fire! **192.** Our Lord! For whomever You commit to the Fire, You have surely disgraced. Wrongdoers will have no helpers. **193.** Our Lord! We have certainly heard the caller call to faith, saying, "Believe in your Lord," So we believed. Our Lord! Forgive us our sins and pardon us of our iniquities and take us unto You with the pious. **194.** Our Lord! Give us what you have promised us through Your messengers, and do not disgrace us on the Day of Resurrection. Truly You will not forsake the meeting." **195.** So their Lord answered them, "I will not let the work of any worker among you, male or female, be lost. Each of you is like the other. So those who emigrated and expelled from their homes were hurt in My way, slayed and were slain, I will absolve of their iniquities and will admit them to Gardens with rivers running beneath, a reward from God. God, with Him is the most beautiful reward. **196.** Do not be deluded by the disbelievers who are strutting about the land. **197.** It is but minor enjoyment, and then their refuge is Hell, an evil resting place! **198.** Those who revere their Lord will have Gardens with rivers running underneath, abiding there forever, as a gift from God. What is with God is better for the righteous. **199.** Truly, among the People of the Book are those who believe in God and what has been sent down to you, and what has been sent down to them; be humble before God, and do not sell God's signs for a trivial price. It is they who will have their reward with their Lord. Truly God is swift in reckoning. **200.** O you who believe! Be patient, strive for patience, persevere, and revere God that perhaps you may prosper.

Surah 4

Women

al-Nisā

In the Name of God, the Compassionate, the Merciful

1. O mankind! Revere your Lord, Who created you from a single soul and from it created his mate, and from the two has disseminated countless men and women. Revere God through Whom you demand your rights of one another, and of relatives. Truly God watches over you. **2.** Give orphans their property and do not substitute the bad for the good, nor combine their property with your property, for that would be a great sin. **3.** If you fear you will not deal justly with the orphans, then marry such women of your pleasing—two, three, or four. But if you fear you cannot deal justly, then only one, or those whom your right hands possess. That is to prevent you from being unjust. **4.** Offer women their dowry as a free gift, but if they wish to remit any of it back to you, then consume it with comfort and joy. **5.** Do not give the feeble-minded ones the wealth God has given you for your support. Use it to provide them with food and clothing and say words of kindness to them. **6.** Test the orphans until they reach the age of puberty, then if you sense them to be of sound judgment, deliver their property to them. Do not consume it wastefully or in haste before they come of age. Whoever is wealthy should abstain, but whoever is poor should partake of it in a reasonable way. When you deliver their property to them, let there be witnesses on their behalf and God suffices as a Reckoner. **7.** Unto men, a share of what parents and kinsfolk leave. Unto women, a share of what their parents and kinsfolk leave—whether it is a small or large share—a determinate share. **8.** When relatives, orphans, and the indigent are present at the division, provide them with some of it and say kind words to them. **9.** Those who dread leaving their own helpless progeny behind, should revere God and speak appropriate words. **10.** Indeed, those who consume unjustly the property of orphans will instead consume fire in their bellies and they will burn in a blazing flame. **11.** God directs you concerning your children: to the male, a share equal to that of two females, but if there are only daughters, two or more, then to them is two-thirds of what he leaves, if only one, then to her, a half. To his parents, for each one of them, a sixth of what he leaves if he is with child, but if he is without child, and his parents are his heirs, then, to his mother, a third, but if he has brothers, then, to his mother, a sixth, after payment of debt and legacies. Whether it is your parents or your children, you do not know which of them is closer to you in benefit, a duty ordained by God. Truly God is Knowing and Wise. **12.** To you, a half of what your wives leave if they are without child, but if they are with child, to you, a fourth of what they leave after paying off any bequest they may have bequeathed or any debt. To them, a fourth of what you leave if you are without child, but if you are with child, then to them, an eighth of what you leave after paying off any bequest you may have bequeathed or any debt. If a man or woman leaves no direct heir, but has a brother or a sister, then, to each one of them, a sixth, but if there are more than two, they will share equally a third after payments of legacies and debts, without harm to anyone, a duty ordained by God. God is Knowing and Clement. **13.** Those are the limits set by God. Whoever obeys God and His Messenger, He will admit him to Gardens with rivers running beneath, to abide there forever. That is the great triumph. **14.** Whoever disobeys God and His Messenger and transgresses His limits, He will admit him to the Fire, to abide there forever. He will have a humiliating punishment. **15.** For women who commit an indecency, call four witnesses among you to bear witness against them. If they bear witness, then confine them to houses until death claims them, or until God ordains another way for them. **16.** If two of those among you are guilty thereof, punish them both, but if they repent and make amends, then leave them alone. Truly God is Relenting and Merciful. **17.** God only accepts the repentance of those who do evil out of ignorance, then immediately repent. These are the ones to whom God relents and God is Knowing and Wise. **18.** Repentance is not accepted from those who do evil deeds until death approaches one of them, and he says, "Truly now, I repent," nor from those who die as disbelievers. For those, We have prepared a painful punishment. **19.** O you who believe! It is not lawful for you to inherit women through coercion, nor to prevent them from remarrying that you may take back some of what you had given them, unless they commit a flagrant indecency. Associate with them in kindness, for if you dislike them, it may be that you dislike something from which God will generate much good. **20.** If you wish to replace one wife with another wife and you had given one of them a hefty sum, do not take any of it back. Would you take it by slander and clear sin? **21.** How could you take it back when you have lain with one another, and they have taken a solemn covenant from you? **22.** Do not marry women who were married to your fathers, save for what has passed. Truly it is an indecent, loathsome, and evil course. **23.** Prohibited unto you are: your mothers, daughters, sisters, fathers' sisters, your mothers' sisters, your brothers' daughter, your sisters' daughter, your milk-mothers and milk-sisters, the mothers of your wives, step-daughters under your guardianship born of your wives within whom you have consummated marriage, but if you have not consummated the marriage with them, then there is no blame on you — the wives of your sons who are from your loins, or two sisters simultaneously, save for what is past for truly God is Forgiving and Merciful — **24.** and all married women, save those whom your right hands possess. This is God's decree for you. Lawful to you are all others provided you seek them in marriage with offerings from your property, while desiring chastity, not lust. Those women whom you enjoy thereby, offer them their dowries, as an obligation, but there is no blame on you for what you agree to after the obligation. God is Knowing and Wise. **25.** Whoever among you does not have the means to marry free-believing women, then believing girls among those whom your rights hands possess. God is well aware of your faith. You are from one another, so marry them with permission from their people and properly give them their dowries as married women, not as fornicators or paramours. Once they are married, should they commit an indecency, they will be liable to half the punishment of free women. This applies to the one among you who fears he will sin. However, it is better for you to be patient. God is Forgiving and Merciful. **26.** God desires to make this clear to you and to guide you through the traditions of those before you and to relent unto you. God is Knowing and Wise. **27.** God desires to redeem you, but the wish of those who follow their lusts desire that you should go tremendously astray. **28.** God desires to lighten your burden, for He created humans weak. **29.** O you who believe! Do not wrongfully consume each other's property, but trade by mutual consent. Do not kill yourselves, for Truly God is Merciful toward you. **30.** Whoever does so out of malice and injustice, We will cast him into the Fire to burn, and that is easy for God. **31.** If you avoid the grave sins that you are forbidden, We will exonerate you of your evil deeds, and We will admit you honorably through the Gate. **32.** Do not covet what God has favored for some of you over others. To men a share of what they earned, and to women a share of what they earned, but ask God for His Bounty. Truly God has knowledge of all things. **33.** To each, We have appointed heirs from what parents and kinsfolk leave. To those whom you pledged with your right hand, give them their portion. Truly God is Witness over all things. **34.** Men are upholders of women in that God has favored some above others and by virtue of what they spend from their wealth. So righteous women are devoutly obedient in guarding themselves during absenteeism for what God would have them guard. As for those from whom you fear discord and animosity, admonish them, desert them in their beds and strike them, but if they conform, you must not pursue an alternate means against them. Truly God is Exalted and Great. **35.** If you fear a breach between the two, appoint an arbiter from his people and an arbiter from her people. If they desire reconciliation, God will consent to reconciliation between them. Truly God is Knowing and Aware. **36.** Worship God and do not attribute partners to Him. Be good to parents and kinsfolk, to orphans and the indigent, to the neighbor who is kin and to the neighbor who is not kin, to the companion at your side, to the wayfarer, and to those whom your right hands possess. Truly God Does not love a conceited braggart. **37.** For those who are miserly and direct people to be miserly, concealing what God has given them of His Bounties, and for the disbelievers, We have prepared a humiliating punishment. **38.** Those who spend of their wealth to be seen by people, but do not believe in God or the Last Day, and take on Satan as a companion, has an evil companion, indeed! **39.** What would they have lost had they believed in God and the Last Day, and spent what God had given them? But God Knows them well. **40.** Truly God does not do so much as an atom's weight of wrong. If a good deed is done, He will double it and grant from His Presence a great reward. **41.** How will it be when We bring forth a witness from every community, and then We bring you as a witness against these? **42.** On that Day, those who disbelieved and disobeyed the Messenger will wish they were flush with the earth, but they will not hide anything from God. **43.** O you who believe! Do not approach prayers while you are drunk until you know what you are saying, nor while in the state of ritual impurity—unless you are traveling—and until you have washed. But if you are ill or on a journey or one has come from relieving himself from a call of nature, or you have had contact with women and you find no water, then use clean earth, and wipe your faces and your hands. Truly God is Pardoning and Forgiving. **44.** Have you not observed those who were given a portion of the Book? They purchase falsehood and wish that you too, should stray from the path. **45.** God knows best your enemies and God is enough of a Protector, and God is enough of a Helper. **46.** Among those who are Jews are those who distort the Word by taking it out of context. They say, "We hear and disobey" and "Hear but are not hearing" and "Attend to us" while twisting their tongues and being reproachful of religion. Had they said, "We hear and obey" and "Listen" and "Look at us," it would have been better and more proper for them. But God cursed them for their disbelief. Therefore, they do not believe, except for a few. **47.** O you to whom the Book has been given! Believe in what We have sent down, confirming what is with you, before We alter faces and turn them inside out or curse them as We cursed the Sabbath breakers. For indeed, the Command of God must be carried out. **48.** Truly God does not forgive should any partner be attributed to Him, but He forgives for anything less than that for whoever

He desires. Whoever attributes partners to God has surely contrived a tremendous sin. **49.** Have you not observed those who claim sanctity upon themselves? Rather it is God Who purifies whomever He desires. They will not be wronged so much as a speck on a datestone. **50.** See how they make up lies against God! That alone is clearly a sin. **51.** Have you not observed those who were given a portion of the Book? They believe in idols and false deities, and say of those who disbelieve, "These are better guided than those who believe in the right way." **52.** It is they whom God has cursed. Whomever God has cursed; you will not find a helper for him. **53.** Or do they have a share of the dominion? If they did, they would not offer people so much as the speck on a datestone. **54.** Or do they envy people for what God has given them of His Bounty? We have indeed given the House of Abraham the Book and wisdom, and We gave them a great kingdom. **55.** Among them are those who believed in him and among them are those who turned away from him. Hell is a sufficient inferno! **56.** Indeed, We will surely cause those who disbelieve in Our signs to burn in the Fire. Each time a new skin surfaces, We will replace them with fresh skins so they may taste the penalty. Truly God is Mighty and Wise. **57.** But for those who believe and perform righteous deeds, We will admit them to the Gardens with rivers running beneath, forever abiding there. They will have purified spouses, and We will admit them into ever-deepening shade. **58.** God commands you to return things entrusted to you to their owners. And if you judge between people, you must do so with justice. Indeed, God gives you excellent instruction! Truly God is All-Hearing and All-Seeing. **59.** O you who believe! Obey God and obey the Messenger, and those who are in authority among you. For if you differ on anything among yourselves, turn it over to God and the Messenger if you believe in God and the Last Day. That will lead to a better and more reasonable outcome. **60.** Have you not observed those who claim they believe in what was sent down to you, and in what was sent down before you, yet they seek judgment from false deities in spite of being commanded not to believe in them? Satan wants to lead them to remote darkness. **61.** When they are told, "Come to what God has sent down to you and to the Messenger," you will see the hypocrites turn from you in repulsion. **62.** How will it be when misfortune strikes from them what their hands have sent forth? They come to you swearing by God: "We only intended goodwill and reconciliation." **63.** God knows what is in their hearts. So turn away from them and admonish them and speak to them about their souls with piercing words. **64.** We have not sent a messenger but that he be obeyed—by God's Leave. If they had only come to you when they had wronged themselves to seek God's forgiveness, the Messenger would have sought forgiveness for them, and they would have found God to be Relenting and Merciful. **65.** But no, by your Lord, they will not believe until they have made you arbitrate between them in their disputes and then find no resistance in their souls to what you have ruled and submit themselves completely. 66. If We had prescribed for them: "End your lives" or "Leave your homes," they would not have done so except for a few. If they had done what they were pressed to do, it would have been better for them and more robustly confirming. 67. Then We would certainly have granted them a great reward from Our Presence. 68. We surely would have guided them to a straight path. 69. Whoever obeys God, and the Messenger will be with those whom God has blessed, namely, the prophets, the truthful ones, the witnesses, and the virtuous. What righteous companions they are! 70. Such is the Bounty from God and God suffices as All-Knowing. 71. O you who believe! Take your precautions, then go forth in groups or go forth all together. 72. Indeed, among you are some who would tarry, then if misfortune should ensue, he would say, "God has blessed me that I was not martyred with them." 73. But should good fortune come to you from God, he would certainly say—as if there were no goodwill between you and him— "I wish I had been with them. I would have achieved a great triumph." 74. Let those who would sell the life of this world for the Hereafter fight in the way of God. Whoever fights in the way of God, whether he is slain or triumphant, We will grant him a great reward. 75. Why would you not fight in the way of God and for the weak and oppressed men, women, and children who cry out, "Our Lord! Deliver us from this town whose people are oppressors and appoint for us a protector from You and appoint for us a helper from You." 76. Those who believe, fight in the way of God. Those who disbelieve fight in the way of false deities. Therefore, fight against the allies of Satan for truly, the cunning of Satan is weak. 77. Have you not observed those unto whom it was said, "Restrain your hands, perform prayer, and give alms?" But when fighting was prescribed for them, a group of them certainly feared people as God ought to be feared, or even more. They said, "Our Lord! Why have You prescribed fighting for us? If only You would grant us reprieve for a while." Say, "The enjoyment of this world is minimal, and the Hereafter is better for those who are reverent, and you will not be wronged so much as a speck on a datestone." 78. Wherever you are, death will overtake you, even if you were in highly risen towers. If good arises for them, they say, "This is from God," but if misfortune befalls them, they say, "This is from you." Say, "Everything is from God." What is it with these people that they barely understand discourse? 79. Whatever good happens to you, it is from God, and whatever bad happens to you, it is from yourself. We sent you as a messenger to humanity, and God is witness enough. 80. Whoever obeys the Messenger, obeys God, but as for those who turn away—We did not send you to be their guardian. 81. They profess obedience, but when they leave you, some of them conspire by night on things other than what you tell them, but God records what they conspire about by night. So turn away from them and trust in God. God is Guardian enough. 82. Do they not contemplate the Quran? Had it been from other than God, they would have certainly found much discrepancy in it. 83. Whenever news of safety or fear comes to them, they spread it about, but had they referred it to the Messenger and to those in authority among them, those whose charge it was to investigate would have understood it. Were it not for God's Grace and His Mercy toward you, you would have certainly followed Satan, except for a few. 84. So fight in the way of God. You are only accountable for yourself and to rouse the believers. Perhaps God will restrain the might of the disbelievers, for God is stronger in might and more severe in punishment. 85. Whoever intercedes for a good cause will receive a share of it and whoever intercedes for an evil cause will share in its burden. God is the Sustainer of all things. 86. If someone greets you courteously, greet them back with a better one, or return it. Truly God takes everything into account. 87. God, there is no god but He. He will indeed gather you all on the Day of Resurrection, in which there is no doubt. Who is truer in discourse than God? 88. What is it with you that you are divided into two factions regarding the hypocrites when God turned them to disbelief for what they have earned? Do you seek to guide those whom God has led astray? You will not find a way for him who God leads astray. 89. They want you to disbelieve as they disbelieve, that you may be on equal grounds with them. So do not take them as protectors until they migrate in the way of God. But if they turn away, seize them, and slay them wherever you find them; do not take a protector or helper from them 90. except for those who join people with whom you have a covenant, or those who approach you with hearts that restrain them from fighting you, or from fighting their own people. Had God willed, He could have had given them power over you, and then they certainly would have fought you. If they withdraw from you, and do not fight you, and offer you peace, then God does not allow you a way against them. 91. You will find others who want security from you, and security from their own people, yet whenever they are enticed to aggression, they lurch back into it. Therefore, if they do not withdraw from you, nor offer you peace, nor restrain their hands, then seize them and slay them wherever you find them. We have provided you clear authorization against them. 92. It is not for a believer to slay a believer unless it is in error. Whoever has slain a believer in error, should set a believing slave free and compensate the deceased victim's family, unless they remit it in charity. If he belonged to a people at war with you, but was a believer, then a believing slave should be set free. If he belonged to a people with whom you have a covenant, then compensation should be paid to the victim's family and a believing slave set free. However, as an atonement from God, whoever cannot find the means should fast two consecutive months

God has all knowledge and wisdom. **93.** Whoever intentionally slays a believer, his reward is Hell, abiding there forever. God's wrath and curse is upon him, and He has prepared a dreadful penalty for him. **94.** O you who believe! When you go forth in the way of God, be discerning and do not say to he who offers you peace, "You are not a believer," coveting the goods of worldly life. For with God, are abundant spoils. You, yourselves were like this previously, but God has been gracious to you. So be discerning. Truly God is aware of whatever you do. **95.** Believers who stay behind, except for the disadvantaged, are not equal to those who strive with their goods and whole being in the way of God. God favors those who strive with their goods and their whole being a degree above those who stay behind. To each, God has promised goodness, but He bestows greater favor and a significant reward upon those who strive over those who remain behind — **96.** levels bestowed by Him, accompanied by forgiveness and mercy. Truly God is Forgiving and Merciful. **97.** When the angels took the souls of those who wronged themselves, they say, "In what state were you?" They say, "We were weak and oppressed on earth." They say, "Was God's earth not spacious enough for you to migrate around?" These will have their refuge in Hell. What a wretched final destination. **98.** Except for the weak and oppressed among men, women, and children who do not have the means nor the guidance to act. **99.** So for these, it is possible for God to forgive them for God is Pardoning and Forgiving. **100.** Whoever migrates in the way of God will find an abundance of sanctuaries on the vast earth. Whoever leaves his home, emigrating to God and His Messenger, and then death overtakes him, his reward has fallen upon God. God is Forgiving and Merciful. **101.** When you journey upon the earth, you will not be blamed for shortening your prayers if you fear the disbelievers may attack you, for the disbelievers are indeed your clear enemy. **102.** When you are with them to lead them in prayer, let one group take their weapons with them while standing with you in prayer. When they have performed their prostrations, they should withdraw to the rear to allow another group that has not yet prayed to come and pray with you while taking precautions and bearing arms. The disbelievers would hope for you to be unmindful of your arms and gear that they may assault you all at once. There is no blame on you if you lay aside your weapons when you are troubled by heavy rain or illness but maintain your precautions. Truly God has prepared for the disbelievers a humiliating punishment. **103.** If you have completed the prayers, you are to remember God while standing, sitting, or lying on your sides. Then when you feel safe, perform all prayers. For indeed, prayers are prescribed upon believers to take place at fixed times. **104.** Do not slacken in pursuit of these people. If you are suffering, they are certainly suffering even as you suffer, while you hope from God for what they do not hope. Truly God is Knowing and Wise. **105.** We have indeed sent the Book down to you in truth, that you might judge between people according to what God has shown you. So do not be an advocate for those who betray their trust. **106.** Seek forgiveness of God, for God is certainly Forgiving and Merciful. **107.** Do not plead on behalf of those who betray their own souls. Truly God does not like one who has given in to perfidy and sin. **108.** They try and hide from people, but they cannot hide from God since He is with them when they conspire by night with words displeasing to Him. God encompasses whatever they do. **109.** There you are, pleading on their behalf concerning the life of this world, but who will intercede with God on their behalf on the Day of Resurrection or act as a protector for them? **110.** Whoever does evil or wrongs himself, and then seeks the forgiveness of God, will find God Forgiving and Merciful. **111.** Whoever earns a sin, earns it solely against his own soul. God is Knowing and Wise. **112.** Whoever earns a fault or a sin, and then blames it on one who is innocent, bears the burden of defamation and obvious sin. **113.** Were it not for God's Bounty and His Mercy toward you, a faction of them would have plotted to lead you astray, but they only lead their own souls astray and they cannot harm you in any way. God has sent the Book and Wisdom down unto you and has taught you what you did not know. Indeed, God's Bounty toward you is great. **114.** There is no good in most of their secret talks except for he who enjoins charity, kindness, or reconciliation between people. For whoever does that while seeking God's Satisfaction, We will grant him a great reward, **115.** but whoever opposes the Messenger after guidance has been made clear to him and follows other than the way of the believers, We will leave him to what he has taken in and We will transport him to Hell. What an evil final destination! **116.** Truly God does not forgive that any partners be attributed to Him, but He forgives what is less than that for whomever He wills. Whoever attributes partners unto God has surely, gone distantly astray. **117.** Verily, they only call upon female deities in His stead and surely, they only call upon a defiant Satan **118.** whom God had cursed, and who had said, "I will certainly take of your servants an appointed share, **119.** and I will certainly lead them astray and arouse desires in them. I will command them, and they will slit the ears of livestock. I will command them, and they will alter God's creation." Whoever takes Satan as a protector instead of God has surely suffered a clear loss. **120.** He makes them promises and stirs desires in them, but Satan promises nothing but delusion. **121.** Such will find their refuge in Hell and will not find a way out. **122.** For those who believe and perform righteous deeds, We will admit them to Gardens with rivers running beneath, abiding there forever. God's Promise is true, and who is truer in discourse than God? **123.** It will not be in accordance with your desires nor the desires of the People of the Book. Whoever does evil will pay for it, and he will find no protector or helper besides God. **124.** Whoever performs righteous deeds, whether male or female and a believer — they will enter the Garden, and they will not be wronged so much as the speck on a datestone. **125.** Who is better in religion than he who submits his face to God, is virtuous, and follows the creed of Abraham as a *ḥanīf*? For God did take Abraham for a friend. **126.** To God belongs whatever is in the heavens and whatever is on the earth, and God surrounds all things. **127.** They seek a ruling from you concerning women. Say, "God gives you a ruling concerning them, and what has been recited to you in the Book concerning the orphan females to whom you do not give what was prescribed to them though you desire to marry them. Also, the helpless among children — you should uphold justice for the orphans. Surely, God is well-acquainted with whatever good you do." **128.** If a wife fears animosity or desertion by her husband, there is no blame upon them should they reach an agreement, for an agreement is much better. Souls are disposed to greed, but if you are virtuous and reverent, truly God is Aware of whatever you do. **129.** You cannot maintain fairness between women even if it is your ardent desire, but do not turn away from one entirely that you leave her as if suspended. However, if you come to an agreement and are reverent, truly God is Forgiving and Merciful. **130.** But if they separate, God will enrich both out of His Abundance. God is All-Encompassing and Wise. **131.** To God belongs whatever is in the heavens and whatever is on the earth. We have warned those who were given the Book before you, and We warn you to revere God. But if you disbelieve, to God belongs everything in the heavens and everything on the earth. God is Self-Sufficient and Praiseworthy. **132.** Unto God belongs everything in the heavens and everything on the earth and God is Guardian enough. **133.** If He so wills, He can remove you, O people, and bring in others, God Has the full power to do so. **134.** Whoever desires the reward of this world know that with God is the reward of this world and the Hereafter. God is Hearing, Seeing. **135.** O you who Believe! Be firm upholders of justice and witnesses for God even if it is against yourselves, or your parents, or kinsfolk. Whether someone rich or poor, God cares for both. So do not follow your impulses that you may act justly, because if you mislead or turn away, God is indeed aware of whatever you do. **136.** O you who believe! Believe in God and His Messenger and the Book He sent down to His Messenger, and the Book He sent down before. Whoever does not believe in God and His angels, His Scriptures, His messengers, and the Last Day has drifted far astray. **137.** Those who believe then disbelieve, and believe then disbelieve, and then increase in disbelief — God will not forgive them nor guide them to the way. **138.** Give news to the hypocrites that a painful punishment awaits them. **139.** Do those who take disbelievers instead of believers as protectors seek power through them? Truly might, in its entirety, belongs to God. **140.** He has already sent down the Book, so that when you hear the signs of God being rejected and mocked, do not sit with them until they engage in some other subject, or else you will certainly be like them. God will gather the hypocrites and the disbelievers all together in Hell. **141.** These are the ones who lie in wait for you: when victory comes to you from God, they say, "Were we not with you?" But if the disbelievers were fortunate, they say, "Did we not gain advantage over you, and did we not protect you from the believers?" God will judge between you on the Day of Resurrection, and God will not grant the disbelievers a way over the believers. **142.** Truly the hypocrites seek to deceive God, but it is God Who deceives them. When they perform prayer, they perform it idly and to be seen by people. They barely hold God in remembrance **143.** while vacillating between matters, being neither for one group nor for the other. You will not find a way for whomever God leads astray. **144.** O you who believe! Do not take the disbelievers as protectors instead of the believers. Do you wish to give God a clear cause against you? **145.** Truly the hypocrites will be in the lowest depth of the Fire, and you will not find a helper for them, **146.** except for those who repent, make amends, hold fast to God, and devote their religion entirely to God. Those are among the believers and God will grant the believers a great reward. **147.** Why should God punish you if you give thanks and believe? God is Thankful and Knowing. **148.** God does not love for evil to be spoken of openly except by one who has been wronged. God is Hearing and Knowing. **149.** Whether you display a good deed openly or conceal it, or pardon an evil, truly God is Pardoning and Powerful. **150.** Those who disbelieve in God and His messengers and seek to make a distinction between God and His messengers say, "We believe in some, but disbelieve in others," are seeking to take a middling between the two. **151.** It is they who are disbelievers, and We have prepared a humiliating punishment for disbelievers. **152.** But those who believe in God and His messengers and make no distinction among any of them, it is they who will be given rewards. God is Forgiving and Merciful. **153.** The People of the Book ask you to bring a book down upon them from Heaven. They have indeed asked Moses for something greater than that. Therefore, they said, "Show us God publicly," and the thunderbolt seized them for their wrongdoing. Then they took up the calf even after clear signs had come to them, yet We pardoned this, and We gave Moses clear authority. **154.** We raised the Mount over them along with their covenant and We told them, "Enter the gate, prostrating," and We said to them, "Do not transgress the Sabbath," and We made a solemn covenant with them. **155.** Then for their breaking of the covenant, disbelieving in the signs of God, slaying of the prophets without right, and their saying, "Our hearts are casings," God has certainly set a seal upon them for their disbelief so they will not believe, except for a few **156.** and for their disbelief, and their utterance against Mary—a tremendous defamation, **157.** and for their saying, "We slew the Messiah, Jesus, son of Mary, the messenger of God," though indeed they did not slay him, nor did they crucify him, but so it appeared to them. Those who differ concerning him are indeed, in doubt. They have no knowledge of it and only follow conjecture. Certainly, they did not slay him. **158.** Rather, God raised him up unto Himself and God is Mighty and Wise. **159.** Indeed, there is none among the People of the Book who will not believe in him before his death, and on the Day of Resurrection, he will be a witness against them. **160.** For the wrongdoing among those who are Jews, We forbade them certain good things that had been made lawful to them, for turning many from the way of God. **161.** For their taking of usury, although they had been forbidden it, and for falsely consuming people's wealth. We have prepared for the disbelievers among them a painful punishment. **162.** But those among them who are firmly rooted in knowledge, and the believers, believing in what was sent down to you, and in what was sent down before you, and those who perform prayer, give alms, and believe in God and the Last Day, unto them We will grant a great reward. **163.** Truly We have revealed to you, as We revealed to Noah and the prophets after him, and as We revealed to Abraham, Ishmael, Isaac, Jacob, the Tribes, Jesus, Job, Jonah, Aaron, and Solomon. And to David, We gave the Psalms. **164.** Some messengers We have narrated unto you before, while some messengers We have not narrated unto you. Unto Moses, God spoke directly. **165.** Messengers bearing good news, and bearing warnings, that mankind should have no plea against God after the messengers. God is Mighty and Wise. **166.** But God Himself bears witness to what He has sent down to you—He sent it down with His Knowledge and the angels bear witness. God is witness enough. **167.** Truly those who disbelieve and turn from the way of God have certainly wandered far astray. **168.** Those who disbelieve and do wrong—God will not forgive them, nor will He guide them to any path, **169.** except to the path of Hell to abide there forever, and that is easy for God. **170.** O People! The Messenger has come to you with truth from your Lord, so believe! It is better for you. But if you disbelieve, to God belongs whatever is in the heavens and the earth. God is Knowing and Wise. **171.** O People of the Book! Do not exaggerate in your religion, nor say anything concerning God except the truth. Truly the Messiah, Jesus, son of Mary, is a messenger of God, and His Word which He bestowed on Mary, and a Spirit from Him. So believe in God and His messengers and do not say, "Three." Refrain! It is better for you. God is only One God. Glory be to Him that He should have a child. To Him belongs whatever is in the heavens and the earth and God is enough of a Guardian. **172.** The Messiah would never refuse to be a servant of God, nor would the angels who are near to Him. Whoever disdains His service and is arrogant, He will gather them unto Himself all together. **173.** As for those who believe and perform righteous deeds, He will pay them their rewards in full and will increase them from His Bounty. But as for those who are disdainful and arrogant, He will punish them with a painful punishment, and they will find no protector or helper for themselves besides God. **174.** O People! A proof has come to you from your Lord. We have sent down to you a clear light. **175.** As for those who believe in God and hold fast to Him, He will cause them to enter His Mercy and Bounty and will guide them to Himself on a straight path. **176.** They seek a decree from you. Say, "God gives you a decree regarding the one without a direct beneficiary. If a man dies without child, but he has a sister, then to her belongs half of what he leaves, and he will inherit her if she is without child. If there are two sisters, then unto them belongs two-thirds of what he leaves. If there are brothers and sisters, then to the male a share equal to that of two females." Thus does God make this clear to you in case you should go astray. God is aware of all things.

Surah 5

THE TABLE SPREAD

al-Mãi'dah

In the Name of God, the Compassionate, the Merciful

1. O you who believe! Fulfill your covenants. Permitted to you are grazing livestock, except what is recited unto you. Forbidden to you are hunted game when you are in the state of pilgrim sanctity. Indeed, God decrees whatever He desires. **2.** O you who believe! Do not violate the sanctity of the symbols of God, nor the sacred month, nor the offerings, nor the garlands, nor those in route to the Sacred House seeking Bounty and Satisfaction from their Lord. But when you are no longer in the state of sacred sanctity, you may hunt for game. Do not let the hatred of a people who had once turned you away from the Sacred Mosque lead you to transgress. Help one another toward piety and reverence but do not help one another toward sin and enmity. Revere God. Truly God is severe in retribution. **3.** Forbidden to you are carrion and blood, the flesh of swine, offerings other than to God, the strangled or beaten to death, the killed by falling or gored to death, what has been mangled by beasts of prey, except for what you can purify, what is sacrificed on stone altars, and what you ration with divining arrows. That is sinful! This day, those who disbelieve are despairing of your religion. So do not fear them but fear Me! This day I have perfected your religion for you, completed My Blessing upon you, and have approved Islām for you as religion. But whoever is compelled by hunger without leaning toward wrongdoing, then God is Forgiving and Merciful. **4.** They ask you what is lawful for them. Say, "Lawful for you are all good things." As for the hunting animals you have trained, direct them by what God has taught you. Eat of what they catch for you and mention the Name of God over this. Revere God for truly, God is quick in reckoning. **5.** This day, all good things are made lawful for you. The food of those who have been given the Book is lawful to you and your food is lawful to them. Also, [lawful to you] are the believing chaste women and the chaste women of those who were given the Book before you after you have given them their dowry as married women, not as fornicators, nor as paramours. The deeds of he who rejects belief will come to nothing, and he will be among the losers in the Hereafter. **6.** O you who believe! If you rise to perform prayer, wash your faces, your hands up to the elbows, wipe your heads, and your feet up to the ankles. If you are in a state of ceremonial impurity, then purify yourselves. If you are ill or on a journey, or come from a call of nature, or you have had contact with women and cannot find water, then resort to clean earth, and wipe your faces and your hands with it. God does not want to place a burden on you, but He wants to purify you and to complete His Blessings upon you, that perhaps you may give thanks. **7.** Remember God's Blessing upon you, and His Covenant which He ratified when you said, "We hear, and we obey." Revere God, for truly God Knows what lies within breasts. **8.** O you who believe! Stand firmly for God, bearing witness to justice, and do not let your hatred toward a certain people lead you to be unjust. Be just! That is closer to you in reverence. Revere God, for truly God is Aware of whatever you do. **9.** To those who believe and perform righteous deeds, God has promised forgiveness and a great reward. **10.** However, those who reject faith and deny Our signs will be the inmates of Hell. **11.** O you who believe! Remember God's blessings upon you when a people prepared to stretch forth their hands against you, but He withheld their hands from you. So revere God, and in God believers must trust. **12.** Indeed, God had made a covenant with the Children of Israel, and We raised among them twelve chieftains. God said, "I am with you!" Surely, if you perform prayer and give alms, believe in My messengers, support them, and lend a goodly loan unto God, I will certainly wipe away your evil deeds, and admit you to Gardens with rivers running beneath. But whoever among you disbelieves afterward has truly strayed from the path of righteousness. **13.** For breaching their covenant, We cursed them and hardened their hearts. They alter words and take them out of context, disregarding part of what they were reminded of. Except for a few of them, you will not cease to discover their treachery. But forgive them, and let it go. Indeed, God loves the virtuous. **14.** We made a covenant with those who say, "We are Christians." Then they forgot part of what they had done. Therefore, We diffused hatred and enmity among them until the Day of Resurrection. God will inform them of what they did. **15.** O People of the Book! Our Messenger has come to clarify much of what you once hid from the Book, and pardoning considerably. A new light and a clear Book have come to you from God. **16.** God guides whoever seeks His Satisfaction to ways of peace, taking them out of darkness into light, and by His Leave, guides them to a straight path.

17. Those who said, "God is the Messiah, son of Mary," were indeed disbelievers Say, "Who would have any power over God if He decided to destroy the Messiah, son of Mary, and his mother, and everyone on the earth?" Unto God belongs sovereignty of the heavens and the earth, and whatever is in between them. He creates whatever He wills, and God is Powerful over all things. **18.** The Jews and the Christians say, "We are the children of God and His beloved ones." Say, "Why then does He punish you for your sins?" Truly, you are but mortals of His making. He forgives whomever he pleases, and He punishes whomever He pleases, and unto God belongs sovereignty over the heavens and the earth and whatever is between them. Unto Him is the final destiny. **19.** O People of the Book! Our Messenger has come to you, making things clear to you — after a long period without messengers — in case you should say, "No bearer of good news or warnings has come to us." But a bearer of good news and warnings has come to you. God is Powerful over all things. **20.** Remember Moses said to his people, "O my people! Remember God's blessings upon you, when He assigned prophets among you, and made you kings, and He gave you what He had given no other in all the worlds. **21.** O my people! Enter the Holy Land, which God has prescribed for you, and do not turn back, else, you will become losers." **22.** They said, "O Moses! This land consists of domineering people, and we will not enter it until they leave it. Therefore, if they leave, we will enter it." **23.** Two fearing men who were blessed by God among those who feared said, "Enter upon them through the gate, for once you have entered it, you will be winners. Trust God, if you are believers." **24.** They said, "O Moses! We will never enter if they remain there. So go forth you and your Lord and fight! We will sit here." **25.** He said, "My Lord! I do not have power over anyone except for my brother and myself, so separate us from the sinful people." **26.** He said, "Then it will be forbidden to them for forty years as they wander the earth. So do not grieve for a sinful people." **27.** Recite to them the true account of Adam's two sons, when each of them offered a sacrifice, but the offering was accepted from one and not accepted from the other. One said, "I will certainly slay you!" He replied, "God only accepts from the reverent. **28.** Even if you stretch forth your hand against me to slay me, I will not stretch forth my hand to slay you. Truly I fear God, Lord of the Worlds. **29.** I wish for you to bear the burden of my sin as well as your own, and you will then be among the inhabitants of the Fire. Such is the reward of wrongdoers." **30.** Then his soul urged him to kill his brother, so he killed him and came to be among the lost ones. **31.** Thereafter, God sent a raven, scratching the earth to show him how to conceal his brother's nakedness. He said, "Woe unto me. I was not able to be like this crow and know how to conceal my brother's nakedness!" He became remorseful.

32. On that account, We ordained for the Children of Israel that whoever slays a soul—unless it is for another soul or causing corruption on earth, it is as if he slew all people; and whoever saves one life, it will be as if he saved the lives of all people. In fact, Our messengers came to them with clear signs, yet even after that, many of them led wasteful lives on earth. **33.** Indeed the punishment of those who wage war against God and His Messenger and strive to create corruption on earth should be execution or crucifixion, or the amputation of hands and feet from the opposite sides, or exile from the land. That is their disgrace in this world, and they will receive great punishment in the Hereafter, **34.** except for those who repent before you overpower them, and know that God is Forgiving and Merciful. **35.** O you who believe! Revere God and seek the means to approach Him. Strive in His way that perhaps you may prosper. **36.** Indeed, even if the disbelievers own everything on the earth twofold that they may ransom themselves from punishment on the Day of Resurrection, it will not be accepted from them, and they will have a painful punishment. **37.** Their wish will be to leave the Fire, but they will not be released, and their penalty will be ongoing. **38.** By way of example from God, cut off the hands of the male thief and female thief. This will be a penalty for what they had earned. Truly God is Mighty and Wise. **39.** But whoever repents after his offense, and makes amends, God will relent unto him. Indeed, God is Forgiving and Merciful. **40.** Do you not know that to God belongs sovereignty over the heavens and the earth? He punishes whomever He wills and forgives whomever He wills. God is Powerful over all things. **41.** O Messenger! Do not be saddened by those who rush into disbelief—those who say, 'We believe,' with their mouths while their hearts do not believe, and the Jews who eagerly listen to lies from others who have not yet come to you. They distort words and take them out of context, saying, 'If you are given this, accept it; but if you are not given it, then beware!' For those whom God wills to test, you have no power to help them against God. It is not God's will to purify their hearts. They will face disgrace in this world, and in the Hereafter, they will suffer a tremendous punishment. **42.** If those who listen to lies and consume what is forbidden come to you, either judge between them or turn away from them. If you turn away, they will not harm you in the least. If you judge, judge between them with justice, for indeed, God loves the just. **43.** How is that they come to you for judgment when they have the Torah expressing God's judgment within? Even after that, they turn away. These are not believers. **44.** We sent down the Torah consisting of guidance and light, by which the prophets who had submitted judged those who are Jews, as did the sages and the rabbis in accordance with God's Book to which they were witnesses. You must not fear people! Fear Me! You must not sell My signs for a trivial price. Whoever does not judge by what God has sent down, it is they who are disbelievers. **45.** We ordained for them in it: a life for a life, an eye for an eye, a nose for a nose, an ear for an ear, a tooth for a tooth, and retribution for injuries. But it will be an act of atonement for he who forgoes it through charity. Whoever does not judge by what God has sent down, it is they who are the wrongdoers. **46.** In their footsteps, We sent Jesus, son of Mary, to confirm the Torah that had come before him. We gave him the Gospel that was comprised of guidance and light, validating that the Torah that had come before him as a guidance and an appeal to the reverent. **47.** Let the people of the Gospel judge by what God had revealed within it. Whomever does not judge by what God sent down; they are the sinners. **48.** We have sent the Book down to you in truth, validating the Book that had come before it, and as a protector over it. So judge between them by what God has sent down, and do not follow their compulsions if they differ from the truth that has come to you. For each among you, We have appointed a law and a way. Had God willed, He would have made you one nation, but He is testing you through what He has given you. Therefore, strive with one another in benevolence. To God will be your return all together. He will inform you of what you differed upon. **49.** Judge between them by what God has sent down and do not follow their compulsions. Beware of them in case they lure you from any of what God has sent down to you. If they turn away, know that God desires to chastise them for some of their sins. Indeed, a great many people are sinful. **50.** Are they seeking judgment from the Age of Ignorance? Who is fairer in judgment than God for a people whose faith is assured? **51.** O you who believe! Do not take the Christians and the Jews as allies. They are the protectors of one another. Whoever takes them as protectors, he is certainly one of them. Truly, God does not guide a wrongdoing people. **52.** However, you see those in whose hearts is a disease racing to them saying, "We fear a change of fortune should befall us." It may be that God will grant victory or a command from Him. Then they will be remorseful for what they secretly hid in their souls. **53.** Those who believe will say, "Are these the ones who swore by God with their strongest oaths that they are with you?" Their deeds have amounted to nothing, and they have become losers. **54.** O you who believe! Whoever among you should turn back on his religion, God will bring forth a people whom He loves and who love Him, humble toward the believers, unyielding toward the disbelievers, endeavoring in the way of God, and not fearing the blame of any critic. That is the Bounty of God that He gives to whomever He desires. God is All-Encompassing and All-Knowing. **55.** Your protector is God and His Messenger and those who believe — those who perform prayer and give alms while bowing down. **56.** Whoever takes God, His Messenger, and those who believe as protector are indeed from the party of God. It is they who are triumphant!

57. O you who believe! Do not take as protectors those who take your religion mockingly and playfully, or from those who received the Book before you, or the disbelievers. Revere God if you are believers. **58.** When you make a call to prayer, they take it as mockery and as play. That is because they are a people who do not understand. **59.** Say, "O People of the Book! Are you vengeful toward us solely because we believe in God and in what was sent down to us and in what was sent down before, and because most of you are sinful?" **60.** Say, "Should I inform you of something worse than that as rewarded by God? Whoever God cursed and had earned His Wrath, He will turn some of them into apes, swine, and idol worshippers. These are in a worse position and astray from the right way." **61.** When they come to you, they say, "We believe." However, they certainly entered with disbelief, and they certainly left with it. God Knows best what they were hiding. **62.** You will see many of them racing one another to sin and enmity and consuming what is forbidden. Indeed, evil is what they were doing. **63.** Why do the sages and the rabbis not forbid them from their sinful speech and their consumption of what is forbidden? What they were working on is truly sinful. **64.** The Jews say, "The Hand of God is shackled." It is their hands that are shackled, and they are cursed for what they say. Truly, His two Hands are outstretched. He bequeaths as He desires. Many of them will certainly increase in rebellion and disbelief against what has been sent down to you by your Lord. We diffused enmity and hatred among them until the Day of Resurrection. Each time they ignite a flame for war, God extinguishes it. They endeavor to spread corruption upon the earth and God does not love the corrupt. **65.** Had the People of the Book believed and been reverent, We would have certainly cleared them of their evil deeds and admitted them to Gardens of Bliss. **66.** Had they practiced the Torah and the Gospel and what was sent down to them from their Lord, they would have certainly been nourished from above and beneath their feet. There are some righteous people among them, but many of them pursue evil. **67.** O Messenger! Proclaim what has been sent down to you from your Lord, and if you do not, you will not have proclaimed His message. God will guard you from people. Truly God does not guide disbelieving people. **68.** Say, "O People of the Book, you have nothing to stand on until you practice the Torah and the Gospel, and what has been sent down unto you from your Lord." What has come down to you from your Lord will surely increase rebellion and disbelief in many of them. So do not grieve over a disbelieving people. **69.** Indeed, those who believe, and those who are Jews, and the Sabeans, and the Christians — and whoever believes in God and the Last Day and works righteousness, no fear will come upon them, nor will they grieve. **70.** We have indeed made a covenant with the Children of Israel and sent messengers to them. Each time a messenger would come to them with what their souls did not desire, they would accuse some of falsehood and others, they would slay. **71.** They assumed there would be no trial, and thus, became blind and deaf. Then God relented unto some, but many were blinded and deafened. God Sees whatever they do. **72.** Indeed, those who say, "Truly God is the Messiah, son of Mary," are disbelievers. But the Messiah said," O Children of Israel! Worship God my Lord and your Lord." Verily, whoever assigns partners unto God, God has forbidden him the Garden, and his refuge will be the Fire. Wrongdoers will have no helpers. **73.** Those who say, "Truly God is the third of three," certainly disbelieve, since there is no god but the One God. If they do not refrain from what they say, a painful punishment will happen to those among them who disbelieved. **74.** Will they not turn to God in repentance and seek His forgiveness? God is Forgiving and Merciful. **75.** The Messiah, son of Mary, was but a messenger. There were messengers before him that have passed. His mother was truthful. They both had to eat their daily food. Observe how We have shown them clear signs yet observe how deluded they are! **76.** Say, "Instead of God, do you worship what has no power to benefit or harm you when God is the Hearing and the Knowing?" **77.** Say, "O People of the Book! Do not expand your religion beyond the truth, and do not follow the impulses of a people who have previously gone astray, led many astray, and deviated from the right path." **78.** Those who disbelieved among the Children of Israel were cursed by the tongue of David and Jesus, son of Mary. That was because they disobeyed and transgressed. **79.** They would not forbid one another from the wrong they committed. Indeed, evil is what they practiced. **80.** You see many of them associating with those who disbelieved. Indeed, evil is what they have sent forth for their souls. The wrath of God is upon them, and they will abide in punishment. **81.** Had they believed in God and the Prophet and what was sent down to him, they would have not taken them as protectors, but many of them are sinful. **82.** You will certainly find the most hostile people toward believers, to be the Jews and those who attribute partners to God. You will find the closest in affection toward those who believe are those who say, "We are Christians." That is because among them are priests and monks, and because they are not arrogant. **83.** When they hear what was sent down to the Messenger, you will see their eyes overflow with tears as they recognize as the truth. They say, "Our Lord! We believe, so inscribe us among the witnesses. **84.** How can we not believe in God and the truth that has come to us when we yearn for our Lord to admit us among the righteous?" **85.** Therefore, God rewarded them for what they said with Gardens that have rivers flowing beneath, to abide there forever. That is the recompense of the righteous. **86.** As for those who disbelieved and denied Our signs—such will be the inhabitants of Hellfire. **87.** O you who believe! Do not forbid the good things that God has made lawful unto you and do not transgress. Truly, God does not love transgressors. **88.** Eat of what God has provided you that is lawful and good and revere God in Whom you are believers. **89.** God will not call you to account for what is futile in your oaths, but He will call you to account for the solemn oaths you have pledged. For its compensation, feed ten indigent persons to the equivalent of what you would feed your own family, or clothe them, or free a slave. Whoever cannot, must fast for three days. If you have sworn, that is the compensation for your oaths but keep your oaths. Thus does God make His signs clear to you that perhaps you may show gratitude. **90.** O you who believe! Intoxicants, gambling, idols, and divining arrows are an abomination of Satan's work. So avoid these that perhaps you may prosper. **91.** Surely, Satan desires to implant enmity and hatred among you through intoxicants to turn you away from the remembrance of God and prayer. Will you then refrain? **92.** Obey God and the Messenger and be heedful, but if you turn away, know that it is only incumbent upon the Our Messenger to proclaim a clear message. **93.** There is no blame on those who believe and perform righteous deeds for what they have eaten so long as they are reverent and believe, and perform righteous deeds, then, are reverent and believe, and then, are reverent and goodly. God loves the goodly. **94.** O you who believe! God will certainly try you with something of the game your hands and spears obtain so God may know who fears Him unseen. Then whoever transgresses after that, his punishment will be painful. **95.** O you who believe! You must not slaughter any game while you are in a state of pilgrim sanctity. Whoever among you slaughters it intentionally, compensation of cattle or the like of what he slaughtered, to be adjudicated by two just men among you, as an offering taken to the Ka'ba, or the compensation of feeding the indigent, or its equivalent in fasting that he may taste the evil consequences of his affair. God has forgiven what has passed, but whoever relapses, God will retaliate against him. God is Mighty and the Possessor of retaliation. **96.** Made lawful unto you is the game of the sea and the food thereof as an enjoyment for you and for travelers. Forbidden unto you is the game of the land so long as you remain in a state of pilgrim sanctity. So revere God to Whom you will be gathered. **97.** God has made the Ka'ba, the Sacred House, an edifice for people, the Sacred Month, the offerings, and the garlands, that you may know that God knows whatever is in the heavens and on the earth, and that God has knowledge of all things. **98.** Know that God is strict in punishment and that God is Forgiving and Merciful. **99.** It is solely the proclamation that is incumbent upon the Messenger. God Knows what you reveal and what you conceal. **100.** Say, "Good and bad are not equal though you may be amazed by the abundance of bad." Therefore, revere God, O possessors of insight, that you may thrive. **101.** O you who believe! Do not ask about things that might appear troublesome to you. If you ask about them while the Quran is being sent down, they will be made clear to you. Yet God has forgiven this. God is Forgiving and Clement. **102.** A people before you had asked about these things, and by doing so, they became disbelievers. **103.** God did not establish *bahira, sa'ibah, wasila, or ha'min*, but those who disbelieve invent lies against God, and most of them do not understand. **104.** When it was said to them, "Come to what God has sent down and to the Messenger," they say, "What we found our fathers practicing is enough for us." What? Even though their fathers knew nothing and were not rightly guided! **105.** O you who believe! The responsibility of your souls is on you. Those who go astray cannot harm you if you are rightly guided. Your return will be to God all together. He will inform you of what you did. **106.** O you who believe! The witness between you, when death approaches one of you, at the time of the bequest, shall be two just men from among you or two from among other than yourselves if you are journeying upon the earth when death befalls you. If you are in doubt, confine both of them after prayer, and they must both swear by God; "We will not sell our testimony for any price, even if he were a relative, nor will we hide the witness of God, for then we would certainly be among the sinners." **107.** But if it is determined that the two of them are guilty of sin, then two others should stand in their place from those most eligible as primary claimants, and swear by God, "Indeed, our testimony is truer than their testimony, and we have not transgressed, for then we would certainly be among the wrongdoers." **108.** This is more likely that they will bear true testimony or fear their oaths will be contradicted by oaths thereafter. Revere God and listen. God does not guide disobedient people. **109.** On the day when God will gather the messengers and say, "What was the response you received?" They will say, "We have no knowledge. You are truly the Knower of the Unseen." **110.** When God said, "O Jesus, son of Mary! Remember My Blessing upon you and upon your mother when I strengthened you with the Holy Spirit so you might speak to people in the cradle and in maturity. When I taught you the Book, Wisdom, the Torah, and the Gospel, by My leave, you created the shape of a bird out of clay, and how by My leave, you breathed into it and it became a bird; and how by My leave, you healed the blind and the leper; and how by My leave, you brought forth the dead; and how I restrained the Children of Israel from you after you had brought them clear signs. But those who disbelieved among them said, 'This is nothing but clear sorcery.' **111.** And when I instilled in the apostles the faith to believe in Me and My Messenger, they said, 'We believe and bear witness that we are Muslims.'" **112.** When the apostles said, "O Jesus, son of Mary! Is your Lord capable of sending down to us a table spread with food?" He said, "Revere God, if you are believers." **113.** They said,

"We want to eat from it that our hearts may be at peace, and that we may know you have spoken truthfully to us and that we may be among the witnesses to it." **114.** Jesus, son of Mary said, "O God, our Lord! Send down a table to us from heaven spread with food to be a feast for us, for the first of us and the last of us, and a sign from You. Provide for us, for You are the best of providers." **115.** God said, "I will indeed send it down to you, but whoever among you disbelieves thereafter, I will certainly punish him with a punishment in a way I have not punished any other in all the worlds." **116.** When God said, "O Jesus, son of Mary! Did you tell people, 'Take me and my mother as gods instead of God?'" He said, "Glory be to You! It is not for me to say that to which I have no right. Had I said it, You would certainly have known it. You Know what is in my depth and I do not know what is in Your Depth. Truly You are the Knower of the Unseen. **117.** I said nothing to them except for what You commanded me: 'Worship God, my Lord and your Lord.' I was a witness over them so long as I remained among them. But when You ended my life, it was You Who was the Watcher over them. You are Witness over all things. **118.** If You punish them, they are indeed Your servants, but if You forgive them, then indeed, You are the Mighty and the Wise." **119.** God said, "This is the Day wherein the truthful will benefit from their truthfulness. For them will be Gardens with rivers running beneath, abiding there forever. God is Satisfied with them, and they are satisfied with Him. That is the great triumph!" **120.** Unto God belongs sovereignty over the heavens and the earth and whatever is in it. He has power over all things.

Surah 6

THE LIVESTOCK

al-An'ām

In the Name of God, the Compassionate, the Merciful

1. Praise be to God Who created the heavens and the earth and made darkness and light. Yet those who do not believe attribute equals to their Lord. **2.** It is He Who created you from clay, then decreed a term. The appointed term is with Him, yet, you still have doubt! **3.** He is God in the heavens and on the earth. He knows your secret and what you reveal, and He knows what you earn. **4.** Never did a sign among the signs of their Lord come to them without them turning away from it. **5.** Indeed, they denied the truth when it came to them, but news will soon come to them of what they used to mock. **6.** Have they not observed how many generations We destroyed before them? We had established them on the earth more firmly than We have established you, and We sent the sky upon them with an abundance of rain, and We made rivers flow beneath them. Then We destroyed them for their sins and established another generation after them. **7.** Had We sent down to you a Book inscribed on parchment that they could touch with their hands, those who do not believe would have said, "Indeed, this is nothing but obvious sorcery." **8.** They would say, "Why has an angel not been sent down unto him?" Had We sent down an angel, then the matter would be settled, but they would not have been granted relief. **9.** Had We made him an angel, We would have sent him down as a man to wrap them in confusion beyond their state of confusion. **10.** Indeed, many messengers were mocked before you. Then those who ridiculed them were besieged by what they ridiculed. **11.** Say, "Journey upon the earth and observe the fate of the deniers." **12.** Say, "To whom belongs whatever is in the heavens and on the earth?" Say, "To God. He has prescribed Mercy for Himself. There is no doubt that He will gather you on the Day of Resurrection. As for those who have lost their souls, they do not believe. 13. To Him belongs all that dwells during the night and during the day. He is the Hearing and the Knowing." 14. Say, "Should I take as a protector anyone other than God, the Originator of the heavens and the earth, who feeds and is not fed?" Say, "I was commanded to be the first among those who submit, and not to be among the idolators." 15. Say, "I truly fear the punishment of a tremendous Day should I disobey my Lord." 16. Whoever is released on that Day, He has truly been merciful to him, and that is the discernable victory. 17. If God should touch you with affliction, no one can remove it but Him, and should He touch you with goodness, He is Powerful over all things. 18. He is Supreme over His servants. He is the Wise and the Aware. 19. Say, "What thing is greatest in testimony?" Say, "God is Witness between you and me. This Quran has been revealed unto me that I may thereby warn you and whomever it may reach. Do you truly bear witness that there are other gods besides God?" Say, "I do not bear such witness." Say, "He is only One God, and Truly I am quit of what you attribute as partners unto Him." 20. Those unto whom We gave the Book identify it as they would identify their own children. As for those who have lost their souls, they do not believe. 21. Who does more wrong than one who invents lies against God or denies His signs. Surely, He does not allow wrongdoers to prosper. 22. On the Day when We will gather them all together, We will say to those who attributed partners unto God, "Where are those partners that you claimed?" 23. Then their contention will be but to say, "God is our Lord, and we were not idolaters." 24. See how they lie against themselves and what they invented has abandoned them. 25. Among them are those who listen to you, but We have placed casings over their hearts and deafness in their ears, so that they do not understand it. Were they to see every sign, they would not believe in it even when they come to you and dispute with you. Those who disbelieve say, "Indeed, this is nothing more than ancient fables." 26. They prevent it and keep away from it. Indeed, without realizing, they only destroy their own souls. 27. If you could only see when they stand before the Fire, they will say, "We wish we could be sent back! We would not deny the signs of our Lord and would become among the believers!" 28. Truly, what they had previously hidden had become clear to them. Even if they were sent back, they would return to all they were forbidden. They are liars indeed. 29. They say, "There is nothing but our life in this world and we will not be resurrected." 30. If you could only see when they stand before their Lord, He will say, "Is this not the truth?" They will say, "Yes, indeed." God said, "Then taste the punishment for having disbelieved." 31. Those who deny the meeting with God are truly lost until the Hour comes upon them suddenly, they will say, "It's regrettable for us that we neglected it!" As such, they will bear their burdens on their backs, and what they bear is evil! **32.** The life of this world is nothing more than play and distraction. Indeed, the Dwelling of the Hereafter is better for those who are reverent. Do you not understand? **33.** We certainly know that what they say saddens you. However, it is not you they reject. Rather, it is the signs of God that the wrongdoers rejected. **34.** Indeed, messengers were denied before you. They patiently tolerated their denial and persecution until Our help came to them. No one can alter the Words of God, and you have already received some accounts of the messengers. **35.** If their objection is stressful to you, then if you could have, you would have sought a tunnel in the earth, or a ladder that reached the sky, that you might bring them a sign. Had God willed, He would have gathered them all to guidance. So do not be among the ignorant. **36.** Indeed, those who can hear, will respond. As for the dead, God will resurrect them, and unto Him they will be returned. **37.** They say, "Why has a sign not been sent down to him from his Lord?" Say, "Truly God has the power to send down a sign." But most of them do not know. **38.** There is not an animal on earth nor a bird that flies upon its wings that are not communities like yourselves. We have not overlooked anything in the Book. In the end, they will be gathered unto their Lord. **39.** Those who deny Our signs are deaf and dumb, and in darkness. Whomever God pleases, He will lead astray and whomever He pleases, He will place him upon a straight path. **40.** Say, "Think to yourselves if the punishment of God were to come upon you, or were the Hour to come upon you, would you call upon anyone besides God if you are truthful?" **41.** Truly it is upon Him that you would call, and He would remove what led you to call upon Him. If it were His will, you would forget whatever partners you joined with Him. **42.** Indeed, We have commissioned many nations before you and We have seized them with suffering and hardship that they might humble themselves. **43.** If only they had they humbled themselves when Our Might had come upon them, but instead, their hearts hardened, and Satan made what they did seem good to them. **44.** So when they forgot of what they had been reminded of, We opened the gates of all good things for them until they rejoiced in what they were given. We seized them unexpectedly and they were from this time forward, in despair. **45.** As a result, the last remnant of a transgressional people was cutoff. Praise be to the Lord of the Worlds. **46.** Say, "Do you think if God were to take away your hearing, your sight, and seal your hearts that a god besides God would restore them for you?" Observe how We vary the signs, yet they still turn away.

47. Say, "Think to yourselves, if the punishment of God were to come upon you unexpectedly and openly, would any be destroyed except for a people of wrongdoers?" 48. We only send the messengers as bearers of good news and as warners. As a result, whoever believes and makes amends, no fear will come upon them, nor will they grieve. 49. But as for those who deny Our signs, punishment will befall them for the wickedness they committed. 50. Say, "I do not say to you that I possess the treasures of God, that I know of the unseen, nor that I am an angel. I only follow what is revealed to me." Say, "Are the blind equal to the seeing? Then, will you not reflect?" 51. Give warning of this to those who fear they will be gathered unto their Lord. Apart from Him, they have no protector nor intercessor so that they may be reverent. 52. Do not drive away those who call upon their Lord morning and evening, desiring His Countenance. You will not be held accountable for any of their deeds, and they will not be held accountable for any of yours, so that you would turn them away and become one of the wrongdoers. 53. Thus did We try some of them through comparison with others that they might say, "Are these the ones whom God has favored among us?" Does God not know best those who are thankful? 54. When those who believe in Our signs come to you, say, "Peace be upon you! Your Lord has prescribed Mercy for Himself for whoever among you performs evil out of ignorance but then, repents and makes amends, He is truly Forgiving and Merciful." 55. Thus, We explain the signs and expose the path of the unrighteous. 56. Say, "I am forbidden to worship those whom you call upon other than God." Say, "I will not follow your compulsions, for then I would have gone astray and would not be among the rightly guided." 57. Say, "I hold clear proof from my Lord, and you have denied Him. What you are seeking to rush is not within my power. Judgment belongs to God alone. He relays the Truth, and He is the best of deciders." 58. Say, "If what you are rushing for were within my power, the matter would have been resolved between you and me. However, God knows best the wrongdoers." 59. He holds the keys to the Unseen. No one knows of it but He. He knows what is on the land and in the sea. No leaf falls but that He knows of it, nor a seed in the obscurity of the earth, nor anything damp or dry but that it is clearly in the Book. 60. It is He who takes your souls by night and He who knows what you commit by day. He then revives you for an appointed term to be fulfilled. Then, your return is unto Him where He will inform you of what you did. 61. He is Dominant over His servants. He sends guardians over you until, when death comes to one of you, Our messengers take him, and they do not fail in their duty. 62. Then, they are returned to God, their true Master. Truly judgment belongs to Him, and He is the hastiest of reckoners.

63. Say, "Who saves you from the darkness of land and sea when you call upon Him in a humble and discrete voice, 'if only He would save us from this, we would, be among the thankful?'" 64. Say "God saves you from this and from every distress, yet you attribute partners unto Him." 65. Say, "He is the One Who has the power to send a punishment upon you from above you or from beneath your feet, or to cover you with confusion and in partisan strife to allow you to taste the might of one another." Observe how We vary the signs, that they may understand. 66. Your people have denied it though it is the truth. Say, "I am not a guardian over you. 67. For every message is a fixed time, and you will soon know." 68. When you see those who engage in vain discourse about Our signs, turn away from them until they engage in other discourse. If Satan makes you forget, then once you have remembered, do not sit among a company of wrongdoers. 69. Those who are reverent will not be held accountable, but there will be a remembrance that perhaps they too, will be reverent. 70. Turn away from those who treat their religion as a game and distraction, and who are misled by the pleasures of this worldly life. Remind them that every soul will face the consequences of its own deeds. It will have no protector or intercessor except God, and even if it offers every kind of ransom, it will not be accepted. These are the ones doomed by their own actions. They will be given a drink of scalding liquid and suffer a painful punishment for their disbelief. 71. Say, "Truly should we call on others instead of God for what neither benefits us nor harms us, and be turned back on our heels after receiving guidance from God? It will be like one who is bewildered and seduced by the demons on the earth, while he has companions calling him to guidance— 'Come to us!'" Say, "Indeed, the Guidance of God is the 'guidance,' and we have been ordered to submit to the Lord of the Worlds 72. and to perform prayer and to revere Him. It is unto Him that you will be gathered." 73. It is He who created the heavens and the earth in truth. On the day, He says, "Be!" and it is. His Word is the Truth! Sovereignty is His on the Day the trumpet is blown, Knower of the Unseen and the Seen. He is the Wise and the Aware. 74. When Abraham said to his father, Azar, "Do you take idols for gods? Truly I see you and your people in obvious error." 75. Thus, We showed Abraham the dominion of the heavens and the earth that he might be among those endowed with certainty. 76. When the night darkened over him, he saw a star. He said, "This is my Lord!" But when it set, he said, "I do not love things that set." 77. Then when he saw the moon rising, he said, "This is my Lord!" But when it waned, he said, "If my Lord does not guide me, I will surely be among a people who are astray." 78. Then when he saw the sun, he said, "This is my

Lord! This is greater!" But when it set, he said, "O my people, I am truly innocent of attributing partners unto God! **79.** For indeed, and as an *upright*, I have directed my face toward He Who created the heavens and the earth. I am not of the idolators." **80.** His people argued with him. He said, "Do you argue with me about God when He has guided me? Unless my Lord desires, I do not fear the partners you attribute to Him. My Lord encompasses all things in Knowledge. Will you then, not remember? **81.** Why should I fear what you associate with God, when you do not fear associating partners with Him without any authority granted by Him? So which of the two groups is more deserving of security, if you truly understand? **82.** Those who believe and who do not confuse their belief through wrongdoing, it is they who will be secure and rightly guided." **83.** That was Our argument which We gave to Abraham against his people. We raise in degrees whomever We desire. Truly your Lord is Wise and Knowing. **84.** We gave him Isaac and Jacob, wherein We guided each. We had previously guided Noah and among his progeny, David, Solomon, Job, Joseph, Moses, and Aaron. By such, do We reward the righteous. **85.** Each — Zachariah, John, Jesus, and Elias — are among the righteous. **86.** Ishmael, Elisha, Jonah, and Lot — We favored each above the worlds. **87.** From among their fathers, their progeny, and their brethren, We chose them and guided them unto a straight path. **88.** That is God's Guidance in which He guides whomever He pleases among His servants. But if they were to attribute partners unto God, everything they were doing would come to nothing. **89.** Those are unto whom We have given the Book, judgment, and prophethood. So if they do not believe in them, We have entrusted them to a people who will not disbelieve in them. **90.** Those are the ones whom God has guided, so follow their guidance. Say, "I am not asking you to be rewarded for it. It is nothing more than a reminder for the worlds." **91.** They did not quantify God with His true quantifications when they said, "God has sent nothing down to any human being." Say, "Who sent down the Book of guidance and light that Moses had provided people with? You turned it into parchments that you display while concealing considerably. You were taught what you did not know about, neither you, nor your fathers." Say, "God," Then leave them to engage in their vain discourse. **92.** This is a blessed Book that We have sent down, confirming what came before it so you may warn the Mother of Cities and those around her. Those who believe in the Hereafter, believe in it, and they are mindful of their prayers. **93.** Who does greater wrong than one who invents a lie against God, or says, "It has been revealed unto me," though nothing has been revealed unto him, and one who says, "I will send down the like of what God has sent down?" If you could only see when the wrongdoers are in the distress of death and the angels stretch forth their hands to say, "Surrender your souls! You will be rewarded this day with a punishment of disgrace for having spoken untruths about God while you were growing arrogant over His signs." **94.** "Now, you have come to Us alone just as We created you the first time and you have left behind what We gave you. We do not see your intercessors with you, those whom you had declared were partners. Now, the bond between you has been cut off and what you once declared has left you." **95.** Indeed, God is the Cleaver of grain and the fruit stone. He retrieves the living from the dead and He is the One Who retrieves the dead from the living. That is God! How then, are you deviant? **96.** As the Cleaver of dawn, He has made night for rest, and the sun and the moon for reckoning. Such is the decree of the Mighty and the Knowing. **97.** It is He Who made the stars that you may be guided by them amid the darkness of the land and sea. We have clarified the signs for a people who know. **98.** It is He Who generated you from a single soul, then a dwelling place and a depository. We have clarified the signs for a people who understand. **99.** It is He Who sends water down from the sky. From it, We bring forth the sprout of every plant and from it, We bring forth vegetation from which We bring forth grain heaped up. From the date palm and from its sheaths are clusters of dates hanging low, gardens of grapes, olives, and pomegranates, like one another, yet not alike. Look upon their harvests as they grow and ripen. Truly in that are signs for a people who believe. **100.** They made the jinn partners unto God though He created them, and falsely attributed sons and daughters to Him without knowledge. Glory be to Him! He is Exalted above what they attribute. **101.** The prime Originator of the heavens and the earth! How could He have a child when He has no consort? God created all things, and He has knowledge of all things! **102.** That is God, your Lord! There is no god but He, Creator of all things. So worship Him. He is the Guardian over all things. **103.** No vision can grasp Him, but He can grasp all vision. He is the Subtle and the Aware. **104.** Perception has come to you from your Lord, so whoever perceives clearly, it will be to the benefit of his own soul, and whoever is blind, it will be on him. I am not a keeper over you. **105.** As such, We vary the signs in case they should say, "You have studied," and that We might make it clear to a people who know. **106.** Follow what has been revealed unto you from your Lord — there is no god but He — and turn away from the idolators. **107.** Had God willed, they would not have joined partners unto God. We have not made you a keeper over them, nor are you, their guardian. **108.** Do not curse those who call upon any other than God in case they should curse God out of enmity without knowledge. As such, We made the deeds of every people seem alluring to them. Then to their Lord will be their return, and He will inform them of what they did. **109.** They swear by God with their most intense oaths that if a sign were to come to them, they would genuinely believe in it. Say, "Indeed, all signs are with God." Still, what will make you realize that even if it were to come to them, they would not believe? **110.** We will cause their hearts and sight to overturn as they did not believe in it the first time. We will leave them to wander confused in their rebellion. **111.** Even if We were to send angels down to them and the dead were to speak to them, and We were to gather all things in front of them, they would still not believe, unless God wills, but most of them are ignorant. **112.** Thus, for each prophet We made an enemy: the demons from among people and jinn, to inspire one another with flowery discourse in order to deceive. Had your Lord willed, they would not have done so. Therefore, abandon them and what they invent, **113.** so that the hearts of those who do not believe in the Hereafter may incline toward it, be satisfied with it, and therefore act on what they are acting upon. **114.** "Should I seek a judge other than God when it is He who has sent down to you the Book, explained?" Those to whom We have given the Book know that it has been sent down in truth from your Lord. So do not be among the doubters. **115.** The Word of your Lord is fulfilled in truth and justice. No one can alter His Words. He is the Hearing and the Knowing. **116.** If you were to obey most of those on earth, they would lead you astray from His way, and He knows best the rightly guided. Most certainly, they only follow speculation. All they do is make assumptions. **117.** Indeed, your Lord knows best those who stray from His way, and He knows best the rightly guided. **118.** So if you are believers in His signs, eat of that in which the Name of God has been invoked. **119.** What is it that stops you from eating that in which His Name has been invoked when He has explained to you that which He has forbidden you? Indeed, many are led astray through their own caprices, without any knowledge. Truly your Lord is He who knows best the transgressors. **120.** Renounce sin, both inwardly and outwardly since surely, those who commit sin will be rewarded for what they practiced. **121.** Do not eat that over which the name of God has not been invoked. Truly it is sinning. Indeed, the demons inspire their friends to argue with you and if you obey them, you are certainly idolators. **122.** Is he who was dead, and to whom We give life, making light for him to walk amid people, like one who dwells in darkness and does not come out? As such, for the disbelievers, what they did was made to seem pleasing to them. **123.** That is why We placed some of the greatest of the guilty in every town to plot there. However, without realizing, they only plot against themselves. **124.** When a sign comes to them, they say, "We will not believe until we are given the like of what was given to the messengers of God." God knows best where to carry out His message. Those who plotted will be stricken with humiliation before God and the guilty will be severely punished for what they plotted. **125.** God will guide whomever He desires. He expands his breast for submission, and He narrows and constricts the breast of whomever He desires to lead astray as though he were mounting the sky. Such does God heap the penalty upon those who refuse to believe. **126.** This is your Lord's path made straight. We have explained the signs for a people who are mindful. **127.** They will have an Abode of Peace with their Lord, and He will be their Protector because of what they practiced. **128.** On the Day when He gathers them all together, "O company of the jinn! You have claimed many among people." Their companions among the people will say, "Our Lord! We have profited from each other, but now we have reached our term which You had appointed for us." He will say, "The Fire is your abode, to abide in, barring if God wills. Truly your Lord is Wise and Knowing." **129.** As such, do We make the wrongdoers allies of one another because of what they earned. **130.** "O company of the jinn and human beings! Did messengers not come to you from among yourselves, narrating My signs to you and warning you of this Day's meeting?" They will say, "We bear witness against ourselves." The life of this world deluded them. They bore witness against themselves that they were disbelievers. **131.** That is because your Lord would certainly never destroy peoples' towns for their wrongdoing if they were oblivious. **132.** For each are degrees according to what they practice. Your Lord is not heedless of what they do. **133.** Your Lord is Self-Sufficient and Possessed of Mercy. If He wills, He can remove you and will place whomever He pleases to be your successor just as He brought you into being from the progeny of another people. **134.** Indeed, what you were promised will come to pass and there is nothing you can do. **135.** Say, "O my people! Practice according to your abilities. I too, am practicing. Soon you will know who will reach the threshold of the Abode. Truly the wrongdoers will not prosper." **136.** They assigned to God a share of the crops and livestock He created saying, "This belongs to God," according to their desires, and "This belongs to our partners." But what is for their partners does not reach God, and what is for God reaches their partners. Wicked indeed is the judgment they make! **137.** Similarly, they made the slaying of their children seem fair unto many of the idolators, that they may destroy them and cause them to be confused in their religion. If God willed, they would not have done so. So, leave them and what they make up. **138.** Following their desires, they say, "These livestock and crops are sacred, and no one shall eat from them unless we choose," the livestock whose backs are forbidden and in which they do not invoke the Name of God while fabricating against Him. Soon He will reward them for what they made up. **139.** They say, "What is in the bellies of these livestock is reserved for our males and forbidden to our wives, but if it is stillborn, then, they will all have a share of it." Soon He will reward them for their attributions. Truly He is Wise and Knowing. **140.** Lost are those who slay their children foolishly, without knowledge, and make forbidden what God has provided them while fabricating against God. They have indeed gone astray and were not rightly guided. **141.** It is He who generates gardens trellised and not trellised and the date palm and crops with diverse produce such as olives, pomegranates, alike yet not alike unto one another. Eat of their fruit when they cultivate and pay its due thereof on the day of its harvest, but do not be wasteful. Truly He does not love the wasteful. **142.** Of the livestock, are some for loading, and some for slaughtering. Eat of what God has provided you and do not follow the footsteps of Satan. Truly, he is a clear enemy to you. **143.** Eight pairs of sheep, [two] and of goats, [two]. Say, "Has He forbidden the two males or the two females, or that which is contained in the wombs of the two females? Tell me with knowledge if you are truthful." **144.** Of camels, two and of oxen, two. Say, "Has He forbidden the two males or the two females, or that contained in the wombs of the two females? Or were you present when God commanded this upon you?" Who does greater wrong than one who invents a lie against God that he may lead men astray without knowledge? Indeed, God does not guide a wrongdoing people. **145.** Say, "I do not find in what was revealed to me anything forbidden upon an eater who eats thereof, except for carrion or blood poured forth, or the flesh of swine for that is surely an abomination, or a sinful offering made to other than God. But whoever is compelled by necessity, without willfully disobeying or transgressing, truly your Lord is Forgiving and Merciful. **146.** Unto those who are Jews, We forbade every animal with claws. We forbade them the fat thereof, except for that upon their backs or their entrails or what is mingled with bone. As such, We rewarded them for their willful disobedience, and surely, We are truthful. **147.** If they accuse you of lying say, "Your Lord is possessed of vast Mercy, but His Might will not be averted from a guilty people." **148.** Those who attribute partners unto God will say, "Had God willed, we would not have attributed partners unto God, nor our fathers, nor would we have been forbidden anything." Those who were before them had similarly denied until they tasted Our Wrath. Say, "Do you have any knowledge that you can produce for us? You follow nothing but speculation. Indeed, you are only conjecturing." **149.** Say, "Unto God belongs the conclusive argument. Had He willed, He could have certainly guided all of you." **150.** Say, "Bring forward your witnesses who will testify that God has forbidden this." Then, if they testify, do not testify with them, and do not follow the impulses of those who lie about Our signs, nor those who do not believe in the Hereafter. They attribute equals unto their Lord! **151.** Say, "Come, I will recite what your Lord has forbidden you: do not attribute anything unto Him. Be good to your parents and do not slay your children for fear of scarcity. We will provide for you and them. Do not approach indecencies — outwardly or inwardly — and do not slay the soul that God has made sacrosanct except justly. He has commanded this upon you that perhaps you may understand." **152.** Do not approach the property of orphans except in the best of manners and until he reaches maturity. You must fully observe the measure and the balance justly. We do not commission a soul beyond its capacity. When you speak, be just, even if it is against a kinsman, fulfill the pact of God. He Has commanded this upon you that perhaps you may remember. **153.** Indeed, this is My path, made straight, so follow it, and do not follow other ways, in case they separate you from His way. He Has commanded this upon you that perhaps you may be reverent. **154.** Then, We gave Moses the complete Book for those who would do right, as clarification to all things, and as a guidance and a mercy, that perhaps they believe in the meeting with their Lord. **155.** This is a blessed Book that We have sent down, so follow it and be reverent that perhaps you may receive mercy. **156.** In case you should say, "The Book was only sent down to two groups before us and we were indeed careless of learning about them." **157.** Or in case you should say, "If the Book had been sent down upon us, we would have certainly been better guided than they." Now, there has come unto you clear signs, guidance, and mercy from your Lord, so who does more wrong than one who denies the signs of God and turns away from them? We will soon reward those who will turn away from Our signs with a terrible punishment for having turned away. **158.** Are they envisioning that the angels should come upon them or that our Lord should come, or that one of the signs of your Lord should come? On the Day that one of the signs of your Lord does come, believing will be of no benefit to any soul that did not believe beforehand and did not earn some goodness in its belief. Say, "Wait! We too, are waiting." **159.** Truly as for those who divide their religion and become factions, you have no connection with them whatsoever. Their affair rests with God alone. Then, He will inform them of what they did. **160.** Whoever brings a good deed will have ten times the like of it, but whoever brings an evil deed will only be rewarded with the like of it and they will not be wronged. **161.** Say, "Truly my Lord has guided me unto a straight path, an *upright* religion, the creed of Abraham, a *hanīf*, and he was not of the idolators." **162**. Say, "Truly my prayer, my sacrifice, my living, and my dying are for God, Lord of the Worlds. **163**. He has no partner This, I am commanded, and I am the first of those who submit." **164**. Say, "Should I seek a lord other than God while He is the Lord of all things? No soul does evil except against itself, and none will bear the burden of the other. From this time onward, to your Lord is your return and He will inform you of what you differed over." **165**. It is He who appointed you as vicegerents on earth and raised some of you above others by degrees that He may try you with what He has given you. Truly your Lord is swift in retribution. Indeed, He is Forgiving and Merciful.

Surah 7

THE HEIGHTS

al-A'rãf

In the Name of God, the Compassionate, the Merciful

1. *Alif. Lãm. Mĩm. Sãd.* **2.** A Book sent down upon you, so let there be no doubt in your breast about it, that you to warn of it and be a reminder for believers. **3.** Follow what has been sent down to you from your Lord and do not follow any protectors besides Him. Little are you mindful! **4.** How many a town have We destroyed! Our Might came upon them by night, or while they were taking their afternoon siesta. **5.** So their cry when Our Might came upon them was but to say, "Indeed, we were wrongdoers." **6.** For We will surely question those unto whom Our message was sent, and We will surely question the messengers. **7.** Then We will recount to them with knowledge that We were never absent. **8.** The weighing on that Day will be just. Those whose scales are heavy will be the successful ones, **9.** while those whose scales are light will have brought ruin upon their souls for mistreating Our signs. **10.** We have indeed secured you upon the earth and provided you with sustenance there. Little do you show gratitude! **11.** Truly We created you, then We formed you, then, We said to the angels, "Prostrate before Adam." They all prostrated except for Iblĩs. He was not among those who prostrated. **12.** He said, "What prevented you from prostrating when I commanded you?" He said, "I am better than him. You have created me from fire while you created him from clay." **13.** He said, "Get down from this! It is not for you to be arrogant here. So go forth! You are surely among those who are humiliated." **14.** He said, "Grant me respite until the Day they are resurrected." **15.** He said, "Truly you are among those granted respite." **16.** He said, "Because you have caused me to err, I will definitely lie in wait for them on Your straight path. **17.** Then, I will come upon them from in front of them and from behind them, and from their right, and from their left. You will find most of them ungrateful."

18. He said, "Go forth from here disgraced and banished! Whoever among them follows you, I will certainly fill Hell with you all." **19.** "O Adam! You and your wife can dwell in the Garden and eat from whatever you wish, but do not approach this tree unless you both want to be among the wrongdoers." **20.** Then, Satan whispered to them to expose them to what had been previously hidden from them of their nakedness. He said, "Your Lord has only forbidden you of this tree so you will not become angels or become among those who live eternally." **21.** He swore unto them, "I am truly a sincere advisor to you." **22.** As a result, he enticed them through deception. When they tasted of the tree, their nakedness became apparent to them, and they began to sew together the leaves of the Garden to cover themselves. Their Lord called unto them: "Did I not forbid you from that tree and tell you that Satan was clearly an enemy unto you?" **23.** They said, "Our Lord! We have wronged ourselves. If you do not forgive us and have mercy on us, we will surely be among the losers." **24.** He said, "Get down, each of you as an enemy to the other! You will have on earth a place to dwell and to amuse yourselves for a while." **25.** He said, "You will live in it, and you will die in it, then from there, you will be removed." **26.** O Children of Adam! We have truly sent down upon you clothing and rich adornment to cover your nakedness. But the raiment of reverence is better. This is among the signs of God that perhaps they may remember. **27.** O Children of Adam! Do not let Satan tempt you as he caused your parents to go forth from the Garden stripping them of their raiment to reveal their nakedness to them. He and his tribe can certainly see you though you cannot see them. We have indeed made the demons friends of those who do not believe. **28.** When they commit an indecency, they say, "We found our fathers practicing it, and God has commanded us as such." Say, "Truly God does not command indecency. Do you speak of God that which you do not know?" **29.** Say, "My Lord has ordered justice. So affix your faces at every place of prayer [toward the Ka'ba] and call upon Him. Devote religion entirely to Him. Just as you were originated by Him, you will also be returned." **30.** Some groups were guided, and other groups were misguided. They took demons as their primary protectors rather than God and they assumed they were rightly guided. **31.** O Children of Adam! Wear your adornment at every place of prayer. Eat and drink, but do not be wasteful for He truly does not love the wasteful. **32.** Say, "Who has forbidden the adornment of God which He has brought forth for His servants along with better things of sustenance?" Say, "These are for those who believe in the life of this world, and on the Day of Resurrection — they are for them alone." In this way, We clarify the signs for a people who understand. **33.** Say, "My Lord has only forbidden indecencies, both, outwardly and inwardly, unjustifiable sin and tyranny, the attribution of partners unto God for which He has sent down no authority, and that you should speak of God of what you do not know." **34.** Every community has its appointed time. When their time comes, they can neither delay it by an hour nor advance it. **35.** O Children of Adam! Should messengers among yourselves come to you recounting My signs, then, whoever is reverent and makes amends, no fear will come upon them, nor will they grieve. **36.** But those who reject Our signs and are arrogant of them, it is they who are the inhabitants of the Fire where they will abide forever. **37.** Who is more unjust than he who invents a lie against God or rejects His verses? These will have earned their fate from the Book until Our messengers reach them and take their souls, they will say, "Where is what you called upon instead of God?" They will respond, "They have forsaken us." They bear witness against themselves as disbelievers. **38.** He will say, "Enter the Fire wherein nations of jinn and humans that have passed before you!" Each time a nation enters, it curses its sister until they have all successively arrived there. The last of them will say of the first of them, "Our Lord, it was they who led us astray. Therefore, give them double the punishment of Fire." He will say, "You do not know, but it will be doubled for each of you." **39.** The first of them will say to the last of them, "You are no better than us, so taste the punishment for what you have earned." **40.** Truly those who deny Our signs and are arrogant toward them, the gates of Heaven will not be opened for them, nor will they enter the Garden until the camel passes through the eye of a needle. As such We reward the guilty. **41.** With coverings above them, Hell will be their resting place. That is how We reward the wrongdoers. **42.** We task no soul beyond its capacity, so as for those who believe and perform righteous deeds, it is they who will be the inhabitants of the Garden. They will abide there forever. **43.** We will remove whatever malice lies within their hearts. Rivers will run beneath them, and they will say, "Praise be to God, who guided us unto this. We would not have been rightly guided had God not guided us. The messengers of Our Lord surely came with the truth." A call will be made unto them, "This is the Garden! You have inherited it for what you practiced." **44.** The inhabitants of the Garden will call out to the inhabitants of Fire, "We have found what Our Lord promised us to be true. Have you found what your Lord promised to be true?" They will say, "Yes." Subsequently, an announcer will declare from amidst them, "May the curse of God be upon the wrongdoers!" **45.** In the end, those who turn from the way of God and try to make it crooked, it is they who are disbelievers in the Hereafter. **46.** There will be a veil between them. Upon the Heights will be men who know each person by their marks. They will call out to the inhabitants of the Garden, "Peace be upon you!" They will not have entered it, though they hope to. **47.** When their eyes turn toward the inhabitants of the Fire, they will say, "Our Lord! Do not place us among the wrongdoing people!" **48.** The inhabitants of the Heights will call out to men whom they know by their marks, "How did your hoarding and arrogance benefit you? **49.** Are these the ones upon whom you swore that God would not extend any mercy?" "Enter the Garden! No fear will come upon you, nor will you grieve." **50.** The inhabitants of the Fire will call out to the inhabitants of the Garden, "Pour some water down on us, or some of what God has provided you." They will respond, "God has truly forbidden them to the disbelievers," **51.** who took their religion to be amusement and play and were deceived by the life of this world. Therefore, this Day, We will forget them since they forgot the meeting of this Day of theirs and had rejected Our signs. **52.** Indeed, We have brought them a Book that We have clarified with knowledge. It is a guidance and a mercy for a people who believe. **53.** Do they wait for anything but for it to be fulfilled? The Day when its complete fulfillment arrives, those who had previously forgotten it will say, "The messengers of Our Lord indeed brought the truth! Do we have any intercessors who will intercede for us, or might we be returned to practice other than what we practiced?" They have surely lost their souls and what they made up will have abandoned them. **54.** Truly your Lord is God Who created the heavens and the earth in six days, then ascended the Throne. He veils the night over the day that pursues it rapidly. The sun, the moon, and the stars are made subservient by His Command. Do creation and command not belong to Him? Blessed is God, Lord of the Worlds! **55.** Call upon your Lord humbly and privately, for indeed, He does not love transgressors. **56.** Do not instill corruption upon the earth after it has been set in order but call upon Him in fear and in hope. Surely, the Mercy of God is ever close to the righteous. **57.** It is He who sends the winds as glad tidings ahead of His Mercy, so that when they bear heavy-laden clouds, We may drive them toward a land that is dead and send water down upon it for every kind of fruit to be extracted. Accordingly, We will revive the dead that perhaps you may remember. **58.** As for the good land, its vegetation comes forth through the will of its Lord. As for the bad, it will barely come forth. As such, do We vary the signs for a people who are grateful. **59.** Indeed, We sent Noah unto his people and he said, "O my people! Worship God! You have no god other than Him. Truly I fear for you the punishment of a monumental day!" **60.** The notables said, "Truly we perceive you to be in obvious error." **61.** He said, "O my people! I am not mistaken but rather, I am a messenger from the Lord of the Worlds. **62.** I deliver unto you the messages of my Lord and advise you sincerely, and I know from God what you do not know. **63.** Or are you surprised that a reminder from your Lord came from a man among yourselves warning you to be reverent that perhaps you may receive mercy?" **64.** But they accused him of lying and so We saved him and those who were with him in the Ark while We drowned those who rejected Our signs. Truly they were a blind people. **65.** Unto the Ād, their brother Hŭd said, "O my people! Worship God! You have no god other than Him. Will you not be reverent?" **66.** The notables among his people who disbelieved said, "Truly we perceive you to be foolish, and we believe you to be among the liars." **67.** He said, "O my people! There is no foolishness in me. I am rather a messenger from the Lord of the Worlds. **68.** I deliver unto you the messages of my Lord, and truly I am a trustworthy advisor to you, **69.** or are you surprised that a reminder from your Lord came to you by a man from among yourselves to warn you? Remember when He made you vicegerents after the people of Noah and significantly elevated your status. By such, remember the compensation of God that perhaps you may prosper." **70.** They said, "Have you come to us that we may worship God alone and abandon what our fathers worshiped? Then bring on what you have threatened us with if you are truthful." **71.** He said, "Desecration and wrath have already come upon you from your Lord. Do you dispute with me over names that you have named, you and your fathers, from which God has not sent down any authority? Then wait! Truly I am waiting along with you." **72.** Therefore, We saved him and those who were with him out of Our mercy and We cut off the last remnant of those who rejected Our signs and were not believers. **73.** Unto the Thamŭd, their brother Sālih said, "O my people! Worship God! You have no other god than Him. There has come to you clear signs from your Lord. This she-camel of God is a sign to you. So let her graze freely on God's earth and do not cause her harm else, a painful punishment will overtake you. **74.** Remember when He made you vicegerents after the Ād and established you upon the earth wherein you built castles for yourselves on the open plain and carved out dwellings in the mountains. Therefore, remember the compensations of God. Do not instill corruption or behave wickedly upon the earth." **75.** The notables among his people who were arrogant said to those among them whom they believed were weak, "Do you know that Sālih has been sent by his Lord?" They said, "Truly we believe in what was sent to him." **76.** Those who were arrogant said, "Truly we do not believe in what you believe." **77.** Thereafter, they hamstrung the she-camel and audaciously challenged the Command of their Lord. They said, "O Sālih! Bring upon us that which you have threatened us with if you are among the messengers." **78.** As a result, the earthquake seized them, and by morning they were lifeless in their homes. **79.** So he turned away from them and said, "O my people! Indeed, I delivered the message of my Lord to you. I sincerely advised you, but you do not love sincere advisors." **80.** And Lot when he said to his people, "What! Do you commit an indecency like no one in the world has committed before you? **81.** Truly you approach men with longing instead of women. You are truly a dissolute people!" **82.** The response of his people was but to say, "Expel them from your town! Truly they are a people who desire to be pure." **83.** Thereafter, We saved him and his family, except for his wife. She was among those who lagged behind. **84.** We rained a 'deluge' upon them. So observe how the guilty were reprimanded! **85.** To the Midian, their brother Shu'ayb said, "O my people! Worship God! You have no god other than Him. There has come to you clear proof from your Lord. So be just with the scale and the weighing pan and do not deprive people of their properties and do not instill corruption or behave wickedly upon the earth after it has been orderly established. That is better for you, if you are believers. **86.** Do not sit around at every path threatening and turning away those who believe in Him from the way of God while seeking to make it crooked. Remember when there were a few of you and He made you numerous. Observe what the punishment of evildoers was like! **87.** If a group of you believe in what I have been sent with, and a group of you do not believe, then be patient until God judges between us. He is the best of judges." **88.** The notables among his people who were arrogant said, "O Shu'ayb! We will certainly expel you from our town and those who believe along with you unless you return to our creed." He said, "What! Even though we are haters. **89.** We would be inventing a lie against God if we were to return to your creed after God had delivered us from it. It is not for us to return unless God, our Lord, wills it. Our Lord encompasses knowledge of all things. In God, we trust. Our Lord! Decide between us and our people in truth, and You are the best of deciders." **90.** The notables among his people who disbelieved said, "Truly if you follow Shu'ayb, you will certainly be the losers." **91.** So the earthquake seized them, and by morning they were lying lifeless in their homes. **92.** For those who rejected Shu'ayb, it was as though they had never dwelt there. Those who denied Shu'ayb ended up being the true losers. **93.** So he turned away from them and said, "O my people! I have indeed delivered unto you the messages of my Lord and have sincerely advised you. So how can I lament over a disbelieving people?" **94.** We did not send a prophet to a town but that We overtook its people with misfortune and hardship that perhaps they would be humble. **95.** We then replaced evil with good until they proliferated and said, "Hardship and ease has touched our fathers," so, We seized them swiftly while they were unaware. **96.** If the people of the towns had believed and been reverent, We would have certainly released blessings unto them from Heaven and earth, but they denied, so We seized them for what they earned. **97.** Did the people of the towns feel safe enough from Our Might as We came upon them by night while they were sleeping? **98.** Or did the people of the towns feel safe enough from Our Might coming upon them in broad daylight while they were playing? **99.** Did they feel secure from God's plotting? No one feels secure from God's plotting save a population of losers. **100.** Or does it not serve as guidance to those who inherited the earth after its former inhabitants that had We willed, We would have stricken them for their sins and sealed their hearts such that they could not hear? **101.** These are the towns whose stories We have narrated unto you. Their messengers had indeed brought them clear signs, but they would not believe in what they had previously rejected. Thus does God seal the hearts of the disbelievers. **102.** We did not find that most of them had a covenant, but We certainly found most of them to be sinful. **103.** Then after them, We sent Moses with Our signs to Pharoah and his notables, but they treated them wrongfully. Therefore, observe what the punishment of evildoers was like! **104.** Moses said, "O Pharoah! I am truly a messenger from the Lord of the Worlds, **105.** obligated to speak nothing but the truth about God. I have brought you a clear sign from your Lord. From this time forward, send the Children of Israel with me." **106.** He said, "If you have brought a sign, bring it forth if you are among the truthful." **107.** He then cast his staff that noticeably became a serpent. **108.** He then drew forth his hand and it was noticeably white to the observers. **109.** The notables among Pharoah's people said, "Indeed, this is a learned sorcerer!" **110.** He aims to expel you from your land, so what do you command? **111.** They said, "Delay him and his brother while you send deputies to the cities **112.** to bring you every learned sorcerer. **113.** The sorcerers came to the Pharoah. They said, "Incidentally, will we be rewarded if we are among the victorious? **114.** He said, "Yes indeed! You will be brought in proximity." **115.** They said, "O Moses! Either you cast or we will be the ones who cast." **116.** He said, "Cast!" when they cast, they bewitched the eyes of people and struck them with apprehension. They came with mighty sorcery. **117.** We disclosed unto Moses, "Cast your staff!" Observe! It engulfed all their trickeries. **118.** Thus the truth came to pass and whatever they performed had no effect. **119.** They were vanquished on the spot and were belittled. **120.** The sorcerers threw themselves down in prostration. **121.** They said, "We believe in the Lord of the Worlds, **122.** the Lord of Moses and Aaron." **123.** Pharoah said, "You believe in him before I grant you leave? This is surely a plot you have plotted in the city to drive its people out, but soon you will know. **124.** I will indeed cut off your hands and your feet from opposite sides, then, I will then crucify you all!" **125.** They said, "Truly we invert to Our Lord." **126.** You take vengeance upon us only because we believed in the signs of Our Lord when they came to us. Our Lord! Shower us with patience and let us die as submitters." **127.** The notables among the Pharoah's people said, "Are you going to let Moses and his people spread corruption in the land and forsake you and your gods?" He said, "We will slay their sons and spare their women. Truly we are dominant over them." **128.** Moses said to his people, "Seek support from God and be patient. Truly the land belongs to God. He bequeaths it to whomever He wills among His servants. The end belongs to the reverent." **129.** They said, "We were victimized before you came to us and after you came to us." He said, "Perhaps your Lord will destroy your enemies and make you vicegerents upon the earth that He may observe how you behave." **130.** Over the years, We actually inflicted the House of Pharoah with a shortage of crops that perhaps they would be reminded. **131.** But whenever good came to them, they would say, "This is ours," and when something bad happened to them, they would consider it an ill omen on behalf of Moses and those who were with him. Truly their ill omen lies with God, but most of them do not know. **132.** They said, "No matter how many signs you bring to bewitch us with, we will not believe in you." **133.** We sent upon them floods, locusts, lice, frogs, blood, and signs explained, but they grew arrogant and were a guilty people. **134.** When the penalty came down upon them, they said, "O Moses! Call upon your Lord for us by the covenant He has made with you. If you lift this penalty from us, we will surely believe on your behalf, and we will certainly send the Children of Israel with you." **135.** Once We lifted the penalty from them for a designated term, they broke their promise. **136.** So We took vengeance upon them and drowned them at sea for having denied Our signs and being unmindful of them. **137.** We bequeathed unto a people who were oppressed, the eastern and western parts of the land that We had blessed. The most beautiful Word of your Lord was fulfilled for the Children of Israel because they were patient. We destroyed everything that Pharaoh and his people had created and constructed. **138.** We took the Children of Israel across the sea until they came upon a people gripping to their idols. They said, "O Moses! Make gods for us like the gods they have." He said, "Truly you are an ignorant people! **139.** As for these, what they practice will perish and what they did will be in vain." **140.** He said, "Should I seek a god for you other than God when He favored you above the worlds?" **141.** When We saved you from the House of Pharoah, who had inflicted terrible punishment upon you, slaying your sons and letting your women live. In this was a great trial from your Lord. **142.** We appointed thirty nights for Moses, and We completed them with an additional ten. He fulfilled the term of his Lord—forty nights. Moses said to his brother Aaron, "Take my place among my people, do what is right, and do not follow the ways of the wrongdoers." **143.** When Moses came to Our appointed meeting and his Lord spoke unto him, he said, "My Lord, show me that I might look at You." He said, "You will not see Me, but look upon the mountain. If it remains firm in its place, then you will see Me." When His Lord revealed Himself to the mountain, He made it crumble to dust and Moses fell down in a swoon. When he recovered, he said, "Glory be to You! I turn unto you in repentance and I am the first of believers." **144.** "O Moses! I have chosen you above all people through My messages and My discourse. So take what I have given you and be among the grateful." **145.** We wrote for him upon the Tablets all things commanded and clarified. "Take hold of them with strength and command your people to hold on to the best of them. Soon, I will show you the abode of the sinful." **146.** I will turn My signs away from those who unjustifiably grow in arrogance upon the earth. Even if they were to see every sign, they would not believe in it. If they were to see the way of sound judgment, they would not take it as a way, but if they were to see the way of error, they would take it as a way. That is because they rejected Our signs and were unmindful of them. **147.** As for those who deny Our signs and the meeting in the Hereafter, their deeds will plummet. Are they rewarded for anything other than what they did? **148.** After Moses had gone away, his people took up a calf from their ornaments. Its body was hollow. Did they not see that it did not speak to them, nor guide them toward the way? They took it up and they were among the wrongdoers. **149.** When it fell upon their hands and they realized they had erred, they said, "If our Lord does not have mercy upon us and forgive us, we will truly be among the losers!" **150.** When Moses returned to his people angry and distressed, he said, "Evil is what you have followed after me! Have you advanced the Command of your Lord?" He put down the Tablets and seized his brother by the head, dragging him toward himself. He said, "Son of my mother! Truly the people saw me weak, and they were about to kill me. So do not let the enemies jeer at my misfortune, and do not unite me with people of sin." **151.** He said, "My Lord, forgive me and my brother and take us into Your mercy for You are the most Merciful of the merciful." **152.** Indeed, for those who took up the calf, anger from their Lord will seize them and humiliate them in the life of this world. As such, do We reward those who embrace falsehood. **153.** Those who perform evil deeds, but repent afterward and believe, then God is indeed Forgiving and Merciful. **154.** When the anger of Moses appeased, he procured the Tablets. In their inscription lay a guidance and a mercy for those who are in fear of their Lord. **155.** Moses chose seventy men from his people for Our meeting. When the earthquake seized them, he said, "My Lord! Had you willed, You would have destroyed them and me earlier. Will You destroy us for what the fools among us have done? It is no more than Your trial. From it, You lead astray whomever You will and guide whomever You will. You are our Protector, so forgive us and have mercy upon us and You are the best of forgivers! **156**. Prescribe good for us in the life of this world and in the Hereafter. Truly we have turned unto You." He said, "I cause My Punishment to strike whomever I will, though My Mercy encompasses all things. I will prescribe it for those who are reverent, and give alms, those who believe in Our signs, **157**. those who follow the Messenger, and the unlettered Prophet whom they find inscribed in the Torah and the Gospel that is with them. He enjoins them to do what is right, and forbids them from doing what is wrong, and makes good things lawful unto them, and forbids them from doing bad things, and relieves them of their burden and the shackles that were upon them. Thereafter, those who believe in him, honor him, help him, and follow the light that has been sent down with him, it is they who will prosper." **158**. Say, "O People! Truly I am God's Messenger to all of you. Sovereignty over the heavens and the earth belong to Him. There is no god but He. He gives life and death. Therefore, believe in God and His Messenger, the unlettered Prophet who believes in God and His Words. Follow Him that perhaps you may be guided." **159**. Among the people of Moses is a group that guides by the truth and does justice in it. **160**. We divided them into twelve tribal groups. When his people asked him for water, We revealed to Moses, "Strike the rock with your staff." Then twelve springs gushed forth from it. Everyone knew their drinking place. We shaded them with clouds and sent down manna and quail upon them. "Eat of the good things We have provided you." But they did not wrong Us, they wronged themselves. **161**. Then it was said to them, "Dwell in this town and eat as you wish there, and say, 'Remove the burden!' and enter the gate prostrating, that We may forgive you for your sins. We will increase the righteous." **162**. Then those among them who did wrong had substituted a word for one different than the one they were told. Therefore, We sent down upon them a torment from heaven for the wrong they performed. **163**. Ask them about the town that was by the sea when they transgressed the Sabbath. Their fish would come to them on the day of their Sabbath, but on the day, when they did not observe the Sabbath, they would not come to them. Thus, did We try them for having been sinful. **164**. When a group among them said, "Why do you admonish a people whom God is about to destroy or punish with a severe punishment?" They said, "To be an excuse before your Lord that perhaps they may be reverent." **165**. When they forgot what they were reminded of, We saved those who refrained from evildoing, and We provided those who wronged with severe punishment for having practiced sin. **166**. When they were insolent about what they had been forbidden, We said to them, "Become outcasted apes!" **167.** Remember your Lord declared that He would truly send against them those who would inflict them with a terrible punishment until the Day of Resurrection. Truly your Lord is hasty in retribution, and truly He is Forgiving and Merciful. **168.** We divided them into nations on the earth. Some are righteous and some are otherwise. We tried them with good things and with evil things that perhaps they would yield back. **169.** Then an ensuing generation had subsequently inherited the Book. They took the vanities of this impermanent world only to say, "We will be forgiven." If other, similar vanities came their way, they would seize them. Did not the covenant of the Book commit them to say nothing but the truth about God? They have studied its contents. The Abode of the Hereafter is better for those who are reverent. Will you not understand? **170.** We will certainly not neglect the reward of the righteous for those who embrace the Book and perform prayer. **171.** When We lifted the mountain over them as if it were a canopy, they thought it would fall on them. "Take what We have given you with might and remember what lies in it that perhaps you may be reverent." **172.** Remember your Lord took from the progeny of the Children of Adam, from their loins and made them testify about themselves, "Am I not your Lord?" They said, "Yes, we testify," in case you should say on the Day of Resurrection, "Truly we were oblivious to this," **173.** or in case you should say, "Our fathers had previously joined partners unto God, and we were the succeeding progeny after them. Will You destroy us for what the falsifiers have done?" **174.** As such, do We explain the signs that perhaps they will yield back. **175.** Recite unto them the account of the one to whom We gave Our signs, but he pulled away. Thereafter, Satan followed up with him, and he became among the deviant. **176.** Had We willed, We certainly would have elevated him by it, but he leaned toward the earth and pursued his impulses. Thus, his likeness is that of a dog: if you attack him, he breathes heavily, and if you leave him alone, he breathes heavily. Such is the likeness of a people who reject Our signs. So recount the stories that perhaps they may reflect. **177.** Evil is the parable of the people who rejected Our signs and wronged themselves. **178.** Whomever God guides, he is rightly guided and whomever He leads astray, it is they who are the losers. **179.** Indeed, We have created for Hell many among the jinn and men. They have hearts with which they do not understand, they have eyes with which they do not see, and they have ears with which they do not hear. These are like livestock, but they are even further astray. It is they who are heedless. **180.** Unto God belong the Most Beautiful Names. So call Him by them and shun those who distort His names. They will soon be rewarded for what they practiced. **181.** Among those We have created is a nation that guides by the truth and thereby, does justice. **182**. As for those who deny Our signs, We will gradually lead them on though they will not know. **183**. I will grant them respite. Truly My scheme is firm. **184**. Have they not reflected? Their companion is not— insane; he is no more than a clear warner. **185**. Or have they not reflected upon the dominion of the heavens and the earth, and the things God has created, or that their term may have already drawn near? So in what message after this will they believe? **186**. Whomever God leads astray will have no guide. He lets them wander about confused in their rebellion. **187**. They question you about the Hour and when its appointed time will be. Say, "Its knowledge lies with my Lord. No one but He will manifest it at its proper time. It will weigh heavy upon the heavens and the earth. It will not come upon you but suddenly." They question you as if you had knowledge of it, say, "Knowledge of it lies only with God, but most people do not know." **188**. Say, "I do not gain benefit or harm for myself except for what God wills. If I had knowledge of the Unseen, I would have acquired much good, and no evil would have touched me. I am nothing more than a bearer of good news unto a people who believe. **189**. It is He who created you from a single soul and made from it a mate that he might find rest in her." Then, when he united with her, she bore a light burden and carried it about, but when she grew heavy, they called upon God their Lord, "If You give us a righteous child, we will surely be among the grateful." **190**. Then, when He gave them a goodly child, they attributed partners to Him for what He had given them. But God is exalted above the partners they attribute. **191**. Do they attribute as partners those who created nothing but are themselves created? **192**. Those who cannot help them, nor help themselves. **193**. If you call them to guidance, they do not follow you. It is the same for you whether you call upon them or whether you remain silent. **194**. Truly those whom they call upon instead of God are servants like you. So call upon them! Let them answer you if you are truthful. **195**. Do they have feet to walk with, or hands to hold with, or eyes to see with, or ears to hear with? Say, "Call upon your partners, then scheme against me, and do not award me respite. **196**. Indeed, my Protector is God Who sent down the Book, and He shields the righteous. **197**. Those whom you call upon instead of Him can neither help you, nor help themselves." **198**. If you call them unto guidance, they do not hear. You see them looking at you, but they do not see. **199**. Hold to forgiveness, command righteousness, and abandon the ignorant. **200**. Should a temptation from Satan provoke you, seek refuge in God. Truly He is Hearing and Knowing. **201**. Indeed, when those who are mindful are affected by an encounter from Satan, they remember and gain clear insight. **202**. But as for their brethren, the plunge them into error, and they do not stop. **203.** When you do not bring them a revelation they say, "Why do you not choose it?" Say, "I only follow what is revealed unto me from my Lord. These are insights from your Lord and a guidance and a mercy for people who believe." **204.** When the Quran is recited, hearken unto it, and listen that perhaps you may receive mercy. **205.** Remember your Lord within your soul, humbly and in awe. Do not raise your voice in the morning and in the evening and do not be among those who are heedless. **206.** Indeed, those who are with your Lord are not too arrogant to worship Him. They glorify Him and prostrate unto Him.

Surah 8

THE SPOILS

al-Anfāl

In the Name of God, the Compassionate, the Merciful

1. They question you about the spoils. Say, "The spoils belong to God and the messenger." Therefore, if you are believers, revere God, settle matters righteously among yourselves, and obey God and His messenger. **2.** For indeed, believers are those whose hearts tremble with fear when God is mentioned and when His signs are recited unto them, they increase them in faith, and they trust in their Lord. **3.** Whereas, whoever prays and spends from what We have provided them, **4.** it is they who are true believers. They will have high standing with their Lord, forgiveness, and a generous provision. **5.** Just as your Lord removed you from your home in truth while a group of believers were averse **6.** and disputed with you concerning the truth after it had become clear, as if they were being driven to death while they were watching. **7.** Remember, God had promised you that one of the two forces would be yours when you had hoped the unarmed one would be yours. But God wishes to verify the truth through His Words and to cut off the roots of the disbelievers, **8.** so He can show truth to be truth and falsehood to be falsehood, though the guilty were averse. **9.** When you sought assistance from your Lord, He responded to you: "I will assist you with a thousand angels, arrayed rank after rank." **10.** God solely made it a message of good news that your hearts may be at peace. Victory comes from God alone. Truly God is Mighty and Wise. **11.** Remember He covered you with sleepiness as security from Him and sent water down upon you from the sky to purify you thereby, remove the defilement of Satan from you, fortify your hearts, and fixate your steps thereby. **12.** Remember the Lord revealed to the angels, "Truly I am with you, so fortify those who believe. I will cast terror into the hearts of those who disbelieve. So strike them above the neck and strike each of their fingertips." **13.** That is because they are in schism with God and His Messenger. Truly God is strict in retribution. **14.** These are the consequences, so taste it. Indeed, the penalty of Fire is for the transgressors. **15.** O you who believe! When you meet those who disbelieve arrayed and ready, do not turn your backs on them. **16.** Whoever turns their back on them on that day, unless it is a stratagem of war or to withdraw to another company, will certainly have earned the wrath of God. His abode will be Hell. What a wretched final destination! **17.** You did not slay them, but God slew them, and you did not cast when you had casted, but God casted, so He may try the believers with a beautiful trial from Him. Truly God is Hearing and Knowing. **18.** These are the consequences. Indeed, God makes feeble the scheming of the disbelievers. **19.** If you seek victory then, victory has come to you, but if you abstain, it will be better for you. If you return, We will return, but your troop will be useless even if they were numerous. God is indeed with the believers. **20.** O you who believe! Obey God and His Messenger and do not turn away from him while you are listening. **21.** Do not be like those who say, "We hear," though they do not hear. **22.** Truly from God's perspective, the worst of human animals are the deaf and dumb who do not comprehend. **23.** Had God known of any good in them, He would have caused them to hear, yet had He caused them to hear, they would have still turned away in denial. **24.** O you who believe! Respond to God and the Messenger when He calls you unto what will give you, life. Know that God comes between a man and his heart, and that unto Him you will be gathered. **25.** Be mindful of civil contention since it does not only affect those who do wrong. Know that God is severe in retribution. **26.** Remember when there were a few of you feeling defenseless throughout the land and fearing people will abduct you, He then, sheltered you and strengthened you with His help and provided you with good provisions that perhaps you may offer gratitude. **27.** O you who believe! Do not betray God and the Messenger and do not betray your trusts knowingly. **28.** Know that your property and your children are but a trial and that truly God holds the great reward. **29.** O you who believe! If you revere God, He will grant you a criterion, absolve you of your evil deeds, and forgive you. God is the Possessor of Tremendous Bounty. **30.** Remember when those who disbelieved plotted against you to capture you, or to slay you, or to expel you. They plotted, and God plotted, and God is the best of plotters! **31.** When Our signs are recited unto them, they say, "We have already heard. Had we willed, we could have said something comparable. This is nothing but ancient tales." **32.** Remember when they said, "O God! If this is the truth from You, rain down stones upon us from the sky, or bring us a painful punishment." **33.** But God will not punish them while you are among them. God will not punish them while they seek forgiveness. **34.** What do they possess to keep God from punishing them while they deter people from the Sacred Mosque, though they are not its protectors? Its protectors are but the reverent, but most of them do not know. **35.** Their prayer at the House was nothing but whistling and clapping. Therefore, taste the punishment for having disbelieved! **36.** Truly those who disbelieve spend of their wealth to divert from the way of God. They will spend it, but then it will become a source of regret upon them when they are overcome. The disbelievers will be gathered unto Hell. **37.** God separates the bad from the good and places the bad one over the other, heaps them all together, and places them in Hell. It is they who are the losers. **38.** Say to the disbelievers that if they cease, what has passed will be forgiven for them, but if they revert, prior practices will take precedence. **39.** Fight them until there is no contention. Religion belongs entirely to God. But if they cease, God is truly observant of what they do. **40.** If they turn away, know that God is your Master, an excellent Master, and an excellent Helper! **41.** Know that whatever you take as spoils, a fifth is for God and the Messenger, and for kinsfolk, orphans, the indigent, and the wanderer, that is if you believe in God and what We sent down upon Our servant on the Day of Discrimination — the day the two forces met for God is Powerful over all things. **42.** When you were situated on the nearby slope, they on the far-out slope, and the caravan was below you, had you planned a meeting with each other, you would have missed the meeting. But for God to conclude a matter that was to be concluded, so that whoever should die, dies according to a clear sign, and whoever should live, lives according to a clear sign. Truly God is Hearing and Knowing. **43.** Remember when God showed them to you in your dream as being a few. Had He shown them to be numerous, you would have hesitated and argued over the matter, but God saved you. Truly He knows what lies within breasts. **44.** Remember when you met them, He showed them to be few in your eyes and made you appear to be few in their eyes, that God may conclude a matter that needed to be concluded. Unto God all matters are returned. **45.** O you who believe! When you meet a force in battle, be firm and copiously believe in God that perhaps you may prosper. **46.** Obey God and His Messenger and do not argue among yourselves lest you lose courage, and your strength be depleted. Be patient. Truly God is with the patient. **47.** Do not be like those who left their homes boastfully to be seen by people while they hinder men from the way of God. God encompasses whatever they do. **48.** Remember when Satan made their deeds seem fair to them and said, "No one among mankind will overcome you today and I am indeed Your defender." But when the two forces saw each other, he turned on his heels and said, "I am clear of you! Truly I see what you do not see. Truly I fear God and God is severe in retribution." **49.** Remember when the hypocrites and those in whose hearts is a disease said, "Their religion has deceived them." But whoever trusts in God, truly God is Mighty and Wise. **50.** If you could only see when the angels take those who disbelieve, striking their faces and their backs: "Taste the punishment of the burning." **51.** This is the result of what your own hands have done, for God does not wrong His servants— **52.** just as it was with the House of Pharaoh and those before them. They denied the signs of their Lord, so God seized them along with their sins. Truly God is Strong and severe in retribution. **53.** That is because God never changes a blessing by which He blesses a people until they change what is in themselves. God is Hearing and Knowing— **54.** just as it was with the House of Pharoah and those before them. They denied the signs of their Lord, so We destroyed them along with their sins. We drowned the House of Pharoah for they were all wrongdoers. **55.** Truly the worst of human animals from God's perspective are those who disbelieve and will not believe! **56.** Those among them with whom you have a made a covenant and always break their covenant, are not reverent. **57.** So if you come upon them in war, use them to disperse those who will come after them that perhaps they might be reminded. **58.** If you fear treachery from a people, withdraw from them equitably. Indeed, God does not like the treacherous. **59.** Do not let those who disbelieve assume they have outperformed. Truly they will not escape. **60.** Prepare for them what you can of strength and horses tethered to frighten thereby, the enemy of God, your enemy, and others besides them who you do not know, but God knows them. Whatever you spend in the way of God will be paid unto you in full and you will not be wronged. **61.** If they lean toward peace, you should lean toward it, and trust in God. Truly He is the Hearing and Knowing. **62.** If their goal is to trick you, then God is enough for you. It is He Who supports you with His help, and with the believers. **63.** He had joined their hearts. Had you spent all that is on the earth, it would not have joined their hearts, but God joined them together. Truly He is Mighty and Wise. **64.** O Prophet! God is enough for you and the believers who follow you. **65.** O Prophet! Incite the believers to fight. If there were twenty who are patient among you, they will overcome two hundred. If there were one hundred of you, they will overcome a thousand of those who disbelieve because they are a people who do not understand. **66.** Now God has lightened your burden for He knows there is faintness in you. If there were one hundred who are patient among you, they will overcome two hundred and if there were a thousand, they will overcome two thousand by God's Leave. God is with the patient. **67.** It is not for a prophet to take captives until he dominates in the land. You desire the transient things of this world, while God desires the Hereafter. God is Mighty and Wise. **68.** If it had not been previously ordained by God, a great punishment would have transpired upon you for what you took. **69.** So consume the spoils you have taken lawfully in a good way, and revere God. Truly God is Forgiving and Merciful. **70.** O Prophet! Say to those captives in your custody, "If God knows there to be any good in your hearts, He will give you what is better than what was taken from you and will forgive you. God is Forgiving and Merciful." **71.** But if they desire to betray you, they have already betrayed God, so We gave you power over them. God is Knowing and Wise. **72.** Truly those who believed and migrated and strived with their wealth and themselves in the way of God, and those who sheltered and helped, are the protectors of one another. As for those who believe and did not migrate, you owe them no protection until they migrate. But if they ask for your help for the sake of religion, then assistance is a duty upon you, except against a people with whom you have a covenant. God sees whatever you do. **73.** As for those who disbelieve, they are protectors of one another. Unless you do the same, there will be contention and great corruption in the land. **74.** Those who believe, migrate, and strive in the way of God and those who gave refuge and helped, truly it is they who are believers. They will acquire forgiveness and a generous provision. **75.** Those who believe after you, migrate and strive with you, will be of you while blood relatives have primary rights among one another in the Book of God. Truly God has knowledge of all things.

Surah 9

Repentance

al-Tawbah

1. A repudiation from God and his Messenger to those idolators with whom you have made a treaty. **2.** So move freely throughout the land for four months but know that you cannot escape God, and that God will humiliate the disbelievers. **3.** An announcement from God and His Messenger to the people on the day of the Greater Pilgrimage that God and His Messenger have repudiated the idolators. Therefore, if you repent it will be better for you. If you turn away, then know that you cannot frustrate God. Inform the disbelievers of a painful punishment, **4.** except for the idolaters upon whom you have made a treaty and who have not failed you in anything, nor supported anyone against you. Thus fulfill the treaty with them for its duration. Truly God loves the reverent. **5.** Then, when the sacred months have passed, slay the idolators wherever you find them, seize them, surround them, and lie in wait for them at every stratagem. But if they repent, perform prayer, and give alms, let them go their way. God is indeed Forgiving and Merciful. **6.** If any of the idolators seek asylum with you, grant him asylum until he hears the Word of God. Then, transfer him to his place of safety since they are a people who do not know. **7.** How can the idolators have a treaty with God and His Messenger except for those with whom you have entered into a treaty at the Sacred Mosque? If they stand true to you, stand true to them. Truly God loves the reverent. **8.** How, then if they prevail over you, do they not observe any kinship or treaty with you? They please you with their mouths while their hearts decline. Most of them are sinful. **9.** They have sold God's signs for a trivial price and have turned from His way. Indeed, evil is what they did by **10.** neither observing kinship nor treaty with any believer. It is they who are the transgressors. **11.** However, if they repent, practice prayer, and give alms, then they are your brethren in religion. We have clarified the signs for a people who know. **12.** If they revoke their oaths after having entered into a treaty and vilify your religion, then fight the leaders of disbelief for indeed, they have no oaths to be terminated. 13. Will you not fight a people who broke their oaths and intended to expel the Messenger when it is they who initiated? Do you fear them? For if you are believers, God is worthier of your fear. 14. Fight them and God will punish them with your hands and disgrace them. He will grant you victory over them, heal the breasts of a believing people, 15. and dispel the rage within their hearts. God relents unto whomever He wills. God is Knowing and Wise. 16. Or did you assume you would be left alone while God had yet to know whom among you endeavored and took no associate besides God, His Messenger, and the believers? God is Aware of whatever you do. 17. It is not for the idolators to maintain the mosques of God, holding witness of disbelief against themselves. They are those whose deeds have plummeted, and they will abide in the Fire. 18. However, only those who believe in God, the Hereafter, practice prayer, give alms, and fear only God, will maintain the mosques of God. Indeed, they will be among the rightly guided. 19. Or do you assume giving drink to the pilgrims, maintaining the Sacred Mosque, is like those who strive in God's way, and believe in God and the Last Day? From God's perspective, they are not equal. God does not guide a wrongdoing people. 20. From God's perspective, those who believe, emigrate, and strive in the way of God with their wealth and their persons are greater in rank. It is they who are the triumphant. 21. Their Lord gives them good news of mercy and satisfaction from Him and Gardens from which they will have eternal bliss, 22. abiding there forever. Truly with God is a great reward. 23. O you who believe! Do not take your brothers and fathers as protectors if they favor disbelief over belief. As for those among you who take them as protectors, it is they who are the wrongdoers. 24. Say, "If our fathers, your children, your brothers, your spouses, your tribe, the wealth you have acquired, the commerce you fear declining, the dwellings you find pleasing, are dearer to you than God and His Messenger, or than to strive in His way, then wait until God comes with His Command." God does not guide a sinful people. 25. God has indeed granted you victory on many grounds. Then on the Day of *Hunain* when you were impressed at how numerous you were and nothing availed you, and the earth, despite its breadth, closed in on you, you then, turned your backs. 26. Then God sent down His Tranquility upon His Messenger, and upon the believers. He sent down forces that you could not see and punished those who disbelieved. That is the reward of the disbelievers. 27. Thereafter, God will relent unto whomever He wills. God is Forgiving and Merciful. 28. O you who believe! Truly the idolators are impure, so after this year of theirs, do not let them come near the Sacred Mosque. If you fear poverty, God will enrich you from His Bounty, if He so wills. Truly God is Knowing and Wise.

29. Fight those who do not believe in God and the Last Day, who do not forbid what God and His Messenger have forbidden, who do not follow the Religion of Truth among those who were given the Book, until they pay their compensation-tax humbly, and with a willing hand. **30.** The Jews say that Ezra is the son of God, and the Christians say the Messiah is the son of God. Those are words from their mouths. They resemble the words of those who had previously disbelieved. God curse them for their waywardness. **31.** They have taken their rabbis and monks as lords instead of God, and the Messiah, son of Mary, though they were only commanded to worship One God. There is no God but He! Glory be to Him above the partners they attribute. **32.** They desire to extinguish the Light of God with their mouths, but God refuses to do anything but carry on with His Light despite the adversity of the disbelievers. **33.** It is He who sent His Messenger with guidance and the religion of Truth to make it prevail over all religions despite the adversity of the idolators. **34.** O you who believe! Truly many of the rabbis and priests falsely consume the wealth of people and turn from the way of God — those who hoard gold and silver and do not spend it in the way of God, inform them of a painful punishment. **35.** On the Day when it will be heated up in the Fire of Hell, their foreheads, their sides, and their backs will be branded with it. "This is what you hoarded up for yourselves, so taste of what you hoarded." **36.** Indeed, from God's perspective, the number of months is twelve months in His Book starting from the day He created the heavens and the earth. Of them, four are sacred. That is the upright religion. So do not wrong yourselves. Fight the idolators all together just as they fight you all together and know that God is with the reverent. **37.** Verily, postponement is but an increase in disbelief that leads the disbelievers to go astray. They make it lawful one year and forbid it another in order to reconcile it with the number made sacred by God to validate what God has forbidden. The evilness of their deeds is made to seem agreeable to them, but God does not guide a disbelieving people. **38.** O you who believe! What bothers you when you are told, "Go forth in the way of God," and you sink heavily unto the earth? Are you content with the life of this world over the Hereafter? The life of this world is but little enjoyment compared to the Hereafter. **39.** If you do not go forth, He will punish you with a painful punishment and replace you with another people. You will not harm Him in the least. God is powerful over all things. **40.** If you do not help him, God has already helped him. Remember when the disbelievers expelled him and while in the cave, the second of the two, said to his companion, "Do not grieve, God is truly with us." Then, God sent down His Serenity upon him and supported him with combatants that you could not see. He made the word of those who disbelieve to be bottommost and the Word of God to be the uppermost. God is Mighty and Wise.

41. Go forth in the way of God, lightly or heavily, and strive with your wealth and your persons in the way of God. That is better for you if you only knew. **42.** Were it something transient nearby and an easy journey, they would have followed you, but the distance was too long for them. They will swear by God, "Had we been able, we would have gone out with you." They destroy themselves and God knows they are liars. **43.** God forgive you! Why did you give them permission to leave before it became clear to you who was telling the truth that you may know who the liars were. **44.** Those who believe in God and the Last Day do not ask for exemption from striving with their wealth and their persons. God knows the reverent. **45.** It is only those who do not believe in God and the Last Day who ask to be exempt. Their hearts are in doubt. Consequently, they waver in doubt. **46.** Had they desired to go forth, they would have made some preparations for it. But God abhorred for them to be sent forth, so He held them back. It was said to them, "Stay back with those who stay back." **47.** Had they gone forth with you, they would have only added to your troubles and would have hurried about in your midst seeking sedition amidst you. Among you are some who listen to them, but God knows well the wrongdoers. **48.** Indeed, they had previously plotted sedition and overturned matters for you until the truth came and the Command of God was clear, something much to their aversion. **49.** Among them some say, "Grant me exemption and do not tempt me." They have surely fallen into temptation, and truly, Hell encompasses the disbelievers. **50.** If 'good' ensues you, it bothers them, but if 'affliction' ensues you, they say, "We took our precautions beforehand," and they turn away rejoicing. **51.** Say, "Nothing transpires except what God has decreed for us. He is our Master, so let believers place their trust in God." **52.** Say, "Do you anticipate that nothing will happen to us except for one of the two great things? We anticipate for you that God will afflict you with a punishment from Him, or by our hands. So wait! Indeed, we are waiting along with you." **53.** Say, "Spend willingly or unwillingly, but it will not be accepted by you. Truly you are a sinful people." **54.** The only thing that prevented their spending from being accepted from them is their disbelief in God and His Messenger. They go to prayer lazily and only spend reluctantly. **55.** Do not let their wealth or their children impress you because God wants to punish them in the life of this world so their souls will depart as disbelievers. **56.** They swear by God that they are indeed of you, but they are not of you. Rather, they are a fearful people. **57.** Were they to find refuge, or caves, or a place to enter, they would run in haste. **58.** Among them, some criticize you over charitable offerings. If they are given of it, they are satisfied, but if they are not given of it, they grow resentful. **59.** If only they had been satisfied with what God and His Messenger had given them and said, "God suffices us. God will give us from His Bounty as will the Messenger.

Our desire is truly for God." 60. As a duty from God, charitable offerings are solely for the poor, the indigent, those working with them, those whose hearts are to be reconciled, ransoming slaves, debtors, those who pursue the way of God, and the traveler. God is Knowing and Wise. 61. There are some among them who offend the Prophet and say, "He is an ear." Say, "An ear that is good for you! He believes in God, and he has faith in the believers. He is a mercy to those among you who believe." As for those who offend the Messenger of God, they will have a painful punishment. 62. They swear by God to please you, but if they are believers, God and His Messenger are worthier of being pleased. 63. Do they not know that whoever opposes God and His Messenger, that the Fire of Hell will indeed be for him to abide there? That is the great disgrace. 64. The hypocrites dread that a sūrah be sent down against them informing them of what is in their hearts. Say, "Go on mocking! Truly God will carry out what you dread." 65. If you ask them, they will certainly say, "We were only chatting and playing." Say, "Is it God, His signs, and His Messenger that you were mocking?" 66. Do not make excuses. You disbelieved after having believed. If We pardon a group of you, We will punish another group for being guilty. 67. Male and female hypocrites are similar to one another for enjoining wrong, forbidding right, and withholding their hands. They forgot God, so He forgot them. Indeed, the hypocrites are sinful. 68. Truly God has promised the Fire of Hell to male and female hypocrites, and the disbelievers for them to abide therein. That is sufficient for them. God has cursed them, and their punishment will be enduring. 69. Similar to those before you, they were mightier than you in power and greater in wealth and children. They enjoyed their portion, and you enjoyed your portion just as those before you enjoyed their portion. You have engaged in vain discourse as they engaged in vain discourse. Their deeds came to nothing in this world and in the Hereafter, and it is they who are the losers. 70. Has not the account come to them of those who were before them—the people of Noah, the Ād, the Thamŭd, the people of Abraham, the inhabitants of Midian, and the overthrown cities? Their messengers had brought them clear signs, but God did not wrong them—they wronged themselves. 71. Believing men and believing women are protectors of one another by enjoining right and forbidding wrong, performing prayer, giving alms, and obeying God and His Messenger— they are those whom God will have Mercy upon. Truly God is Mighty and Wise. 72. God has promised believing men and believing women Gardens with rivers running beneath to abide there forever along with goodly dwellings in the Garden of Eden. Satisfaction from God is huge. That is the great victory! 73. O Prophet! Strive against the disbelievers and the hypocrites and be hardy with them. Their refuge is Hell. What a wretched destination! 74. They swear by God that they did not say it, but they indeed spoke the word of disbelief and disbelieved after having submitted. They had fantasies that they did not realize. They were resentful only because God and His Messenger had enriched them from His Bounty. If they repent, it would be better for them, but if they deter, God will punish them with a painful punishment in this world and in the Hereafter. They will have neither protector nor helper on the earth. **75.** Among them are those who make a covenant with God saying, "If He gives us of His Bounty, we will certainly spend in charity and we will certainly be among the righteous." **76.** But when He gave them of His Bounty, they were miserly with it and turned away in rejection. **77.** So He penalized them with insincerity in their hearts until the Day they will meet Him for having broken their promise with God and for having lied. **78.** Do they not know that God knows their secret and their private discourse, and that God is the Knower of all that is Unseen? **79.** There are those who condemn and ridicule believers who give in charity and those who can only give of their keep. However, God ridicules them, and their punishment will be painful. **80.** Seek forgiveness for them or do not seek forgiveness for them. If you seek forgiveness for them seventy times, God will not forgive them. That is because they disbelieved in God and His Messenger. God does not guide a sinful people. **81.** Those who were left behind rejoiced in retiring behind the Messenger of God. They were opposed to striving with their wealth and with their persons in the way of God. They said, "Do not go forth in the heat." Say, "The Fire of Hell is of a more intense heat," if they only understood. **82.** Let them laugh a little but weep intensely as a reward for what they earned. **83.** If God returns you to a group of them and they ask you for permission to leave, say, "You will never go forth with me, nor will you fight with me against any enemy. You were satisfied in retiring the first time so retire with those who stay behind." **84.** Never pray over any of them who dies, nor stand by his grave. Truly they disbelieved in God and His Messenger and died in sin. **85.** Do not let their wealth or their children impress you. God wants to punish them in the life of this world that their souls will depart as disbelievers. **86.** When a sūrah is sent down, "Believe in God and strive with His Messenger," the affluent among them ask you for permission to leave, saying, "Let us be among those who retire." **87.** They are satisfied in being among those who lag behind, but a seal is on their hearts, and they do not understand. **88.** Yet the Messenger and the believers strive with their wealth and with their persons. It is they who will have good things and it is they who will prosper. **89.** God has prepared for them Gardens with rivers running beneath to abide there forever. That is the great victory! **90.** Then, came the Bedouins asking for permission to be excused while those who had lied to God and His Messenger sat back. A painful punishment will strike those among them who disbelieve. **91.** There is no blame upon the weak, the sick, or those who find nothing to spend so long as they are sincere toward God and His Messenger. God is Forgiving and Merciful. There is no argument against the righteous, **92.** nor upon those who came to you to give them a mount. You said to them, "I did not find anything for you to mount on." They then turned back, their eyes flowing with tears, saddened because they found nothing to spend. **93.** The argument falls on those who ask you to grant them leave though they are wealthy and are content to be among those who remain behind. God has set a seal upon their hearts, so they do not know. **94.** They will offer you excuses when you return to them. Say, "Do not offer excuses! We will not believe you. God has already informed us of you." God and His Messenger will see your deeds and you will then be brought back to the Knower of the Unseen and the Seen. He will inform you of what you did. **95.** They will swear by God to you when you return to them so you may turn away from them. So turn away from them. Truly they are an abomination, and their refuge is Hell as compensation for what they earned. **96.** They swear to you that you may be satisfied with them. Though you may be satisfied with them, God is not satisfied with a sinful people. **97.** The Bedouin are more severe in disbelief and hypocrisy and more inclined not to know the limits of what God has sent down unto His Messenger. God is Knowing and Wise. **98.** Among the Bedouin are those who take what they spend as a loss, and they await a change in fortune for you, but an evil change in fortune will be on them. God is Hearing and Knowing. **99.** Among the Bedouin are those who believe in God and the Last Day and take what they spend to draw them in proximity to God and the prayers of the Messenger. Indeed, it will be proximity for them. God will cause them to enter His Mercy. Truly God is Forgiving and Merciful. **100.** As for the predecessors among the emigrants, the helpers, and those who virtuously followed them, God is satisfied with them, and they are satisfied with Him. He has prepared Gardens with rivers running beneath for them to abide there forever. That is the great victory! **101.** Among the Bedouin around you there are hypocrites, and among the people of Madinah are those who are obstinate in hypocrisy. You do not know them. We know them and We will punish them doubly and they will then be relegated to a greater punishment. **102.** [There are] others who acknowledge their sins, having combined good deeds with evil ones. Yet, it is possible that God will turn to them in forgiveness, for God is Forgiving and Merciful. **103.** You are to take a charitable offering from their wealth to purify, sanctify, and thus, bless them. Truly your prayers are a security for them. God is Hearing and Knowing. **104.** Do they not know that God accepts repentance from His servants and receives the charitable offerings and that God is indeed Relenting and Merciful? **105.** Say, "Perform your deeds. God will see your deeds as well as the Messenger and the believers. You will be brought back to the Knower of the Unseen and the Seen, and He will inform you of what you did." **106.** Others are in suspense of God's Command. He will either punish them or He will relent unto them. God is Knowing and Wise. **107.** Those who established a mosque for malice, disbelief, to divide the believers, and to be a station for those who previously created war against God and His Messenger, will definitely swear, "We desire only what is best." But God testifies that they are, indeed, liars. **108.** Never stand in it! A mosque founded on piety from day one is worthier for you to stand in. In it are men who love to purify themselves, and God loves those who purify themselves. **109.** So is the one who founded his structure on piety and God's satisfaction better, or the one who founded his structure on the crumbling vertical face of a cliff which then, crumbles with him into the Fire of Hell? God does not guide a wrongdoing people. **110.** The structures they have built will not stop being distressing to their hearts until their hearts are torn apart, for God is Knowing and Wise. **111.** Truly God has purchased from the believers their souls and wealth for the Garden to be theirs. They fight in the way of God, slaying and being slain, a promise binding upon Him in the Torah, Gospel, and the Quran. Who is Truer to His promise than God? So rejoice in the deal you have made. Indeed, that is the great victory! **112.** So give good news to the believers, the repentant, the worshippers, the gracious, the travelers, those who bow, those who prostrate, those who enjoin right, those who forbid wrong, and those who maintain the limits set by God. **113.** It is not for the Prophet and those who believe to seek forgiveness for the idolators even if they were of kin after it was made clear to them that they will be the inhabitants of Hellfire. **114.** Abraham's plea for forgiveness for his father was only because of a promise he had made to him. But when it became clear to him that he was an enemy of God, he repudiated him. Truly Abraham was compassionate and forbearing. **115.** It is not on God to lead a people astray after having guided them until He makes it clear to them that which they should guard against. Truly God has knowledge of all things. **116.** Truly unto God belongs sovereignty over the heavens and the earth. He gives life and death. You have no protector nor helper besides God. **117.** God has indeed relented unto the Prophet and the emigrants and the helpers who followed him during a period of distress. This is after the hearts of a group of them had nearly swerved. He subsequently relented unto them. Truly He is Kind and Merciful to them, **118.** and to the three who were left behind until despite its breadth, the earth had closed in on them and their own souls had closed in on them and they realized there was no refuge from God, save with Him. Then, He relented unto them so they might repent. Truly God is Relenting and Merciful. **119.** O you who believe! Revere your Lord and be among the truthful. **120.** It is not for the people of Madinah and the Bedouin who live around them to lag behind from the Messenger of God, or to give themselves preference over him. That is because no thirst, nor fatigue, nor hunger befalls them in the way of God, nor do they tread a path that infuriates the disbelievers, nor do they endure anything at the hands of the enemy, but that a righteous deed is recorded for them on account of it. Truly God does not waste the reward of the righteous. **121.** They do not spend anything, whether small or large, nor traverse any valley, without it being recorded for them, so that God may reward them according to the best of what they used to do. **122.** It is not for the believers to all go forth. Why shouldn't a group from each community go forth to gain a deeper understanding of the religion and, upon returning, warn their people—so that they might become mindful? **123.** O you who believe! Fight those disbelievers who are close to you and let them find hardiness in you. Know that God is with the reverent. **124.** Whenever a sūrah is sent down, some among them say, "Which of you has had his faith increase by it?" For those who believe, it has increased them in faith, and they rejoice. **125.** But as for those in whose hearts is a disease, it has added defilement to their defilement, and they die as disbelievers. **126.** Do they not see that they are tried each year, once or twice—but they neither repent nor take notice? **127.** Whenever a sūrah is sent down, they look at each other: "Does anyone see you?" Then they turn away. God has turned their hearts away because they are a people who do not understand. **128.** Indeed, a messenger has come to you from among your own. He is troubled and concerned by your suffering, but he is kind and merciful to the believers. **129.** But if they turn away say, "God suffices me. There is no god, but He. In Him, I trust. He is the Lord of the Supreme Throne."

Surah 10

Jonah

Yŭnus

In the Name of God, the Compassionate, the Merciful

1. *Alif. Lām. Rā.* These are the signs of the Book of Wisdom. **2.** Is it a wonder for people that We sent revelations to a man from among themselves to warn people and give good news to those who believe they will have a level of sincerity with their Lord? The disbelievers say, "Indeed, this is clearly a sorcerer." **3.** Truly your Lord is God Who created the heavens and the earth in six days, then ascended the Throne to take charge of the matter. There is no intercessor save by His Leave. That is God your Lord. Therefore, worship Him! Will you not remember? **4.** Unto Him, you will all be returned. God's promise is real. Truly He devised creation, and He will bring it back, so He can justly reward those who believe and perform righteous deeds. But the disbelievers will have a drink of boiling liquid and a painful punishment for having disbelieved. **5.** It is He who made the sun a shining light and the moon a light measured out in stages that you may know the number of years and the computation of time. God did not create this but in truth. He explains the signs for a people who know. **6.** Truly in the alteration of night and day and whatever God has created in the heavens and on the earth are signs for people who are reverent. **7.** Verily those who do not anticipate the meeting with Us, who are pleased with the life of this world feeling secure from within, and who are oblivious to Our signs, **8.** it is they whose refuge will be the Fire for what they earned. **9.** Truly those who believe and perform righteous deeds, their Lord guides them by their faith. They will have rivers running below them in Gardens of bliss. **10.** Their supplication in it will be, "O God! Glory is to You." Their greeting in it will be, "Peace." The completion of their supplication will be, "Praise be to God, Lord of the Worlds!" **11.** If God were to expedite evil for people, even as they would advance the good, their destiny would have ended. However, We leave those who do not anticipate the meeting with Us to wander around in their diversion. **12.** When harm afflicts a human, he calls on Us to be by his side whether he is sitting or standing. Then, when We remove his affliction from him, he moves on as if he did not call on Us regarding the affliction that had touched him. As such, the transgressors assumed that what they did was fair. **13.** We have certainly destroyed generations before you when they did wrong. Their messengers had brought them clear signs, but they would not believe. Thus, do We avenge the guilty people. **14.** Then, We made you deputies on the earth after them to observe your behavior. **15.** When Our signs are recited unto them as clear proofs, those who do not anticipate the meeting with Us say, "Bring a different Quran to us, or change this one." Say, "It is not for me to change it of my own will. I only follow what is revealed unto me. Truly I fear the punishment of a tremendous day if I disobey my Lord." **16.** Say, "Had God willed, I would not have recited it unto you, nor would He have made it known to you. Indeed, I have existed among you for a lifetime prior to it. Do you still not understand?" **17.** Who does more wrong than one who invents a lie against God or lies about His signs. The guilty will truly, not prosper. **18.** They worship, besides God, that which will neither harm them nor benefit them, and they say, "These are our mediators with God." Say, "Would you inform God of something in the heavens or the earth that He does not know about? Glory be to Him and exalted is He above the partners they attribute!" **19.** People were but one nation, then, they differed. Had it not been for a Word that had preceded from your Lord, their differences would have been settled between them. **20.** They say, "Why has no sign been sent down unto him from his Lord?" Say, "The Unseen belongs to God alone. So wait! Truly I am among those waiting along with you." **21.** When We give people a taste of mercy after some calamity touches them, observe, they take to plotting against Our signs. Say, "God is swifter in plotting." Indeed, Our messengers record whatever you plot. **22.** He is the One who leads you over land and sea even when sailing through a favorable wind, and they are rejoicing in it. But when a violent tempest comes upon them, and waves come at them from every side, and they assume they will be encompassed by them, they call upon God, devoting religion entirely to Him. "If you save us from this, we will certainly be among the appreciative." **23.** Then when He saves them, observe, they behave tyrannically on the earth without justification. O people! Your tyranny is only against yourselves as an enjoyment in the life of this world, then unto Us will be your return so We can inform you of what you did. **24.** The allegory of the life of this world is that of the water We send down from the sky. The earth's vegetation from which people and livestock eat, mingles with it until the earth takes on its gleam and is embellished. Its inhabitants think they have gained mastery over it.

Our Command comes upon it by night or by day, whereupon We make it a mown field as if it had not flourished the day before! Thus, do We explain the signs for a people who reflect. **25.** God calls to the Home of Peace and guides whomever He wills unto a straight path. **26.** To those who are virtuous and beyond, neither darkness nor shame will come over their faces! They are the inhabitants of the Garden, and they will abide there forever. **27.** Those who commit evil deeds will be rewarded with a similar evil and shame will overcome them. There will be no one to protect them from God—as though their faces are covered with blotches from night's darkness. They are the inhabitants of Fire, and they will abide there forever. **28.** On the Day We gather them all together, We will say to those who attributed partners to God, "Partner in your turf, you and your partners!" Then We will separate them, and their partners will say, "It was not us whom you worshipped. **29.** God is witness enough between you and us. We were unmindful of your worship!" **30.** It is there and then that every soul will experience what it did in the past, and they will all be returned unto God, their true Master, and what they invented will desert them. **31.** Say, "Who is it that sustains you from Heaven and earth? Or who possesses your hearing and sight? Who brings out the living from the dead and the dead from the living, and who is in charge of the affair?" They will say, "God." So say, "Will you then not be reverent?" **32.** So that is God, your true Lord. What exists beyond truth besides error? How then are you turned away? **33.** Consequently, the Word of your Lord proved to be true for those who are sinful. Indeed, they do not believe. **34.** Say, "Is there any among your partners, one who originates creation and then, retrieves it?" Say, "God originates creation and then, retrieves it. Then, how is it that you are deluded?" **35.** Say, "Is there any among your partners who can guide to the truth?" Say, "God guides to the truth. Is one who guides to the truth worthier to follow or one who cannot guide unless he were guided? What is it with you! How do you judge?" **36.** But most of them only follow assumptions. Truly assumptions are of no benefit at all compared to the truth. Indeed, God is Aware of what they do. **37.** This Quran could not have been produced by any besides God. It is from the Lord of the Worlds, and a confirmation of what came before it, and an explanation of the Book in which there is no doubt. **38.** Or do they say, "He forged it?" Say, "Bring a sūrah like it and call upon whoever you can aside from God if you are truthful." **39.** Truly they lie about the knowledge they do not comprehend and the interpretation that has not yet reached them. So have those before them. Observe how the wrongdoers fared. **40.** Among them are those who believe in it and among them are those who do not believe in it. Your Lord knows best the wrongdoers. **41.** If they call you a liar, say, "I have my work, and you have your work. You are clear of what I do, and I am clear of what you do.

42. Among them are those who listen to you, but can you make the deaf hear, though they do not understand? 43. Among them are those who look at you, but can you guide the blind, though they cannot see? 44. Truly God does not wrong people at all, but people wrong themselves. 45. On the Day when He will gather them, it will be as if they tarried no more than a day's hour while addressing one another. Indeed, those who denied the meeting with God have lost. They were not rightly guided. 46. Whether We show you a part of what We promise them, or We take your soul, their return will be to Us. Subsequently, God is Witness over what they do. 47. There is a messenger for every nation. When their messenger comes, he will impartially judge between them. They will not be wronged. 48. They say, "When will this promise take place, if you are truthful?" 49. Say, "I have no power over what harm or benefit may come to me except for what God wills. For every nation there is a time appointed. When their time comes, they will not delay it by a single hour, nor will they advance it." 50. Say, "Have you contemplated if His punishment were to come upon you by day or by night, what part thereof would the sinful wish to expedite?" 51. Then, when it comes to pass, will you believe in it? Now? When you previously wanted to expedite it? 52. Then, it will be said to the wrongdoers, "Taste the everlasting punishment. Are you rewarded for anything besides for what you had earned?" 53. They inquire of you, "Is this true?" Say, "Indeed, by my Lord, it is true. You cannot impede it." 54. Indeed, if every soul that had sinned possessed all that is on the earth, he would try to ransom himself, and they will hide their remorse when they see the punishment. Judgment will take place between them with justice, and they will not be wronged. 55. Truly unto God belongs whatever is in the heavens and on the earth. Undeniably, God's promise is true, but most of them do not know. 56. He gives life and death, and unto Him you will be returned. 57. O People! Advice has come to you from your Lord, and a cure for what lies within hearts, and a guidance and a mercy for the believers. 58. Say, "In the Bounty of God and in His Mercy, in that, let them rejoice. That is better than what they accumulate. 59. Say, "Have you seen what God sent down unto you as sustenance? Then, you made some of it forbidden and some lawful." Say, "Did God give you permission or do you make up lies against God?" 60. What will those who make up lies against God surmise on the Day of Resurrection? Truly God is Possessed of Bounty for people, but most of them do not show gratitude. 61. You will not be doing any business, nor will you be reciting any part of the Quran, nor undertaking any action, save that We will be standing Witness over you while you are engaging there. Not a mote's weight evades your Lord on the earth or in Heaven, no smaller than that, nor larger, but that it is in a clear Book. 62. Watch! Truly no fear will come upon the friends of God, nor will they grieve.

63. For those who believe and are reverent 64. is good news in the life of this world and in the Hereafter. There is no substitution for the Words of God. That is the great victory! 65. Do not let their speech grieve you. Truly, honor belongs entirely to God. He is the Hearing and the Knowing. 66. Behold! Truly, whoever is in the heavens and whoever is on the earth belongs to God. What is it that they follow, those who attribute partners to God? They make assumptions and follow nothing but conjecture. 67. It is He who made the night for you to rest in, and the day for you to see. Truly in that are signs for a people who listen. 68. They say, "God has taken a child." Glory be to Him! He is the Self-Sufficient. To Him belongs whatever is in the heavens and whatever is on the earth. You have no authority over this. Do you speak about God that which you do not know? 69. Say, "Certainly, those who invent a lie against God will not prosper." 70. There may be pleasure in this world, but to Us will be their return. We will make them taste severe punishment for having disbelieved. 71. Recite unto them the story of Noah when he said to his people, "O my people! If my presence and remembrances of God's signs is too much for you, then in God I trust. Therefore, you and your partners decide on your plan, and let there be no doubt in your plan. Carry it out and grant me no respite! 72. But if you turn your backs, I have not asked you for any reward. My reward lies only with God, and I am commanded to be among those who submit. 73. Yet, they denied him, so We saved him and those with him in the Ark. We made them successors and We drowned those who denied Our signs. So consider the end of those who were warned. 74. Then after him, We sent messengers to their people, and they brought them clear signs. But they would not believe in what they had previously rejected. So do We set a seal on the hearts of transgressors. 75. Then after them, We sent Moses and Aaron with Our signs to Pharoah and his notables. But they were arrogant, and they were a guilty nation. 76. So when the Truth from Us came to them, they said, "Surely, this is clearly sorcery!" 77. Moses said, "Do you speak of the truth when it comes to you? Is this sorcery? The sorcerers will not prosper." 78. They said, "Have you come to us to turn us away from what we found our fathers following, so that you may both possess the grandeur of the land? We will not believe in the two of you!" 79. Pharoah said, "Bring me every known sorcerer." 80. When the sorcerers came, Moses said to them, "Cast what you would cast." 81. When they cast, Moses said, "What you produced is sorcery. God will soon make it futile. Surely, God does not allow the work of those who do mischief to be useful. 82. Through His Words, God verifies truth, though the sinners hate it." 83. But none except for some from his progeny believed in Moses, out of fear that Pharoah and his notables would oppress them. Truly Pharoah was exalted in the land and was indeed, among the transgressors. 84. Moses said, "O my people! If

you believe in God, then trust in Him if you are Muslims." **85.** They said, "In God we trust, Our Lord! Do not make us victims of wrongdoing people. **86.** Save us through Your Mercy from a disbelieving people." **87.** We revealed unto Moses and his brother, "Assign for your people houses in Egypt. Make your houses places of worship and perform prayer and give good news to the believers." **88.** Moses said, "Our Lord! Truly You have given Pharoah and his notables adornment and wealth in the life of this world. Our Lord! They will mislead men from Your way. Our Lord! Destroy their wealth and harden their hearts — they will not believe until they see painful punishment." **89.** He said, "Your supplication has been answered. Stand firm and do not follow the way of those who do not know." **90.** We transported the Children of Israel across the sea and Pharoah and his forces pursued them out of envy and enmity until drowning overtook them. Then he said, "I believe there is no god, but the One the Children of Israel believe in. I am among those who submit." **91.** Now? After you disobeyed, and you were among the unscrupulous! **92.** Today, We will save you in your body so you might become a sign for those who come after you. Yet many among people are unmindful of Our signs. **93.** We certainly settled The Children of Israel in a genuine establishment, and We provided them with good things. They did not dispute with one another until after knowledge came to them. Truly your Lord will judge between them regarding their differences on the Day of Resurrection. **94.** So if you are in doubt of what We have sent down to you, ask those who recited the Book before you. The truth has indeed come to you from your Lord. So do not be among the doubters. **95.** Do not be among those who deny the signs of God, to avoid being among the losers. **96.** Indeed, those for whom the Word of your Lord has been verified will not believe **97.** even if every sign should come to them, until they observe the painful punishment. **98.** Why has not a single town believed and benefited from its belief, other than the people of Jonah? When they believed, We removed them from the punishment of shame in the life of this world, and We granted them amusement for a while. **99.** Had your Lord willed, everyone on earth would have believed, all in all. Would you coerce people until they become believers? **100.** It is not for a soul to believe except through the will of God. He places doubt upon those who do not understand. **101.** Say, "Observe what is in the heavens and on the earth." But neither signs nor warnings will benefit a people who do not believe. **102.** Are they waiting for anything except what is similar to the days of those who passed away before them? Say, "Then wait! Indeed, I am waiting along with you." **103.** Then We save Our messengers and those who believe. As such, it is incumbent on Us to save the believers. **104.** Say, "O people! If you are in doubt of my religion, I do not worship what you worship instead of God. Rather, I worship God Who will retrieve you and I am commanded to be among the believers. **105.** Truly set your face toward the religion as a *hanīf*, and do not be among the idolators. **106.** Do not call on other than God for what neither benefits nor harms you. For if you do, you will certainly be among the wrongdoers." **107.** If God touches you with affliction, no one can remove it except Him. If he wishes you well, no one can hold back His Bounty. He delivers it to whomever He desires among His servants. He is the Forgiving and the Merciful. **108.** Say, "O people! The Truth has come to you from your Lord. Whoever is rightly guided, is rightly guided for his own soul and whoever is misguided, is solely misguided to its detriment. I am not a guardian over you." **109.** Follow what has been revealed to you and be patient until God yields judgment. He is the best of judges.

Surah 11

HŬD

Hŭd

In the Name of God, the Compassionate, the Merciful

1. *Alif. Lãm. Rã.* A Book whose signs have been adjudicated, then clarified by One who is Wise and Aware. **2.** "Worship none but God. Truly I am a warner from Him and a bearer of good news. **3.** Seek forgiveness from your Lord, then turn to Him in repentance. He will satisfy you with ample pleasure for an appointed term and give His Bounty unto all possessors of grace. But if you turn away, then I fear for you the punishment of a great day. **4.** To God is your return. He is powerful over all things." **5.** Observe! They fold up their breasts to hide from Him. But when they cover themselves with their garments, He knows what they conceal and what they reveal. Truly He knows what lies within breasts. **6.** There is no creature that crawls upon the earth but that its sustenance lies with God. He knows of where it lives and where it rests. All is in a clear Book. **7.** It is He Who created the heavens and the earth in six days while His Throne was on the waters, so He may test which of you performs the most virtuous deeds. Yet if you say, "You will indeed be resurrected after death," the disbelievers will certainly say, "This is nothing but obvious sorcery!" **8.** If We delay their punishment for a limited time, they will surely say, "What holds it back?" But then, on the day it comes upon them, nothing will turn it away from them, and what they used to mock will close in on them. **9.** If We allow man to taste Mercy from Us and then withdraw it from him, he will sink into hopelessness and ingratitude. **10.** But if We allow him to taste something favorable after adversity has touched him, he will surely say, "All evils have left me." He becomes elated with pride, **11.** except for those who are patient and perform righteous deeds. For them there is forgiveness and a great reward. **12.** Perhaps you might dismiss some of what was revealed to you and your breast might feel constrained because they say, "Why has a treasure not been sent down to him or an angel not come down to him?" But you are only a warner, and God is Guardian over all matters. **13.** Or do they say, "He invented it?" Say "Then, bring ten sūrahs like it that are forged and call upon whomever you can instead of God, if you are truthful." **14.** But if they do not answer you, know that it has been sent down with God's Knowledge and that there is no god but He. So are you Muslims? **15.** Whoever desires the life of this world and its adornment, We will pay them in full for their practices in it, and they will not be denied. **16.** They are those who will have nothing in the Hereafter save the Fire. Whatever they achieved there will plummet, and what they had accomplished will become useless. **17.** So what of the one who rests on clear signs from His Lord, and for whom it is recited by a witness from Him? Before it was the Book of Moses, a guide, and a mercy. It is they who believe in it. Whoever disbelieves in it from among the parties, Fire will be their encounter. From this time forward, do not be in doubt of it. Indeed, it is the truth from your Lord, but most people do not believe. **18.** Who does greater wrong than those who make up lies against God? They will be brought before their Lord and witnesses will say, "These are the ones who lied against their Lord." Observe! The curse of God is on those who do wrong, **19.** those who turn from the way of God, seeking to make it crooked, and those who disbelieve in the Hereafter. **20.** Those are the ones who cannot escape on earth, and they will have no protector besides God. Their punishment will be doubled. They were not able to hear, nor were they able to see. **21.** They are those who have lost their souls, and what they invented had deserted them. **22.** There is no doubt that in the Hereafter, they will be the utmost losers. **23.** Those who believe and perform righteous deeds and are humble before their Lord, will certainly be the inhabitants of the Garden where they will abide forever. **24.** The similarity of these two groups is like the blind and the deaf and the hearing and the seeing. Are they equal when compared? Will you not remember? **25.** Indeed, We sent Noah to his people. "Truly I am a clear warner unto you, **26.** that you might worship none but God. Truly I fear for you the punishment of a painful day." **27.** But the notables among his people who disbelieved said, "We see you as no more than a human being like us, and we see no one following you except for obviously, the downcast among us. Nor do we see that you have merit over us. Rather, we think you are liars." **28.** He said, "O my people! Do you think if I stand upon a clear sign from my Lord and that He has granted me Mercy from Himself, that you are blind to it? Should we impose it on you though you hate it? **29.** O my people! I am not asking you for any wealth in return for it. My reward lies only with God. I will not drive away those who believe. Truly they will meet their Lord, but I see that you are an ignorant people! **30.** O my people! If I were to drive them away, then who would help me against God?? Will you not be mindful? **31.** I am not telling you that the treasures of God are with me, nor that I know of the Unseen. I am not saying I am an angel, nor am I saying that those who are despicable in your eyes, will not receive any good from God. God knows best what is in their souls — otherwise, I would indeed be among the wrongdoers." **32.** They said, "O Noah! You have argued with us and have prolonged the arguments, so bring on us that which you have threatened us with if you are among the truthful." **33.** He said, "God alone will bring it to you if He so desires, and you cannot prevent it. **34.** As much as I want to offer my advice, it will not benefit you if God desires to lead you astray. He is your Lord and to Him you will be returned." **35.** Or do they say, "He has invented it?" Say, "If I invented it, then my guilt is on me, but I am clear of what you slander." **36.** It was revealed unto Noah, "None of your people will believe except for those who have already believed. So do not be distressed by what they do. **37.** Build the Ark before Our eyes and by Our Revelation. Do not address Me about those who did wrong; surely, they will be drowned." **38.** He was building the Ark and whenever notables among his people passed by him, they ridiculed him. He said, "If you mock us, we will surely mock you in the same way you do. **39.** Soon, you will know upon whom will come a punishment that will disgrace him and upon whom will be an enduring punishment." **40.** Until the time Our Command arrived, and the reservoir gushed forth, We said, "Carry on board two pairs of every kind, and your family, except the one upon whom the Word has preceded and those who believe." No one believed along with him, except a few. **41.** He said, "Embark on it. In the name of God be its course plotting and arrival. Truly my Lord is Forgiving and Merciful." **42.** It carried them through their course over mountainous waves. Noah called out to his son, who remained aloof, "O my son! Embark with us and do not be among the disbelievers." **43.** The son replied, "I will take refuge on a mountain. It will protect me from the water." He replied, "There is no protector on this day from the Command of God, except for those upon whom He has Mercy." The waves came between them, and he was among the drowned. **44.** It was said, "O earth! Swallow your water! O sky! Hold back." The water receded and the command was carried out. It settled on Jūdī. It was said, "Let the wrongdoing people be faraway!" **45.** Noah called out to his Lord and said, "O my Lord! Truly my son is from my family. Indeed, Your promise is true! You are the most just of judges." **46.** He said, "O Noah! Truly he is not from your family, and he is certainly not a work of righteousness. Do not question me about what you have no knowledge of. Truly I caution you not to be among the ignorant." **47.** He said, "My Lord! Truly I seek refuge in You and from questioning You about that in which I have no knowledge. If You do not forgive me and have Mercy upon me, I will be among the losers." **48.** It was said, "O Noah! Disembark in peace from Us with blessings upon you, the populations among you, and their progeny. There are also populations upon whom

We will grant pleasures, but then, a painful punishment from Us will befall them." **49.** These are among the parables of the Unseen that We reveal to you. Neither you nor your people knew of them beforehand. So be patient. Truly the end belongs to the reverent. **50.** Unto the Ãd, their brother Hŭd said, "O my people! Worship God! You have no other than Him. You are nothing but liars. **51.** O my people! I do not ask you of any reward for it. Indeed, my reward lies only with the One Who created me. Do you not understand? **52.** O my people! Seek forgiveness from your Lord, then turn to Him for repentance. He will send the skies to pour abundant rain upon you and add strength to your strength. Do not turn away as villains." **53.** They said, "O Hŭd! We are not believers in you. You have not brought us clear signs and we will not forsake our gods based on your word. **54.** Verily, we are only saying that one of our gods has afflicted you with evil." He said, "I call God as witness, and I testify that I am clear of what you attribute as partners **55.** instead of Him. So then, plot against me all together and do not grant me respite. **56.** Truly I trust in God, my Lord, and your Lord. There is not a creature that crawls, but that He holds it by its forelock. Truly my Lord is on a straight path. **57.** I have delivered the message to you that was sent to me by Him, but if you turn away, my Lord will exchange you with a nation other than yourselves and you will not harm Him in the least. Truly my Lord is Guardian over all things." **58.** When Our Command came, We saved Hŭd and those who believed with him through Our Mercy. We saved them from a severe punishment. **59.** That was the Ãd. They rejected the signs of their Lord, disobeyed the messengers, and followed the Command of every stubborn oppressor. **60.** They were pursued by a curse in this world, and on the Day of Resurrection. Observe! Truly the Ãd disbelieved in their Lord. Observe! Away with the Ãd, the people of Hŭd! **61.** To the Thamŭd, was their brother Sãlih who said, "O my people! Worship God! You have no god other than Him. He brought you forth from the earth and settled you there. So seek forgiveness from Him, then turn to Him in repentance. Truly my Lord is Near and Responsive." **62.** They said, "O Sãlih! You were a source of hope among us before this. Are you forbidding us from worshipping what our fathers worshipped while we remain in doubt and suspicion of your call to us?" **63.** He said, "O my people! Do you think that if I stand on clear proof from my Lord, and that He has granted me Mercy from Himself that I would disobey Him? Then who would help me against God were I to disobey Him? For you would be doing nothing more than increasing my loss. **64.** O my people! This she-camel of God is a sign to you. Leave her to feed freely from God's earth and do not inflict her with harm or you will be seized by a punishment close by." **65.** But they hamstrung her. Therefore, he said, "Enjoy yourselves in your homes for three days. That is a promise that will not be disproven." **66.** Thereafter, Our

Command came. Through a Mercy from Us. We saved Sālih and those who believed with him from the disgrace of that day. Truly your Lord, He is the Strong and the Mighty. **67.** The Cry seized those who did wrong. By morning, they were found lifeless in their homes **68.** as though they had never lived there. Observe! Truly the Thamūd disbelieved in their Lord. Observe! Away with the Thamūd. **69.** Indeed, Our messengers came to Abraham with good news. They said, "Peace." "Peace," he replied, and without hesitation, he brought them a roasted calf. **70.** Then, he was apprehensive when he noticed their hands did not reach out toward it. They said, "Do not fear. Truly we have been sent to the people of Lot." **71.** His wife was standing there, and she laughed. Then, We gave her good news of Isaac, and after Isaac, of Jacob. **72.** She said, "O woe unto me! Will I bear a child when I am old woman, and my husband here is an old man? This is certainly a shocking thing." **73.** They said, "Are you shocked by the Command of God? The Mercy of God and His Blessings be upon you O People of the House. Truly He is Praised and Glorious!" **74.** So when fear had left Abraham and good news had come to him, he pleaded with Us regarding the people of Lot. **75.** Truly Abraham was forbearing, soft-hearted, and penitent. **76.** "O Abraham! Turn away from this! Indeed, the Command of your Lord has come for they will receive a punishment that cannot be recalled." **77.** When Our messengers came to Lot, he was feeling distraught on their account, helpless and powerless regarding them. He said, "This is a distressful day." **78.** His people came rushing toward him, while they had been practicing evil deeds previously. He said, "O my people! These are my daughters. They are purer for you. So revere God and do not disgrace me in front of my guests. Is there not a right-minded man among you?" **79.** They said, "You certainly know that we have no right to your daughters, and you certainly know what we want." **80.** He said, "If only I had power over you or the ability to take refuge in some mighty support!" **81.** They said, "O Lot! We are the messengers of your Lord. They will not reach you. So set out with your family during the night and no one is to look back except for your wife. Truly what happens to them will occur to her. Indeed, the morning will be their encounter. Is not the morning close?" **82.** Hence when Our Command arrived, We made its topmost to be its bottommost, and We rained down upon them stones of dried clay one upon another, **83.** marked by your Lord. They are never far from the wrongdoers. **84.** Unto the Midian, their brother Shu'ayb said, "O my people! Worship God! You have no god other than Him. Do not short-weight the scale. Truly I see you making headway, but I fear for you the punishment of an all-encompassing Day. **85.** O my people! Fully observe the scale and the weighing pan, be just, and do not deprive people of their goods. Do not work corruption by behaving wickedly upon the earth. **86.** If you are believers, what is left for you by God is better for you, and I am not an attendant over you." 87. They said, "O Shu'ayb! Do your prayers require that we leave what our fathers worshipped or that we should not do as we wish with our wealth? You are surely, a man of tolerance and sound judgment." 88. He said, "O my people! Do you not see that I hold a clear sign from my Lord, and that He has provided me with goodly provision from Himself? I do not wish to oppose you and act on what He has forbidden you to do. For as long as I can, I only want what is best for you, but my success lies with God alone. In Him I trust and unto Him I turn. 89. O my people! Do not let your conflict with me cause you to sin, such as what happened to the people of Noah, or the people of Hŭd, or the people of Sālih. The people of Lot are not far from you! 90. Seek forgiveness from your Lord, then turn unto Him in repentance. Truly my Lord is Merciful and Loving." 91. They said, "Shu'ayb! We do not understand much of what you say and truly, we perceive you to be weak among us. If it were not for your family, we would have certainly stoned you, for you have no greatness over us." 92. He said, "O my people! Does my family have more power over you than God for you to place Him behind your backs? Truly my Lord encompasses all that you do. 93. O my people! Practice whatever you can for I am practicing too. You will soon know who will receive punishment that will shame him and who is a liar. So keep watching, for I am watching with you." 94. When Our Command arrived, through a Mercy from Us, We saved Shu'ayb and those who believed with him. The Cry seized those who did wrong. By morning, they were found lying lifeless in their homes 95. as though they had never lived there. Observe! Away with the Midian, just as the Thamŭd were done away with. 96. Indeed, We sent Moses with Our signs and a clear authority 97. to Pharoah and his notables. But they followed the command of Pharoah, and the command of Pharoah was not rational. 98. He will go before his people on the Day of Resurrection and lead them to the Fire. Evil is indeed the watering place to which they are led! 99. From this, they will be pursued by a curse as well as on the Day of Resurrection. Woeful is the gift they will be given. 100. These are some of the stories We have recounted to you of the towns. Among the towns are some that are still standing and some that have been mown down. 101. We did not wrong them, but they wronged themselves. When the Command of your Lord had arrived, their gods — or whatever they called on instead of God — did not benefit them in the least. They did not increase them in anything but their ruin. 102. That is the grip of your Lord when He seizes the wrongdoing townspeople. Indeed, His undertaking is painful and severe. 103. Truly that is a sign for those who fear the punishment of the Hereafter. That is the Day when people will be gathered together and that is a Day that will be witnessed. 104. We will not delay it, save for a limited term. 105. On the day it comes, no soul will speak, save by His Leave. Among them will be the wretched and the joyous.

106. As for those who are wretched, they will be in the Fire, wherein there will be moaning and wailing for them **107.** while abiding there for so long as the heavens and the earth endure, save as your Lord wills. Surely, your Lord does whatever He wills. **108.** As for those who are joyous, they will be in the Garden, living there for so long as the heavens and the earth endure — save as your Lord wills — a gift without end. **109.** So do not be in doubt concerning what these people worship. They only worship what their fathers had worshipped, but We will surely give them their undiminished share. **110.** Indeed, We gave Moses the Book, then differences arose about it. Were it not for a Word that had preceded from your Lord, the matter would have been settled between them. Yet, they certainly remained in confounding doubt of it. **111.** Surely your Lord will pay each of them in full for their actions. He is truly Aware of what they do. **112.** So stand firm as you have been commanded as well as those who turn in repentance with you. Do not be rebellious. Truly He sees whatever you do. **113.** Do not lean toward the wrongdoers in case the Fire should touch you and you will have no protector besides God. Thereafter, you will not be helped. **114.** Perform prayer at the two ends of the day and in the early hours of the night. Truly good deeds remove those who are evil. This is a reminder for those who remember. **115.** Be patient. Truly God does not neglect the reward of the virtuous. **116.** So why were there not among the generations before you those who possessed merit and who would forbid corruption upon the earth other than a few among them whom We saved? Those who did wrong pursued the luxuries they had been given, and they were guilty. **117.** Your Lord would never destroy towns unjustifiably while its people were amending. **118.** Had your Lord willed, He would have turned people into one nation; however, they would have remained in disagreement **119.** except for those for whom your Lord has Mercy — for this He created them. The Word of your Lord is fulfilled: "I will surely fill Hell with jinn and people all together!" **120.** Everything We have recounted to you about the stories of the messengers is to solidify your heart. Here, the Truth has come to you as an appeal and a reminder for believers. **121.** Say unto those who do not believe, "Practice as much as you can. We, too, are practicing. **122.** Wait! We too, are waiting." **123.** To God belongs the Unseen in the heavens and on the earth. To Him all matters are returned. So worship Him and trust in Him. Your Lord is not Unmindful of what you do.

Surah 12

Joseph

Yŭsuf

In the Name of God, the Compassionate, the Merciful

1. *Alif. Lām. Rā.* These are the signs of the clear Book. 2. Truly We sent it down as an Arabic Quran that perhaps you may understand. 3. We recount to you the best of parables by Our having revealed unto you this Quran, though prior to this, you were among the unaware. 4. When Joseph said to his father, "O my father, truly I have seen eleven stars, and the sun, and the moon. I saw them prostrating before me." 5. He said, "O my son! Do not tell your brothers of your vision in case they devise some scheme against you. Indeed, Satan is a clear enemy unto people. 6. As such, your Lord will choose you, teach you the interpretation of events, and complete His Blessing upon you, and upon the House of Jacob, just as He completed it upon your forefathers, Abraham, and Isaac. Indeed, your Lord is Knowing and Wise." 7. Surely, there are signs in Joseph and his brothers for those who inquire. 8. Remember when they said, "Truly Joseph and his brother are more loved by our father than we are though we are more of a team. Indeed, our father is clearly at fault. 9. Slay Joseph or cast him out to some land to free up your father's mind. By such, you will become righteous people thereafter." 10. One among them said, "Do not slay Joseph, but if you wish to take action, cast him into the depths of a well where some caravan might pick him up." 11. They said, "O father! What is it with you that you do not trust us with Joseph? Truly we wish him well. 12. Send him with us tomorrow to play and enjoy himself. We will certainly take care of him." 13. He said, "Truly it grieves me for you to take him. I fear the wolf might eat him while you are not paying attention to him." 14. They said, "If the wolf should eat him while we are a team, then, we are losers!" 15. Subsequently, when they went with him and agreed to throw him into the depths of the well, We revealed to

him, "You will eventually inform them of this affair of theirs and they will not even be aware." 16. They returned to their father in the evening, weeping. 17. They said, "O father! We went racing with one another and left Joseph to tend to our things and the wolf ate him. But you will not believe us even though we are truthful." 18. They brought his shirt with fake blood. He said, "Indeed your souls have seduced you in this matter. Comely patience! It is God Whose help I seek after what you have described." 19. Then a caravan came along, and they sent their water carrier. He lowered his pail, and he said, "Good news! Here is a boy!" Subsequently, they hid him as merchandise. God knew well what they were doing. 20. They sold him for a trivial price, a few dirhams, since they did not consider him valuable. 21. The man from Egypt who bought him said to his wife, "Give him decent accommodation. It is possible that he may benefit us or that we may take him as a son." So did We establish Joseph in the land that we may teach him the interpretation of events. God has full control over His affairs, but most people do not know. 22. When he reached his utmost maturity, We gave him wisdom and knowledge. So do We reward those who are righteous. 23. But she in whose home he was staying, sought to seduce him from himself. She locked the doors and said, "You, come here!" He said, "I seek refuge in God! Truly my Lord has made my sojourn agreeable. Indeed, wrongdoers will not prosper." 24. She emphatically leaned toward him, and he would have leaned toward her had he not seen the evidence of his Lord. As such, We turned evil and indecency away from him. He was indeed among Our sincere servants. 25. As they raced to the door, she ripped his shirt from behind. They encountered her master at the door. She said, "What is the punishment for one who wishes ill toward your wife unless he be imprisoned or painfully chastised?" 26. He said, "She was the one who tried to seduce me." A witness from her own people testified, "If his shirt is ripped from the front, then, she is telling the truth, and he is among the liars. 27. But if his shirt is ripped from the back, then she has lied, and he is among the truthful." 28. Thereafter, when he saw his shirt was ripped from behind, he said, "Truly this is from the scheming of women. Indeed, your scheme is great! 29. Joseph, turn away from this, and you, seek forgiveness for your sin! Truly you were among the faulty." 30. Some of the townswomen said, "The viceroy's wife sought to seduce her slave-boy from himself! He has enamored her with love. We perceive her to be in obvious error." 31. So when she heard of their cunning, she sent for them, prepared a banquet for them, and gave each of them a knife. She said to Joseph, "Come out before them!" Then, when they saw him, they cut their hands out of admiration and said, "Praise be to God! This is no human being. This is nothing but an honorable angel!" 32. "This is the one upon whom you blamed me for. I truly sought to seduce him from himself, but he remained chaste. If he does not do as I command, he will be imprisoned and become among the bottommost." **33.** He said, "My Lord! I would love to be in prison than to comply with what they are asking me to do. If you do not deter their scheming from me, I will become among the ignorant." **34.** Therefore, his Lord answered him and deterred their scheming away from him. Truly He is the Hearing and the Knowing. **35.** Then, it appeared to them after having seen the signs that they should imprison him for a limited time. **36.** Two young men entered prison with him. One of them said, "Truly, I envisioned myself pressing wine." The other said, "I envisioned myself carrying bread on top of my head and the birds were eating from it." "Inform us of its interpretation. Truly we perceive you to be among the righteous." **37.** He said, "No food with which you are provided will come to you except that I will inform you of its interpretation before it comes. This is among the things that my Lord has taught me. I abandoned the ways of a people who do not believe in God. They will be among the disbelievers in the Hereafter. **38.** I follow the creed of my forefathers Abraham, Isaac, and Jacob. It is not for us to attribute any partners to God. That is from the Bounty God has bestowed upon us and upon people, but most people do not show gratitude. **39.** O my prison companions! Is a variety of lords better, or God, the One, the Supreme? **40.** You worship nothing besides Him aside from the names you and your fathers have named. God did not send down authority by any means. Judgment belongs to God alone. He commands that you worship none but Him. That is the *upright* religion, but most people do not know. **41.** O my prison companions! As for one of you, he will serve wine to his lord, but as for the other, he will be crucified, and the birds will eat from his head. The matter about which you inquired has been decreed." **42.** He said to one of them whom he knew would be saved, "Mention me to your lord." But Satan caused him to forget to make mention of him and Joseph lingered in prison for a few more years. **43.** The king said, "Truly I envision seven fat cows being eaten by seven lean ones, and seven green heads of grain, and others dry. O notables! Give me your opinion on my dream if you can interpret visions." **44.** They said, "Confusing dreams! We are not experts in the interpretation of dreams!" **45.** A short while later, the one among the two who had been saved remembered and said, "I will inform you of its interpretation, just send me out." **46.** "Joseph, O truthful one! Give us your opinion concerning seven fat cows being eaten by seven lean ones, and seven green heads of grain and others dry, that perhaps I will return to the people to help them understand." **47.** He said, "You will sow diligently for seven years. As usual, whatever you harvest, leave it in its ear, saving a little for consumption. **48.** Then, after this, will come seven that are hard that will devour what you have saved for them except a modest amount from what you have stored.

49. Then afterwards will come a year wherein people will be granted relief, and they will be pressing on." **50.** The king said, "Bring him to me!" Subsequently, when the messenger came to him, he said, "Return to your lord and ask him, 'What of the women who cut their hands? Surely, my Lord knows well of their cunning!'" **51.** He said, "What was your intention in trying to seduce Joseph?" They said, "Praise be to God! We have no knowledge of any evil against him." The king's wife said, "Now that the truth has come to light, I am the one who sought to seduce him and verily, he is among the truthful." **52.** "This is for him to know that I did not betray him during his absence. Truly God does not guide the cunning and the treacherous. **53.** But I do not absolve my own soul. Indeed, the soul commands evil, except for those upon whom my Lord has mercy. Truly my Lord is Forgiving and Merciful." **54.** The king said, "Bring him to me so I may reserve him entirely to myself." Then, when he had spoken with him, he said, "Truly today, you will be safely entrusted in our hands and firmly established." **55.** He said, "Establish me over the storehouses of the land for indeed, I am a competent guardian." **56.** As such, did We establish Joseph in the land to make of it whatever he wills. We bestow Our Mercy upon whomever We will, and We do not neglect the reward of the righteous. **57.** The reward of the Hereafter is better for those who believe and are reverent. **58.** Joseph's brothers came and entered upon him. He recognized them, but they did not recognize him. **59.** When he provided them with their provisions, he said, "Bring me a brother of yours from your father. Do you not see that I give full measure and that I am the best of hosts? **60.** But if you do not bring him to me, you will have no measure from me, nor will you come near me." **61.** They said, "We will seek to draw him from his father. Indeed, we are doers." **62.** He said to his young male servants, "Place their merchandise in their saddlebags. Perhaps they will recognize it when they return to their people — that is, if they return." **63.** Then when they returned to their father they said, "O father! The measure has been withheld from us, so send our brother with us to obtain our measure. We will certainly be his guardians." **64.** He said, "Should I entrust him to you as I had previously entrusted his brother to you? But God is the best of guardians, and He is the most Merciful of the merciful." **65.** When they opened their belongings, they found that their merchandise had been returned to them. They said, "O father! What more do we need? This is our merchandise. It has been returned to us. Now, we can provide for our family and remain guardians over our brother while adding another camel-load. These are meager provisions!" **66.** He said, "I will not send him with you until you give me a solemn pledge before God that you will surely bring him back to me unless you are bounded." Then when they gave their solemn pledge, he said, "God is Guardian over what we say."

67. He said, "O my sons! Do not enter through one gate but enter through separate gates. I cannot prevail you at all against God. Judgment belongs to God alone. I trust in Him and let those who trust, trust in Him." **68.** When they entered from where their father had ordered them, it did not prevail them against God at all, but it was something out of Jacob's soul that he felt he had to do. Truly he was knowledgeable by what We had taught him, but most people do not know. **69.** When they entered upon Joseph, he drew his brother close to himself and said, "Truly I am your brother, so do not be upset over what they had done." **70.** As a result, when he prepared their provisions for them, he placed a drinking cup into his brother's saddlebag. Then, an announcer cried out, "O you in the caravan! Truly, you are thieves!" **71.** Turning toward them, they said, "What are you missing?" **72.** They said, "We are missing the king's goblet." "For whoever brings it forth, there will be a camel-load, and I will be responsible." **73.** They said, "By God, you certainly know that we did not come to create corruption in the land, and we are not thieves." **74.** They said, "What will the compensation be if you are liars?" **75.** They said, "Its compensation will be in whoever's saddlebag it is found, he himself, will be its reward. Thus, do we compensate the wrongdoers." **76.** Then, he began with their baggage before the baggage of his brother. He then removed it from his brother's baggage. Thus, did We devise a plot for Joseph. Under the king's law, he could not have taken his brother unless God had willed. We elevate in rank whomever We will, and above everyone endowed with knowledge, there is One who knows better. **77.** They said, "If he has stolen, one of his brothers had stolen beforehand." But Joseph kept it a secret in his soul and did not disclose it to them. He said, "You are in a worse position! God knows best regarding what you describe." **78.** They said, "O viceroy! He has a father who is venerable in age, so take one of us in his place. Truly we see you to be among the righteous." **79.** He said, "God be my refuge that we should take anyone besides he with whom we found our property! For then, we would certainly be wrongdoers." **80.** Subsequently, when they were disheartened by him, they conferred privately. The eldest of them said, "Do you not know that your father has taken a solemn pledge from you before God, because you had previously neglected Joseph? Thus, I will not depart from this land until my father grants me leave, or God renders judgment upon me. He is the best of judges! **81.** Return to your father and say, 'O father! Verily, your son has committed theft. We bore witness to what we knew, but we are not attendants over the unseen. **82.** So ask the town that we were in and the caravan with which we approached. Surely, we are truthful.'" **83.** He said, "Indeed, your souls have enticed you in this matter. Comely patience! It may be that God will bring them to me all together. Truly He is the Knowing and the Wise."

84. He turned away from them and said, "Oh how great is my grief for Joseph!" His eyes had turned white from grief, and he was agonized and upset. 85. They said, "By God! Will you go on remembering Joseph until you become ill to the point of dying? 86. He said, "I complain of my grief and my sorrow to God alone. I know from God what you do not know. 87. O my sons! Go and inquire about Joseph and his brother and do not despair of God's Comfort. Verily, no one despairs of God's Comfort except for disbelieving people." 88. So when they entered upon him, they said, "O viceroy! Hardship has seized us and our people. We brought but meager merchandise, so pay us full measure and be charitable unto us. Indeed, God will reward the charitable." 89. He said, "Do you know what you have done with Joseph and his brother while you were ignorant?" 90. They said, "Are you truly Joseph?" He said, "I am Joseph, and this is my brother. God has been gracious unto us. Truly, it is for whoever is reverent and patient. Indeed, God does not neglect the reward of the righteous." 91. They said, "By God! God has preferred you over us and we were at fault." 92. He said, "There is no reproach against you this day. God will forgive you. He is the most Merciful of the merciful. 93. Take this shirt of mine and place it over my father's face and he will be able to see. Bring me your entire family." 94. After the caravan left, their father said, "If you do not think me weak-minded, I truly sense the scent of Joseph." 95. They said, "By God! You have been weak-minded for a long time." 96. When the bearer of good news came, he placed it over his face, and his sight returned. He said, "Did I not tell you I know what you do not know?" 97. They said, "O father! Seek forgiveness for us from our sins. Truly we were at fault." 98. He said, "I will indeed seek forgiveness for you from my Lord for truly He is Forgiving and Merciful." 99. Subsequently, when they entered upon Joseph, He drew his parents close to himself and said, "If God wills, you will safely enter Egypt." 100. He raised his parents to the throne, and they fell, prostrating before him. He said, "O my father! This is the fulfillment of my vision. My Lord has made it come true. He was good to me when he took me out of prison and brought you from the desert after Satan had incited evil between my brothers and me. Indeed, my Lord is benevolent toward what He desires. Truly He is the Knower and the Wise. 101. My Lord! You have given me some power and taught me the interpretation of events. Originator of the heavens and the earth! You are my Protector in this world and in the Hereafter! Allow me to die as a submitter unto You and unite me with the righteous." 102. These are among the accounts of the unseen which We reveal unto you. You were not among them when they decided upon their affair and plotted. 103. No matter how much you desire it, most people are not believers. 104. You are not asking of them any reward for it. It is no more than a reminder for the worlds.

105. How many signs from the heavens and the earth do they pass by, yet they turn away from them? **106.** Most of them do not believe in God, but they attribute partners to Him. **107.** Do they feel secure from the overwhelming arrival of God's punishment or from the sudden coming of the Hour while they are unaware? **108.** Say, "This is my way. I call unto God with clear sight, I and those who follow me. Glory be to God! I am not among those who attribute partners unto God." **109.** We did not send anyone before you to receive Our revelations except for men from among the townspeople. Have they not traveled the earth and observed the final repercussions of those before them? The Abode of the Hereafter is better for those who are reverent. Do you not understand? **110.** Until the messengers despaired and thought they were considered liars, Our help came to them, and We saved whoever We desired. Our Might will not be turned back from sinful people. **111.** Indeed, in their stories is a lesson for those endowed with insight. It is not an invented account; it is, rather, a confirmation of what had come before it, an explanation of all things, and guidance and mercy for a people who believe.

Surah 13

THE THUNDER
al-Ra'd

In the Name of God, the Compassionate, the Merciful

1. *Alif. Lām. Mīm. Rā.* These are the signs of the Book. What has been sent down to you from your Lord is the truth, but most people do not believe. **2.** It is God Who raised the heavens that you see without pillars, then then ascended the Throne. He made the sun and the moon subservient each running its course for an appointed term. He regulates the affair by explaining the signs that you may believe with certainty of the meeting with your Lord. **3.** It is He Who spread out the earth and established firm mountains and streams there, and of all its fruits, He placed two pairs. He causes the night to cover the day. Truly, in that are signs for a people who reflect. **4.** Upon the earth are neighboring tracts, vineyards, sown fields, date palms of a shared root and not of a shared root irrigated by a single water. We have made some to be more favorable than others when consumed. Truly in that are signs for a people who understand. **5.** If you are marveled, then marvelous is their saying, "When we are dust, will we really be raised to a new creation?" Those are the ones who disbelieved in their Lord, and those are the ones who will have shackles upon their necks, and those are the ones who will be the inhabitants of the Fire where they will abide forever. **6.** Yet they would want you to rush onto evil before good, though examples have gone by before them. Truly, your Lord is Possessed of Forgiveness for people despite their wrongdoing, and truly your Lord is Severe in Retribution. **7.** Those who disbelieve say, "Why has a sign not been sent down upon him from his Lord?" You are but a warner and for every people there is a guide. **8.** God knows what every female bears, and how some wombs end prematurely and how others reach full term. Everything before Him is balanced— **9.** Knower of the Unseen and the Seen, the Great, and the Exalted. **10.** It is the same for he who speaks secretly, and he who does so openly, he who lies low at night, or he who advances by day. **11.** For him there are attending angels to his front and to his rear, guarding him by God's Command. Truly God does not change what is in people until they change what is in themselves. When God desires evil for people, there is no turning back and they will have no protector except Him. **12.** It is He Who shows you lightning, provoking fear and hope, and Who produces heavy-laden clouds. **13.** The thunder glorifies His praise as do the angels in awe of Him. He hurls the thunderbolts, striking with them whom He wills. Yet they argue about God, but He is severe in wrath. **14.** To Him is the supplication of truth; and those who supplicate apart from Him, do not answer them in the least, save as one who stretches forth his palms toward water that it may reach his mouth, though it does not reach him. The supplication of disbelievers is nothing but delusion. **15.** To God prostrates whoever is in the heavens and on the earth, willingly or unwillingly, as do their shadows in the morning and in the evening. **16.** Say, "Who is the Lord of the heavens and the earth?" Say, "God." Say, "Then have you taken protectors besides Him that do not have power over what may harm or benefit them?" Say, "Are the blind and the seeing equal, or are darkness and light equal?" Or have they attributed to God partners who have created the like of His creation, such that what was created appeared comparable to them? Say, "God is the Creator of all things, and He is the One, the Dominant." **17.** He sends water down from the sky for riverbeds to flow according to their allotment, and the torrent carries a rising foam like the foam that rises from fire while making ornaments for mere pleasure. Thus does God set forth truth from falsehood. As for the foam, it moves along as waste, but what benefits people remains on the earth. Thus does God relate the parables. **18.** Those who respond to their Lord will have what is virtuous and those who do not respond to Him, even if they had all that is in the heavens and on the earth or more, they would seek to offer it for ransom. For them will be a horrible reckoning. Their refuge is Hell. What an evil resting place! **19.** Is one who knows what has been sent down to you from your Lord is the truth like one who is blind? Only those endowed with insight reflect, **20.** who fulfill the pact with God, and do not break the covenant; **21.** who join what God has Commanded be joined, fear their Lord, and dread an evil reckoning; **22.** who are patient, seeking the Countenance of their Lord, perform prayer, spend from what We provided them discreetly and openly, and repel evil with good. They are the ones who will receive the reward of the Abode. **23.** They will enter Gardens of Eden along with those who were righteous among their fathers, their spouses, and their progeny. Angels will enter upon them from every gate. **24.** "Peace be upon you because you were patient." How excellent is the Final Abode! **25.** As for those who break God's pact after accepting His covenant, sever what God has Commanded be joined, and work corruption upon the earth, it is they who will receive the curse. The evil abode will be theirs. **26.** God spreads out sustenance for whomever He wills. They enjoy the life of the world, but the life of this world is no more than entertainment compared to the Hereafter. **27.** Those who disbelieve say, "Why has some sign not been sent down to him from his Lord?" Say, "Truly God leads astray whomever He wills and guides to Himself whomever turns to Him in repentance, **28.** such as those who believe and whose hearts are at peace in the remembrance of God. Are hearts not at peace through the remembrance of God? **29.** For those who believe and perform righteous deeds, theirs is blessedness and a beautiful return." **30.** Thus, We have sent you to a nation before which other nations had passed away that you may recite to them that which We have revealed to you; yet they still disbelieve in the Compassionate. Say, "He is my Lord. There is no God but He. I trust in Him, and I turn to Him. **31.** Were there a Quran that would set mountains in motion, or split the earth, or the dead were made to speak, but no, unto God belongs the entire affair. Do the believers not understand that had God willed, He would have guided people all together? Misfortune will never cease to follow those who disbelieve for what they practiced or settle closely to their homes until God's Promise arrives. Truly God will not forsake the appointed term. **32.** Indeed, messengers before you were mocked, and I granted respite to those who disbelieved, but then I seized them. How then was My Reprisal? **33.** Then what of He Who attends to every soul for what it has earned, yet they attribute partners unto God? Say, "Name them! Or will you inform Him of something about the earth that He does not know about, or is this a show of words?" Their scheming has certainly made them seem reasonable to those who disbelieve. They have turned from the path! Whoever God leads astray will have no guide. **34.** They will be punished in the life of this world and their punishment in the Hereafter will be even more severe. They will have no one to protect them from God. **35.** The parable of the Garden that has been promised to the reverent with rivers running beneath, its food and shade everlasting. That is the ultimate end for those who were reverent; the ultimate end for the disbelievers will be Fire! **36.** Those to whom We have given the Book are happy about what has been sent down unto you. Among the clans are those who reject some of it. Say, "I have only been Commanded to worship God, and not to attribute partners unto Him. To Him I call and to Him is my return." **37.** Thus, We have sent it down as a Judgment in Arabic. Yet if you follow their desires after the knowledge that has come to you, you will not have a protector nor a defender against God. **38.** Indeed, We sent messengers before you and provided them with wives and progeny. It is not for a messenger to bring a sign except if God permits. For each period, there is a Book. **39.** God eradicates and secures what He wills. With Him is the Mother of the Book.

40. Whether We show you a part of what We promise them, or We take your soul, your duty is to proclaim and Our duty is to call them to account. **41.** Do they not perceive how We come upon the land and reduce its outlying borders? God judges. No one repeals His Judgment, and He is swift in calling to account. **42.** Indeed, those who were before them schemed, but unto God belongs all scheming. He knows what every soul earns, and the disbelievers will know to whom belongs the Ultimate Abode. **43.** Those who disbelieve say, "You are not a messenger." Say, "God is enough of a witness between you and me along with those who have knowledge of the Book."

Surah 14

Abraham

Ibrāhīm

In the Name of God, the Compassionate, the Merciful

1. *Alif. Lām. Rā.* A Book We have sent down to you to bring people out of darkness and draw them into light—by the leave of their Lord, to the path of the Mighty and the Praised. **2.** It is God to Whom belongs whatever is in the heavens and whatever is on the earth. Woe unto the disbelievers for a severe punishment. **3.** Those who prefer the life of this world over the Hereafter and who deter men from the way of God and seek to make it crooked, it is they who are far astray. **4.** We have not sent a messenger who does not speak the tongue of his people, so that he may make matters clear unto them. Then God leads astray whomever He wills and guides whomever He wills. He is the Mighty and the Wise. **5.** Indeed, We sent Moses with Our signs, "Take your people from darkness into light, and remind them of the Days of God. Truly in that are signs for every patient and grateful person." **6.** Remember when Moses said to his people, "Remember God's Blessing upon you when He saved you from the House of Pharoah, who inflicted terrible punishment upon you, slaying your sons and sparing your women. In that was a great trial from your Lord. **7.** Remember your Lord proclaimed, 'If you show gratitude, I will surely grant you increase, but if you are ungrateful, truly, My punishment is severe.'" **8.** Moses said, "If you disbelieve, you and whoever is on the earth all together, God is definitely Self-Sufficient and Praiseworthy." **9.** Have you not received the story of those before you—the people of Noah, the Ād, the Thamŭd, and those who came after them? No one knows them but God. Their messengers brought them clear signs, but they turned their hands into their mouths and said, "Truly we disbelieve in what you have been sent, and we are in serious doubt about what you call us to." **10.** Their messengers said, "Is there any doubt concerning God, the Originator of the heavens and the earth? He invites you that He may forgive some of your sins and grant you reprieve until an appointed term?" They said, "You are but human beings like us. You wish to turn us away from what our forefathers worshipped. So bring us a clear authority." **11.** Their messengers said to them, "We are but human beings like yourselves, but God is gracious to whomever He wills among His servants. It is not for us to bring you an authority, except by God's Leave. Therefore, in God, let the believers trust. **12.** Why should we not trust in God when He has guided us in our ways? We will surely endure patiently despite the infliction you have caused us. Let those who trust, trust in God." **13.** Those who disbelieved said to their messengers, "We will definitely expel you from our land, or you should revert to our creed." So their Lord revealed to them, "We will abolish the wrongdoers. **14.** We will indeed allow you to reside in the land after them. This is for those who fear My Position and fear My Warning." **15.** They sought victory, but every obstinate tyrant fails. **16.** Before him lies Hell and he will be given oozing purulence to drink **17.** which he will sip but can barely swallow. Death will come upon him from every direction, yet he will not die. Before him lies severe punishment. **18.** The simile of those who disbelieve in their Lord is that their deeds are like ashes in which the winds blow furiously on a stormy day. They have no power over anything they have earned. That is utmost error. **19.** Have you not observed that God created the heavens and the earth in truth? If He wills, He can remove you and deliver a different creation. **20.** That is no great matter for God. **21.** They will appear before God all together, and the weak will say to those who displayed arrogance, "Truly we were your followers, so can you benefit us in any way against the Punishment of God?" They will say, "Had God guided us, we would have guided you. It is the same for us whether we are anxious or patient. There is no way out for us." **22.** Satan will say when the matter has been decreed, "God has indeed promised you the Promise of truth. I promised you, but I failed you. I had no authority over you, except that I called upon you and you responded to me. So do not blame me but blame yourselves. I cannot respond to your cries for help, nor can you respond to my cries for help. I surely disbelieved in your past claim of associating me as a partner. Truly the wrongdoers will be subjected to a painful punishment." **23.** By the leave of their Lord, those who believe and perform righteous deeds will be admitted to Gardens with rivers running beneath to abide there forever. Their greeting within will be "Peace!" **24.** Have you not observed how God sets forth an equivalence? A good word is like a good tree. Its roots firm, and its branches in the sky. **25.** By the leave of its Lord, it produces fruit in every season. God sets forth parables for people that perhaps they may remember. **26.** The simile of a bad word is like a bad tree — uprooted from the face of the earth, it has no solidity. **27.** God holds firm those who believe in well-founded speech in the life of this world and in the Hereafter. God leads the wrongdoers astray and God does whatever He wills. **28.** Have you not observed those who exchanged the Blessing of God for ingratitude and caused their people to occupy the House of Perdition? **29.** They will reach Hell, an evil abode! **30.** They set up equals unto God, in order to lead others astray. Say, "Enjoy yourselves! Truly your destination is unto the Fire!" **31.** Tell My servants who believe to perform prayer and to give of what We have provided them, secretly and openly, before the day comes where there will be neither bargaining, nor befriending. **32.** It is God Who created the heavens and the earth and sent water down from the sky, then with it produced fruits for your sustenance. He has made the ships subservient to you that they may sail upon the sea by His Command. He has made rivers subservient to you, **33.** and made the sun and the moon constant and subservient to you. He made night and day subservient to you. **34.** He gives you something of everything you ask for and were you to number the Blessings of God, you would not be able to count them. Mankind is, indeed, wrongdoing and ungrateful. **35.** Remember when Abraham said, "My Lord! Make this land safe and spare me and my children from worshipping idols? **36.** My Lord! They have indeed led astray many among people, so whoever follows me, he is of me; whoever disobeys me, You are certainly Forgiving and Merciful. **37.** Our Lord! Truly, I have settled some of my progeny in an uncultivated valley near Your Sacred House, our Lord, that they might perform prayer. So motivate the hearts of some people to lean toward them and provide them with fruits that perhaps they may show gratitude. **38.** Our Lord! Truly You know what we conceal and what we disclose. Nothing is hidden from God on earth or in Heaven. **39.** Praise be to God Who granted me Ishmael and Isaac in my old age. Truly my Lord is the Hearer of supplications. **40.** My Lord! Make me one who performs prayer along with my progeny. Our Lord! Accept my supplication. **41.** Our Lord! Forgive me and my parents and the believers on the Day the Reckoning arrives." **42.** Do not assume that God is oblivious to the deeds of the wrongdoers. He only grants them respite until the Day when their eyes stare, transfixed. **43.** Running with necks outstretched and heads uplifted, their gaze unblinking and hearts empty. **44.** Warn people of the Day when the punishment will come upon them. For those who did wrong will say, "Our Lord! Grant us respite for a short while so we may respond to Your Call and follow the messengers." "Did you not swear earlier that there will be no end for you? **45.** You settled in the homes of those who had wronged themselves though it was made clear to you how We dealt with them, and we outlined parables for you." **46.** They devised their scheme, but their scheme lies with God, though their scheming could move mountains. **47.** So do not assume that He would fail to keep His Promise to His messengers. God is indeed

Mighty and the Possessor of Retribution. **48.** On that Day, the earth will be changed into other than earth as will the heavens. They will appear before God, the One, the Dominant. **49.** On that Day you will see the guilty bound together in fetters, **50.** their garments made of tar and their faces covered with Fire, **51.** that God may compensate each soul for what it had earned. Truly God is swift in reckoning. **52.** This is a proclamation unto people that they may be warned and that they may know that He is the One God. Let those endowed with insight take heed.

Surah 15

Hijr

al-Hijr

In the Name of God, the Compassionate, the Merciful

1. *Alif. Lām. Rā.* These are the signs of the Book and Quran that makes things clear. **2.** It may be that those who disbelieved wish they had been Muslims. **3.** Leave them to eat and enjoy themselves and to be distracted by hope, but they will soon know. **4.** Never did We destroy a town but that it had a decree that was known. **5.** No nation can advance its term, nor delay it. **6.** They say, "O you unto whom the Remembrance has been sent down, indeed you are possessed. **7.** If you are among the truthful, why do you not bring us the angels?" **8.** We do not send down the angels except in truth. Were We to do so they would not be granted respite. **9.** It is We Who undoubtedly sent down the Remembrance and We are truly its Preserver. **10.** We have definitely propelled those of old before you; **11.** however, never did a messenger approach them but that they mocked him. **12.** Thus do We infiltrate it into the hearts of the sinners. **13.** They did not believe in it, though the ways of the old had already passed. **14.** Were We to open a gate for them unto Heaven, they would continue to ascend through it **15.** and would say, "Our eyes are hypnotized. We are, indeed, a bewitched people." **16.** We have set constellations in the sky and made them beautiful for observers. **17.** We have guarded them from every outcast demon, **18.** except for the one who secretly listens, only to be pursued by a blazing flame. **19.** We spread out the earth and cast in firm mountains. We produced therein everything in due balance. **20.** We provided in it a means of livelihood for you and for those whose sustenance is not on you. **21.** Nothing is there but that its treasures are with Us. We only send it down in a known measure. **22.** We sent forth fertilizing winds. We sent water down from the sky to provide you with sufficient drink, but you are not the keepers of its storage. **23.** Indeed it is We Who give life and cause death, and We are the Inheritor. **24.** We certainly know those among you who advance, and We certainly know those who lag behind, **25.** and it is surely your Lord Who will gather them. He is indeed Wise and Knowing. **26.** Truly We created man from dried clay, molded of black mud, **27.** and earlier, We created the jinn from scorching fire. **28.** Remember when your Lord said unto the angels, "Behold! I am creating a human being from dry clay, molded of black mud. **29.** So when I have proportioned him and breathed of My Spirit into him, drop down before him prostrating." **30.** Then all of the angels prostrated together, **31.** except for Satan. He refused to be with those who prostrated. **32.** He said, "O Iblīs! What bothers you that you are not with those who prostrate?" **33.** He said, "I am not one to prostrate to a human being whom You have created from dried clay, molded of black mud." **34.** He said, "Then leave this place! Surely, you are outcast, **35.** and surely, the curse will be upon you until the Day of Judgment!" **36.** He said, "My Lord! Grant me respite until the Day they are resurrected." **37.** He said, "Truly you are among those granted respite **38.** until the Day of the Moment Known." **39.** He said, "My Lord! Since you have led me astray, I will surely make things on the earth seem sound to them and I will lead them astray, all together, **40.** except for Your sincere servants among them." **41.** He said, "That is a straight path to Me. **42.** As for My servants, you certainly do not have authority over them except for the wrongdoers who follow you. **43.** Truly, Hell will be their meeting, all together." **44.** It has seven gates and for each gate among them there is a designated section. **45.** "Indeed, the righteous will dwell in gardens and springs—**46.** 'Enter them in peace and security.' **47.** We will cleanse their hearts of any malice, and they will sit as brothers on raised couches, facing one another. **48.** They will experience no exhaustion there, nor will they be removed from it." **49.** Tell My servants that I am, indeed, the Forgiving and the Merciful, **50.** and that My Punishment is a painful punishment. **51.** Tell them of the guests of Abraham, **52.** when they entered upon him and said, "Peace!" He said, "Truly we are afraid of you." **53.** They said, "Do not be afraid. Truly we bring you good news of a knowledgeable son." **54.** He said, "Do you bring me good news when old age has overcome me? So of what do you bring me good news?" **55.** They said, "We bring you good news in truth, so do not be among those who despair." **56.** He said, "Who despairs of the Mercy of his Lord except for those who are astray?" **57.** He said, "What is your business, O messengers?" **58.** They said, "We have been sent to a sinful people, **59.** except for the family of Lot. We will surely save them all together, **60.** except his wife. We have determined that she will certainly be among those who will lag behind." **61.** Then when the messengers came to Lot's family, **62.** he said, "Truly you are an unknown people." **63.** They said, "Even so, We come to you to accomplish that which they doubted. **64.** We bring you the truth and we are certainly truthful. **65.** So leave with your family during the night, follow behind them, and do not allow anyone to turn around. Go forth to wherever you are commanded." **66.** We decreed this matter unto him so the last remnants of those people will be cut off by morning. **67.** The people of the city arrived, celebrating. **68.** He said, "Truly these are my guests, so do not dishonor me! **69.** Revere God and do not disgrace me." **70.** They said, "Did we not forbid you from associating with all people?" **71.** He said, "These are my daughters, if you must act." **72.** By your life! They wandered confused in their drunkenness. **73.** So the Cry overtook them by sunrise, **74.** then We made its uppermost to be its lowermost and We rained down stones of dried clay upon them. **75.** Truly in that is a sign for those who discern, **76.** and truly, they are on a road still standing. **77.** Truly in that is a sign for the believers. **78.** Indeed, the inhabitants of the Wood were wrongdoers. **79.** So We avenged them and truly they are both on an open highway. **80.** Indeed, the inhabitants of *al-Hijr* denied the messengers. **81.** We gave them Our signs, but they turned away from them. **82.** They carved dwellings in the mountains for security, **83.** yet by morning, the Cry seized them, **84.** and what they earned did not benefit them. **85.** We did not create the heavens and the earth and whatever is between them but in truth. The Hour is certainly coming, so overlook with gracious forgiveness. **86.** Truly your Lord is the Knowing Creator. **87.** We have indeed given you the seven oft repeated, and the Mighty Quran. **88.** Do not strain your eyes toward the pleasures We have given certain classes of them and do not grieve over them. Lower your wing unto the believers. **89.** Say, "Truly I am clearly the warner." **90.** Such as We have sent down on the dividers **91.** who turned the Quran into fragments. **92.** So by your Lord! We will interrogate them all **93.** about what they did. **94.** So proclaim as you have been commanded and turn away the idolators. **95.** Truly We are enough for you against those who mock, **96.** and those who set up another god along with God; yet they will soon know. **97.** We certainly know that your breast is confined because of what they say. **98.** So glorify the praise of your Lord and be among those who prostrate. **99.** Worship your Lord until certainty approaches you.

Surah 16

THE BEE

al-Nahl

In the Name of God, the Compassionate, the Merciful

1. The Command of God is coming so do not seek to hasten it. Glory to Him! He is exalted beyond the partners they attribute. **2.** He sends angels down with the Spirit from His Command to whomever He wills among His servants, "Give warning that there is no god but I, so revere Me!" **3.** He created the heavens and the earth in truth. Exalted is He above the partners they attribute. **4.** He created humans from a drop of semen, yet he is a clear adversary. **5.** He has created livestock for you that offers warmth and benefits. From it, you eat, **6.** and in them is a sense of beauty as you take them home or take them out to pasture. **7.** They carry your heavy load to a land that you would have never reached without distress and hardship to yourselves. Your Lord is indeed Kind and Merciful. **8.** Horses, mules, and donkeys are for you to ride and for adornment. He created that which you know not of. **9.** It is for God to show the way though some have been turned aside. Had He willed, He would have guided you all together. **10.** It is He Who sends water down from the sky. Some of it you drink, and some provides vegetation to feed your livestock. **11.** From it, He makes the crops grow for you, such as, olives, date palms, grapevines, and every kind of fruit. Truly in that is a sign for a people who reflect. **12.** He has made the night and day subservient unto you. The sun, the moon, and the stars are subservient by His Command. Truly in that are signs for a people who understand. **13.** What He has created for you on the earth of varying colors, truly is a sign for a people who reflect. **14.** It is He Who made the sea subservient, that you may eat from its tender meat, and extract from it the ornaments that you wear. You see the ships plowing through it to seek His Bounty that you may perhaps show gratitude.

15. He placed sturdy mountains on the earth to keep it stable beneath you, and created rivers and pathways so that you may find your way **16.** He also set landmarks, and it is by the stars that they find guidance. **17.** Is He Who creates like one who does not create? Will you not then, reflect? **18.** Were you to keep score of the Blessings of God, you would not be able to count them. Truly God is Forgiving and Merciful. **19.** God knows what you conceal and what you disclose. **20.** Those whom they call upon instead of God create nothing and are themselves created; **21.** dead, not alive, as they are not aware of when they will be resurrected. **22.** Your God is One God and as for those who do not believe in the Hereafter, their hearts are in denial, and they are arrogant. **23.** There is no doubt that God knows what they conceal and what they disclose, for truly He does not love the arrogant. **24.** When it was said to them, "What has your Lord sent down?" They say, "Ancient tales!" **25.** Let them carry their entire burden on the Day of Resurrection along with some of the burdens of those who were unknowingly led astray. Lo! evil is what they bear! **26.** Those before them also plotted. Then God came upon their structure from its foundation, and the roof fell upon them from above. Punishment came at them while they were not aware. **27.** Then on the Day of Resurrection He will humiliate them and say, "Where are My partners that made you defiant?" Those who were given knowledge will say, "Indeed today, disgrace and evil are upon the disbelievers" — **28.** since those whose lives were taken by the angels had wronged their own souls. Then they will offer submission: "We were not doing any evil." Even so, God knows best what you were doing. **29.** So enter the gates of Hell to abide there forever. For indeed the abode of the arrogant is evil! **30.** It will be said to those who are reverent, "What has your Lord sent down?" They will say, "Goodness." For those who are virtuous in this world, there will be contentment. The Abode of the Hereafter is better. The abode of the reverent is excellent, indeed. **31.** They will enter the Gardens of Eden with rivers running beneath. They will have whatever they wish for there. Thus does God reward the reverent. **32.** Those whom the angels take while they are in a state of goodness will say, "Peace be upon you! Enter the Garden for what you practiced." **33.** Do they await anything but for the angels to come upon them or for the Command of your Lord to arrive? Those before them did the same. God did not wrong them, rather, they wronged themselves. **34.** So they were stricken by the evil deeds they practiced and were overcome by what they used to mock. **35.** Those who attribute partners to God say, "Had God willed, we would not have worshipped anything besides Him, neither us nor our fathers, nor would we have observed anything sacred besides Him." Those before them did the same. Is anything incumbent upon the Messenger besides the clear proclamation? **36.** We have certainly sent a messenger unto every nation —

"Worship God and avoid false deities." Then, among them were those whom God guided, and among them those who had earned error. Therefore, travel through the earth and observe the fate of the deniers. **37.** Though you are anxious that they be guided, truly God does not guide those who go astray, and they will have no helpers. **38.** They swear by God their most solemn oaths that God will not resurrect those who die. Even so, it is a promise binding upon Him though most people do not know, **39.** so that He might make clear to them where they differed and so disbelievers know that they were truly liars. **40.** Indeed, for anything which We have willed, We but say the word, "Be", and it is. **41.** Those who emigrate for the sake of God, after having been wronged, We will surely settle them in a good place in this world. If they only knew, the reward in the Hereafter is greater **42.** for those who are patient and trust in their Lord. **43.** We did not send any messengers before you except men to whom We have revealed, so ask the people of the Remembrance if you do not know the **44.** clear signs and scriptures. We have sent down the Remembrance to you so you may explain to people what We have sent to them, that perhaps they may reflect. **45.** Do those who have plotted evil deeds feel secure that God will not cause the earth to engulf them? Or that punishment will not come upon them while they are not aware? **46.** Or that He will not seize them in the midst of their going back and forth as they are powerless to stop it? **47.** Or that He will not seize them by causing gradual loss? Truly your Lord is Kind and Merciful. **48.** Do they not see that whatever God has created casts its shadow to the right and to the left, prostrating to God while in a state of complete humility? **49.** To God prostrates all crawling creatures or angels in the heavens or on the earth, and they do not show arrogance. **50.** They fear their Lord above them, and they do whatever they are commanded. **51.** God says, "Do not take on two gods. Truly He is only One God. So be in awe of Me." **52.** To Him belongs whatever is in the heavens and on the earth. Religion belongs to Him forever. Will you then revere something other than God? **53.** Whatever blessing you have is from God, and when misfortune touches you, it is unto Him that you cry for help. **54.** However, when He removes the misfortune from you, a group among you attributes partners unto their Lord. **55.** So let them be ungrateful for what We have given them: "Enjoy yourselves! For soon, you will know." **56.** They dedicate a share of what We have provided them to what they do not know. By God! You will certainly be questioned about what you invent. **57.** They assign daughters to God. Glory be to Him as they obtain what they desire! **58.** When one of them receives the news of a newborn female, his face darkens, and he is filled with anger. **59.** He hides from people because of the bad news he was given. Should he keep it in humiliation, or should he bury it in the dust? How evil is the judgment they make! **60.** Those who do not believe in the

Hereafter, have an evil disposition, yet unto God belongs the highest of dispositions. He is the Mighty and the Wise. **61.** Were God to chastise people for their wrongdoing, He would not exclude a single creature therefrom. But He puts them off to a term appointed. When their term comes, they will not delay it a single hour, nor will they advance it. **62.** They attribute to God to what they are averse. Their tongues describe the lie that all good will surely be theirs. There is no doubt that the Fire will be theirs and they will be hustled toward it. **63.** By God! We have indeed sent messengers to nations before you, but Satan made their deeds seem reasonable to them. Therefore, he is their protector on this day, and their punishment will be painful. **64.** We did not send the Book down to you except for you to make it clear to them where they differed, and as a guidance and a mercy for those who believe. **65.** God sends water down from the sky to revive the earth after its death. Truly this is a sign for a people who listen. **66.** There is certainly a lesson for you in livestock. We give drink for you from what is in their bellies, between refuse and blood, as pure milk, agreeable to those who ingest it. **67.** You derive strong drink and goodly provision from the fruits of the date palm and the vine. Certainly, in this is a sign for a people who understand. **68.** Your Lord revealed unto the bee, "Build your hives amid the mountains, the trees, and from what they construct. **69.** Then eat of every kind of fruit and follow the ways of your Lord submissively." A drink of diverse colors comes from their bellies wherein there is healing for people. Truly in that is a sign for a people who reflect. **70.** God created you, and then, He takes you. Among you are those who are taken back to the feeblest of ages, such that they know nothing after having had knowledge. Truly God is Knowing and Powerful. **71.** God has favored some of you above others in provision. Those who have been favored do not hand over their provision to those whom their right hands possess to grant equality. Would they thus deny the blessings of God? **72.** God has ordained mates for you from among yourselves, and from your mates, He has ordained for you children and grandchildren. He provided you with good things. Will they then believe in untruthful things and be ungrateful toward God's blessings? **73.** They worship instead of God what has no power and will never have power over any provision that may come to them from the heavens and the earth. **74.** So do not set forth parables for God. Truly God Knows and you do not know. **75.** God sets forth the parable of an enslaved servant who has power over nothing, yet he, to whom We have provided a goodly provision from Us, then spends of it secretly and openly. Are they equal? Praise be to God! No, most of them do not know. **76.** God sets forth the parable of two men. One is simple-minded with power over nothing, and he is a burden to his master, and wherever he directs him, he brings no good. Is he equal to one who commands justice and who is on a straight path?

77. Unto God belongs the Unseen of the heavens and the earth. The affair of the Hour is like the blinking of an eye, or even sooner. Truly God is powerful over all things. 78. God brought you forth from the bellies of your mothers knowing nothing. He endowed you with hearing, sight, and hearts, that perhaps you may show gratitude. 79. Do they not perceive that birds are controlled in mid-air, and nothing holds them up except God? Truly in this are signs for a people who believe. 80. God has destined a place of rest for you in your homes. He has made homes for you from cowhide that you can carry with ease on the day you travel and on the day you settle. Out of their wool, their fur, and their hair are furnishings, and temporary pleasantries. 81. God has made shade for you from among what He created. He made places of shelter for you in the mountains. He made garments for you to protect you from the heat and shields to protect you from your own might. Thus does God complete His Blessings unto you that perhaps you may submit. 82. Then if they deter, only the clear message is incumbent upon you. 83. They acknowledge the Blessing of God and then deny it. Most of them are disbelievers. 84. On that Day We will raise up a witness from every nation, then, those who disbelieved will not be allowed excuses, nor can they make amends. 85. When those who did wrong see the punishment, it will not be lightened for them, nor will they be given respite. 86. When those who attribute partners unto God see the partners, they attributed, they will say, "Our Lord! These are our partners upon whom we called instead of You." But they will retort, "Indeed you are liars." 87. On that Day, they will offer submission unto God and what they made-up will abandon them. 88. Those who disbelieved and turned from the way of God, We will add punishment on top of punishment upon them for the corruption they implemented. 89. On that Day, We will bring forth from every nation a witness from among them to testify against them, and We will have you as a witness against these people. We revealed the Book to you as a clarification for all matters, and as guidance, mercy, and good news for those who submit. 90. Indeed, God demands justice, virtue, giving to kinsfolk, and forbids indecency, wrongdoing, and rebelliousness. He admonishes you that perhaps you may remember. 91. Fulfill the Covenant of God when you have pledged to it, and do not break your oaths after solemnly affirming them and having made God a witness over you. God knows whatever you do. 92. Do not be like the woman who undoes her yarn after it has been tightly spun, breaking it apart. Do not use your oaths deceitfully with one another just because one group may be greater in number than another. God is testing you through this, and on the Day of Resurrection, He will make clear to you what you disagreed about. 93. Had God willed, He would have made you one nation, but He leads astray whomever He wills and guides whomever he wills. You will surely be

interrogated about what you practiced. **94.** Do not take your oaths to practice deception among yourselves just in case your foot slips after having been firmly planted, and you taste evil for having turned away from God. Your punishment will be great. **95.** Do not sell the Covenant of God for a trivial price. What is with God is indeed better for you if you only knew. **96.** What is with you comes to an end, but what is with God is permanent. We will indeed reward those who are patient for the best of what they practiced. **97.** Whoever is a believer and practices righteousness, whether male or female, We will give them a new life, and a good life. We will indeed, render unto them their reward according to the best of what they practiced. **98.** So when you recite the Quran, seek protection in God from the outcast Satan. **99.** Truly he has no authority over those who believe and trust in their Lord. **100.** His authority is only over those who take him as a protector, and those who take him as a partner. **101.** When We replace one sign with another, God knows best what He sends down. They say, "You are a forger," but most of them do not know. **102.** Say, "The Holy Spirit has brought it down from your Lord in truth, to strengthen those who believe and as guidance and good news for those who submit." **103.** Verily We know they say, "He has only been taught by a human being." The tongue of the one whom they falsely implicate is foreign while this is a clear Arabic tongue. **104.** Truly those who do not believe in the signs of God, will not be guided by God and their punishment will be painful. **105.** It is only those who do not believe in the signs of God who make up lies though they are the liars. **106.** Whoever disbelieves in God after having believed, except for he who is coerced while his heart is at peace in faith, or whoever opens his breast unto disbelief, the Wrath of God will be upon them, and their punishment will be great. **107.** That is for having preferred the life of this world over the Hereafter. God truly does not guide a disbelieving people. **108.** God has placed a seal on their hearts, their hearing, and their vision. It is they who are unmindful. **109.** There is no doubt that in the Hereafter, they are the losers. **110.** Truly, those who emigrated after being persecuted, then strove and remained patient, will find that your Lord is indeed Forgiving and Merciful. **111.** The Day every soul will come disputing on its own behalf, every soul will be compensated in full for what it practiced. They will not be wronged. **112.** God sets forth the parable of a town that was secure and at peace. It was receiving abundant provisions from every locale, but it was ungrateful of God's blessings. From this time forward, God let it taste the garment of hunger and fear for what they had wrought. **113.** A messenger among themselves had indeed come to them, but they denied him. As a result, punishment seized them in the midst of their iniquities. **114.** From this time forward, eat of the lawful and good things God has provided you and be grateful of God's Blessings, if it is

He Whom you worship. **115.** He has only forbidden you carrion, blood, the flesh of swine, and what has been offered to an entity other than God. But whoever is compelled out of necessity without willfully disobeying or transgressing, God is indeed Forgiving and Merciful. **116.** Do not speak lies that your tongues describe, "This is lawful, and this is forbidden," such that you make up lies about God. Those who make up lies about God will certainly not prosper. **117.** For little enjoyment, there will be a painful punishment. **118.** Unto those who are Jews, We forbade what We had previously narrated unto you. We did not wrong them, but they wronged themselves. **119.** Then truly your Lord—for those who commit evil out of ignorance, then later repent, and make amends, thereafter,—your Lord is indeed, Forgiving and Merciful. **120.** Abraham was indeed a nation devoutly obedient to God, an *upright*, and was not among the idolators. **121.** He was grateful for His Blessings. He chose him and guided him unto the straight path. **122.** We granted him good in this world. He will indeed be among the righteous, in the Hereafter. **123.** Then We revealed unto you, "Follow the creed of Abraham, a *ḥanīf*, and he was not among the idolators." **124.** The Sabbath was solely ordained for those who differed about it. Your Lord will truly judge between them on the Day of Resurrection concerning what they differed upon. **125.** Call unto the way of your Lord with wisdom and goodly appeal and dispute with them in the most virtuous manner. Your Lord is, indeed, He Who knows best those who have strayed from His way, and He knows best the rightly guided. **126.** If you are to reprimand them, reprimand them as you were reprimanded, but if you are patient, then, that is better for the patient. **127.** So be patient, and your patience is only with God. Do not grieve on their account, nor be distressed by what they plot. **128.** Truly God is with those who are reverent and those who are virtuous.

Surah 17

THE NIGHT JOURNEY

al-Isrã

In the Name of God, the Compassionate, the Merciful

1. Glory to Him Who carried His servant by night from the Sacred Mosque to the Farthest Mosque. We blessed its precincts that We might show him some of Our signs. Truly He is the Hearer and the Seer. **2.** We gave Moses the Book. We made it a guidance for the Children of Israel — "Do not take as guardian any other than Me" — **3.** the progeny of those whom We carried with Noah. Truly he was a grateful servant. **4.** In the Book, We decreed for the Children of Israel, "You will certainly work corruption upon the earth twice, and you will rise to a great height." **5.** So when the first Promise arrived, We sent servants of Ours against you who were possessed of powerful strength, and they ravaged your homes. It was a promise fulfilled. **6.** Then in turn, We reinforced you against them. We increased you in wealth and children and We made you more numerous. **7.** If you are virtuous, you are virtuous for yourselves, and if you do evil, it would be for its own sake. So when the second promise comes to pass, they will bring misery to your faces, enter the Temple as they did the first time, and completely destroy whatever they conquer. **8.** It may be that your Lord will have mercy on you, so if you revert, We will revert. We made Hell a detention for the disbelievers. **9.** Truly this Quran guides toward what is most upright and informs the believers who perform righteous deeds that they will indeed receive a great reward. **10.** Truly We have prepared a painful punishment for those who do not believe in the Hereafter. **11.** Man supplicates for evil as he supplicates for good. Man is always in a hurry. **12.** We made the night and the day two signs. Then We erased the sign of the night and made the sign of the day for sight that you may seek bounty from your Lord and that you may know the number of years and how to compute. We have explained everything in detail. **13.** We have fastened every person's fate upon his neck. We will bring it forth to meet him on the Day of Resurrection as a wide-open book. **14.** "Read your book! On this Day, your soul is enough of a reckoner against you." **15.** Whoever is rightly guided is only rightly guided for the sake of his own soul, and whoever is astray, is solely astray to its detriment. No one will bear the burden of the other, and never do We punish until We have sent a messenger. **16.** When We want to destroy a town, We command those who live a life of luxury, but they transgress therein. Thus, the Word comes due against it and We completely, demolish it. **17.** How many a generation have We destroyed after Noah! Your Lord suffices as One Who Perceives and Knows of the sins of His servants. **18.** Whoever desires the transient, We advance it for him, except for whatever We desire for whomever We desire. Then We provide Hell for him, wherein he will burn, be culpable and rejected. **19.** Whoever desires the Hereafter, earnestly labors for it, and is a believer, their efforts will be appreciated. **20.** We will help each, these and those, with the Gift of your Lord, and the Gift of your Lord is not restricted. **21.** Observe how We have favored some of them over others. Verily the Hereafter is greater in rank and greater in favoritism. **22.** Do not set up another god with God or you will sit in disgrace and restitution. **23.** Your Lord decrees that you worship none but Him, and to be virtuous to parents. Whether one or both of them reaches old age, do not say to them, "Uff!" nor chide them, but speak kind words to them. **24.** Lower the wing of humility unto them out of mercy, and say, "My Lord! Have mercy upon them, as they raised me when I was young." **25.** Your Lord knows more what is in your souls. If you are righteous, then truly He is Forgiving toward the penitent. **26.** Give the relative their due, as well as the needy and the traveler, but do not squander resources recklessly. **27.** Truly the wasteful are the brethren of demons, and Satan is ungrateful to his Lord. **28.** But if you turn away from them by seeking mercy that you would hope for from your Lord, then say a kind word to them. **29.** Do not let your hand be shackled to your neck, nor let it be entirely open, that you become blameworthy and destitute. **30.** Indeed your Lord feasibly outspreads provision for whomever He wills. He is indeed knowledgeable and perceptive of His servants. **31.** Do not slay your children from fear of poverty. We will provide for them and for you. Truly slaying them is a great sin. **32.** Do not approach adultery. Verily it is immoral and an evil route. **33.** Do not slay a soul that God has made sacred, save justifiably. Whoever is slain unjustly, We have given his heir authority, but do not let them slay excessively. Truly he will be helped. **34.** Do not approach an orphan's property except in the best of manners and until he reaches maturity. Fulfill the engagement. Surely the engagement will be enquired into. **35.** Give full measure when you measure, and weigh with a scale that is steady. That is better and more advantageous in the end. **36.** Do not pursue what you have no knowledge of. Truly the hearing, the sight, and the heart will all be called to account. **37.** Do not walk boastfully upon the earth. You certainly do not penetrate the earth, nor reach the mountains in height. **38.** The evilness of everything is hateful to your Lord. **39.** That is from the wisdom your Lord has revealed unto you. Do not set up a god along with God, else you will be thrown into Hell, blameworthy and rejected. **40.** Did your Lord favor you with sons while He took females from among the angels? You utter monstrous talk indeed! **41.** Truly We have variations in this Quran that they might reflect upon, but it will do no more than add to their aversion. **42.** Say, "If there were gods with Him, as they say, they would surely seek a way to the Possessor of the Throne." **43.** Glory be to Him! Exalted is He above whatever they say. **44.** The seven heavens and the earth, and whoever is in them, glorify Him. There is not a thing that does not celebrate His praise though you do not understand their praise. Truly He is Most-Forbearing and Forgiving. **45.** When you recite the Quran, We place an invisible veil between you and those who do not believe in the Hereafter. **46.** We have placed casings over their hearts and deafness in their ears such that they do not understand it. Whenever you mention your Lord alone in the Quran, they turn their backs in aversion. **47.** We know best when they converse in secret, what they listen for when they listen to you, and when the wrongdoers say, "You are following nothing more than an ensorcelled man!" **48.** Look how they strike you with examples, but they have gone astray and cannot find a way. **49.** They say, "What! When we are bones and dust, will we really be resurrected as a new creation?" **50.** Say, "Be of stone or iron **51.** or any other created matter that expands in your minds." Then they will say, "Who will bring us back?" Say, "He Who originated you the first time." They will shake their heads at you and say, "When will it be?" Say, "It could be soon." **52.** The Day when He calls you, you will respond by praising Him, and you will think that you tarried for only a short while. **53.** Tell My servants that they should only speak righteousness. Satan truly provokes dissent among them. Truly Satan is a clear enemy of people. **54.** Your Lord knows you best. If He wills, He will have Mercy upon you, and if He wills, He will punish you. We have not sent you as a guardian over them. **55.** God knows best whoever is in the heavens and the earth. We have indeed favored some of the prophets over others, and unto David, We gave the Psalms. **56.** Say, "Call upon those whom you claim besides Him, for they do not have the power to remove nor change difficulties from you." **57.** It is they who make supplication to find the means to access to their Lord. Which of them is nearer? They hope for His Mercy and fear His Punishment. Truly the Punishment of your Lord is something of which to be wary. **58.** There is no town but that We will destroy it before the Day of Resurrection or punish it with a severe punishment. That is recorded in the Book.

59. Nothing stops Us from sending signs but that former generations have denied them. We gave unto the Thamūd the she-camel as visible sign, but they wronged her. We do not send down Our signs but to inspire panic. 60. Remember when We said to you, "Surely your Lord encompasses all people." We only ordained the vision that We showed you as a trial for people like the Accursed Tree in the Quran. We inspire fear in them, but that only adds to massive transgression. 61. When We said unto the angels, "Prostrate before Adam," they all prostrated, save Iblīs. He said, "Should I prostrate before one whom You have created from dried clay?" 62. He said, "Do You see this, which You have honored above me? If You grant me reprieve until the Day of Resurrection, I will surely gain mastery over all of his progeny, save a few." 63. He said, "Go! And whoever among them should follow you, truly Hell will be your reward, an abundant compensation! 64. Therefore, provoke whomever you can among them with your voice, and assault them with your cavalry and your infantry, be their partner in wealth and children, and make them promises." Satan promises them nothing but deceitfulness. 65. "As for my servants, you truly have no authority over them." Your Lord is enough of a guardian. 66. Your Lord is He Who makes the ships sail upon the sea, that you might seek of His Bounty. Truly He is Merciful unto you. 67. Whenever you face difficulties at sea those who you call upon instead of Him, abandon you, but when He delivers you safely to land, you deter. Yet man is ungrateful! 68. Do you feel secure that He will not allow you to be engulfed near the shoreline, or release a storm of stones against you? Then you would find no guardian for yourselves. 69. Or do you feel secure enough that He will not return you to it and release upon you a turbulent wind to drown you for having been ungrateful? Then you would find no avenger there against Us. 70. We have indeed honored the Children of Adam. We carry them over land and sea, provide them with good things, and We favor them above the many that We have created. 71. On the Day We call every people alongside their imam, whoever is given his book in his right hand, it is they who will read their book. They will not be wronged so much as a speck on a datestone. 72. Whoever was blind to this, will be blind in the Hereafter, and further astray from the way. 73. They were about to tempt you away from what We revealed unto you that you might falsely attribute something else unto Us, whereupon they would have certainly taken you as a friend. 74. Had We not made you well-rounded, you would truly have leaned toward them somewhat. 75. Consequently, We would have made you taste double in life and double in death. Then you would have found yourself without a helper against Us. 76. Indeed, they were about to rouse you from the land in order to expel you from there, where they would have not lingered after you, save for a short period, 77. similar to the ways

of those among Our messengers whom We had sent before you. You will find no change in Our ways. **78.** Perform prayer as the sun declines until the darkening of night, and the recitation at dawn, for indeed, the recitation at dawn is ever witnessed! **79.** Keep vigil in prayer for part of the night as additional for you. It may be that your Lord will resurrect you to a station worthy of praise. **80.** Say, "My Lord! Admit me in a truthful manner and exit me in a truthful manner and grant me from Your Presence an authority to assist me." **81.** Say, "Truth has arrived, and falsehood has perished. Truly falsehood is bound to perish." **82.** We send down in the Quran what serves as a cure and a mercy for the believers. It increases the wrongdoers in nothing but loss. **83.** Whenever We confer a blessing upon mankind, he turns aside and withdraws, but whenever evil touches him, he is in despair. **84.** Say, "Each acts according to his disposition, and your Lord knows best who is more rightly guided to the way." **85.** They ask you about the Spirit. Say, "The Spirit is from the Command of my Lord, and you have not been given knowledge, except for a little." **86.** If We willed, We could have taken away what We revealed unto you. Then you would not find a guardian for yourself against Us, **87.** except for mercy from your Lord. His Bounty toward you is great indeed. **88.** Say, "Surely if people and jinn group together to bring the like of this Quran, they would not bring the like then, even if they backed each other up." **89.** We have indeed explained every kind of parable for people in this Quran. Yet most people avoid it with mere disbelief. **90.** They say, "We will not believe in you until you make a spring burst forth from the earth for us, **91.** or until you have a garden of date palms and grapevines, and make streams burst forth for us in the midst of it, **92.** or until you make the sky fall on us in pieces, as you have claimed, or until you bring God and the angels before us, **93.** or until you have a house made of gold ornaments, or until you rise to Heaven. We will not believe in your ascent until you bring down to us a book we can read." Say, "Glory be to my Lord! Am I not but a human being, and a messenger?" **94.** What prevented people from believing when guidance came to them, except for their claim, "Has God sent a human being as a messenger?" **95.** Say, "If there were angels walking about on the earth in peace, We would have sent down upon them an angel from Heaven as a messenger." **96.** Say, "God is enough of a witness between you and me. Truly He is Aware and Perceptive of His servants." **97.** Whomever God guides, he will be rightly guided, and whomever He leads astray, you will find no protectors for them instead of Him. We will gather them on the Day of Resurrection prone on their faces—blind, dumb, and deaf. Their refuge will be Hell, and each time it abates, We will increase the blazing flame upon them. **98.** That is their reward for disbelieving in Our signs. They say, "What! When we are bones and dust, will we really be resurrected as a new creation?" **99.** Have they not observed that God, Who created the heavens and the earth, has the power to create the like of them? He has decreed for them a term in which there is no doubt. Yet, the wrongdoers only refuse in disbelief. **100.** Say, "Were you to possess the treasuries of my Lord's Mercy, you would certainly hold back out of fear of spending. Mankind is ever niggardly." **101.** We have indeed, given Moses nine clear signs. So ask the Children of Israel. When he came to them, Pharoah said, "Truly, I think that you, O Moses, are bewitched!" **102.** He said, "You truly know that no one has sent these down except the Lord of the heavens and the earth as clear warnings. I think, O Pharoah that you are truly doomed!" **103.** He desired to rouse them from the land, so We drowned him and those with him all together. **104.** Afterward, We said to the Children of Israel, "Live in the land, but when the promise of the Hereafter comes to pass, We will bring you as a mixed assembly." **105.** In truth, We sent it down, and in truth, it descended. We did not send you except as a bearer of good news and as a warner, **106.** a Quran in segments, that you may recite it to people in intervals. We sent it down in sequential revelations. **107.** Say, "Believe in it or do not believe." For indeed those who were given prior knowledge, when it is recited unto them, fall down prostrate on their faces. **108.** They say, "Glory be to our Lord! The Promise of our Lord is indeed fulfilled." **109.** They fall on their faces weeping and it increases them in humility. **110.** Say, "Call upon God, or call upon the Compassionate. Whichever you call upon, to Him belong the Most Beautiful Names. Do not be loud in your prayer, nor too quiet, but seek a way in between." **111.** Say, "Praise be to God Who begets no child! He has no partner in sovereignty, nor does He have a protector from humiliation." Proclaim Him with the utmost glorification.

Surah 18

THE CAVE

al-Kahf

In the Name of God, the Compassionate, the Merciful

1. Praise be to God Who sent the Book down unto His servant free of crookedness, **2.** standing upright to warn of a great disaster coming from Him, to inform believers who perform righteous deeds that they will receive a goodly reward, **3.** remaining there forever, **4.** and to forewarn those who say, "God has taken a child." **5.** They have no such knowledge, nor do their fathers. This is an outrageous word that comes out of their mouths. What they say is indeed nothing but a lie. **6.** Perchance you will devastate yourself out of grief over their ways if they do not believe in this account. **7.** We have truly fashioned whatever is on the earth as an adornment for it, that We may try them to see which of them is the most virtuous in conduct. **8.** Truly We will make whatever is upon it a barren dust. **9.** Do you figure that the Companions of the Cave and the Inscription are wonders among Our signs? **10.** When several youths took refuge in the cave, they said, "Our Lord! Grant us mercy from Your Presence and righteously dispose of our affair for us." **11.** So while in the cave, We capped their ears for a number of years. **12.** Then We raised them up again, that We might know which of the two parties had best calculated how long they had tarried. **13.** We relate their story to you in truth. They were indeed youths who believed in their Lord. We increased them in guidance, **14.** and We fortified their hearts. When they arose, they said, "Our Lord is the Lord of the heavens and the earth. We will not call upon a god besides Him, for then, we would have indeed uttered an outrage. **15.** These people of ours have taken gods other than Him. Why do they not produce clear evidence for their worship? Who could be more unjust than someone who fabricates a lie against God? **16.** When you distance yourselves from them and from all they worship besides God, seek refuge in the cave. Your Lord will shower you with His mercy and make your situation easier to manage." **17.** You would have seen the sun rising, veering to the right of their cave, and setting, turning away to the left, while they lay in a spacious area within it. That is among the signs of God. Whomever God guides will be rightly guided and whomever He leads astray will find no protector to lead him to the right way. **18.** You would have thought they were awake, but they were asleep. We turned them to the right and to the left with their dog stretching his forelegs at the threshold. Had you come upon them, you would have been filled with terror on their account and ran away from them. **19.** Subsequently, We raised them up again that they might question one another. One of them said, "How long have you tarried?" They said, "We have tarried a day, or part of a day." They said, "Your Lord knows best how long you have tarried. So send one among you with this money to the city to observe which of them has the purest food and bring sustenance afterward. Be modest and do not let anyone be mindful of you. **20.** Truly, if they learn of you, they will stone you or make you revert to their creed. Then you will never prosper." **21.** By this, We caused them to be discovered that they might know God's Promise is true and there is no doubt about the Hour. When the townsfolk were arguing about the affair among themselves, they said, "Erect a building over them. Their Lord knows them best." Those who were perplexed over their affair said, "We will build a place of worship over them." **22.** They will say, "Three and the fourth was their dog," and they will say, "Five and the sixth was their dog" — guessing at the unseen. Then they will say, "Seven and the eighth was their dog." Say, "My Lord knows best their number. No one knows them, except for a few." So do not enter into controversies about them except with clear argument, nor consult with anyone about them. **23.** Do not say, "Surely, I will do that tomorrow," **24.** save by God's will. Remember your Lord when you forget and say, "It may be that my Lord will guide me closer to this in righteousness." **25.** They tarried in their cave for three hundred years plus an additional nine. **26.** Say, "God knows best how long they tarried. Unto Him belongs the Unseen of the heavens and the earth. How well He sees and hears! They have no protector besides Him, and He makes no one a partner unto Him in His Judgment." **27.** Recite what has been revealed to you from the Book of your Lord. No one will alter His Words, and you will not find refuge except with Him. **28.** Draw patience to your soul with those who call upon their Lord morning and evening, desiring His Countenance. Do not turn your eyes away from them to seek the adornment of the life of this world, nor obey one whose heart We have made unmindful of the remembrance of Us, one who follows his craze, and whose affair has gone beyond all bounds. **29.** Say, "It is the truth from your Lord! Therefore, whoever wills, let him believe, and whoever wills, let him disbelieve." We have indeed prepared a Fire for the wrongdoers to be enclosed by its walls. If they plead for relief, they will be relieved with water similar to molten lead that will scald their faces, an evil drink indeed. What an evil resting place! **30.** As for those who believe and perform righteous deeds, We will truly not let the reward of their righteous performance succumb. **31.** For such things, there will be Gardens of Eden with rivers flowing below. They will be adorned with bracelets of gold and wear green garments of fine silk woven with gold threads while reclining on couches there. What a great reward and beautiful resting place! **32.** Present to them the parable of two men: for one of them, We made two gardens of grapevines, surrounded them with date palms, and placed crops between them. **33.** Both gardens did not fail in the least to bring forth their fruit. We made a stream gush in their midst. **34.** He obtained his harvest and said to his comrade as he conversed with him, "I am greater than you in wealth and stronger in men." **35.** He entered his garden wronging himself and said, "I do not think that this will ever perish, **36.** nor do I think that the Hour is forthcoming. If I am brought back to my Lord, I will surely find something better than this in the Hereafter." **37.** His comrade said to him while conversing with him, "Do you disbelieve in the One Who created you from dust, then from a drop of semen, then fashioned you into a man? **38.** He is God, my Lord and I do not attribute none as partner unto Him. **39.** When you entered your garden, why did you not say, 'As God wills. There is no strength except in God.' If you see that I am less than you in wealth and children, **40.** it may be that my Lord will give me something better than your garden and that He will send upon it a reckoning from the sky that it becomes a smooth leveled plain, **41.** or its water may sink deep so that you will never be able to find it." **42.** His fruit was encompassed by ruin, and he began to wring his hands on account of what he had spent on it while it lay in waste on its trellises, saying, "I wish I had never attributed anyone as partner unto my Lord!" **43.** He had no force to help him besides God, nor could he help himself. **44.** There, protection belongs to God, the True One. He is the best in reward and the best in the end. **45.** Set forth to them the similarity in the life of this world. It is like the water We send down from the sky. It mixes with the vegetation of the earth and then it becomes dry stalks, scattered by the winds. God is capable of all things. **46.** Wealth and children are the adornment of life in this world, but what endures — righteous deeds — are better in reward from your Lord and better in what people would hope for. **47.** On the Day We set the mountains in motion; you will see the earth as an open plain. We will gather them and not leave anyone behind. **48.** They will be marshaled before your Lord in ranks. "You have indeed come to us as We created you the first time. Truly you claimed We would never appoint a meeting for you." **49.** The Book will be set down. Then you will see the guilty fearful of what is in it. They will say, "Oh! Woe unto us! What a book this is! It leaves nothing out, big or small but that it has taken it into consideration." They will find what they did readily presented. Your Lord wrongs no one. **50.** When We said unto the angels, "Prostrate before Adam," they prostrated, save Iblīs. He was one of the jinn and he deviated from the command of his Lord. Will you then take him and his progeny as protectors instead of Me, though they are your enemy? How evil an exchange for the wrongdoers! **51.** I did not make them witnesses to the creation of the heavens and the earth, nor to their own creation. I do not take those who lead astray as a support. **52.** On the Day He says, "Call upon those whom you claimed are my partners," they will call upon them; however, We will place a partition between them, and they will not respond to them. **53.** The guilty will see the Fire, knowing they will fall into it, and will find no means of escape from it. **54.** In this Quran, We have certainly employed every kind of parable for people. Man is the most contentious of beings. **55.** What is there to keep people from believing and seeking forgiveness of their Lord when guidance has come to them, unless the old ways arise upon them, or punishment will arrive at them face-to-face. **56.** We do not send the messengers save as bearers of good news and warnings. Those who disbelieve dispute with vain argument to weaken the truth. They take My signs and what they were warned of in mockery. **57.** Who does greater wrong than one who has been reminded of the signs of his Lord, then turns away from them and forgets what his hands had sent forth. We have placed casings over their hearts and deafness in their ears such that they do not understand it. Even if you call them to guidance, they will never be rightly guided. **58.** Your Lord is Forgiving and Possessed of Mercy. Were He to take them to account for what they had earned; He would have advanced their punishment. They will indeed have their meeting upon which they will find no refuge. **59.** Those towns, We destroyed them for the wrong they did and fixed an appointed time for their destruction. **60.** Remember when Moses said to his attendant, "I will not quit until I reach the junction of the two seas even if I must travel for a long time." **61.** Then, when they reached the junction of the two, they forgot their fish. It had made its way to the sea while slithering away. **62.** Then when they had passed elsewhere, he said to his attendant, "Bring us our meal. This journey of ours has certainly exhausted us." **63.** He said, "Did you see that when we sheltered near the rock, I had indeed forgotten the fish? No one but Satan made me forget to mention it. It took its course through the sea in an amazing way." **64.** He said, "That is what we were seeking!" As a result, they turned back, retracing their footsteps. **65.** So there, they had found one of Our servants upon whom We had bestowed a mercy from Us and to whom We had taught knowledge from Our Presence. **66.** Moses said to him, "Can I follow you that you may teach me from what you have been taught of in sound judgment?" **67.** He said, "Truly you will not be able to bear patiently with me. **68.** How can you bear patiently with knowledge you do not encompass?"

69. He said, "You will find me patient, if God wills, and I will not disobey you in any way." 70. He said, "If indeed you follow me, do not ask me questions about anything until I communicate with you about it." 71. So they went on until they had embarked upon a ship. He punctured a hole in it. He said, "Did you puncture a hole in it to drown its people? You have done an outrageous thing!" 72. He said, "Did I not tell you that you will not be able to bear patiently with me?" 73. He said, "Do not blame me for having forgotten, nor make me suffer from my complicated situation." 74. Then they went on until they encountered a young boy, and he slew him. He said, "Did you slay a pure soul who had not slain any other soul. You have surely committed a terrible thing!" 75. He said, "Did I not tell you that you will not be able to bear patiently with me?" 76. He said, "If I question you about anything after this, do not keep me in your company. I have informed you of my apology." 77. Then they went on until they came upon the people of a town and asked them for food, but they denied them any hospitality. Then they discovered a wall there that was about to fall, and he set it up straight. He said, "Had you willed, you could have charged for it." 78. He said, "This is the parting between you and me. I am going to inform you of the meaning of what you had no patience for. 79. As for the ship, it belonged to indigent people who worked at sea. I wanted to damage it, since just beyond them, there was a king who was confiscating every ship by force. 80. As for the young boy, his parents were believers, and we feared he would make them suffer through his rebellion and disbelief. 81. So we desired that their Lord give them one who is better than him in purity and closer in affection. 82. As for the wall, it belonged to two orphan boys in the city, and beneath it was a treasure that belonged to them. Their father was upright, therefore, as mercy from your Lord, your Lord willed that once they reach maturity, He would give them strength in order to extract their treasure. I did not do this of my own accord. This is the meaning of what you had no patience for." 83. They questioned you about Dhu'l Qar'nayn. Say, "I will recite to you a recount of him." 84. Truly We established him in the land and gave him the way to all things. 85. So he followed a way, 86. until he reached the place of the setting sun. He found it setting in a murky spring. There, he found a people and We said, "Dhu'l Qar'nayn! You may punish or you may treat them well." 87. He said, "As for the one who has done wrong, we will punish him. Then he will be taken back to his Lord, where He will punish him with a terrible punishment. 88. But as for the one who believes and works righteousness, he will have a goodly reward, and We will speak to him of what is easy from Our command." 89. Then he followed a path 90. until he reached the place of a rising sun. He found it rising over a people for whom We had not provided any protection. 91. Thus, We encompassed the knowledge he possessed. 92. Then he followed a path 93. until he reached a place

between two mountain barriers. He found beside them a people who could barely understand speech. **94.** They said, "O Dhu'l Qar'nayn! Truly Gog and Magog transgress upon the land. Can we assign you a tribute that you might set a barrier between them and us?" **95.** He said, "What my Lord has established for me is better, so help me with might. I will set a barrier between you and them. **96.** Bring me pieces of iron." Then when he had leveled the two mountainsides, he said, "Blow!" until he turned it into a fire. He said, "Bring me molten copper to pour over it." **97.** Thus, they were not able to surmount it, nor could they penetrate it. **98.** He said, "This is a mercy from my Lord. When the Promise of my Lord comes, He will crumble it to dust, and the Promise of my Lord is real!" **99.** We will leave them on that Day to surge like waves on one another. The trumpet will be blown, and We will gather them together. **100.** We will present Hell on that Day for the disbelievers **101.** who cannot hear and whose eyes would be veiled in remembrance of Me. **102.** Do those who disbelieve figure they may take My servants as protectors instead of Me? Truly We have prepared Hell to be a welcoming for disbelievers. **103.** Say, "Should I inform you who the greatest losers are with respect to their deeds? **104.** Those whose efforts go astray in the life of this world, while they figure they are virtuous in their works." **105.** They are those who disbelieve in the signs of their Lord, and in the meeting with Him. Thus, their deeds have come to nothing, and We will not ration any weight to their deeds on the Day of Resurrection. **106.** Hell! That is their reward for having disbelieved and for having taken My signs and My messengers in mockery. **107.** Those who believe and perform righteous deeds, the Gardens of Paradise will be their welcome, **108.** abiding there forever. They do not seek to change anything there. **109.** Say, "If the sea were ink for the words of my Lord, it would run dry before the words of my Lord were completed, even if We brought another sea like it as a supplement." **110.** Say, "I am only a human being like you. It is revealed to me that your God is One God. So whoever inspires for the meeting with his Lord, let him perform righteous deeds and make no one a partner to his Lord in worship."

Surah 19

MARY

Maryam

In the Name of God, the Compassionate, the Merciful

1. *Kāf. Hā. Yā. 'Ayn. Sād.* **2.** A reminder of the Mercy of your Lord unto His servant Zachariah. **3.** Remember when he called out to his Lord in a secret plea. **4.** He said, "My Lord! Truly my bones have grown feeble, and my head glistens with grayish hair. I have never been distressed in calling upon You, my Lord. **5.** My wife is barren, and I truly fear for my relatives after me. So grant me from Your Presence an heir **6.** who will inherit from me and inherit from the House of Jacob—and my Lord, make him well-pleasing." **7.** "O Zachariah! Truly We bring you good news of a boy whose name is John [*Yehya*], a name We have not given previously to any before him." **8.** He said, "How will I have a boy when my wife is barren, and I have grown quite decrepit from old age?" **9.** He said, "Thus it will be. Your Lord says, "It is easy for Me! I had created you before when you were nothing!" **10.** He said, "My Lord! Designate a sign for me." He said, "Your sign will be that you should not speak with anyone for three nights—though you can speak." **11.** Subsequently, he came out of the sanctuary unto his people and signaled to them that they should glorify morning and evening. **12.** "O John! Take hold of the Book with might!" We gave him judgment as a child, **13.** and sympathy from Our Presence. He was reverent, **14.** dutiful to his parents, and he was not insolent or domineering. **15.** Peace be upon him the day he was born, the day he dies, and the day he comes forth to life. **16.** Remember Mary in the Book when she withdrew from her family to an eastward location, **17.** and she secluded herself from them. Then We sent Our Spirit to her in the likeness of a respectful man. **18.** She said, "I seek refuge in my Lord from you, if you truly fear God!" **19.** He said, "I am only a messenger from your Lord to bestow upon you a pure boy." **20.** She said, "How will I have a boy when no man has touched me, nor have I been unchaste?" **21.** He said, "Thus will it be. Your Lord says, 'It is easy for Me.'" We will make him a sign unto people as a mercy from Us. It is a decreed manner. **22.** So she conceived him and withdrew with him to a distant location. **23.** The violent pangs of childbirth drove her to the trunk of a date palm. She said, "Ah! I wish I had died before this, so I could have been forgotten and disremembered." **24.** He called out to her from below her, "Do not grieve! Your Lord has placed a rivulet beneath you. **25.** Shake the trunk of the date palm toward you, and fresh, ripe dates will fall upon you. **26.** So eat, drink, and freshen your eye. If you see any human say, 'Truly I have vowed a fast unto the Compassionate, so I will not speak this day to any man.'" **27.** Then she went to her people carrying him. They said, "O Mary! You have brought an appalling thing! **28.** O sister of Aaron! Your father was not an evil man nor was your mother unchaste." **29.** Then she pointed at him. They said, "How can we speak to one who is an infant in the cradle?" **30.** He said, "Truly I am a servant of God. He has given me the Book and made me a prophet. **31.** He has blessed me wherever I may be and bided me with prayer and almsgiving for as long as I live. **32.** He bid me to be compliant toward my mother. He has not made me overbearing and despicable. **33.** Peace be upon me the day I was born, the day I die, and the day I am raised alive!" **34.** That is Jesus, the son of Mary, a statement of truth that they doubt. **35.** It is not for God to take a child. Glory be to Him! When He decrees a thing, He only says to it, "Be!" and it is. **36.** "Truly God is my Lord and your Lord, so worship Him. This is a straight path." **37.** Yet the parties differed among themselves. Woe unto those who disbelieve from the witnessing of a tremendous day! **38.** How well will they hear and how well will they see on the Day they come unto Us? But today, the wrongdoers will be in obvious error. **39.** Warn them of the Day of Regret, when the matter will have been decreed, while they were unmindful and did not believe. **40.** Indeed, We will inherit the earth and whatever is on it. Unto Us, they will be returned. **41.** Remember Abraham in the Book. He was indeed truthful, and a prophet **42.** when he said to his father, "O my father! Why do you worship what does not hear or see, nor benefit you in any way? **43.** O my father! Truly knowledge has come to me that has not come to you. Therefore, follow me and I will guide you toward a straight path. **44.** O my father! Do not worship Satan. Satan is indeed disobedient toward the Compassionate. **45.** O my father! Truly I fear that a punishment from the Compassionate will adjoin you such that you will become a friend of Satan." **46.** He said, "Do you reject my gods, O Abraham? If you do not stop, I will certainly stone you. Go away from me for a long period of time!" **47.** He said, "Peace be upon you! I will seek forgiveness for you from my Lord. Truly

He has been gracious to me. 48. I will remove myself from you and what you call upon besides God. I will call upon my Lord. Perhaps if I call upon my Lord, I will not be desolate." 49. So when he had withdrawn from them and what they called upon besides God, We granted him Isaac and Jacob, and We made a prophet of each. 50. We bestowed some of Our mercy upon them and ordained for them a sublime lingua of truth. 51. Remember Moses in the Book. He was indeed devoted, a messenger and a prophet. 52. We called out to him from the right side of the Mount and drew him near in private discourse. 53. We bestowed upon him from Our Mercy, his brother Aaron, a prophet. 54. Remember Ismael in the Book. He was indeed true to the promise. He was messenger and a prophet. 55. He used to bid his people to prayer and almsgiving, and he was pleasing to his Lord. 56. Remember Idrīs in the Book. He was indeed truthful and a prophet. 57. We raised him to a sublime station. 58. Those are whom God has blessed among the prophets of the progeny of Adam, and of those whom We carried with Noah and the progeny of Abraham and Israel, and of those whom We had chosen and guided. When the signs of the Compassionate were recited to them, they would drop in prostration, weeping. 59. They were then succeeded by a generation who ignored their prayer and followed their desires. As such, they will embrace evil, 60. except those who repent, believe, and perform righteousness. It is they who will enter the Garden and they will not be wronged in the least. 61. Gardens of Eden, those which the Compassionate promised His servants in the Unseen. His Promise will indeed come to pass. 62. They will only hear "Peace" and no vain talk there. There, they will have their sustenance in the morning and evening. 63. This is the Garden We will bequeath unto those among Our Servants who were reverent. 64. "We will not descend except by the Command of your Lord. Unto Him belongs what is before us and what is behind us and what lies in between. Your Lord is not forgetful—65. the Lord of the heavens and the earth and whatever is between them, worship Him and be persistent in His worship. Do you know of any who carries His name?" 66. A human says, "When I am dead, will I be brought forth alive?" 67. Does man not remember that We created him before, when he was nothing? 68. By your Lord! We will certainly gather them and the demons. We will certainly bring them around Hell on their knees. 69. Then We will indeed yank from every group whoever among them was most insolent toward the Compassionate. 70. We will then assuredly know those who mostly deserve to burn therein. 71. There is not one of you, but that he will approach it. It is a decree determined by Your Lord. 72. We will then save those who are reverent and leave the wrongdoers there on their knees. 73. When Our signs are recited unto them as clear proof, those who disbelieve say to those who believe, "Which of the two groups is better in position or greater in influence?" 74. How many a generation have We destroyed before them who were finer in possessions and outer appearance. 75. Say, "Whoever is in error, the Compassionate will extend his term until they see what they have been promised, be it the punishment or the Hour, they will know whose position is worse, and whose forces are weaker." 76. God increases in guidance those who are rightly guided. Enduring good deeds are better in reward with your Lord, and better in return. 77. Have you not observed the one who disbelieves in Our signs, and says, "I will be given wealth and children." 78. Has he penetrated the Unseen or made an agreement with the Compassionate? 79. No, but instead, We will record what he says, and We will prolong his punishment. 80. We will inherit from him what he claims, and he will come to Us alone. 81. They have taken gods besides God to be their idols. 82. But instead, they will disavow what they worshipped and become adversaries unto them. 83. Have you not observed how We unleash the demons on the disbelievers to provoke them cleverly? 84. So do not rush against them. We are indeed counting the number of days out to them. 85. On the Day We gather the reverent to the Compassionate as an honored delegation, 86. We drive the guilty into Hell as a thirsty herd. 87. They will have no power of intercession except for the one who has made an agreement with the Compassionate. 88. They say, "The Compassionate has taken a child." 89. You have indeed alleged a terrible thing. 90. The heavens are ready to burst and the earth to split apart and the mountains to fall in ruins, 91. that they should claim the Compassionate has a child! 92. It is not fitting for the Compassionate to take on a child. 93. There is none in the heavens and on the earth but that it comes to the Compassionate as a servant. 94. He has taken account of them and has precisely numbered them. 95. Each of them will approach him alone on the Day of Resurrection. 96. Indeed, those who believe and perform good deeds will be granted love by the Compassionate. 97. We have only made this easy on your tongue that you may give good news to the reverent and warn a contentious people. 98. How many a generation before them have We destroyed? Do you see even one of them or hear so much as a whisper from them?

Surah 20

TĀ HĀ

Tā Hā

In the Name of God, the Compassionate, the Merciful

1. *Tā Hā* **2.** We did not send down the Quran to you that you should be distressed, **3.** but only as a reminder to one who fears **4.** a revelation from He who created the earth and the high heavens. **5.** The Compassionate ascended the Throne. **6.** To Him belongs whatever is in the heavens, whatever is on the earth, whatever is between them, and whatever lies beneath the ground. **7.** If you speak aloud, He truly knows what is secret and how much more is still hidden. **8.** God, there is no god but He. To Him belong the Most Beautiful Names. **9.** Has the story of Moses come to you? **10.** When he saw a fire and said to his family, "Stay here. Truly I perceive a fire. Perhaps I will bring you a firebrand or find guidance at the fire." **11.** Then when he arrived at it, We called on him, "O Moses! **12.** Truly I am your Lord. Take off your shoes. You are in the sacred valley of Tuwā. **13.** I have chosen you! Therefore, listen to what is revealed. **14.** Indeed, I am God. There is no god but I, so worship Me and perform prayer for the remembrance of Me. **15.** The Hour is certainly coming. I keep it hidden that every soul will be rewarded for its endeavors. **16.** So do not let he who disbelieves and follows his desires divert you from it, else you will perish. **17.** What is that in your right hand, O Moses?" **18.** He said, "It is my staff. I lean upon it, beat down fodder for my sheep, and I find other uses for it." **19.** He said, "Cast it, O Moses!" **20.** Then he cast it and behold, it was a serpent moving swiftly. **21.** He said, "Do not fear. Take hold of it! We will restore it to its former condition. **22.** Draw your hand to your side. It will come forth 'white,' unharmed, as another sign **23.** that We may show you some of Our greatest signs. **24.** Go unto Pharoah! Truly he has transgressed." **25.** He said, "My Lord! Expand my breast for me! **26.** Make my affair easy for me, **27.** and untie a knot from my tongue, **28.** so they may understand my speech. **29.** Appoint a manager for me among my family,

30. namely, my brother, Aaron. 31. Increase my strength through him, 32. And make him a partner in my affair, 33. that we may glorify You abundantly, 34. and remember You abundantly. 35. For indeed, You see us both." 36. He said, "You have been granted your request, O Moses! 37. We have indeed conferred a favor upon you another time, 38. when we inspired your mother with the revelation: 39. 'Place him in a crate and cast it at sea. Then the sea will discharge him upon the bank. An enemy unto Me and an enemy unto him will take him.' I bestowed on you a love from Me, that you might be reared under My eye. 40. When your sister went forth and said, 'Should I show you one who can nurse him?' Thus We returned you to your mother, that she might be comforted, and she would not grieve. Then you slew a man, but We saved you from distress, and We tested you through trials. Thereafter you spent years among the people of Midian. Then you came at the decreed time, O Moses. 41. I have selected you for Myself. 42. Go forth with My signs, you and your brother, and do not tire in remembrance of Me. 43. Go to Pharoah, both of you! Truly he has transgressed! 44. Yet speak gently to him that perhaps he may remember or be afraid." 45. They said, "Our Lord! We indeed fear that he will deal hastily with us or that he will transgress." 46. He said, "Do not fear! I am truly with both of you. I hear and I see." 47. So approach him and say, "We are truly the two messengers of your Lord. So send forth with us the Children of Israel and do not punish them. We have brought you a sign from your Lord. Peace be upon him who follows guidance! 48. Truly it has been revealed to us that punishment will come upon he who lies and turns away." 49. He said, "Who is the Lord of you two, O Moses?" 50. He said, "Our Lord is He who gives everything its creation and then guides it." 51. He said, "Then what is the situation with former generations?" 52. He said, "Knowledge of that is with my Lord in a Book. He does not make a mistake, nor does He forget—53. the One Who made the earth a cradle and spread pathways for you there. He sent water down from the sky, by which We extracted diverse pairs of vegetation, saying, 54. 'Eat and pasture your livestock.'" Truly in that are signs for those endowed with insight. 55. From it We created you and to it We will bring you back. Then from it, We will bring you out once again. 56. Indeed, We showed him Our signs—all of them, yet he denied and rejected them. 57. He said, "Have you come to us to expel us from our land with your sorcery, O Moses? 58. We will certainly produce sorcery like it for you. So appoint a meeting between you and us at a neutral place, which neither you nor we will fail to keep." 59. He said, "Your meeting will be on the Day of Adornment. Let the people be gathered when the sun has risen high." 60. Then Pharoah turned away, devised his scheme, and then returned. 61. Moses said to them, "Woe unto you! Do not fabricate a lie against God, else He will destroy you by chastisement

Whoever fabricates will fail." **62.** So they debated their matter among themselves and kept their discourse a secret. **63.** They said, "These two are sorcerers who wish to do away with your exemplary way of life and to expel you from your land with their sorcery. **64.** So gather your plans and come in ranks. Today, whoever gains the upper hand will have certainly prospered!" **65.** They said, "O Moses! Either you cast or we will be the first to cast." **66.** He said, "You cast instead." Then, behold, their ropes and their staffs appeared to him, moving swiftly through their sorcery **67.** to a point where Moses sensed fear in his soul. **68.** We said, "Do not fear! Truly you are uppermost. **69.** Cast what is in your right hand. It will devour what they have produced. They have only produced a sorcerer's trick. A sorcerer does not prosper, wherever he may go." **70.** Then the sorcerers fell down in prostration. They said, "We believe in the Lord of Aaron and Moses." **71.** He said, "Do you believe in him before I give you permission? He is indeed your topmost leader, who has taught you sorcery. Now, I will cut off your hands and feet on opposite sides and I will crucify you on the trunks of palm trees. Then you will certainly know which of us has a more severe and longer-lasting punishment!" **72.** They said, "We will not favor you over the clear signs that have come to us, and He Who originated us. Therefore, decree whatever you decree — You only decree in the life of this world. **73.** Truly we believe in our Lord that He may forgive us our sins and the sorcery you compelled us to perform. God is better and more lasting!" **74.** Truly, whoever comes guilty to his Lord, Hell will be for him. He will not live or die in that place. **75.** But whoever comes unto Him as a believer and has indeed performed righteous deeds, they will be exalted in ranks — **76.** Gardens of Eden with rivers running beneath, abiding there forever. That is the reward of one who purifies himself. **77.** We indeed revealed unto Moses, "Set forth with My servants by night and strike a dry path for them through the sea. Do not be afraid of being overtaken, and fear not." **78.** Then Pharoah pursued them with his forces, but they were overtaken by the sea that engulfed them. **79.** Pharoah led his people astray and did not guide them. **80.** O Children of Israel! We have saved you from your enemies and have arranged a meeting for you on the right side of the Mount. We sent down manna and *quail* to you. **81.** Eat of the good things We have provided you, but do not exceed the limits therein, else My Wrath will be unleashed upon you. He upon whom My Wrath is unleashed will indeed perish. **82.** I am certainly most forgiving toward one who repents, believes, performs righteousness, and is rightly guided afterward. **83.** "What has made you hasten ahead of your people, O Moses?" **84.** He said, "They are close upon my footsteps, and I hurried to You my Lord that You may be satisfied." **85.** He said, "Truly We have tried your people during your absence, and the Samaritan led them astray." **86.** Then Moses returned to his people, angry and sorrowful. He said, "O my people! Did your Lord not make you a goodly Promise? Did the promise seem too long for you or did you desire that the anger of your Lord be unleashed on you such that you broke your promise with me?" **87.** They said, "We did not break our promise with you of our own will, but we were burdened by the weight of people's ornaments, so we tossed them in, and so did the Samaritan toss as well." **88.** Then he brought out a calf with a body that lowed, and they said, "This is your god and the god of Moses, for he had forgotten." **89.** Have they not observed that it does not respond to them with words, and it has no power over what harm or benefit may come to them? **90.** Aaron had indeed said to them earlier, "O my people! You are only being tested by this, and surely your Lord is the Compassionate. So follow me and obey my command!" **91.** They said, "We will not stop being its devotees until Moses returns to us." **92.** He said, "O Aaron! What held you back that when you saw them going astray, **93.** that you did not follow me? Did you disobey my command?" **94.** He said, "O son of my mother! Do not seize my beard or my head. I feared you would say, 'You have caused division among the Children of Israel, and you have not respected my word.'" **95.** He said, "What was your purpose, O Samaritan?" **96.** He said, "I saw what they did not see, so I took a handful of dust from the footprints of the messenger, and I threw it in. Thus did my soul induce me." **97.** He said, "Be gone! While in this life you can say 'Do not touch me,' but truly, for you there is a meeting that you cannot fail to keep. Now look at your god to which you remain devoted. We will certainly burn it and throw its ashes in the sea!" **98.** Your only god is God, besides Whom there is no other God. He encompasses all things in knowledge. **99.** Thus do We relate to you some of the accounts of what took place in the past. We have given you a Reminder from Our Presence. **100.** Whoever turns away from it, he will truly bear it as a burden on the Day of Resurrection, **101.** abiding in that place. The Day of Resurrection will be a burden for them. **102.** The Day the trumpet will be blown, We will gather the guilty on that Day, bleary-eyed. **103.** They will whisper among themselves, "You have only tarried ten days." **104.** We know well what they will say, "You have only tarried a day!" **105.** They ask you about the mountains. Say, "My Lord will scatter them as ashes, **106.** and will leave it a level plain. **107.** You will see no crookedness or curvature therein." **108.** On that Day, they will follow the Caller Who has no crookedness. Voices will be humbled before the Compassionate, and you will hear nothing but a murmur. **109.** On that Day, intercession will be of no benefit except for he whom the Compassionate has granted permission and is satisfied with his word. **110.** He knows what is before them and what is behind them. They do not encompass Him with knowledge. **111.** Faces will be humbled before the Living, and the Self-Subsisting. Whoever carries inequity will have failed, **112.** but whoever performs righteous deeds and is a believer will not fear neither wrong nor deprivation. **113.** Thus We have sent it down as an Arabic Quran, and We have varied the threat in that perhaps they may be reverent, or that a remembrance might occur to them. **114.** Exalted is God, the True Sovereign. Do not be in haste with the Quran before its revelation is completed for you, but rather say, "My Lord! Increase me in knowledge!" **115.** We have indeed made a covenant with Adam previously, but he forgot, and We found no dedication in him. **116.** When We said unto the angels, "Prostrate yourselves before Adam," they prostrated, except for Iblīs. He refused. **117.** We said, "O Adam! Truly this is an enemy unto you and your wife. So do not let him expel the two of you from the Garden, such that you would be miserable. **118.** Truly you will not be hungry or appear nude there. **119.** Indeed you will not go thirsty or suffer from the sun's heat there." **120.** Then Satan whispered to him. He said, "O Adam! Can I show you the Tree of Eternity and a kingdom that never decays?" **121.** As a result, they both ate from it. Their nudity became exposed to them, and they began to sew together the leaves of the Garden. Adam disobeyed his Lord, and so he erred. **122.** Then his Lord chose him, relented to him, and guided him, yet **123.** He said, "Get down from it! Both of you together, where each of you will be an enemy unto the other. If guidance should come to you from Me, then whoever follows My Guidance will not go astray or be miserable. **124.** But whoever turns away from remembrance of Me, truly he will have a miserable life, and We will raise him blind on the Day of Resurrection." **125.** He will say, "My Lord! Why have you raised me blind when I used to see?" **126.** He will say, "So it is. Our signs came to you, but you had forgotten them. As such, you will be forgotten on this Day!" **127.** Thus, do We reward whoever was reckless and did not believe in the signs of his Lord. Surely the punishment of the Hereafter is more severe and more enduring. **128.** Does it not serve as guidance for them? How many a generation have We destroyed before them amid whose dwellings they walk? In that are indeed signs for those endowed with of insight. **129.** Were it not for a Word that had already gone forth from your Lord and a term appointed, it would have been inevitable. **130.** So bear patiently with what they say and glorify the praise of your Lord before the rising of the sun and before its setting, in the hours of the night, and at the ends of the day, glorify Him that perhaps you may be content. **131.** Do not strain your eyes toward the pleasures and splendors of the life of this world that We had granted unto certain groups, that We may test them with it. The provision of your Lord is better and more enduring. **132.** Bid your family to prayer and be dedicated to it. We do not ask you for provision, but We provide for you. The end belongs to reverence. **133.** They say, "Why has he not brought us a sign from his Lord?"

Have they not received a clear sign from former scriptures? **134.** Had We destroyed them with a punishment before it, they would have said, "Our Lord! If only You had sent a messenger to us, we would have followed Your signs before being humbled and put to shame." **135.** Say, "Every person is waiting! So wait! For you will come to know those who are the companions of the straight path and those who were rightly guided."

Surah 21

THE PROPHETS

al-Anbiyã

In the Name of God, the Compassionate, the Merciful

1. People's reckoning is drawing near as they unmindfully turn away. **2.** No new Reminder came to them from their Lord, but that they listened to it while they played, **3.** their hearts distracted. The wrongdoers confide in secret conversation, "Is this not a human being like yourselves? Will you then yield to sorcery with open eyes?" **4.** He said, "My Lord knows what is spoken in Heaven and on the earth. He is the Hearing and the Knowing." **5.** Rather, they said, "Confused dreams! Maybe he made it up! Maybe he is a poet! Let him bring us a sign like those of former times were sent." **6.** No town that We destroyed before them believed, will these, then, believe? **7.** We sent no messenger before you except for men to whom We had revealed. So ask the people of Remembrance if you do not know. **8.** We did not make them bodies that did not eat food, nor were they immortal. **9.** Then We fulfilled the promise to them and saved them and whomever We desired, and We destroyed the transgressors. **10.** We have indeed sent a Book down to you as a Reminder. Do you not understand? **11.** How many a town engaged in wrongdoing have We destroyed, and then, brought other nations thereafter, into existence? **12.** When they sensed Our Might, behold, they ran away from it. **13.** "Do not run away! Return to the luxury you have been given and to your homes that perhaps you may be questioned." **14.** They said, "Oh, woe unto us! Truly we have been transgressors." **15.** Their cry did not stop until We made them as a mown field, as ashes silent and motionless. **16.** We did not create Heaven and earth and whatever is between them as an idle sport. **17.** Had We desired to take up a diversion, We would have surely taken it from what was with Us—that's if We were to do so. **18.** Rather, We cast truth against falsehood. It crushes it, and behold, it perishes. Woe unto you for what you describe! **19.** To Him belongs whoever is in the heavens and on the earth. Those who are with Him are not too arrogant to worship Him, nor do they ever grow weary. 20. They glorify night and day without tiring. 21. Or have they taken gods from the earth who resurrect? 22. Were there gods other than God in them, they would have certainly been corrupted. Therefore, glory be to God, Lord of the Throne, above what they describe. 23. He will not be questioned about what He does, but they will be questioned. 24. Or have they taken gods instead of Him? Say, "Bring me your proof! This is a Reminder for those who are with me, and a Reminder for those before me. Rather, most of them do not know the truth, so they turn away." 25. We sent no messenger before you except that We revealed to him, "Indeed there is no god but I, so worship Me!" 26. They say, "The Compassionate has taken a child." Glory be to Him! They are rather honored servants. 27. They do not precede Him in speech, and they act by His Command. 28. He knows what is before them and what is behind them. They do not intercede, save for one with whom he is satisfied. They are anxious with fear of Him. 29. Subsequently, whoever among them should say, "Truly I am a god instead of Him," will be rewarded with Hell. Thus, do We reward the transgressors. 30. Have those who disbelieve not observed that the heavens and the earth were joined together, and We split them, and We made every living thing from water. Will they then not believe? 31. We placed firm mountains in the earth in case it should shake beneath them. We made broad passages between them as pathways that perhaps they may be guided. 32. We made the sky a preserved canopy, yet they turn away from its signs. 33. It is He Who created night and day, the sun, and the moon, each gliding in an orbit. 34. We have not ordained eternal life for any human being before you, so if you die, will they live forever? 35. Every soul will taste death. As a test, We try you with evil and with good, and to Us you will be returned. 36. Whenever those who disbelieve see you, they take you in nothing but mockery— "Is this the one who mentions your gods?" It is they who are disbelievers in remembrance of the Compassionate. 37. Man is a creature of haste. I will soon show you My signs, so do not seek to hasten Me! 38. They say, "If you are truthful, when will this promise take place?" 39. If those who disbelieved but knew of the time when they will not be able to hold the Fire back from their faces or from their backs, and nor will they be helped. 40. Instead, it will arrive at them suddenly and confound them. They will then not be able repel it, nor will they be granted respite. 41. Messengers were certainly mocked before you. Then those who mocked them were overtaken by what they used to mock. 42. Say, "Who will protect you night and day from the Compassionate?" But they would rather turn away from the remembrance of their Lord. 43. Or do they have gods to defend them instead of Us? They cannot help themselves, nor are they given protection against Us. 44. Rather, We allowed them and their fathers to enjoy themselves until their lives were prolonged. Do they not perceive how We come upon the land, reducing it of its outlying borders? Is it they who will prevail? **45.** Say, "I only warn you through a revelation," but the deaf do not hear the Call when they are warned. **46.** If a breath of your Lord's Punishment were to touch them, they would certainly say, "Oh woe unto us. Truly, we were transgressors." **47.** We will set up the scales of justice on the Day of Resurrection, and no soul will be wronged in the least. Even if it were the weight of a mustard seed, We will bring it forth, and We are sufficient as Reckoners. **48.** Indeed We gave Moses and Aaron the Criterion, a radiant light, and a reminder for the reverent **49.** who fear their Lord unseen, and who are wary of the Hour. **50.** This is a blessed Reminder that We have sent down. Will you then deny it? **51.** Indeed We gave Abraham his uprightness in past conduct. We knew him well **52.** when he said to his father and his people, "What are these figures that you are worshipping?" **53.** They said, "We found our fathers worshipping them." **54.** He said, "You and your fathers have surely been in evident error." **55.** They said, "Have you brought us the truth or are you among those who play around?" **56.** He said, "Indeed your Lord is the Lord of the heavens and the earth, Who originated them. I am among those who bear witness unto this. **57.** By God! I will plot against your idols after you have turned your backs." **58.** Subsequently, he broke them into pieces except for the largest among them that perhaps they might resort to it. **59.** They said, "Who has done this to our gods? Truly he is among the transgressors!" **60.** They said, "We heard a young man mention them. He is called Abraham." **61.** They said, "So bring him before the eyes of the people that perhaps they may bear witness." **62.** They said, "Was it you who did this to our gods, O Abraham?" **63.** He said, "Indeed it was the largest among them who did this. Therefore, question them if they speak!" **64.** As a result, they consulted among themselves and said, "Truly, you are the wrongdoers!" **65.** Then they reverted: "You certainly know that these do not speak!" **66.** He said, "Do you worship besides God what will not benefit or harm you in any way? **67.** Repulsion be upon you, and upon what you worship besides God. Do you not understand?" **68.** They said, "Burn him, and protect your gods, if you are willing to take action!" **69.** We said, "O Fire! Be of coolness and peace for Abraham." **70.** They desired to plot against him, but We made them the greatest losers. **71.** We delivered him and Lot to the land that We had blessed for all nations. **72.** We bestowed upon him Isaac and Jacob as an additional gift. We made each of them virtuous. **73.** We made them imams guiding according to Our Command. We revealed to them to perform good deeds, perform prayer and to give of alms. They were worshippers of Us. **74.** As for Lot, We gave him judgment and knowledge and We saved him from the town that was committing evil deeds. They were indeed an evil and sinful people. **75.** We admitted him to Our Mercy. He was indeed among the righteous. **76.** Remember Noah when he cried out previously; We answered him and saved his family from great distress. **77.** We helped him against those who rejected Our signs. Truly they were an evil nation, so We drowned them all together. **78.** Remember David and Solomon when they rendered judgment regarding the tilth when the people's sheep had strayed there by night. We were Witness to their judgment. **79.** We clarified it to Solomon, and to both, We gave judgment and knowledge. We compelled the mountains and the birds to glorify along with David. We were the performers. **80.** We taught him how to make garment-shields for you to protect you against your own violence, but are you thankful? **81.** And to Solomon, the wind blew violently. It ran by his command to the land that We had blessed. We are aware of all things. **82.** Among the demons are those who dove deep for him and performed other deeds besides this. We guarded them. **83.** Remember Job when he cried unto his Lord. "Truly affliction has seized me! You are the most Merciful of the Merciful." **84.** Therefore, We answered him and removed the affliction that was upon him. We gave him his family and the like to be with them as a Mercy from Us and a reminder to the worshippers. **85.** Remember Ismael, Idrīs, and Dhu'l-Kifl—each was among the patient. **86.** We admitted them to Our Mercy. Truly they are among the righteous. **87.** Remember Dhu'l-Nūn, when he departed in wrath and thought We had no power over him. Then he cried out from the depths of darkness, "There is no god but You! Glory be to You! Truly I have been among the transgressors." **88.** We answered him and saved him from grief. Thus, do We save the believers. **89.** Remember Zachariah when he cried out to his Lord, "My Lord! Do not leave me childless though You are the best of inheritors." **90.** So We answered him. We cured his wife and granted him Yehya. Truly they were quick to perform good deeds. They called upon Us with desire and with apprehension, and they were humble before Us. **91.** As for she who guarded her chastity, We breathed of Our Spirit into her and made her and her son a sign for the worlds. **92.** Indeed this is your nation, a single nation, and I am your Lord. Therefore, worship Me! **93.** But they partitioned their affair among one another. However, each will return unto Us. **94.** There will be no ingratitude for whoever performs righteous deeds and is a believer. We are indeed the recorders for him. **95.** There will be a prohibition for any town We have destroyed. They will not return **96.** until the time Gog and Magog are let through, and they swiftly swarm from every hill. **97.** The true promise is drawing near. Behold! There will be the fixed stare of those who disbelieved, "Oh woe to us! We have certainly been unmindful of this! We have indeed been transgressors." **98.** What you worshipped besides God will indeed serve as fuel for Hell. You will surely arrive at it. **99.** If these had been gods, they would not have arrived at it, but each will abide therein. **100.** They will be sighing therein and not be able to hear. **101.** Indeed those who had previously received Our Blessings will be far removed of it. **102.** They will not hear the slightest sound of it and will abide in what their souls had desired. **103.** The great terror will not grieve them, and the angels will greet them. "This is your Day, which you were promised!" **104.** On that Day, We will roll up the sky like the rolling of scrolls for Scriptures. Just as We produced the first creation, We will return it. This is a promise binding upon Us. We will indeed fulfill it. **105.** We have truly written in the Psalms after the Reminder that My righteous servants will inherit the earth. **106.** Indeed in this, is a proclamation for a worshipful people. **107.** We did not send you except as a mercy unto the worlds. **108.** Say, "It has only revealed unto me that your God is One God. So will you be Muslims?" **109.** But if they turn away, say, "I have proclaimed equally to all of you and I certainly do not know whether what you were promised is near or far. **110.** He indeed, knows of what is overtly spoken, and He knows of what you conceal. **111.** I do not know. Perhaps it is a trial for you—an enjoyment for a while." **112.** He said, "My Lord, judge with justice! And our Lord, the Most Compassionate, is the One whose help is sought against what you claim."

Surah 22

THE PILGRIMAGE
al-Hajj

In the Name of God, the Compassionate, the Merciful

1. O people! Revere your Lord. Truly the quaking of the Hour is a tremendous thing! **2.** On the Day you perceive it, every nursing woman will forget about what she nurses, and every pregnant woman will deliver her unborn, and people will appear to be drunk when they are not drunk. Rather, the Punishment of God is severe. **3.** Among people will be those who dispute about God without knowledge and follow every defiant demon, **4.** whereupon it is decreed that whoever takes him as a protector, will be led astray. He will guide him unto the punishment of the Inferno. **5.** O people! If you are in doubt of the Resurrection, remember that We created you from dust, then from a drop of semen, then from a blood clot, then from a lump of flesh, formed and unformed, that We have made clear to you. We cause what We will to remain in the wombs for a term appointed. Then We bring you forth as an infant that you may reach full-fledged adulthood. Some are taken by death, and some are sent back to the geriatric age, that he will no longer know what he once knew. You see the earth lifeless, but when We send water down upon it, it stirs and swells and produces a delight from every pair. **6.** That is because God is the Truth, because He gives life to the dead, because He is Powerful over all things, **7.** because the Hour is coming in which there is no doubt, and because He will resurrect whoever is in the graves. **8.** Among people are those who argue about God without knowledge, without guidance, and without a Book of Enlightenment, **9.** while turning aside and causing others to stray from the way of God. Such will be disgraced in this world, and We will make him taste the penalty of Burning Fire on the Day of Resurrection. **10.** That is because of what your hands have sent forth for truly, God does not wrong His servants. **11.** Among people are some who worship God while on the edge. If good arises for him, He is comforted by it, but if a trial befalls him, he is turned over on his face losing in this world and in the Hereafter. That is the manifest loss. **12.** He calls upon what is apart from God and what neither harms him nor benefits him. That is straying far indeed. **13.** He calls upon one whose harm is more probable than his benefit. What an evil affiliate and what an evil companion. **14.** God will indeed admit those who believe and those who perform righteous deeds to Gardens with rivers running beneath. Truly God does whatever He desires. **15.** Whoever believes that God will not support him in this world and the Hereafter, let him extend a rope to the Heaven and sever, then see if this act removes his frustration. **16.** So do We send it down as clear signs, and so does God guide whomever He wills. **17.** God will indeed judge among those who believe and those who are Jews, the Sabeans, the Christians, the Magians, and the idolators, on the Day of Resurrection. Truly God is Witness over all things. **18.** Have you not observed that unto God prostrates whoever is in the heavens and whoever is on the earth: the sun, the moon, the stars, the mountains, the trees, the beasts, and many from among people? But punishment has come due for many of them. No one will be honored from whomever God disgraces. Truly God does whatever He wills. **19.** These two adversaries dispute about their Lord. As for those who disbelieve, clothing of fire will be cut out for them, and boiling liquid will be poured over their heads. **20.** It will scald their insides and melt their skin. **21.** For them, there will be iron hooks. **22.** While in their grief, and whenever they desire to leave it, they will be returned to it, and told, "Taste the penalty of Burning Fire!" **23.** God will indeed admit those who believe and perform righteous deeds to Gardens with rivers running beneath. There, they will be adorned with gold and pearl bracelets, and their garments made of silk. **24.** They will be shown to what is pure speech and will be guided to the path of the Praised. **25.** Truly, for those who disbelieve and turn from the way of God and the Sacred Mosque, which We have made equal for all people, those living there and those who come from abroad, and whoever chooses to deviate wrongfully therein, We will make him taste a painful punishment. **26.** Remember when We assigned for Abraham the location of the Sacred House: "Attribute no partners unto Me and purify My House for those who circumambulate, those who stand, and those who bow and prostrate. **27.** Proclaim the *hajj* for people. They will come to you on foot and on every kind of lean beast. They will come from the depth of mountainous highways **28.** to observe the benefits for themselves and to mention the Name of God on designated days, over the four-legged livestock He has provided them. So eat thereof and feed the desolate poor. **29.** Then let them complete their prescribed rites, fulfill their vows, and circumambulate the Ancient House." **30.** So it is! From his Lord's perspective, whoever honors the sacred rites of God, it will be better for him. Livestock is lawful for you, save what is recited unto you. Therefore, avoid the filth of idols, and avoid false speech **31.** while being upright before God. Do not attribute partners unto Him. Whoever attributes partners unto God, it is as if he fell from the sky and the birds snatched him, or the wind swept him to a faraway place. **32.** So it is. Whoever honors the rituals of God, it truly comes from the piety of hearts. **33.** You will have benefits in them for the appointed term. Thereafter, their legitimate place of sacrifice is near the Ancient House. **34.** We have appointed a rite for every nation that they may mention the name of God over the livestock He has provided them. Your God is One God, so submit unto Him, and give good news to the humble **35.** whose hearts tremble when God is mentioned, who patiently endure what happens to them, who perform prayer, and who spend of what We have provided them. **36.** We have placed the sacrificial camels for you among God's rituals. There is good for you in them, so mention the name of God over them as they line up. Then when they have fallen upon their flanks, eat of them, and feed the satisfied and the supplicant. Consequently, We have made them subservient unto you that perhaps you may be thankful. **37.** Neither their flesh nor their blood will reach God, but your reverence will reach Him. So He has made them subservient to you that you might magnify God for having guided you. Give good news to the virtuous. **38.** Indeed God defends those who believe. Truly God does not love any ungrateful traitor. **39.** Permission is given to those who fight because they were wronged. God is indeed able to help those **40.** who were wrongfully expelled from their homes only for saying, "Our Lord is God." If God did not restrain one group of people through another, monasteries, churches, synagogues, and mosques—where God's name is abundantly commemorated—would surely have been demolished. God will certainly help those who help Him—God is indeed Strong and Mighty— **41.** and those who, if We were to establish them on the earth, would establish prayer, give alms, enjoin what is right, and forbid what is wrong. Ultimately, all matters rest with God. **42.** If they deny you, the people of Noah denied before them as did the Ād, the Thamŭd, **43.** the people of Abraham, the people of Lot, **44.** and the inhabitants of Midian. Moses was denied as well, but I granted the disbelievers a respite. Then I seized them in punishment. How terrible was My rejection! **45.** How many towns have We destroyed for their wrongdoing, leaving them collapsed upon their roofs, with abandoned wells and towering castles! **46.** Have they not traveled through the land, that they might have hearts to understand with or ears to hear with. It is indeed not the eyes that go blind, but it is hearts within hearts that go blind. **47.** They want you to expedite the punishment. But God will not fail His promise. Truly a day with your Lord is like a thousand years from what you reckon. **48.** How many a town did I grant respite while it did wrong, then I apprehended it, and to Me is the final destiny. **49.** Say, "O people! I am only a clear warner to you!" **50.** As for those who believe and perform righteous deeds, for them there will be forgiveness and a generous provision. **51.** However, those who strive to thwart Our signs will be the inhabitants of Hellfire. **52.** We did not send a messenger or a prophet before you, but that when he had a desire, Satan would launch into his desire, and God would revoke what Satan launched. Then God makes His signs firm. God is Knowing and Wise, **53.** that He might make what Satan launched to be a trial for those who have a disease in their hearts and, and those whose hearts are stiffened. Truly the wrongdoers are in distant schism. **54.** Those who have been given knowledge know that 'this is the truth from your Lord' and thus believe in it, that their hearts may be humbled before Him. God truly guides those who believe unto a straight path. **55.** Yet those who disbelieve remain in doubt over it, until the Hour suddenly comes upon them, or the punishment of an empty day comes upon them. **56.** Sovereignty on that Day will be God's. He will judge between them. Those who believe and perform righteous deeds will be in Gardens of Bliss, **57.** but those who disbelieve and deny Our signs will have a humiliating punishment. **58.** As for those who emigrate in the way of God, and are slain or die, God will certainly provide them with a goodly provision. God is indeed the best of providers. **59.** He will surely admit them through an entrance in which they will be well pleased. God is indeed Knowing and Clement. **60.** So it is. Whoever punishes with the like of what he was punished and was re-assaulted, God will certainly help him. Truly God is Pardoning and Forgiving. **61.** That is because God fuses night into day and fuses day into night. God is indeed Hearing and Seeing. **62.** That is because God is the Truth and what they call upon instead of Him is false because God is the Exalted and the Great. **63.** Have you not observed that God sends water down from Heaven and then the earth becomes green? Truly God is Kind and Knowledgeable. **64.** To Him belongs whatever is in the heavens and whatever is on the earth. God is indeed the Self-Sufficient and the Praised. **65.** Have you not observed that God has made whatever is on the earth subservient to you while the ship sails over the sea by His Command? He withholds the sky from falling on the earth, save by His Leave. God is indeed Kind and Merciful unto people. **66.** It is He Who gave you, life then He causes you to die, then He gives you, life. Truly man is ungrateful. **67.** For every nation We have appointed a rite for them to perform, so do not let them argue with you over the matter. Appeal to your Lord. You are indeed following straight guidance. **68.** If they argue with you say, "God knows best what you do. **69.** God will judge between you on the Day of Resurrection regarding what you differed upon." **70.** Do you not know that God knows whatever is in Heaven and on the earth? That is indeed in a Book. Truly that is easy for God. **71.** They worship instead of God that for which He has sent down no authority, and that in which they have no knowledge of. The wrongdoers will have no helpers. **72.** When Our signs are recited unto them as clear proofs, you will see denial on the faces of those who disbelieve. They nearly attack those who rehearse Our signs unto them. Say, "Should I inform you of what is worse than that? The Fire God has promised to those who disbelieve. What an evil final destiny!" **73.** O People! A parable is set forth, so listen to it! Truly those who you call upon instead of God will never create a fly, even if they all gather to do so. If the fly should snatch anything away from them, they cannot retrieve it from it. Feeble are the pursuer and the pursued. **74.** They did not measure God with His True measure. Truly God is Strong and Mighty. **75.** God chooses messengers from among the angels and from among people. God is indeed Hearing and Seeing. **76.** He knows of what is before them and what is behind them and unto God all matters are returned. **77.** O you who believe! Bow, prostrate, and worship your Lord and do good that perhaps you may prosper. **78.** "Strive for God as He deserves to be striven for. He has chosen you and placed no difficulty upon you in the religion. This is the way of your father Abraham. He named you Muslims in the past, and now as well, so that the Messenger may bear witness over you, and you may bear witness over humanity. Therefore, establish prayer, give alms, and hold firmly to God. He is your Protector — what an excellent Protector and what an excellent Helper!"

Surah 23

THE BELIEVERS

al-Mu'minūn

In the Name of God, the Compassionate, the Merciful

1. Successful are the believers **2.** who are humble in their prayers, **3.** who avoid vain speech, **4.** who give alms, **5.** and who guard their chastity, **6.** except from their spouses or those whom their right hands possess, for they are not to be blamed — **7.** and whoever seeks beyond that, are transgressors. **8.** Those who guard their trusts and their covenants, **9.** and those who guard their prayers, **10.** it is they who are the heirs, **11.** and those who will inherit Paradise to abide therein. **12.** We certainly created man from an extract of clay, **13.** then We made him a drop of semen in a secure lodging, **14.** then of the drop of semen, We created a blood clot, then of the blood clot, We created a lump of flesh, then of the lump of flesh, We created bones where We covered the bones with flesh, then We brought him into existence as another creation. Blessed is God, the best of creators! **15.** Then indeed, after that, you will die. **16.** Then, on the Day of Resurrection, you will certainly be raised up. **17.** We have indeed created seven paths above you. We were not unmindful of creation. **18.** We sent water down from Heaven in a measured amount and established it upon the earth. We are indeed capable of taking it away. **19.** In doing so We brought forth gardens of date palms and grapevines from which you will have many fruits to eat, **20.** and a tree springing from Mount Sinai to produce oil and a seasoning for food. **21.** In livestock, there is certainly a lesson for you. We give you drink from what is in their bellies and You have many benefits from them. You eat from them, **22.** and you are carried upon them and upon ships. **23.** Indeed, We sent Noah to his people, and he said, "O my people! Worship God! You have no other God than Him. Will you not be reverent?" **24.** But the notables among his people who disbelieved said, "This is only a human being like yourselves. He desires to set himself above you. Had God willed, He would have sent angels down. We did not hear of this from our forefathers. 25. He is no more than a man possessed, so let us wait a while." 26. He said, "My Lord! Help me, for they deny me." 27. Subsequently, We revealed unto him, "Build the Ark before Our eyes and by Our revelation. Then when Our Command arrives and the reservoir gushes forth, place there two of every kind, and your family, except for those against whom the Word has already gone forth. Do not address Me concerning those who did wrong, for indeed, they will be drowned. 28. When you and those with you have mounted the Ark, say, "Praise be to God Who has saved us from the wrongdoing people." 29. Say, "My Lord! Harbor me in a blessed harbor. You are the best of those who harbor." 30. Indeed, in that are signs and indeed We are putting people to the test. 31. We then produced another generation after them. 32. We sent them a messenger from among themselves stating, "You must worship God! You have no other god than him! Will you not be reverent?" 33. The notables of his people who disbelieved and denied the meeting in the Hereafter, and unto whom We had given luxury in the life of this world said, "This is but a human being like you. He eats from what you eat and drinks from what you drink. 34. So if you obey a human being like yourselves, you will certainly be losers. 35. Does he promise you that when you are dead and are dust and bones, that you will truly be resurrected? 36. Improbable, improbable is what you are promised. 37. There is nothing but our life in this world. We die and we live, and we will not be resurrected. 38. He is only a man making up lies against God and we are not ones to believe him." 39. He said, "My Lord! Help me for they deny me." 40. He said, "They will soon become remorseful." 41. Subsequently, the Cry righteously seized them, and We turned them into rubbish. So away with a wrongdoing nation. 42. We then produced another generation after them. 43. No nation can advance or delay its term. 44. We then sent Our messengers in succession. Whenever a messenger arrived at its people, they would deny him. Therefore, We caused them to follow one another and made them the objects of stories. So away with a people who do not believe. 45. Then We sent Moses with his brother Aaron with Our signs and a clear authority 46. to Pharoah and his notables. But they were arrogant and were an insolent nation. 47. They said, "Should we believe in two human beings like us, while their people are the slaves we possess?" 48. But they denied them and thus were among the destroyed. 49. We truly gave the Book to Moses that perhaps they may be guided. 50. We made the son of Mary and his mother a sign and We gave them refuge on a high ground with stability and a flowing spring. 51. O messengers! Eat of the good things and perform righteousness. Truly I know of what you do. 52. Indeed, this nation of yours is one nation and I am your Lord, so revere Me. 53. But they set forth their affair upon different scriptures, each party rejoicing in what it held. 54. So leave them in their confusion for a while. 55. Do they figure that after We provided them with wealth and children, 56. We will advance unto them with good? Truly, they are unaware. 57. Indeed, those who are in awe for fear of their Lord, 58. those who believe in the signs of their Lord, 59. those who do not attribute partners unto their Lord, 60. and those who give what they give while their hearts quiver with fear that they will return to their Lord, 61. it is they who rush toward good deeds by taking the lead in them. 62. We task no soul beyond its capacity, and with Us is a Book that speaks in truth. They will not be wronged. 63. Their hearts are confused over this, and there are other deeds they continue to perpetrate, 64. until We overtake those who lived in luxury by punishment. As a result, they will beg! 65. Do not plead today! Truly you will not be helped by Us! 66. My signs were recited unto you, but you used to turn on your heels, 67. arrogant in relation to it and speaking foolishly by night. 68. Have they not contemplated the Word, or has there come to them what did not come to their forefathers? 69. Or do they not know their messenger and so deny him? 70. Or do they say, "He is possessed?" Rather, he has brought them the truth, but most of them are opposed to the truth. 71. Were the truth to follow their desires, the heavens, and the earth and those contained in that place would have been corrupted. We truly gave them their reminder, but they turned away from their reminder. 72. Do you ask for compensation though the reward of your Lord is better? He is the best of providers. 73. You have certainly called them unto a straight path. 74. Surely those who do not believe in the Hereafter are deviating from the path. 75. Were We to show them mercy and remove whatever wrong was upon them, they would certainly persist and wandering confused in their transgression. 76. We seized them with punishment. They did not surrender to their Lord, nor did they humble themselves 77. until We opened a gate of severe punishment upon them. Observe how they despair there! 78. It is He Who formed your hearing, vision, and hearts. Little do you show gratitude! 79. It is He Who created you on the earth, and unto Him you will be gathered. 80. It is He who gives life and death. Unto Him belongs the alternation between night and day. Will you not understand then? 81. On the contrary, they speak in the likeness of their forefathers. 82. They say, "What, when we die and become dust and bones, we will be resurrected? 83. We and our fathers were truly warned of this beforehand. This is nothing but tales of the ancients." 84. Say, "To whom belongs the earth and whoever is upon it, if you know?" 85. They will say, "To God." Say, "Will you not, then, be mindful?" 86. Say, "Who is the Lord of the seven heavens and the Lord of the great Throne?" 87. They will say, "God." Say, "Will you not then be reverent?" 88. "In Whose Hand is the governance of all things? He protects but is not protected against, if you truly know." 89. They will say, "In God's." Say, "How then are you deluded?" 90. Rather, We have sent them the truth, but they are indeed liars. 91. God has not taken a child, and neither are there any gods with Him because each god would have taken what he created and some of them would have overcome others. Glory be to God above what they attribute! 92. Knower of the Unseen and the Seen! He is exalted above the partners they attribute. 93. Say, "My Lord! If only You would show me what they are promised! 94. So my Lord, do not place me among the wrongdoing people!" 95. We are certainly able to show you what We promised them. 96. Take charge by practicing what is better than evil. We know best what they attribute. 97. Say, "My Lord! I seek refuge from You from the temptations of demons. 98. I seek refuge in You, my Lord, in case they approach me." 99. Until death reaches one of them, he says, "My Lord! Return me, 100. that perhaps I will work righteousness in what I left behind," but indeed, these are words that he speaks. Behind them is a barrier until the Day they are resurrected. 101. When the trumpet is blown, there will be no kinship between them that Day, nor will they question one another. 102. As for those whose scales are heavy, it is they who will prosper. 103. As for those whose scales are light, it is they who will have lost their souls and will abide in Hell. 104. The Fire will blast across their faces, and they will grin there. 105. "Were My signs not recited unto you, and you denied them?" 106. They will say, "Our Lord! Our wretchedness overwhelmed us, and we were a people astray. 107. Our Lord! Remove us from it. Then if we revert, we will indeed be wrongdoers." 108. He will say, "Be gone therein and do not speak to Me." 109. Truly there was a group of My servants who would say, "Our Lord! We believe, so forgive us and have mercy upon us. You are the best of those who are merciful." 110. But you took them in mockery until it made you forget My remembrance. You used to laugh at them. 111. Truly, I have rewarded them today for having been patient. They are indeed the triumphant. 112. He will say, "How many years did you tarry on earth?" 113. They will say, "We tarried a day or part of a day but ask those who keep count." 114. He will say, "You tarried but a little, if you only knew." 115. "Did you assume then, that We created you frivolously, and that you would not be returned to Us?" 116. So exalted is God, the True Sovereign. There is no god but He, the Lord of the noble Throne. 117. Whoever calls upon another god along with God, for which he has no proof, his reckoning is with God. The disbelievers will truly not prosper. 118. Say, "My Lord! Forgive and show mercy, for you are the most Merciful of the merciful."

Surah 24

LIGHT

al-Nūr

In the Name of God, the Compassionate, the Merciful

1. A sūrah that We have sent down and ordained, and revealed in clear signs, so that perhaps you may remember. 2. As for the adulterer and the adulteress, flog them each one hundred lashes. Do not let sympathy for them overcome you regarding God's Judgment if you believe in God and the Last Day. Let their punishment be witnessed by a group of believers. 3. The adulterer should only marry an adulteress or idolatress, and the adulteress should only be married to an adulterer or idolater. Such a thing is forbidden to the believers. 4. As for those who accuse chaste women, but do not produce four witnesses, flog them eighty lashes and never accept any testimony from them. It is they who are the sinful, 5. save those who repent thereafter and make amends. God is indeed Forgiving and Merciful. 6. As for those who accuse their spouses and have no witnesses but themselves, then the testimony of one of them should be four testimonies, swearing by God that he is among the truthful, 7. and the fifth should be that the curse of God be upon him if he is among the liars. 8. The punishment should be averted from her should she give four testimonies, swearing by God that he is among the liars, 9. and the fifth that God's Wrath should come upon her if he is among the truthful. 10. It is only because of God's Bounty and Mercy upon you, for indeed God is Relenting and Wise. 11. Indeed those who brought forth the lie were a group from among you. Do not assume it to be evil for you; on the contrary, it is good for you. Unto each man among them is the sin he committed, and he among them who partook in the greater part of it will receive a significant punishment. 12. Why is it when the believing men and women heard of it, they did not think positively and say, "This is an obvious lie?" 13. Why did they not bring four witnesses to the matter? From God's perspective, when they do not bring onward

four witnesses, it is they who are liars. **14.** Were it not for God's Bounty and His Mercy upon you, in this world and in the Hereafter, you would have received a significant punishment for what you engaged in. **15.** When you accepted it with your tongues and spoke with your mouths of what you had no knowledge of, you have taken the matter lightly, though from God's perspective it is significant. **16.** Why, when you heard of it, did you not say, "It is not for us to speak of this! Glory be to You! This is a tremendous defamation!" **17.** If you are believers, God will admonish you if you ever repeat something similar. **18.** God makes the signs clear unto you. God is Knowing and Wise. **19.** Truly those who would like for indecency to be spread among those who believe, their punishment will be painful in this world and in the Hereafter. God knows and you do not know. **20.** If it were not for God's Bounty and Mercy upon you, and that God is Kind and Merciful. **21.** O you who believe! Do not follow the footsteps of Satan! Whoever follows the footsteps of Satan, truly he enjoins indecency and immorality. If it were not for God's Bounty and Mercy upon you, not one of you would be pure. But God purifies whomever He wills. God is Hearing and Knowing. **22.** Do not let the men of abundance and means among you take an oath against giving to kinsfolk and the indigent and those who emigrated in the way of God. Let them forgive and forbear. Do you not want for God to forgive you? God is Forgiving and Merciful. **23.** Indeed those who accuse chaste and heedless believing women are cursed in this world and in the Hereafter. Their punishment will be significant **24.** on the day their tongues, their hands, and their feet will bear witness against them for their actions. **25.** On that Day, God will pay them in full their fair dues. They will know that God is the Manifest Truth. **26.** Wicked women are for wicked men, and wicked men are for wicked women. Good women are for good men, and good men are for good women. They are cleared of what they say. For them, is forgiveness and a generous provision. **27.** O you who believe! Do not enter houses other than your own until you ask for permission and greet its residents. That is better for you that perhaps you may remember. **28.** If you do not find anyone there, then do not enter until you are given permission. If it is said to you, "Turn back," then turn back. That is purer for you and God knows of what you do. **29.** There is no blame on you for entering uninhabited houses wherein there is some good for you. God knows what you reveal and what you conceal. **30.** Tell the believing men to lower their eyes and to guard their privates. That is purer for them. God is indeed Aware of what they do. **31.** Tell the believing women to lower their gaze and to guard their chastity, and to not display their adornment except for what is visible thereof. Let them draw their kerchiefs over their breasts, and not display their adornment except to their husbands, or their fathers, or their sons, or their husbands' sons or their brothers, or their brothers' sons, or their sisters' sons, or their women, or those whom their right hands possess, or male attendants free of desire, or children who are unaware of the private areas of women, and they should not stomp their feet such that the ornaments they conceal become known. O believers, repent unto God all together that perhaps you may prosper. **32.** Marry those who are single among you, and the righteous among your male slaves and your female slaves. If they are poor, God will enrich them from His Bounty. God is All-Encompassing and All-Knowing. **33.** Let those who are unable to marry remain chaste until God enriches them from His Bounty. If any of those whom your right hands possess, seek a contract with you, contract with them if you know of any good in them and give them from the Wealth of God that He has provided for you. Do not compel your female slaves into prostitution if they want to remain chaste that you may gain from the goods of this world. Whoever compels them, then after having been compelled, God will truly be Forgiving and Merciful. **34.** Indeed, We have sent down to you clear signs and a description of those who have passed before you, as an admonition for the reverent. **35.** God is the Light of the heavens and the earth. The simile of His Light is like a niche with a lamp in it. The lamp is in a glass. The glass is like a shining star kindled from a blessed olive tree, neither of the East nor of the West. Its oil will thoroughly shine forth even if no fire has touched it. Light upon light. God guides unto His Light whomever He wills and sets forth parables for people. God has knowledge of all things. **36.** In Houses that God has permitted to be raised and wherein His name is remembered, He will be glorified there, morning and evening **37.** by men whom neither their trade nor their buying and selling distract from the remembrance of God, the performance of prayer, and the giving of alms. They fear the day when eyes and hearts will be turned about, **38.** that God may reward them for the best of what they performed and increase His Bounty. God provides for whomever He wills without measure. **39.** But those who disbelieve, their deeds are like a mirage on a desert plain where a thirsty man assumes it is water until he arrives upon it, then he does not find it to be anything, but he finds God there. He will then, pay him his reckoning in full, and God is swift in reckoning. **40.** Or like the darkness of a fathomless sea, covered by waves above waves with clouds above them—darknesses, one above the other. When one puts his hand out, he can hardly see it. He for whom God has not appointed any light, has no light. **41.** Have you not observed that God is glorified by whoever is in the heavens and on the earth, and by the birds and their wings? Truly each knows its prayer and its glorification, and God knows what they do. **42.** To God belongs sovereignty over the heavens and the earth and to God is the final destination. **43.** Have you not considered how God drives the clouds, joins them together, turns them into a heap, and then you see the rain pour forth from amidst these? He sends down from the sky, from the mountains of clouds, hail from which He strikes whomever He wills and from which he turns away from whomever He wills. The flash of His lightning practically takes away sight. **44.** God alternates the night and the day. In that is indeed an indication for those possessed of sight. **45.** God created every animal from water. Among them are those that walk on their bellies, and among them are those that walk on two legs, and among them are those that walk on four. God creates whatever He wills. God is indeed powerful over all things. **46.** We have indeed sent down clear signs. God guides whomever He wills unto a straight path. **47.** They say, "We believe in God and in the Messenger, and we obey." Subsequently, a group of them turns away, but those are not believers. **48.** When they are called to God and His Messenger that He may judge between them, observe how a group of them will turn away. **49.** But if they were in the right, they would have gone to Him submissively. **50.** Is there a disease in their hearts? Or do they doubt or fear that God and His Messenger will deal with them unjustly? Truly, it is they who are the wrongdoers. **51.** The only words of the believers when they are called unto God and His Messenger, that He may judge between them, will be to say, "We hear, and we obey." It is they who will prosper. **52.** Whoever obeys God and His Messenger, and who fears God and reveres Him, it is they who will triumph. **53.** They swear by God with their most solemn oaths that were you to command them, they would have certainly gone forth. Say, "Do not swear! Obedience is honorable. For indeed God is Aware of whatever you do." **54.** Say, "Obey God and obey the Messenger." But if they turn away, upon him, is his burden, and upon you, is your burden. However, if you obey him, you will be rightly guided, and nothing is ordained upon the Messenger save to preach the clear message. **55.** God has promised those among you who believe and perform righteous deeds that He will surely, make them vicegerents upon the earth just as He made those before them to be vicegerents. He will solidify their religion for them, that which He has approved for them, and He will indeed change them from a state of fear to one of safety. They will worship Me and not attribute any partners unto Me. Thereafter, whoever disbelieves, it will be they who are sinful. **56.** Perform prayer, give alms, and obey the Messenger that perhaps you may receive mercy. **57.** Do not assume that the disbelievers will obstruct on the earth. The Fire will be their abode. What a wretched final destination! **58.** O you who believe! Let those whom your right hands possess and those who have not reached maturity ask for permission to be in your presence three times: before the dawn prayer, when you remove your clothes at noon, and after the night prayer. These are the three times of privacy for you. Outside of these, there is no fault on you or them if they move about among one another. Thus does God make the signs clear to you. God is Knowing and Wise. **59.** When children among you come of age, let them ask for permission as those before them asked for permission. In this way, God makes His signs clear unto you. God is Knowing and Wise. **60.** As for women in their declining years who no longer feel a desire for intimacy, there is no blame on them to lay aside their garments without displaying any ornament, but it is better for them to modestly refrain. God is Hearing and Knowing. **61.** There is no fault against the blind, nor fault against the lame, nor against the sick, nor upon yourselves in that you eat from your houses, or your fathers' houses, or your mothers' houses, or your brothers' houses, or your sisters' houses, or your paternal uncles' houses, or your paternal aunts' houses, or your maternal uncles' houses, or your maternal aunts' houses, or those whose keys you possess, or your friend. There is no blame on you whether you eat together or separately. Therefore, when you enter houses, greet each other with a blessed and kind salutation from God. Thus does God make the signs clear to you that perhaps you may understand. **62.** The believers who believe in God and His Messenger, and who when they are with you regarding a collective matter, should not leave until they ask you for permission to leave. Truly those who ask for your permission to leave, it is they who believe in God and His Messenger. So when they ask for your permission to leave regarding some matter of theirs, give leave to whomever you will and seek forgiveness for them from God. Truly God is Forgiving and Merciful. **63.** Do not deem the Messenger's calling among you to be like you calling unto one another. Truly God knows those among you who slip away covertly. Let those who oppose his command be cautious, lest they face a trial or suffer a severe punishment. **64.** Rest assured that to God belongs whatever is in the heavens and on the earth. God certainly knows of your intentions. On the Day they will be returned unto Him, He will inform them of what they did. God has knowledge of all things.

Surah 25

THE CRITERION

al-Furqān

In the Name of God, the Compassionate, the Merciful

1. Blessed is He who sent down the Criterion to His servant that he may be a warner to the worlds. 2. He unto Whom belongs sovereignty over the heavens and the earth, Who did not take a child, Who has no partner in sovereignty, Who created everything, and then assessed it with the best of assessments. 3. Yet they have taken gods instead of Him, that create nothing and are themselves created. They have no power over what harm or benefit may come to them, and they have no power over death, or life, or resurrection. 4. The disbelievers say, "This is nothing but a lie that he has invented, and another people have helped him with it." They have indeed put forward falsehood and defamation. 5. They say, "They are ancient tales which he has had written down, and they are recited unto him morning and evening." 6. Say, "It was sent down by He Who knows the secret behind what is in the heavens and on the earth." He is indeed Forgiving and Merciful. 7. They say, "What is it with this Messenger who eats food and walks in the markets? Why is there not an angel sent down to him to be a warner with him, 8. or no treasure given to him, or no garden for him to eat from?" The transgressors say, "You follow nothing, but a bewitched man." 9. Look how they struck examples of you, but they went astray and could not find the way. 10. Blessed is He Who, if He willed would produce what is better than that—Gardens with rivers running beneath—He will produce palaces for you. 11. Rather, they deny the Hour. We have prepared an Inferno for those who deny the Hour. 12. When it sees them from a far-off place, they will hear it raging and roaring. 13. When they are bound together and cast in a tight place thereof, they will there and then plead for their own destruction. 14. "Do not beg for a single destruction on this Day but beg for many destructions!" 15. Say, "Is that better or the eternal Garden promised to the reverent?" It is a reward for them and

a final destination. **16.** They will have whatever they desire while abiding there forever. It is a binding promise upon your Lord. **17.** On the Day He gathers them and what they worship instead of God, He will say, "Was it you who caused these servants of Mine to go astray, or did they voluntarily go astray from the path?" **18.** They will say, "Glory be to You! It does not befit us to take protectors besides You. But You granted them and their father's enjoyment until they forgot the Remembrance. They were a ruined people. **19.** They have indeed denied what you said and so, you cannot thwart or assist." Whoever among you does wrong, We will make him taste a great punishment. **20.** We did not send any messengers before you but that they ate food and walked in the markets. We made some of you a trial for others. Will you be patient? Your Lord is Perceptive. **21.** Those who do not hope to meet Us say, "Why have the angels not been sent down to us, or why have we not seen our Lord?" They truly grew arrogant in their souls and insulted with great defiance. **22.** The Day they see the angels, there will be no good news for the guilty on that Day. They will say, "A barrier, forbidden!" **23.** We will turn to whatever deed they performed and make it scattered dust. **24.** That Day, the inhabitants of the Garden will have the best dwelling place and the most beautiful of rests. **25.** The Day when the heavens are riven asunder with clouds and the angels descend, **26.** on that Day, the true sovereignty will belong to the Compassionate. That will be a difficult Day for the disbelievers. **27.** That Day, the wrongdoer will bite his hands, saying, "Oh! I wish I had taken the path with the Messenger! **28.** Oh! Woe unto me! Had I not taken such a person as a friend! **29.** He indeed caused me to deviate from the Remembrance after it had come to me. Satan is the deceiver of man." **30.** The Messenger will say, "O my Lord! Truly my people have considered this Quran to be nonsense." **31.** As such, We made an enemy from among the sinners for every prophet, and your Lord is sufficient as a Guide and Helper. **32.** The disbelievers say, "Why was the Quran not sent down to him in one entity?" It is so, to strengthen your heart thereby. We recited It to you at a reasonable pace. **33.** They do not come to you with any parable but that We bring a better truth and explanation for you. **34.** Those who are gathered to Hell upon their faces will be in a worse place and further astray from the path. **35.** Truly We gave Moses the Book and made his brother his minister. **36.** Then We said, "Go to the people who have denied Our signs." We then destroyed them completely. **37.** When Noah's people denied the messengers, We drowned them and made them a sign for mankind. We have prepared for the wrongdoers a painful punishment. **38.** The Ãd and the and the inhabitants of al-Rass, and many generations between them, **39.** for each We set forth parables, and We utterly destroyed them. **40.** They truly passed through a town where it had rained an evil rain. Have they not seen it? But they did not hope for a resurrection. **41.** When they see you, they simply take you in mockery: "Is this the one whom God sent as a messenger? **42.** He would have indeed practically led us astray from our gods had we not been steadfast to them." They will know when they see the punishment who is further astray from the way. **43.** Have you observed the one who takes his own passion as his god? Would you be a guardian over him? **44.** Or do you assume that most of them hear or understand? They are indeed but like cattle. They are further astray from the way. **45.** Have you not considered how your Lord spread out the shade and had He willed, He could have made it still? Then We made the sun as a marker of it. **46.** We then withdrew it unto Ourselves a smooth withdrawal. **47.** It is He who made the night as a garment for you, made sleep for rest, and made day for resurrection. **48.** It is He who sends the winds as good news ahead of His Mercy. We send down pure water from Heaven **49.** that We may revive a dead land and give drink to the many cattle and people that We have created. **50.** Indeed We have distributed it among them that they may remember. But most people refuse to be anything but ungrateful. **51.** Had We willed, We would have sent a warner to every town. **52.** So do not conform with the disbelievers. Exert with it against them with the utmost exertion. **53.** It is He who mixed the two seas: this one, sweet and satisfying and that one, salty and bitter. He made a barrier between them and a constricted enclosure. **54.** It is He who created a human being from water and made of him lineages and marriages. Your Lord is powerful. **55.** They worship besides God what neither benefits nor harms them. The disbeliever is biased against his Lord. **56.** We only sent you to be a bearer of good news and a warner. **57.** Say, "I do not ask of you any reward for it, save whoever desires to take the path toward his Lord." **58.** Trust in the Living Who does not die and glorify His praise. God is sufficient as One Aware of the sins of His servants. **59.** It is He Who created the heavens and the earth and whatever is between them in six days, then ascended the Throne. He is the Compassionate. Therefore, ask about Him, One Who is aware. **60.** When it is said to them, "Prostrate before the Compassionate," they say, "What is the Compassionate? Should we prostrate in front of what You command us?" It increases their aversion. **61.** Blessed is He who placed the constellations in the sky and placed there a lamp and a shining moon. **62.** It is He Who made the night and the day successively for whoever wills to reflect or wills to be grateful. **63.** The servants of the Compassionate are those who walk modestly upon the earth, and when the ignorant address them they say, "Peace," **64.** and who spend the night before their Lord, prostrating and standing, **65.** and who say, "Our Lord! Avert the punishment of Hell from us! Its punishment is indeed inextricable. **66.** What an evil dwelling place and station!" **67.** Those who when they spend are neither spendthrift nor niggardly, but hold a balance between them, **68.** and who do not call upon another god along with God, and do not slay the soul that God has made sacrosanct, save by right, and who do not fornicate, since whoever does will meet punishment, **69.** and the punishment will be multiplied for him on the Day of Resurrection. He will abide humiliated therein, **70.** except for those who repent, believe, and perform righteous deeds. God will replace their evil deeds with good deeds. God is Forgiving and Merciful. **71.** Whoever has repented and performs righteous deeds has certainly turned to God with veritable repentance. **72.** Those who do not observe falsehood, and who, when they run across vain talk, they run across it with dignity, **73.** and who, when they are reminded of the signs of their Lord, do not fall deaf or blind against them, **74.** and who say, "Our Lord! Grant us delight in our spouses and our progeny and make us leaders for the reverent," **75.** it is they who will be rewarded the lofty station for having been patient, and they will be welcomed within by salutations and peace **76.** to abide there. What a beautiful dwelling and resting place! **77.** Say, "My Lord is not troubled by your failure to supplicate, but you have rejected, so the outcome is certain."

Surah 26

THE POETS

al-Shu'ara

In the Name of God, the Compassionate, the Merciful

1. *Tā. Sīn. Mīm.* **2.** These are the signs of the clarifying Book. **3.** It may be that you torment yourself because they are not believers. **4.** If We desired, We would have sent down a sign from Heaven and their heads would remain bowed before it in humility, **5.** yet no new reminder comes to and from the Compassionate, but that they turn away from it. **6.** Truly they have denied it, but the news which they used to mock will come to them. **7.** Have they not considered the earth and how much of every noble kind We have caused to grow therein? **8.** Truly in that is a sign, but most of them are not believers. **9.** Indeed your Lord is the Mighty and the Merciful. **10.** Remember when your Lord called out to Moses, "Go to the wrongdoing people, **11.** the people of the Pharoah. Will they not be reverent?" **12.** He said, "My Lord, truly I fear they will deny me. **13.** My breast will be distressed, and my tongue constrained, so send Aaron as well. **14.** They have a charge of crime against me, so I fear they will slay me." **15.** He said, "Oh no! Go forth with Our signs. We will be with you, listening. **16.** So go to the Pharoah and say, 'Truly we are sent by the Lord of the Worlds, **17.** that you may send the children of Israel with us.'" **18.** He said, "Did we not raise you among us as a child, and did you not stay among us for years throughout your life? **19.** You committed the act that you committed, and you are among the blasphemous." **20.** He said, "I committed it then, when I was one of those who were astray. **21.** So I fled from you because I feared you. Then my Lord granted me judgment and made me one of the messengers. **22.** That is the favor you are telling me about as you enslave the Children of Israel." **23.** Pharoah said, "What is the Lord of the Worlds?" **24.** He said, "The Lord of the heavens and the earth and all between them, if you want to be assured." **25.** He said to those around him, "Do you not hear?" **26.** He said, "Your Lord and the

Lord of your forefathers." **27.** He said, "Truly your messenger who has been sent to you is possessed!" **28.** He said, "The Lord of the East and the West and whatever is between them, if you understand." **29.** He said, "Truly, if you take a god instead of me, I will place you among the imprisoned!" **30.** He said, "And if I bring you something evident?" **31.** "Then bring it, if you are among the truthful." **32.** Then Moses cast his staff, and it was clearly a serpent. **33.** Then he drew out his hand and behold, it was white to the observers. **34.** He said to the notables around him, "Indeed this is a knowledgeable sorcerer **35.** who desires to expel you from your land with his sorcery. What would you command?" **36.** They said, "Delay him and his brother and send deputies to the cities **37.** to fetch you every known sorcerer." **38.** As a result, the sorcerers were brought together for the meeting of an appointed day. **39.** The people were told, "Will you gather **40.** that perhaps we may follow the sorcerers if they are the winners?" **41.** Then when the sorcerers came, they said to the Pharoah, "Will we truly have a reward if we are the winners?" **42.** He said, "Yes, and you will be among those who are brought in proximity." **43.** Moses said to them, "Cast what you will be casting!" **44.** Subsequently, they cast their ropes and staff and said, "By the might of Pharoah, we will certainly be the winners!" **45.** Then Moses cast his staff, and behold it devoured what they faked. **46.** Then the sorcerers dropped down, prostrating. **47.** They said, "We believe in the Lord of the Worlds, **48.** the Lord of Moses and Aaron." **49.** He said, "Do you believe in him before I give you permission? He is certainly your leader and has taught you sorcery. You will soon learn that I will surely cut off your hands and feet from opposite sides, and I will surely crucify you all!" **50.** They said, "It is no problem. Truly unto our Lord, we will return. **51.** We surely hope that our Lord will forgive us for our sins that we may become foremost among the believers." **52.** Then We revealed unto Moses, "Set forth with My servants by night though you will indeed be pursued." **53.** Then the Pharoah sent deputies to the cities. **54.** "These are indeed a small band, **55.** and have truly stirred our rage. **56.** We are a fully prepared." **57.** Therefore, We drove them out of gardens, springs, **58.** treasures, and an honorable position. **59.** Thereafter, We made the Children of Israel the inheritors. **60.** Then they pursued them at sunrise. **61.** When the two masses saw one another, the companions of Moses said, "We are overtaken!" **62.** He said, "Not at all! Truly my Lord is with me. He will guide me." **63.** Then We revealed unto Moses, "Strike the sea with your staff!" It then divided and each part was akin to a great mountain. **64.** Then We brought the 'others' in proximity. **65.** And We delivered Moses and all who were with him, **66.** and then, We drowned the others. **67.** Truly in that is a sign but most of them are not believers. **68.** Indeed your Lord is the Mighty and the Merciful

69. Recite unto them the story of Abraham 70. when he said to his father and his people, "What are you worshipping?" 71. They said, "We worship idols, and we will always be devoted to them." 72. He said, "Do they hear you when you call, 73. or do they benefit or harm you?" 74. They said, "Truly we found that our fathers were doing so." 75. He said, "Have you considered what you worship, 76. you and your ancestors? 77. For they are all my enemies except for the Lord of the Worlds 78. Who created me, and guides me, 79. Who feeds me and gives me drink, 80. Who, when I am ill, heals me, 81. Who causes me to die, then gives me life, 82. and Who I hope will forgive my sins on the Day of Judgment. 83. My Lord! Grant me wisdom and bind me to the righteous! 84. Grant me the tongue of truth among subsequent generations. 85. Place me among the heirs of the Gardens of Bliss. 86. Forgive my father for he is among the astray. 87. Do not disgrace me on the Day they are resurrected, 88. the Day when neither wealth nor sons will benefit, 89. except for he who goes to God with a sound heart." 90. The Garden will be brought close to the reverent, 91. and Hellfire will be in full view of the sinful. 92. It will be said to them, "Where is what you worshipped 93. instead of God? Are they helping you or helping themselves?" 94. Then they will be thrown into it, they, the sinful, 95. and the forces of Iblīs altogether. 96. They will say as they dispute with one another therein, 97. "By God, we were truly in obvious error 98. when we held you as equal to the Lord of the Worlds. 99. No one caused us to go astray but the guilty. 100. So now we have no intercessors, 101. nor a loyal friend. 102. If we had another turn, we would be among the believers." 103. Truly in that is a sign, but most of them were not believers. 104. Truly your Lord, is indeed the Mighty and the Merciful. 105. The people of Noah denied the messengers, 106. when their brother Noah said to them, "Will you not be reverent? 107. Truly I am a trustworthy messenger unto you. 108. So revere God and obey me. 109. I do not ask of you any reward for it. My reward lies only with the Lord of the Worlds. 110. So revere God and obey me." 111. They said, "Should we believe you when only the downcast follow you?" 112. He said, "What knowledge do I have of what they did? 113. Their reckoning is only by my Lord if you only knew. 114. I will not drive away the believers. 115. I am but a clear warner." 116. They said, "Oh Noah, truly if you do not stop, you will indeed be among the stoned." 117. He said, "My Lord, truly my people have denied me. 118. So decide between me and them and deliver me and the believers who are with me!" 119. Therefore, We delivered him and those who were with him into the loaded Ark. 120. Afterward, We drowned those who remained. 121. Truly in that is a sign but most of them are not believers. 122. Indeed your Lord is the Mighty and the Merciful. 123. The Ād denied the messengers 124. when their brother Hŭd said to them, "Will you

not be reverent? **125.** Truly I am a trustworthy messenger unto you. **126.** So revere God and obey me **127.** I do not ask of you any reward for it. My reward lies only with the Lord of the Worlds. **128.** Do you build a sign at every high locale to amuse yourselves? **129.** Do you occupy fortresses that perhaps you may live forever? **130.** When you destroy, do you destroy as tyrants? **131.** So revere God and obey me. **132.** Revere He who has bestowed on you what you know, **133.** bestowed on you cattle, children, **134.** gardens, and springs. **135.** Truly I fear for you the punishment of a tremendous day!" **136.** They said, "It is the same to us whether you pressure us or whether you are not among those who pressure. **137.** This is nothing but the tenet of the ancient, **138.** and we will not be punished." **139.** Therefore, they denied him, and We destroyed them. Truly in that is a sign but most of them are not believers. **140.** Indeed your Lord is the Mighty and the Merciful. **141.** The Thamūd denied the messengers, **142.** when their brother Sālih said to them, "Will you be reverent? **143.** Truly I am a trustworthy messenger unto you. **144.** So revere God and obey me. **145.** I do not ask of you any reward for it. My reward lies only with the Lord of the Worlds. **146.** Will you be left feeling secure in all that you have here **147.** amid gardens and springs, **148.** sown fields, date palms with ripe stalks, **149.** where you skillfully carve dwellings in the mountains. **150.** So revere God and obey me. **151.** Do not obey the commands of the reckless **152.** who work corruption upon the earth, and do not justly remedy their affairs." **153.** They said, "You are but one of the bewitched. **154.** You are no more than a human being like us. So bring us a sign if you are truthful." **155.** He said, "This is a she-camel. She will drink and you will drink on an appointed day. **156.** Do not touch her with harm or you will be taken by the punishment of a tremendous day." **157.** But they hamstrung her and then became remorseful. **158.** So punishment seized them. Truly in that is a sign, but most of them are not believers. **159.** Your Lord is indeed the Mighty and the Merciful. **160.** The people of Lot denied the messengers **161.** when their brother Lot said to them, "Will you not be reverent? **162.** Truly I am a trustworthy messenger unto you, **163.** so, revere God and obey me. **164.** I do not ask of you any reward for it. My reward lies only with the Lord of the Worlds. **165.** Among all creatures do you approach males, **166.** and leave what God has created for you to be your spouses? You are indeed a sinful people." **167.** They said, "O Lot, if you do not stop, you will be among those who are cast out." **168.** He said, "Truly I am of those who abhor what you do. **169.** My Lord! Deliver me and my family from what they do." **170.** Therefore, We delivered him and his family all together **171.** except for an old woman who was among those who lagged behind. **172.** We then destroyed the others. **173.** We rained a shower of brimstone upon them, and evil was the rain upon those who were warned.

174. Truly in that is a sign, but most of them are not believers. **175.** Indeed your Lord is the Mighty and the Merciful. **176.** The inhabitants of the Wood denied the messengers **177.** when Shu'ayb said to them, "Will you not be reverent? **178.** Truly I am a trustworthy messenger unto you, **179.** so, reverence God and obey me. **180.** I do not ask of you any reward for it. My reward lies only with the Lord of the Worlds. **181.** Give full measure and do not be among those who cause loss. **182.** Weigh with an evenly balanced scale, **183.** and do not reduce people's goods, nor commit evil upon the earth while employing immorality. **184.** Revere Him Who created you and former generations." **185.** They said, "You are but one of the bewitched. **186.** You are no more than a human being like us. We truly suspect that you are among the liars, **187.** so, make pieces of the sky fall upon us if you are among the truthful." **188.** He said, "My Lord knows best what you do." **189.** So they denied him, and the punishment of the day of despair seized them. Truly it was the punishment of a tremendous day. **190.** Truly in that is a sign, but most of them are not believers. **191.** Your Lord is truly the Mighty and the Merciful. **192.** Indeed it is a revelation of the Lord of the Worlds, **193.** brought down by a Trustworthy Spirit **194.** upon your heart that you may be among the warners. **195.** In a clear, Arabic tongue, **196.** it is truly in the scriptures of the ancient. **197.** Is it not a sign for them? Truly the learned among the Children of Israel know of it. **198.** Had We sent it down upon some non-Arab, **199.** and he recited it unto them, they would not have believed in it. **200.** Thus We appended it in the hearts of the guilty. **201.** They will not believe in it until they see the painful punishment. **202.** It will come upon them suddenly while they are heedless. **203.** Then they say, "Will we be granted respite?" **204.** Do they seek to advance Our punishment? **205.** Do you see that We granted them enjoyment for years, **206.** and then, what they were promised came upon them. **207.** So of what benefit was this amusement to them? **208.** Never did We destroy a town but that it had its warners **209.** as a reminder. We are not wrongdoers. **210.** The demons did not descend with it, **211.** nor would it suit them, nor would they be able. **212.** Indeed, they have been excluded from hearing. **213.** So do not call upon another god along with God, else you will be among the punished. **214.** Warn your tribe, your nearest kin, **215.** and lower your wing to the believers who follow you. **216.** Should they disobey you say, "Truly I am clear of what you do." **217.** Trust in the Mighty and the Merciful **218.** Who sees when you rise, **219.** and move among those who prostrate. **220.** Indeed He is the Hearing and the Knowing. **221.** Should I inform you of those upon whom the demons descend? **222.** They descend upon every sinful liar **223.** while eavesdropping, and most of them are liars. **224.** As for the poets, the sinful follow them. **225.** "Have you not noticed that they roam aimlessly in every valley,

226. saying things they do not do— 227. except for those who believe, do good deeds, frequently remember God, and support one another after being wronged? As for those who commit injustice, they will soon know the fate to which they will return."

Surah 27

THE ANTS

al-Naml

In the Name of God, the Compassionate, the Merciful

1. *Tā. Sīn.* These are the signs of the Quran and a manifest Book, **2.** a guide and good news for the believers **3.** who perform prayer and give alms and believe in the Hereafter. **4.** Truly, for those who do not believe in the Hereafter, We have made their deeds pleasing to them as they wander around confused. **5.** It is they who will have the worst of punishments and who will be the greatest losers in the Hereafter. **6.** Indeed you received the Quran from One who is Wise and Knowing. **7.** Remember when Moses said to his family, "Truly I perceive a fire. I will bring you some news therefrom, or a borrowed flame that perhaps you may warm yourselves." **8.** Then when he arrived at it, a call came out him, "Blessed is the One in the fire and the one around it. Glory be to God, Lord of the Worlds! **9.** O Moses! Truly, it is I, God, the Mighty and the Wise, **10.** Cast your staff!" Then when he saw it quivering like a serpent, he retreated and did not retrace his steps. "O Moses! Do not fear! Truly the messengers do not fear in My Presence, **11.** except for one who did wrong, then substituted evil with good. For truly, I am Forgiving and Merciful. **12.** Insert your hand in your bosom. It will become white without blemish, to be among the nine signs to the Pharoah and his people. They have indeed been a sinful people. **13.** When Our signs perceptibly came to them, they said, "This is clearly sorcery!" **14.** They rejected them wrongfully and exultantly though their souls were convinced of them. So observe what the final retribution was like for the transgressors! **15.** Indeed We gave knowledge to David and Solomon. They said, "Praise be to God, Who has favored us among many of His believing servants." **16.** Solomon succeeded David and said, "O people, we have been taught the language of the birds, and we have been given all things. This is indeed clear grace!" **17.** Gathered for Solomon were his forces of jinn, men, and birds. They marshaled 18. until they came to the valley of the ants. An ant said, "O ants! Enter your dwellings, or else Solomon and his forces will unknowingly crush you." 19. He smirked, laughing at her words, and said, "My Lord! Inspire me to show gratitude for the blessings You have blessed me and my parents with that I may work righteousness to please You. Admit me through Your Mercy to be among Your righteous servants!" 20. He surveyed the birds and said, "How is it that I do not see the hoopoe? Or is he among those who are absent? 21. I will certainly punish him severely, or unless he offers me clear cause, I will slaughter him." 22. But it had not been long when he said, "I have understood what you have not understood, and I brought you a valid report from Saba. 23. I truly found a woman ruling over them. She has been given of all things and She has a magnificent throne! 24. I found her and her people prostrating to the sun instead of God, and Satan has made their deeds seem pleasing to them. He steered them from the path so they may not be rightly guided. 25. Will they not prostrate unto God Who brings forth what is hidden in the heavens and on the earth, and Who knows what you hide and what you disclose? 26. God, there is no god but He, Lord of the Mighty Throne!" 27. He said, "We will see if you have spoken the truth or if you are among the liars. 28. Go with this letter of mine and deliver it to them. Then withdraw from them to see what they send back." 29. She said, "O notables! Truly a noble letter has been delivered to me. 30. Indeed it is from Solomon and truly it is: 'In the Name of God, the Compassionate, the Merciful. 31. Do not elevate yourselves against me but come to me in submission.'" 32. She said, "O notables! Give me your opinion in this matter of mine. I am not one to decide on any matter unless you are present." 33. They said, "We are imbued with strength and imbued with great might, but the command is yours. So consider what you would command." 34. She said, "Verily, when kings enter a town, they corrupt it and make the noblest of its people the most abased. They will do the same. 35. I will send them a gift and see what my envoys come back with." 36. But when it came to Solomon, he said, "Do you offer me wealth? What God has given me is better than what He has given you. It is indeed you who rejoice in your gift!" 37. "Return to them for we will indeed arrive upon them with forces they cannot endure. We will expel them from therein humbled and disgraced." 38. He said, "O notables! Which of you will bring me her throne before they come to me in submission?" 39. An *'ifrit* (rebel) among the jinn said, "I will bring it to you before you rise from your place. I certainly have the strength to do it, and I am trustworthy." 40. The one who had knowledge of the Book said, "I will bring it to you in the blink of an eye." Then when he saw it before him, he said, "This is of the Grace of my Lord to try me and to see whether I will give thanks or be ungrateful. Whoever gives thanks, he gives thanks solely to his soul. Whoever is ungrateful, truly my Lord is Self-Sufficient, and Generous." 41. He said, "Disguise her throne for her. We will see if she is rightly guided or if she is among those who are not rightly guided." 42. Then when she came it was said, "Is your throne like this?" She said, "It looks like it." We had been given knowledge before her, and we were Muslims, 43. while what she worshipped rather than God hindered her. She was truly of a disbelieving people. 44. It was said to her, "Enter the palace." But when she saw it, she assumed it was an expanse of water and bared her forelegs. He said, "Truly this is a structure paved with crystal." She said, "My Lord! I have certainly wronged myself and I submit with Solomon to God, Lord of the Worlds." 45. We have indeed sent to the Thamūd their brother Sāliḥ, "Worship God!" but observe, the two factions were quarreling. 46. He said, "O my people! Why do you seek to advance evil before good? Why do you not seek the forgiveness of God that perhaps you may be shown mercy?" 47. They said, "We portend ill of you and of those who are with you." He said, "Your portending ill is with God. Rather you are a people being tried." 48. There were nine persons from the city working corruption in the land who would not reform. 49. They said, "Let us swear by God that we will attack him and his family by night. Then, we will actually say to his heir that we were not present at the ruin of his family and that we are certainly truthful." 50. They plotted a plot, and We plotted a plot, but they were unaware. 51. So observe what the output of their plot was like in the end. We have indeed destroyed them and their people all together. 52. Those are their homes lying deserted for their wrongdoing. Truly in this is a sign for a people who know. 53. We saved those who believed and were reverent. 54. When Lot said to his people, "Do you commit indecency though you can see? 55. Do you really approach men with desire instead if women? Clearly you are but an ignorant people!" 56. Yet the response of his people was no more than to say, "Expel the family of Lot from your town! Truly they are a people who keep themselves pure!" 57. Therefore, We saved him and his family, except for his wife. We destined her to be among those who lagged behind. 58. We poured a rain down upon them. Evil is the rain of those who were warned! 59. Say, "Praise be to God, and peace be upon His servants whom He has chosen." Is God better, or the partners they attribute? 60. Or He, Who created the heavens and the earth, and sent water down for you from the sky through which We made beautiful gardens, whose trees you would not be able to make grow. Is there a god alongside God? Rather, they are a people who attribute equals. 61. He has made the earth a dwelling place, and made rivers run through it, with firm mountains for it, and created a barrier between the two seas. Is there a god alongside God? No, most of them do not know. **62.** Who responds to the distressed one when he calls upon Him and removes the evil, and Who makes you vicegerents of the earth? Is there a god alongside God? Little are you mindful! **63.** Who guides you in the darkness of the land and sea, and who sends the winds as good news ahead of His Mercy? Is there a god alongside God? Exalted is God above the partners they attribute! **64.** Who produced creation, then reproduces it, and Who provides for you from Heaven and the earth? Is there a god alongside God? Say, "Bring your proof if you are truthful." **65.** Say, "None in the heavens or on the earth know of the Unseen except for God. They do not know when they will be resurrected." **66.** Even so, does their knowledge reach the Hereafter, or are they in doubt concerning it? They are indeed blind to it. **67.** Those who disbelieve say, "What? When we and our fathers become dust, will we really be resurrected? **68.** Indeed we were promised this, we and our forefathers. This is nothing but ancient tales!" **69.** Say, "Journey upon the earth and observe what it was like for the guilty in the end!" **70.** Do not grieve for them and do not be distressed by what they plot. **71.** They say, "When will this promise come to be if you are truthful?" **72.** Say, "It may be that some of what you seek to expedite is close by you." **73.** Your Lord is indeed Possessed of Grace toward mankind, but most of them are ungrateful. **74.** Truly your Lord knows what their hearts conceal and what they disclose. **75.** There is nothing hidden in the Heaven or on the earth, but that it is in a clear Book. **76.** Truly this Quran recounts unto the Children of Israel most of that wherein they differ, **77.** and truly it is a guidance and a mercy for the believers. **78.** Indeed your Lord will judge between them by His Judgment. He is the Mighty and the Knowing. **79.** So trust in God. Truly you stand upon the clear truth. **80.** You certainly cannot make the dead hear, nor can you make the deaf hear the call when they turn their backs, **81.** nor can you guide the blind away from their mistakes. You can only make those hear who believe in Our signs and are Muslims. **82.** When the Word comes upon them, We will bring forth a beast for them from the earth that will speak to them of how mankind was not certain of Our signs. **83.** On that Day, We will gather from every nation a group of those who denied Our signs and they will be marshaled **84.** until once they arrive, He will say, "Did you deny My signs, though you did not encompass them in knowledge? What is it that you did?" **85.** The Word will fall upon them for their having done wrong and they will not be able to speak. **86.** Have they not observed that We made the night that they may rest therein, and the day for them to, see? In that are indeed signs for a people who believe. **87.** On that Day the trumpet will be blown, and whoever is in the heavens and on the earth will be terrified, save whom God wills. Everyone will come to Him in humility. **88.** You will observe the mountains you had assumed were rock-solid, pass away like clouds. This is the Work of God Who perfects all things, for indeed He is Aware of whatever you do. **89.** Whoever brings a good deed, will have what is better than it. They will be secure from terror on that Day. **90.** Whoever brings an evil deed will have their faces cast down into the Fire. Do you think you will be rewarded for anything other than what you performed? **91.** "Indeed I am commanded to worship the Lord of this city, Who has made it sacred. Unto To Him belong all things. I am commanded to be among those who submit, **92.** and to recite the Quran. So whomever is rightly guided, he is guided solely for his own soul." Say to whomever is astray, "Truly I am but a warner," **93.** and say, "Praise be to God! He will show you His signs, and you will know them." Your Lord is not unmindful of what you do.

Surah 28

THE STORIES

al-Qasas

In the Name of God, the Compassionate, the Merciful

1. Tā. Sīn. Mīm. **2.** These are the signs of a clear Book. **3.** We recite to you the true story of Moses and Pharaoh for a people of believers. **4.** Indeed Pharoah exalted himself in the land and divided his people into groups while oppressing a sect among them by slaying their sons and sparing their women. Truly he was among the makers of corruption. **5.** We wanted to be gracious to those who were oppressed in the land, to make them leaders and heirs, **6.** to establish them on the earth to show Pharoah and Hāmān and their forces the very things about which they were worried. **7.** So We revealed to the mother of Moses: "Nurse him. But if you fear for him, cast him into the river and do not grieve or distress. We will certainly bring him back to you and make him one of the messengers." **8.** Then the House of Pharoah picked him up, whereupon he would become an enemy and a sorrow unto them. Indeed Pharoah, Hāmān, and their forces were sinners. **9.** The wife of Pharaoh said, "A joy to the eye and to you! Do not slay him. He may be of benefit to us, or we can take him as a son," but they were heedless. **10.** However, the heart of Moses's mother became empty, and she would have disclosed the matter had We not fortified her heart that she might be among the believers. **11.** She said to his sister, "Follow him." As a result, she watched him from a distance, while they were unaware. **12.** We prevented him from being suckled by former foster mothers, so she said, "Should I direct you to the people of a house who will take care of him and treat him with good intentions?" **13.** So We returned him to his mother that she may be comforted and not grieve, and that she might know that God's promise is true. But most of them do not know. **14.** When he reached maturity and was fully established, We gave him wisdom and knowledge. Thus, do We reward those who are good. **15.** He had entered the city at a time when its people were distracted. There, he found two men fighting. One from among his own sect and the other from among his enemies. Subsequently, Moses struck him with his fist and killed him. He said, "This is the work of Satan! Truly he is a clear enemy that leads astray." **16.** He prayed, "O my Lord! I have indeed wronged my soul! Forgive me!" As a result, He forgave him. Truly He is the Forgiving and the Merciful. **17.** He said, "My Lord! Because You have blessed me, I will never be a supporter of the guilty." **18.** By morning while in the city, he was fearful and vigilant. Behold, the one who had sought his help the day before cried out to him for help! Moses said to him, "Truly you are clearly in error." **19.** But when he wanted to strike the one who was an enemy to both, he said, "O Moses! Do you desire to slay me as you slew a soul yesterday? You want nothing but to be a tyrant on the earth and do not want to be among the workers of righteousness?" **20.** Then from the outskirts of the city a man came running. He said, "O Moses! Truly the notables are conspiring against you that they might slay you. Therefore, leave! Truly I am among your sincere advisors." **21.** Subsequently, he left there fearful and watchful. He said, "My Lord! Save me from the wrongdoing people!" **22.** When he turned his face toward Midian, he said, "Perhaps my Lord will guide me to the right path." **23.** Then when he arrived at the waters of Midian, he found a community of people watering their flock. He found by them two women standing back. He said, "What is your situation?" They said, "We will not give them water until the shepherds have driven away. Our father is extremely old." **24.** As a result, he gave them water for them. Then he turned toward the shade and said, "My Lord! Truly I need any good that You may send down upon me." **25.** Then one of the two came walking bashfully toward him. She said, "Truly my father invites you, that he may compensate you for watering for us." When he arrived and recited his story to him, he said, "Do not fear. You have been saved from the wrongdoing people." **26.** One of the two said, "O my father! Hire him. It is indeed better to hire the strong and the trustworthy." **27.** He said, "My desire is to have you marry one of these two daughters under the condition that you will lease yourself to me for eight years, but if you complete ten, that would be of your own will. I do not wish to be hard on you. God willing, you will find me to be among the righteous." **28.** He said, "So let it be between you and me. Whichever of the two terms I complete, let there be no enmity toward me. May God be witness over what we say." **29.** Then when Moses fulfilled his term and set out with his family, he perceived a fire on the side of Mount Tūr. He said to his family, "Stay here. I perceive a fire. Maybe I will bring some good news or a firebrand that perhaps you may warm yourselves." **30.** When he arrived at it, he was called upon from the right bank of the valley at the blessed field of the tree, "O Moses!

I am indeed God, Lord of the Worlds!" **31.** "Cast your staff!" Then when he saw it quivering like a serpent, he retreated and did not retrace his steps. "O Moses! Approach and do not fear! You are indeed of those who are protected. **32.** Insert your hand in your bosom. It will become white and unharmed. Let your arms hug your sides against fear. These are two proofs from your Lord to Pharaoh and his notables. Truly they are a sinful people." **33.** He said, "My Lord! I have indeed killed a soul among them, and I fear they will slay me. **34.** My brother Aaron is more eloquent than me in speech. Therefore, send him with me as a helper to endorse me, for I fear they will deny me." **35.** He said, "We will strengthen your arm through your brother, and We will grant authority for both of you such that they cannot reach you. With Our signs, you and those who follow you will be victors." **36.** When Moses brought them clear signs, they said, "This is nothing more than invented sorcery. We have not heard of this from our forefathers." **37.** Moses said, "My Lord knows best who brings guidance from Him and whose end is at the threshold of the Abode. Truly the wrongdoers will not prosper." **38.** Pharoah said, "O notables! I did not know that you have a god other than myself. O Hāmān! Bake bricks out of clay and build me a lofty palace that I may mount up and observe the god of Moses though I truly believe he is among the liars." **39.** He and his forces were unjustifiably arrogant upon the earth. They thought they would not be returned to Us. **40.** We seized him and his forces and cast them into the sea. So observe what the end of the guilty was like. **41.** We made them leaders calling unto the Fire. They will not be helped on the Day of Resurrection. **42.** We caused them to be pursued by a curse in this world. They will be among the despised on the Day of Resurrection. **43.** Truly after We had destroyed former generations, We gave Moses the Book as insight, guidance, and mercy to the people that perhaps they may reflect. **44.** You were not on the western side when We decreed the Commandment unto Moses, and you were not among the witnesses, **45.** yet We raised generations whose lives were long-lasting. You did not dwell among the people of Midian reciting Our signs unto them, rather We were the Senders. **46.** You were not on the side of Mount Tūr when We called out, yet as a mercy from your Lord that you may warn a people unto whom no warner had come before you that perhaps they may remember. **47.** In case an affliction should befall them because of what their hands had sent forth, they will say, "Our Lord! If only you had sent a messenger unto us, we would have followed Your signs and been among the believers!" **48.** But when the truth from Us had arrived them, they said, "Why did he not come with signs similar to what Moses had come with?" Did they not disbelieve in what Moses had received aforetime? They said, "Two sorceries supporting one another." They said, "We are truly disbelievers in each." 49. Say, "So bring a book from God that provides better guidance than these two that I may follow it, if you are truthful." 50. If they do not answer you, then know that they only follow their desires. Who is more astray than one who follows his whim without guidance from God? Truly God does not guide a wrongdoing people. 51. Indeed We allowed the Word to reach them that perhaps they may reflect. 52. Those to whom We had given the Book before it, were believers in it. 53. When it was recited unto them, they said, "We believe in it. Indeed, it is the truth from our Lord. Truly we were Muslim even before it." 54. It is they who will be given double the reward for having been patient. They repel evil with good and spend from what We have provided them. 55. When they hear idle talk, they turn away from it and say, "Unto us our deeds and unto you, your deeds. Peace be upon you! We do not seek out the ignorant." 56. You certainly do not guide whomever you like, but God guides whomever He wills. He knows best those who are rightly guided. 57. They say, "If we follow guidance along with you, we will be snatched away from our land." Have We not established a secure Sanctuary for them where fruits of all things were offered as a provision from Ourselves? But most of them do not know. 58. How many townspeople have We destroyed who exulted in the ease of their lives? There are their homes, uninhabited after them, except for a few. Indeed, We are truly the Inheritors. 59. Your Lord never destroys towns until He sends a messenger to their mother city to recite Our signs unto them. We never destroy towns, except if their people are wrongdoers. 60. Anything you have been given is no more than amusement in the life of this world and its embellishments. However, what lies with God is better and more lasting. Will you not be wise? 61. Is he unto whom We have made a goodly promise and who attains it, the same as he unto whom We have granted enjoyment in the life of this world only to become among those persecuted on the Day of Resurrection? 62. On the Day when He calls out to them and says, "Where are My partners—those who you were claiming?" 63. Those against whom the Word has already come due will say, "Our Lord! These are the ones we caused to deviate. We led them to deviance since we were deviant. We free ourselves before You. It was not us that they worshipped." 64. It will be said, "Call upon your partners." Subsequently, they will call upon them, but they will not answer them. They will see the punishment, if only they were ones to be guided! 65. On the Day He calls out to them, they say, "What was the answer you gave the messengers?" 66. They will be blinded by the news on that Day and will not even be able to question one another. 67. But it is possible for he who repented, believed, and worked righteousness among them to be salvaged. 68. Your Lord creates what He wills, and He chooses accordingly. They will have no choice. Glory be to God. He is exalted beyond the partners they attribute! **69.** Your Lord knows what their hearts conceal and what they disclose. **70.** He is God. There is no god but He! To Him belongs praise at the beginning and at the end. To Him belongs judgment, and unto Him you will be returned. **71.** Say, "Have you considered that if God were to make night perpetual over you until the Day of Resurrection, what god other than God would bring you light? Will you then not listen?" **72.** Say, "Have you considered that if God should make day come over you perpetually until the Day of Resurrection, what god other than God would bring you night, that you might rest therein? Will you not see then?" **73.** It is out of His Mercy that He created night and day for you to rest and to seek His Bounty that perhaps you may be thankful. **74.** On the Day when He calls to them, He will ask, "Where are My partners that you used to claim?" **75.** We will bring forward a witness from every nation and say, "Bring your proof." They will then know that the truth belongs to God, and what they made up will forsake them. **76.** Truly Qarūn was of the people of Moses, but he wronged them. We gave him of the treasures whose keys would have certainly been a heavy burden unto a body of strong men. Remember when his people said to him, "Do not exult! God truly does not like the exultant. **77.** Seek the Abode of the Hereafter with what God has given you, and do not forget your portion in this world. Be good as God has been good to you. Do not seek to create mischief on the earth. Truly God does not like those who do mischief." **78.** He said, "I brought this forth from the knowledge that I possess." Did he not know that God had destroyed generations before him that were mightier in strength and greater than what they had gathered? But the wicked will not be called for their sins. **79.** He came out to his people in his adornment. Those who desired the life of this world said, "We wish we had what Qarūn was given; he truly possesses great wealth!" **80.** But those who had been given knowledge said, "Woe to you! The reward of God is far better for those who have faith and do righteous deeds, and it is granted only to those who remain patient." **81.** We then caused the earth to engulf him and his house. He had no party to help him against God, nor could he help himself. **82.** Those who had hoped to be in his place the day before saying, "Ah! It is God Who extends provision to whomever He desires among His servants. Had God not been gracious to us, He could have caused us to be engulfed. Ah! Those who reject God will not prosper." **83.** That is the Abode of the Hereafter that We have decreed for those who do not desire dominance nor corruption on the earth. The end belongs to the reverent. **84.** Whoever comes forth with a good deed will have better than it, but whoever comes forth with an evil deed, He will not reward those who performed evil deeds, save to the extent of what they performed. **85.** Indeed, the

One Who ordained the Quran for you will certainly bring you back to the place of return. Say, "My Lord knows best those who bring guidance from those who are in obvious error." **86.** You did not hope that the Book would be delivered to you. Rather, it was a mercy from your Lord. Thus, do not be supporters of the disbelievers. **87.** Do not let them hold you back from the signs of God after they have been sent down to you. Call unto your Lord and do not be among those who attribute partners unto God. **88.** Do not call upon another god along with God. There is no God but He! Everything will perish except for His Countenance. Judgment belongs to Him and unto Him, you will be returned.

Surah 29

THE SPIDER

al-Ankabūt

In the Name of God, the Compassionate, the Merciful

1. *Alif. Lām. Mīm.* **2.** Do people assume they will be left to say, "We believe," and that they will not be tested **3.** though We have truly tested those before them? God certainly knows those who are truthful, and He certainly knows the liars. **4.** Or do those who commit evil deeds assume they will get the best of Us? Their judgment is indeed evil! **5.** Whoever hopes for the meeting with God, God's term is coming. He is the Hearing and the Knowing. **6.** Whoever strives, strives only for himself. God is indeed beyond need of the worlds. **7.** For those who believe and perform righteous deeds, We will certainly clear them of their evil deeds, and We will certainly reward them according to the best of their deeds. **8.** We instructed man to be good to his parents, but if they urge you to associate a partner with Me, of which you have no knowledge, then do not obey them. To Me is your return where I will inform you of what you did. **9.** For those who believe and perform righteous deeds, We will allow them to enter among the righteous. **10.** Among people are those who say, "We believe in God," but if he is harmed for the sake of God, he assumes that persecution by people is the persecution of God. Yet if help comes from your Lord, he will truly say, "We were indeed with you." Does God not know best what lies within the hearts of creatures? **11.** God certainly knows those who believe, and He certainly knows those who are hypocrites. **12.** Those who disbelieve say to those who believe, "Follow our path and we will carry your sins." They are indeed liars. They will not carry any of their sins. **13.** They will certainly carry their own burdens and the burdens of others along with them. On the Day of Resurrection, they will definitely be questioned on what they invented. **14.** Indeed We sent Noah unto his people, and he remained among them a thousand years, less fifty. They were wrongdoers, so the flood seized them. **15.** Then We saved him and the companions of the ship. We made it a sign for the worlds. **16.** When Abraham said to his people, "Worship God and revere Him. That is better for you, if you only knew. **17.** You only worship idols instead of God and you only create perversion. Surely those whom you worship besides God have no power over what sustenance may come to you. Therefore, seek your sustenance with God. Worship Him and be thankful to Him. To Him you will be returned. **18.** But if you reject, so did nations before you. Nothing is incumbent upon the Messenger save the clear proclamation." **19.** Have they not considered how God originates creation and then brings it back? That is easy for God indeed. **20.** Say, "Travel through the earth and consider how He originated creation. Then God will bring the next creation into existence. Truly God is powerful over all things." **21.** He punishes whomever He wills and has mercy upon whomever He wills. Unto Him you will be returned. **22.** You will not be able to frustrate on earth or in Heaven, and besides God, you will have no protector, nor helper. **23.** Those who disbelieve in God's signs and in the meeting with Him, despair of My Mercy and for them there will be a painful punishment. **24.** However, the comeback of his people was but to say, "Slay him or burn him!" Then God saved him from the fire. There are certainly signs in that for a people who believe. **25.** Abraham said, "You have taken idols instead of God to maintain a pleasant bond among yourselves and the life of this world. Then on the Day of Resurrection you will disown one another, and you will curse one another, but your refuge will be the Fire, and you will have no helpers." **26.** Lot believed him and said, "Truly I am emigrating unto my Lord. He is truly the Mighty, and the Wise." **27.** We gave him Isaac and Jacob, and We ordained prophethood and scripture among his progenies. We gave him his reward in this world and in the Hereafter. He will indeed be among the righteous. **28.** When Lot said to his people, "Indeed you commit indecency such as none in the worlds has committed before you. **29.** Do you truly approach men, cut off the way, and commit indecency during your assemblies?" His people's response was but to say, "Bring us God's punishment if you are among the truthful." **30.** He said, "My Lord! Help me against the people who commit sin!" **31.** When Our envoys came to Abraham with good news, they said, "We will certainly destroy the people of this town. Its people are indeed wrongdoers." **32.** He said, "Truthfully, Lot is in it." They said, "We know better who is in it." We will indeed save him and his family except for his wife. She was among those who lagged behind. **33.** When Our envoys went to Lot, he was distressed on their account, yet he was constrained from helping them. They said, "Do not be afraid, nor grieve. We will certainly save you and your family except for your wife. She will be of those who lag behind. **34.** We will indeed bring down upon the people of this town a suffering from Heaven for having been sinful."

35. We have truly left it therefrom to be a clear sign for a people who understand.
36. Unto the Midian We sent down their brother Shu'ayb. He said, "O my people! Worship God and hope for the Last Day. Do not behave wickedly on the earth while performing mischief." 37. But they rejected him, so they were seized by the quake. By morning they were found lifeless in their homes. 38. And the people of Ād and Thamŭd—it has already been made clear to you through the ruins of their dwellings. Satan made their actions seem appealing and turned them away from the right path, even though they were wise. 39. And Qarūn, Pharoah, and Hāmān! Moses had indeed brought them clear signs, but they were arrogant on earth and could not overreach. 40. Each We seized for his sin. Among them are some upon whom We sent a torrent of stones, among them are some whom the Cry seized, among them are some whom We caused the earth to engulf, and among them are some whom We drowned. God did not wrong them, but they wronged themselves. 41. The simile of those who take protectors besides God is like that of a spider that makes a house. Truly the weakest of houses is the spider's house if they only knew. 42. Indeed God knows whatever they call upon instead of Him. He is the Mighty and the Wise. 43. These are the parables. We set them forth for people, but none understand them, except for those who know. 44. God created the heavens and the earth in truth. That is indeed a sign for believers. 45. Recite what has been revealed unto you of the Book and perform prayer. Truly prayer prevents against indecency and abomination, but the remembrance of God is certainly greater. God is Aware of whatever you do. 46. Do not dispute with the People of the Book except in kindness save those of them who have done wrong. Say, "We believe in what was sent down unto us and what was sent down to you. Our God and your God are one and unto Him we are submitters." 47. Thus, We have sent down the Book unto you. So those unto whom We have given the Book, believe in it. Among them are some who believe in it, and no one rejects Our signs, except for the disbelievers. 48. You did not recite any Book before this nor did you write it with your right hand, for then the false claimers would have doubted. 49. Rather it is but clear signs in the hearts of those who have been given knowledge. No one rejects Our signs, except for the wrongdoers. 50. They say, "Why have signs been sent down unto him from his Lord?" Say, "Signs are with God alone. I am solely a clear warner." 51. Is it not enough for them that We have sent down unto you the Book that is recited unto them? Surely in that is a mercy and a remembrance for a people who believe. 52. Say, "God is enough of a witness between you and me. He knows whatever is in the heavens and on the earth." Those who believe in what is false and disbelieve in God, it is they who are the losers. 53. They ask you to expedite the punishment. Yet were it not for a term appointed, the punishment would have

come upon them. It will indeed come suddenly upon them while they are heedless. **54.** They ask you to expedite the punishment. Hell will indeed encompass the disbelievers. **55.** On the Day when the punishment will cover them from above and from beneath their feet, We will say, "Taste of what you did!" **56.** O My servants who believe! My earth is indeed spacious. Therefore, worship Me. **57.** Every soul will taste death. Then unto Us you will be returned. **58.** For those who believe and perform righteous deeds, We will indeed settle them in the lofty abodes of the Garden with rivers running beneath to abide there forever, an excellent reward for the performers, **59.** and for those who are patient and trust in their Lord. **60.** How many a creature does not carry its own sustenance, yet God provides for it and for you? He is the Hearing and the Knowing. **61.** Were you to ask them, "Who created the heavens and the earth and made the sun subservient?" They would certainly say, "God." How then are they deluded? **62.** God outspreads sustenance for whomever He wills among His servants. Truly God has knowledge of all things. **63.** Were you to ask them, "Who sends water down from the sky to revive the earth after its death?" They would surely say, "God." Say, "Praise be to God!" However, most of them do not understand. **64.** The life of this world is nothing but diversion and amusement. Truly the Abode of the Hereafter is life indeed if they only knew. **65.** When they board a ship, they call upon God and devote their religion entirely to Him, but when they reach land in safety, they attribute partners. **66.** So let them be ungrateful for what We have given them and let them amuse themselves for soon they will know. **67.** Do they not see that We have made a secure sanctuary while people are being snatched away all around them? Do they believe in what is false? Are they ungrateful of God's Blessing? **68.** Who does greater wrong than one who invents a lie against God or denies the truth when it comes to him? Is there not an Abode in Hell for the disbelievers? **69.** For those who strive for Us, We will indeed guide them to Our ways. God is indeed with the righteous.

Surah 30

THE ROMANS

al-Rūm

In the Name of God, the Compassionate, the Merciful

1. *Alif. Lām. Mīm.* **2.** The Romans have been defeated **3.** in a land nearby. However, after their downfall, they will prevail **4.** within a few years. The matter belongs to God, in the past and in the future. On that day, the believers will rejoice **5.** for God's assistance. He helps whomever He wills. He is the Mighty and the Merciful. **6.** God's Promise — and God does not fail His Promise — but most people do not know. **7.** They know what appears in the life of this world but are heedless of the Hereafter. **8.** Do they not reflect in their own minds? God did not create the heavens and the earth and whatever is between them, except in truth for a term appointed. But indeed, many people do not believe in the meeting with their Lord. **9.** Have they not traveled through the earth and observed the final fate of those before them? They were stronger than them in power. They cultivated the earth and built upon it more than they have. Their messengers had brought them clear signs. God would have never wronged them, but they wronged themselves. **10.** Then, evil is the end of those who committed evil deeds. They denied God's signs and held them up in mockery. **11.** God originates creation, then brings it back, and then, to Him you will be returned. **12.** On the Day when the Hour takes place, the guilty will despair. **13.** They will have no intercessors from among those whom they had attributed as partners. They will then disbelieve in those they attributed as partners. **14.** On the Day when the Hour takes place, on that Day, they will be separated. **15.** However, those who believed and did righteous deeds will roam joyously in a Garden. **16.** But those who disbelieved and rejected Our signs, and the meeting of the Hereafter, will be brought to punishment. **17.** So glorify God when you reach the evening and when you rise in the morning. **18.** Praise belongs to Him in the heavens and on the earth when the evening sets in and when you reach noontide. **19.** He brings forth the living from the dead and brings forth the dead from the living. He revives the earth after its death. As such, you will be brought forth. **20.** Among His signs is that He created you from dust. Then, observe, you are a human being spread-out far and wide. **21.** Among His signs is that He created mates for you from among yourselves to dwell with them in comfort. He established affection and mercy between you. Truly in that are signs for a people who understand. **22.** Among His signs are the creations of the heavens and the earth and the variations in your tongues and colors. Truly in that are signs for those who know. **23.** Among His signs is your sleep by night and by day and your quest for His Bounty. In that are indeed signs for a people who hear. **24.** Among His signs is that He shows you lightning by way of fear and hope. He sends water down from the sky, then revives the earth after its death. In that are indeed signs for a people who understand. **25.** Among His signs is that the sky and the earth stand by His Command. Then when He calls you forth from the earth in a single call, behold, you will come forth. **26.** To Him belongs whoever is in the heavens and on the earth. All are devoutly obedient to Him. **27.** It is He Who produces creation, then reproduces it. That is very easy for Him. To Him belongs the loftiest exemplification in the heavens and on the earth. He is the Mighty and the Wise. **28.** He presents to you an example from yourselves: Do you have partners from among those whom your right hands possess to share as equals from what We have provided for you? Do you fear them as you would fear each other? So do We explain the signs in detail to a people who understand. **29.** Rather, those who do wrong follow their caprices without having knowledge. But who will guide those whom God has led astray? They will have no helpers. **30.** So direct your face toward religion as an upright—God's disposition—upon which He created people. There is no altering in God's creation. That is the upright religion, but most people do not know. **31.** Turn to Him, revere Him, perform prayer, and do not be among the idolators, **32.** or those who divided their religion and became factions where each party is content with what it partakes. **33.** When harm befalls people, they call upon their Lord by turning to Him in repentance. Then when He offers them a taste of His Mercy, observe a group of them attribute partners to their Lord, **34.** as if ungrateful for what We have given them. So "Enjoy yourselves! For soon you will know." **35.** Or have We sent down any evidence to them that validates what they attribute as partners to Him? **36.** When We grant people a taste of mercy, they are happy with it; but if harm befalls them as a consequence of what their own hands have done, they fall into despair. **37.** Do they not perceive that God extends sustenance for whomever He wills? In that indeed are signs for a people who believe. **38.** So give to the kinsman his right, and to the indigent, and the traveler. That is better for those who desire the Countenance of God. It is they who will prosper. **39.** That which you lay out from usury might increase through the wealth of other people, but it does not increase with God. But what you lay out in alms, while desiring the Countenance of God—it is they who receive a manifold increase. **40.** God is the One who creates you, provides for you, causes you to die, and then restores you to life. Is there anyone among those whom you attribute as partners that does any of that? Glory be to Him and exalted is He above the partners they attribute. **41.** Corruption appeared on land and sea because of what people's hands have earned that perhaps they might return. **42.** Say, "Travel upon the earth and observe the fate of those beforehand, most of whom were idolators." **43.** Set your face to the upright religion before there comes a Day from God that no one can repel. That Day, they will be spread apart. **44.** Whoever disbelieves, his disbelief is to his own detriment. Whoever works righteousness will make provision for their own souls, **45.** that He may reward those who believe and perform righteous deeds from His Bounty. Truly He does not like the disbelievers. **46.** Among His signs is that He sends the winds as bearers of good news to let you taste of His Mercy, that the ships may sail by His Command, that you may seek of His Bounty, and that perhaps you may be grateful. **47.** We have indeed sent messengers to nations before you and they brought them clear signs. Then We meted out retribution to those who were guilty. It is incumbent upon Us to help the believers. **48.** God is the One who sends the winds, which then raise the clouds. He spreads them across the sky as He wills and then breaks them apart until you see the rain emerging from within them. Then when He bestows it upon whomever He wills among His servants, they rejoice, **49.** although before it was sent down upon them, they were in despair. **50.** So observe the effects of God's Mercy and how He revives the earth after its death. Indeed this proves that He is the Reviver of the dead for He is Powerful over all things. **51.** If We were to send a wind and they were to see it turn yellow, they would certainly disbelieve. **52.** For indeed, you do not make the dead hear, nor do you make the deaf hear the call when they turn their backs, **53.** nor do you guide the blind from straying. You cannot make anyone hear except for those who believe in Our signs and are Muslim. **54.** God is He. Who created you from weakness, then ordained strength after weakness, then ordained weakness and old age after strength. He creates whatever He wills. He is the Knowing and the Powerful. **55.** On the Day when the Hour takes place, the guilty will swear they tarried no more than an hour. By such, they were deluded by **56.** those who were given knowledge and belief will say, "Indeed you tarried in God's Book until the Day of Resurrection. This is the Day of Resurrection, but you did not know." **57.** On that Day, the excuses of those who did wrong will not benefit them, nor can they make amends. **58.** We have indeed cited every kind of parable for people in this Quran. If you bring them a sign, those who disbelieve will be sure to say, "You make nothing more than false claims." **59.** Thus does God seal the hearts of those who do not know. **60.** So be patient. God's Promise is indeed true. Do not let those with uncertainty cause you unrest.

Surah 31

LUQMĀN

Luqmān

In the Name of God, the Compassionate, the Merciful

1. *Alif. Lām. Mīm.* 2. These are the signs of the Wise Book, 3. guidance and mercy for the righteous 4. who perform prayer, give alms, and who firmly believe in the Hereafter. 5. It is they who are guided by their Lord, and it is they who will prosper. 6. Among people are those who purchase vain discourse without knowledge only to lead astray from the way of God as they take it in mockery. There will be a humiliating punishment for them. 7. When Our signs are recited unto him, he turns away arrogantly as if he did not hear them, as if there was deafness in his ears. So inform him of a painful punishment. 8. Indeed, for those who believe and perform righteous deeds, Gardens of Bliss will be theirs 9. to dwell in forever. This is God's true promise. He is the Mighty, the Wise. 10. As you see, He created the heavens without pillars and cast firm mountains onto the earth, in case it shakes beneath you, and scattered about every kind of beast there. We sent water down from the sky and produced there a pair from every bountiful species. 11. This is the creation of God. So show me what those besides Him have created. The wrongdoers are indeed in obvious error. 12. Truly We gave Luqmān wisdom: "Give thanks to God!" Whoever gives thanks, he gives thanks for himself and whoever disbelieves, truly God is Self-Sufficient and Praised. 13. Behold, Luqmān said to his son, admonishing him, "O my son! Do not attribute partners unto God for indeed, attributing partners is an enormous fallacy." 14. We have commanded man concerning his parents. His mother bore him, effort upon effort and his weaning was two years. Give thanks to Me and to your parents. To Me is the final destination. 15. But if they strive to make you attribute a partner to Me of which you have no knowledge, then do not obey them. Associate with them in the world in a kindly fashion, but follow the way

of those who turn in repentance unto Me. Then to Me is your return, and I will inform you of what you did. **16.** "O my son! If it were but the weight of a mustard seed whether it is in a rock, in the heavens, or on the earth, God will bring it forth. Truly God is Benevolent and Aware. **17.** O my son! Perform prayer, enjoin right, forbid wrong, and bear patiently with whatever might happen to you. That is of the most commendable undertakings. **18.** Do not turn your cheek at people in a condescending manner, nor walk proudly upon the earth. God certainly does not love every conceited boaster. **19.** Be moderate in your pace and lower your voice for the vilest of voices are those of asses." **20.** Have you not considered that God has made whatever is in the heavens and whatever is on the earth subservient to you, and He has poured His Blessings upon you both openly and covertly? Among people are those who dispute about God without knowledge, without guidance, and without an illuminating Book. **21.** "When they are told, 'Follow what God has revealed,' they reply, 'We will follow only what we found our forefathers practicing.' What! Even if Satan is leading them to the punishment of the Inferno?" **22.** Whoever submits his face to God and is righteous has indeed grasped the most trustworthy handhold. Unto God is the end of all affairs. **23.** Whoever does not believe, do not let his disbelief grieve you. Unto Us is their return. We will then inform them of what they did. Truly God knows what lies within breasts. **24.** We will grant them a little enjoyment, but We will then compel them toward a severe punishment. **25.** Were you to ask them, "Who created the heavens and the earth?" they would certainly say, "God." Say, "Praise be to God." Truly most of them do not know. **26.** Unto God belongs whatever is in the heavens and on the earth. Truly God is the Self-Sufficient and Praised. **27.** If all the trees on the earth were pens, and if the sea were ink, and seven oceans added to the supply, the Words of God would not be exhausted. Truly God is Mighty and Wise. **28.** Your creation and your resurrection are but a single soul. God is indeed Hearing and Seeing. **29.** Have you not observed that God fuses night into the day and that He fuses day into night and that He made the sun and the moon subservient, each running for an appointed term and that God is Aware of whatever you do? **30.** That is because God, He is the Truth and whatever they call upon other than Him is false. God is the Exalted and the Great. **31.** Have you not seen how the ships sail upon the sea by God's Blessing so that He may show you, His signs? In that are indeed signs for every patient and grateful person. **32.** When waves cover them like canopies, they call upon God, bestowing religion entirely to Him. Then when He has delivered them safely to land, some of them take an intermediate course. No one rejects Our signs except all who are disloyal and ungrateful.

33. O people! Revere your Lord and fear a day in which no parent will avail his child, and no child will avail his parent. God's Promise is true indeed. So do not let the life of this world delude you, and do not let the deluder delude you regarding God. **34.** God indeed has knowledge of the Hour. He sends down the rain and knows what lies in wombs. No soul knows what it will earn on the morrow and no soul knows in what land it will die. Truly God is Knowing and Aware.

Surah 32

PROSTRATION

al-Sajdah

In the Name of God, the Compassionate, the Merciful

1. *Alif. Lām. Mīm.* 2. The revelation of the Book in which there is no doubt is from the Lord of the Worlds. 3. Or do they say, "He has forged it?" It is indeed the truth from your Lord that you may forewarn a people to whom no warner has come before you that perhaps they may be guided. 4. It is God Who created the heavens and the earth and whatever is between them in six days, and then He then ascended the Throne. Apart from Him, you have neither protector nor intercessor. Will you not then remember? 5. He manages the affair from Heaven to earth, and then it rises to Him in a day that measures a thousand years in your reckoning. 6. Such is the Knower of the Unseen and the Seen, the Mighty and the Merciful, 7. Who made all that He created beautiful, and Who began the creation of mankind from clay. 8. Then He made his progeny from the flow of an insignificant fluid. 9. Then He fashioned him and breathed of His Spirit into him. He endowed you with hearing, sight, and hearts. Little do you show gratitude! 10. They say, "What! When we vanish from the earth, will we become a creation renewed?" Truly, they do not believe in the meeting with their Lord. 11. Say, "The Angel of death in charge of you will take you then; to your Lord you will be returned." 12. If only you could see when the guilty bend their heads low before their Lord: "Our Lord! We have seen and we have heard, so send us back so we may work righteousness. We are indeed convinced." 13. Had We willed, We would have given every soul its guidance. But the Word from Me will come due. "I will indeed fill Hell with jinn and people all together!" 14. So taste—for having forgotten the meeting of this Day of yours—for indeed, We have forgotten you! Taste the everlasting punishment for what you did. 15. However, not so for those who believe in Our signs and who, when reminded of them, fall in prostration, glorify the praise of their Lord, and are not conceited, 16. as their sides forsake their beds to call

upon their Lord out of fear and hope, and who spend from what We have provided them. **17.** No soul knows which delights of the eye remain undisclosed, a reward for what they performed. **18.** Is one who believes like one who is sinful? They are not equal. **19.** As for those who believe and perform righteous deeds, sheltered Gardens will be theirs as a welcoming for what they performed. **20.** As for those who are sinful, their refuge is the Fire. Whenever they want to depart from it, they are returned to it. It is said to them, "Taste the punishment of the Fire that you used to deny!" **21.** We make them taste the lesser punishment before the greater punishment that they might return. **22.** Who does greater wrong than one who has been reminded of the signs of his Lord, then turns away from them? We will take vengeance upon the guilty. **23.** Indeed, We gave Moses the Book. So do not be in doubt regarding the meeting with Him. We made him a guide for the Children of Israel. **24.** We appointed leaders from among them who guided Our Command because of their patience. They were certain of Our signs. **25.** Truly your Lord will distinguish between them on the Day of Resurrection regarding matters in which they differed. **26.** Does it not serve as a guidance for them? How many generations did We destroy before them amidst whose homes they walk? In that are indeed signs. Will they not listen? **27.** Have they not considered how We drive water to a barren earth to produce crops for them and for their cattle to feed? Do they not, see? **28.** They say, "When will this victory be, if you are truthful?" **29.** Say, "On the Day of Victory, faith will not benefit those who disbelieved, nor will they be granted respite." **30.** Then turn away from them and wait. They, too, are waiting.

Surah 33

THE PARTIES

al-Ahzāb

In the Name of God, the Compassionate, the Merciful

1. O Prophet! Revere God and do not obey the disbelievers and the hypocrites. Truly God is Knowing and Wise. **2.** Follow what is revealed to you from your Lord. Truly God is Aware of whatever you do. **3.** Trust in God—God suffices as a Guardian. **4.** God has not placed two hearts in the breast of any man. Nor has He made your wives whom you repudiate with the practice of *zihār* (a pagan form of divorce) your mothers. Nor has He made those whom you claim as your sons, your sons. Those are only words from your mouths. But God speaks Truth and guides the way. **5.** Call them after their fathers. That is more equitable before God. If you do not know their fathers, then they are your brothers in faith or your dependents. There is no blame on you for making a mistake in that respect, but only for what your hearts had intended. God is Forgiving and Merciful. **6.** The Prophet is closer to the believers than they are to themselves, and his wives are their mothers, and blood relations are closer to one another, according to the Book of God, than are the believers and the emigrants. Nonetheless, you should act justly toward your friends. That is inscribed in the Book. **7.** Remember when We took the covenants from the prophets, then from you, from Noah, Abraham, Moses, and Jesus, son of Mary. We took a solemn covenant from them **8.** that the truthful may be questioned concerning their truthfulness. He has prepared a painful punishment for the disbelievers. **9.** O you who believe! Remember the Blessing of God upon you when the forces came upon you, and We sent a wind against them that you did not see. God sees whatever you do. **10.** When they came upon you from above and below you, when their eyes swerved and their hearts reached their throats, you conceptualized many things about God. **11.** It was there that the believers were tried and shaken severely. **12.** The hypocrites and those in whose hearts is a disease said, "God and His Messenger promised us nothing but delusion." **13.** Then a group among them said, "O people of Yathrib! You have no stance, so turn back." Afterward, a group among them sought permission from the Prophet, saying, "Truly our homes are exposed," though they were not exposed. They wanted nothing but to flee. **14.** Had they entered the city from all of its surroundings, then were incited to sedition, they would have readily responded, hesitating only briefly, **15.** though they had previously made a covenant with God not to turn their backs. Truly a covenant with God must be answered for. **16.** Say, "Fleeing will not benefit you if you are fleeing from death or killing, because you will only be granted temporary satisfaction. **17.** Say, "Who is it who will protect you from God if He desires evil for you or if He desires mercy for you?" Besides God, they will find no protector or helper for themselves. **18.** Indeed God knows those among you who deter and who say to their brethren, "Come along with us," They will not go to battle, except for a few **19.** who are envious of you. When fear arises, they look at you with rolling eyes, as if overtaken by death. But when the fear passes, they attack you with sharp tongues, driven by envy of your success. These people lack true faith, so God has nullified their deeds — and this is effortless for God. **20.** They believe the enemy forces have not withdrawn, and if they were to return, they would wish to be in the desert with the Bedouins, seeking news about you from afar. Even if they were with you, they would hardly engage in battle. **21.** Indeed you have in the Messenger of God, a beautiful example for those who hope for God and the Last Day and remember God abundantly. **22.** When the believers saw the parties, they said, "This is what God and His Messenger promised. God and His Messenger were truthful." This only added to their faith and submission. **23.** Among the believers are men who have been true to what they pledged unto God. Among them are those who have fulfilled their vow, and among them are those who wait. They did not change in the least, **24.** that God may reward the truthful for their truthfulness and punish the hypocrites if He so desires or even relent unto them for God is truly Forgiving and Merciful. **25.** God turned back those who disbelieved in their rage. They did not attain good. God was enough for the believers in battle. God is Strong and Mighty. **26.** God brought the People of the Book who supported them down from their strongholds and cast terror into their hearts. Some you slew and some you took captive. **27.** He made you heirs of their land, their homes, their property, and a land you have not frequented. God is Powerful over all things. **28.** O Prophet! Say to your wives, "If you desire the life of this world and its embellishment, then come! I will provide for you and release you in a handsome manner. **29.** But if you desire God, his Messenger, and the Abode of the Hereafter, then indeed, God has prepared a great reward for the virtuous among you."

30. O wives of the Prophet! Whoever among you commits a brazen indecency, her punishment will be twofold, and that is easy for God. 31. But whoever among you is devoutly obedient to God and His Messenger and works righteousness, We will compensate her twofold, and We will have prepared for her a generous provision. 32. O wives of the Prophet! You are not like other women. If you are reverent, then do not be overly complaisant in speech, else one in whose heart is a disease will be moved to desire. So speak with modesty. 33. Live in your homes and do not display your charms as previously displayed during the Age of Ignorance. Perform prayer, give alms, and obey God and His Messenger. God only wants to remove abomination from you — People of the House — and to purify you completely. 34. Remember what is recited unto you in your homes from among the signs of the Wisdom of God. God is indeed Kind and Aware. 35. For Muslim men and Muslim women, believing men, and believing women, devout men and devout women, truthful men and truthful women, patient men and patient women, humble men and humble women, charitable men and charitable women, men who fast and women who fast, men who guard their chastity and women who guard their chastity, and men who remember God and women who remember God, God has prepared forgiveness and a great reward. 36. It is not for a believing man or a believing woman, when God and His Messenger have decreed a matter, to have a choice about the matter. Whoever disobeys God and His Messenger has erred, an obvious error. 37. Remember when you said to the one whom God had blessed and whom you had favored, "Keep your wife and be mindful of God," while concealing within yourself what God was going to reveal, and you feared people, although God is more deserving of being feared. Then when Zayd renounced his marital claim upon her, We wed her to you so there would be no restrictions for the believers with respect to the wives of their adopted sons, when the latter have renounced their marital claims on them. The Command of God will be fulfilled. 38. There is no restriction for the Prophet in what God has ordained for him. That is the practice of God among those who passed before. God's Command is an absolute decree determined 39. for those who convey the messages of God and fear Him, and fear no one but God, for God is enough of a Reckoner. 40. Muhammad is not the father of any man among you, rather he is the Messenger of God and the Seal of the prophets. God has knowledge of all things. 41. O you who believe! Remember God with plentiful remembrance, 42. and glorify him morning and evening. 43. It is He who Blesses you, as do His angels, that He may take you out of darkness into light. He is Merciful unto the believers. 44. Their greeting on the Day they meet Him will be "Peace." He has prepared a generous reward for them. 45. O Prophet! We have indeed sent you as a witness, as a bearer of good news, and

as a warner, **46.** as one who calls unto God by His Leave, and as a luminous lantern. **47.** Give good news to the believers that there will be Great Bounty for them from God. **48.** Do not obey the disbelievers and the hypocrites. Disregard their offenses and trust in God, for God suffices as a Guardian. **49.** O you who believe! If you marry believing women and then divorce them before you have touched them, there will be no waiting [*Iddah*] period to count. Therefore, provide for them and release them benevolently. **50.** O Prophet! We have made lawful for you, your wives to whom you have given them their bridewealth, as well as those whom your right hand possesses from those whom God has granted you as spoils of war, the daughters of your paternal uncles and the daughters of your paternal aunts, the daughters of your maternal uncles and the daughters of your maternal aunts who emigrated with you, and any believing women if she offers herself to the Prophet and if the Prophet wants to marry her — applicable to you only — and not other believers. We know well what We ordained for them in respect to their wives and those whom their right hands possess, so there will be no blame on you. God is Forgiving and Merciful. **51.** You may decline whomever you will among them or receive whomever you will. There is no blame on you if you desire any of those whom you declined. As such, it is possible that they will be comforted, will not grieve, and will be satisfied with what you have given them. God knows what is in your hearts. God is Knowing and Clement. **52.** Beyond that, women are not lawful for you to exchange for other wives, though their beauty impresses you, except for those whom your right hand possesses. God is indeed the Watcher over all things. **53.** O you who believe! Do not enter the homes of the Prophet for a meal without waiting for the prearranged time, but if you are summoned, enter. Then when you have eaten, disperse. Do not linger to seek conversation. That would indeed offend the Prophet, and he would be embarrassed to tell you, but God is not discomfited of the truth. When you ask his wives for anything, ask them from behind a veil. That is purer for your hearts and their hearts. You should not offend the Messenger of God, nor ever marry his wives after him. That would truly be an enormity from God's perspective. **54.** Whether you disclose something or conceal it, truly God has knowledge of all things. **55.** There is no blame upon them to appear before their fathers, or their sons, or their brothers, or their brothers' sons, or their sisters' sons, or their own women, or those whom their right hands possess. Revere God, for God is indeed witness over all things. **56.** Truly God and His angels invoke blessings upon the Prophet. O you who believe! Invoke blessings upon him, and greetings of peace. **57.** Indeed those who offend God and His Messenger, God will curse them in this life and in the Hereafter and has prepared a humiliating punishment for them. **58.** As for those who offend, believing men and believing women for other than what they have committed to, they bear the burden of calumny and clear sin. **59.** O Prophet! Tell your wives and your daughters, and the women of the believers to draw their cloaks over themselves. By such, it is likelier that they will be known and not insulted. God is indeed Forgiving and Merciful. **60.** Because if the hypocrites, those with sickness in their hearts, and those who spread false rumors in the city do not cease, We will surely incite you against them, and they will only remain your neighbors there for a short time. **61.** Accursed wherever they are found! They will be taken and utterly slain **62.** as was the practice of God with past populaces, and you will find no change in the practice of God. **63.** People question you concerning the Hour. Say, "Knowledge of that lies with God alone, and what do you know: the Hour could be soon." **64.** Truly God curses the disbelievers and has prepared a blazing fire for them **65.** to abide there forever. They will find neither protector nor helper. **66.** On the Day when their faces are turned over in the Fire, they will say, "Oh! Had we obeyed God and obeyed the Messenger!" **67.** They will say, "Our Lord! Truly we obeyed our leaders and elders. They made us stray from the path. **68.** Our Lord! Present them with double the penalty and curse them with a greater curse." **69.** O you who believe! Do not be like those who wronged Moses. God cleared him of the false accusations they made, and he was held in high honor by God. **70.** O you who believe! Revere God and speak justly, **71.** that He may appropriate your deeds for you and forgive your sins. Whoever obeys God and His Messenger has attained a great triumph. **72.** We did indeed offer 'the Trust' to the heavens, the earth, and the mountains, but they refused to undertake it. They were wary of it, yet man undertook it. Truly he has proven himself an ignorant transgressor. **73.** As such, God will punish the hypocritical men and hypocritical women, the idolatrous men, and the idolatrous women. God will relent to the believing men and believing women. God is Forgiving and Merciful.

Surah 34

Saba

Saba

In the Name of God, the Compassionate, the Merciful

1. Praise be to God to Whom belongs whatever is in the heavens and whatever is on the earth. Praise is His in the Hereafter. He is the Wise and the Knowledgeable. 2. He knows of what enters the earth, of what comes out of it, what descends from Heaven, and what ascends there. He is the Merciful and the Forgiving. 3. Those who disbelieve say, "The Hour will never come upon us." Say, "Truly by my Lord and by the Knower of the Unseen, it will certainly come to you." Not an iota's weight evades Him in the heavens or on the earth, nor smaller, nor larger than that, but that it is in a clear Book, 4. that He may reward those who believe and perform righteous deeds. Forgiveness and a generous provision will be theirs, 5. but there will be a painful punishment for those who strive tirelessly to thwart Our signs. 6. Those who have been given knowledge perceive that what has been sent down upon you from your Lord is the truth and it guides to the path of the Mighty and the Praised. 7. Those who disbelieve say, "Should we show you a man who will inform you that when you are torn to shreds, you will be in a new creation?" 8. Has he feigned a lie against God, or has a spirit possessed him? Those who do not believe in the Hereafter will indeed be in torment and extreme error. 9. Have they not considered what is before them and what is behind them of the sky and the earth? Had We willed, We could cause the earth to consume them or allow fragments of the sky to fall upon them. In that are indeed signs for every devoted servant. 10. Truly We gave David bounty from Us: "O mountains! Echo God's praises with him—you birds as well!" We made iron pliable for him 11. so, he could create coats of mail and craft the links with precision while working righteousness. I certainly see what you do. 12. For Solomon, the morning sequence of the wind was a month, and the evening sequence was a month. For him, We made a fount of molten copper to flow for him. Of the jinn

are those who worked hand in hand with him by the Leave of his Lord, but as for those of them who deviate from Our Command, We will make them taste the punishment of the Inferno **13.** making for them whatever he willed from elevated stations, statues, basins like reservoirs, and fixed cauldrons. "Work, O family of David, with gratitude, though a few of My servants are grateful." **14.** When We decreed death upon him, the only thing that signified his death to them was a crawling creature of the earth feeding off his staff. When he fell, it was obvious to the jinn that had they known the Unseen, they would not have remained in humiliating punishment. **15.** For the Saba, there was indeed a sign in their homes. There were two gardens, one to the right and one to the left. "Eat of the sustenance given by your Lord and offer Him your gratitude—a bountiful territory and a forgiving Lord." **16.** But they turned away, so We sent the flood of the *Arim* (dam) upon them. We exchanged their two gardens with two gardens that generated bitter fruit, a few lote trees and tamarisks. **17.** Such did We reward them for having disbelieved. Do We reward any but the disbeliever? **18.** We arranged between them and the towns We had blessed, towns that could be easily perceived. We measured the distance between them: "Travel between them safely by night and by day." **19.** But they said, "Our Lord, lengthen the distance of our journeys." They wronged themselves, so We turned them into history. We scattered them in every direction. In this are indeed signs for the patient and the grateful. **20.** Indeed, Iblīs proved his opinion of them to be true. They all followed him, except for a party among the believers. **21.** He had no authority over them, except that We may know who it is that believes in the Hereafter and who among them is in doubt of that. Your Lord guards over all things. **22.** Say, "Call upon those you claim besides God. They do not possess even an iota's weight of authority in the heavens or the earth. They have no share in them, nor does He have any helper among them." **23.** No one will benefit from intercession with Him save for whomever He has granted permission. Even if terror is removed from their hearts, they will say, "What did your Lord say?" They will say, "The truth. He is the Exalted and the Great." **24.** Say, "Who provides for you from the heavens and the earth?" Say, "God. Either we or you are rightly guided or in obvious error." **25.** Say, "You will not be questioned about what we were guilty of, nor will we be questioned about what you do." **26.** Say, "Our Lord will gather us together and He will then decide between us in truth. He is the Judge and the Knower." **27.** Say, "Show me those whom you have joined with Him as partners. But no; rather, He is God the Mighty and the Wise." **28.** We only sent you as a bearer of good news and a warner to all people. But most people do not know. **29.** They say, "When will this promise come to be, if you are truthful?" **30.** Say, "You will have a meeting on a Day that you cannot delay or advance by a single hour." **31.** The disbelievers say, "We will not believe in this Quran, nor in what was held before it." If you could only see when the wrongdoers were standing before their Lord hurling reproaches against one another. Those who were weak and oppressed will say to those who were arrogant, "Were it not for you, we would have been believers." **32.** Those who were arrogant will say to those who were weak, "Did we turn you away from guidance after it had come to you? No, but you were guilty!" **33.** Those who were weak and oppressed will say to those who were arrogant, "No, but there was plotting by night and by day when you ordered us to disbelieve in God and to attribute equals to Him." They will hide their remorse when they see the punishment, and We will place chains around the necks of those who disbelieve. Will they be requitted for other than what they did? **34.** We sent no warner to a town but that the affluent would say, "We disbelieve in that which you have been sent." **35.** They say, "We are greater in wealth and children, and we will not be punished." **36.** Say, "Indeed, my Lord extends provision for whomever He wills and esteems, but most people do not know." **37.** Neither your wealth nor your children will draw you closer to Us, except for those who believe and work righteousness. Their reward will be manifold for what they did, and they will be in secure stations. **38.** Those who strive tirelessly to thwart Our signs, will be brought forth into punishment. **39.** Say, "Indeed my Lord extends provision for whomever He wills and esteems among His servants. Whatever you have spent, He will replace. He is the best of providers." **40.** On the Day when He will gather them all together, He will say to the angels, "Were these the ones worshipping you?" **41.** They will reply, "Glory be to You instead of them! You are our Protector instead of them!" Truly they worshipped jinn. Most of them believed in them. **42.** So on that Day, not one of you will have the power to benefit or to harm the other. We will say to the wrongdoers, "Taste the punishment of the Fire that you used to deny!" **43.** When Our signs are recited unto them as clear proofs, they say, "This is nothing but a man whose desire is to hold you back from what your forefathers worshipped." They say, "This is nothing but a made-up falsehood." Those who disbelieve say to the Truth when it comes to them, "This is nothing but clear sorcery," **44.** though We have not given them scriptures that they could study, nor have We sent them a warner before you. **45.** Their predecessors had denied, though these have not even received a tenth of what We had given them, yet they denied My messengers. How terrible was My rejection! **46.** Say, "I only urge you to do one thing which is to stand before God in pairs or individually and then, reflect. There is no insanity in your companion. He is no more than a warner to you in face of a severe punishment." **47.** Say, "I do not ask of you any reward — for that will be yours — my reward is only with God. He is Witness over all things." **48.** Say, "Truly my Lord casts the truth, the

Knower of things Unseen." **49.** Say, "Truth has arrived. Falsehood does not initiate and or restore anything."**50.** Say, "If I have gone astray, I have only gone astray to my own detriment and if I am rightly guided, it is through what my Lord has revealed unto me. He is indeed Hearing and Near." **51.** If you could only see when they are terrified and there is no escape, and they are seized from a nearby place. **52.** They will say, "We believe in it!" But how can they attain it from a distant location? **53.** They previously rejected it while doubting the Unseen from a far-off place. **54.** A barrier is set between them and what they desire, as it was done to those who were previously like them. They were indeed in disquieting doubt.

Surah 35

THE ORIGINATOR

Fātir

In the Name of God, the Compassionate, the Merciful

1. Praise be to God, Originator of the heavens and the earth, Who appoints the angels as messengers of two, three, and four wings, expanding creation as He desires. Truly God is Powerful over all things. **2.** Whatever mercy God delivers to people, no one will withhold. And whatever He withholds, no one will release afterward. He is the Mighty and the Wise. **3.** O people! Remember God's Blessings upon you. Is there a creator other than God who provides for you from Heaven and earth? There is no god but He. So why are you deluded? **4.** If they reject you, messengers before you were rejected, but to God all matters are returned. **5.** O people! God's Promise is indeed true. So do not let the life of this world deceive you, nor let the deceiver deceive you with respect to God. **6.** Indeed, Satan is your enemy, so take him as an enemy. He only calls on his followers that they may be among the companions of the Inferno. **7.** Those who disbelieve will receive a severe punishment. Those who believe and work righteousness will receive forgiveness and a great reward. **8.** Then what about the one whose evil conduct seems alluring to him such that he perceives it as good? God leads astray whomever He wills and guides whomever He wills. So do not let your soul be carried away in sorrow over them. God truly knows what they do. **9.** It is God Who sends the winds to make the clouds rise, then We drive them to a land that is lifeless to revive the earth after its death. Such will be the Resurrection! **10.** Whoever desires majesty, know that overall majesty belongs to God. To Him ascends the good word, and He elevates the righteous deed. Those who plot evil deeds will be severely punished, and their plotting will perish. **11.** God created you from dust, then from a drop of semen, then He made you pairs. No female will bear or give birth without His Knowledge.

No one will live a lengthy life, nor a shortened life unless it is decreed. Truly that is easy for God. **12.** The two seas are not equal. One is sweet, satisfying, and pleasant to drink from, and the other is salty and bitter. Yet from each, you consume fresh meat and retrieve ornaments that you can wear. You see the ships navigating through there, that you may seek of His Bounty, and that perhaps you may offer gratitude. **13.** He fuses night into day and fuses day into night. He made the sun and the moon subservient, each running for an appointed term. That is God your Lord. To Him, belongs sovereignty. As for those who you call upon instead of Him, they do not possess so much as a speck on a datestone. **14.** If you call upon them, they do not hear your call, and even if they heard it, they would not answer you. On the Day of Resurrection, they will disavow the partnership you attributed. No one will inform you like the One Who is Aware. **15.** O people! You are the needful of God. He is the Self-Sufficient and the Praised. **16.** If He wills, He can remove you and bring forth a new creation. **17.** That is not difficult for God. **18.** No one will bear the burden of another, though one heavily burdened will call for his burden to be borne. But no one will bear any of it, even if they were relatives. You warn only those who fear their Unseen Lord and perform prayer. Whoever purifies himself will indeed be purifying his own soul, and to God is the final destination. **19.** The blind and the seeing are not equal, **20.** nor the darkness and light, **21.** nor the shade and the scorching heat. **22.** The living and the dead are not equal. God can certainly make whomever He wills to hear, but you cannot make those in graves to hear. **23.** You are no more than a warner. **24.** We have indeed sent you with the truth as a bearer of good news and as a warner. There has been no nation but that a warner has passed among them. **25.** If they deny you, those before them have also denied. Their messengers had brought them clear signs, scriptures, and the Book of Enlightenment. **26.** Then I seized those who disbelieved. How terrible was My rejection! **27.** Have you not considered that God sends water down from the sky? With it We bring forth produce of various colors? In the mountains are tracts of white and red, made of different shades, and others, pitch-black. **28.** There are also among people beasts and cattle of diverse colors. Yet only the knowledgeable among His servants, fear God. Truly God is Mighty and Forgiving. **29.** Truly those who recite the Book of God, perform prayer, and spend of what We provided them discreetly and publicly aspire to a trade that will never fail, **30.** that He may pay them their reward and add to it from His Bounty. Truly He is Forgiving and Thankful. **31.** What We have revealed to you from the Book is the truth authenticating what came before it. Truly God is Seeing and Aware of His servants. **32.** Then We passed the Book on to those of Our servants whom We chose. Among them, there are those who wrong themselves, those who follow a moderate path, and those who, by God's permission, are foremost in doing good deeds. This is the greatest blessing. **33.** They will enter Gardens of Eden and will be adorned there with bracelets of gold and pearls. Their clothing there will be of silk. **34.** They will say, "Praise be to God Who has liberated us from grief. Indeed, our Lord is Forgiving and Thankful, **35.** Who, of His Bounty, made us worthy of living in the Abode of an Everlasting Life where no weariness nor fatigue will touch us." **36.** As for those who disbelieved, the Fire of Hell will be theirs that they die incessantly, and their torture from the Fire will not be lightened. As such, We avenge every disbeliever. **37.** They will cry out there, "Our Lord! Let us return so we may do righteous deeds, different from what we used to do." He will say, "Did We not grant you a life long enough for anyone who wished to reflect to do so? And a warner came to you! So taste the consequences, for the wrongdoers will have no helpers." **38.** Truly God knows of the Unseen in the heavens and the earth. Truly He knows what lies within breasts. **39.** It is He Who appointed you vicegerents on the earth. Therefore, whoever disbelieves, will own his disbeliefs. Nothing will be added to the disbelief of the disbelievers but revulsion. Nothing will be added to the disbelief of the disbelievers but loss. **40.** Say, "Have you considered your partners that you call upon instead of God? Show me what they have created of the earth. Do they have a share in the heavens, or did We give them a book with clear signs that they can validate?" Truly the wrongdoers promise one another nothing but delusion. **41.** Truly God supports the heavens and the earth in case, they fall apart. If they were to fall apart, none will support them after Him. Truly He is Clement and Forgiving. **42.** They swore by God their most solemn oaths that were a warner to come to them, they would be more rightly guided than any other nations. Yet, when a warner came to them, it only added to their aversion. **43.** They grew arrogant on earth while plotting evil. Evil plotting will only affect its designers. Are they looking back to the ways of the primordial? You will not find an alternative to the way of God, and you will not find alteration in the way of God. **44.** Have they not traveled the earth to observe how those before them fared in the end, though they were greater than them in strength? God will not be frustrated by anything in the heavens or on the earth. God is truly Knowing and Powerful. **45.** Were God to punish people based on what they deserve, He would not leave a single creature on the face of the earth, but He gives them respite until an appointed term. However, when their term comes, God is indeed perceptive of His servants.

Surah 36

YĀ SĪN

Yā Sīn

In the Name of God, the Compassionate, the Merciful

1. *Yā. Sīn.* 2. By the Wise Quran, 3. you are indeed among the message bearers, 4. and on a straight path 5. sent down by the Mighty and the Merciful, 6. that you may warn a people whose fathers were not warned. As such, they were heedless. 7. Indeed the Word proved true for most of them, but they did not believe. 8. We have surely placed shackles around their necks, up to their chins, to keep their hands forced upward. 9. We placed a barrier before them, a barrier behind them, and blindfolded them, so they cannot see. 10. Whether you warn them or do not warn them, they will not believe. 11. Only warn whoever follows the Remembrance and fears the Compassionate Unseen. So give him good news of forgiveness and a generous reward. 12. Indeed, We give life to the dead, and record what they have sent forth and what they have left behind. We have recorded everything in a clear registry. 13. Set forth for them is the parable of the people of a town where the messengers arrived. 14. When We sent two to them, they rejected them. Therefore, We strengthened them with a third and they said, "Truly, We have been sent as messengers to you." 15. They said, "You are but humans like us and the Compassionate has not sent anything down. You are certainly lying." 16. They said, "Our Lord knows. We have indeed been sent down to you as messengers, 17. and our only charge is to proclaim a clear message." 18. They said, "Indeed, we foretell an evil omen. If you do not stop, we will certainly stone you, and you will be inflicted by us with a painful punishment." 19. They said, "Your projection of an evil omen is upon yourselves, though you have been reminded. You are but a prodigal people!" 20. Then a man came running from the outskirts of the city. He said, "O my people! Follow the messengers! 21. Follow those who do not ask you

for a reward and who are rightly guided. 22. Why should I not worship Him Who originated me and unto Whom you will be returned? 23. Should I take gods instead of Him? If the Compassionate wanted to harm me, their intercession would be of no use to me, nor could they salvage me. 24. Then indeed, I would be in obvious error. 25. Truly, I believe in your Lord, so listen to me." 26. It was said, "Enter the Garden!" He said, "If my people only knew 27. how my Lord forgave me and placed me among the honored." 28. After him, We did not send any forces down from heaven against his people, and nor would We send down. 29. It was but a single cry, then behold, they were quenched. 30. Woe for the servants! A messenger does not come to them, but that they mock him. 31. Have they not considered how many generations We destroyed before them, such that they will not return to them? 32. Indeed, all of them will be present before Us. 33. A sign to them is the dead earth. We revive it and retrieve grain from it, that they may eat there. 34. We produce gardens of date palms and grapevines and make springs gush forth, 35. that they may eat of the fruits made by their hands. Will they not be grateful? 36. Glory be unto He Who has created all of the pairs from what the earth produces from among themselves and from other things that they do not know. 37. A sign unto them is the night. We strip the day from that place and behold, they are in darkness. 38. The sun runs its course to a lodging place of its own. That is the decree of the Mighty and the Knowing. 39. For the moon, We have decreed phases for it until it returns and looks similar to an old palm stalk. 40. It is not allowed for the sun to catch up with the moon, nor for the night to outstrip the day, while each of them orbits in space. 41. A sign to them is that We carried their progeny in the fully loaded Ark. 42. We created for them the like on which they navigate. 43. Had We willed, We could have drowned them with no one to call on and they would not have been delivered 44. save through mercy by Us and for temporary gratification. 45. Then they were told, "Be mindful of what is before you and what is behind you that perhaps you may receive mercy." 46. Not a sign comes to them from the signs of their Lord, but they turn away from it. 47. When it is said to them, "Spend of what God has provided you," those who disbelieved say to the believers, "Are we to feed someone who, if God willed, He would feed him? You are in nothing more than obvious error." 48. They say, "When is this Promise, if you are truthful?" 49. They wait for no more than a single cry that will seize them as they argue among themselves. 50. They will have no chance to make a bequest, nor to return to their people. 51. The trumpet will be blown and watch how they will rush forth from their graves to their Lord. 52. They will say, "Woe to us! Who raised us from our place of rest?" "This is what the Compassionate had promised. "The messengers were right!" 53. There will be but a single cry, then, behold how they will be present before Us! **54.** For on this Day, not a soul will be wronged in any way, and you will not be rewarded for other than what you did. **55.** For indeed it is the Day, the inhabitants of the Garden will be functioning with joy. **56.** They and their spouses will be reclining on couches under the shade. **57.** They will have fruit there and whatever else they call for. **58.** "Peace!" A Word from a most Merciful Lord. **59.** O guilty ones! Stand apart on this Day. **60.** Did I not command you, O Children of Adam not to worship Satan since he is truly a clear enemy unto you **61.** and to worship Me? This is the straight path. **62.** He has indeed led many among you astray. Did you not understand? **63.** This is the Hell that you were promised. **64.** Burn there today for having disbelieved! **65.** On that Day, We will seal their mouths. Their hands will speak to Us and their feet will bear witness to what they earned. **66.** Had We willed, We would have blotted out their eyes. They would then race to the path, but how would they see? **67.** Had We willed, We would have transformed them in their places so they could neither move forward nor backward. **68.** For whomever We give a long life, We will reverse in creation. Do they not understand? **69.** We have not taught him poetry, nor is it befitting for him. It is but a remembrance and a clear Quran, **70.** to warn those who are alive and to confirm the truth of the Word against the disbelievers. **71.** Have they not considered that from among what Our hands have produced, We created cattle to be under their dominion. **72.** We tamed them for them that some they may ride and some of which they may eat. **73.** They take benefits and drinks therefrom. Will they not be grateful? **74.** Yet they have taken gods other than God that perhaps they might be helped. **75.** They cannot assist them, even if a prepared army is on their side. **76.** So do not let their speech sadden you. We truly know what they conceal and what they disclose. **77.** Or does a human not see that We created him from a drop of semen, and that then, he becomes a clear adversary? **78.** He sets out examples for Us and forgets his own creation by saying, "Who will revive these bones while they are disintegrated?" **79.** Say, "He Who brought them forth the first time will revive them. He knows of every creation, **80.** "The One who brought forth fire for you from the green tree, allowing you to ignite flames from it." **81.** Is He Who created the heavens and the earth not able to create the like of that? Absolutely! He is the knowing creator. **82.** When He desires a thing, His Command is but to say the word, "Be" and it is. **83.** So glory be to Him in Whose Hand lies the dominion of all things and unto Him, you will be returned.

Surah 37

THOSE WHO ARE IN RANKS

al-Saffāt

In the Name of God, the Compassionate, the Merciful

1. With the ranks in range, **2.** the drifters drifting, **3.** and the reciters of the Remembrance, **4.** indeed your God is One, **5.** the Lord of the heavens and the earth and everything between them, as well as Lord of the easts. **6.** Truly We beautified the lower heaven with the beauty of stars **7.** to guard against every defiant demon. **8.** They do not listen to the Highest Assembly for they are cast out from every side, **9.** rejected, and will be subjected to perpetual penalty, **10.** except one who snatches a fragment, and then is pursued by a piercing flame. **11.** So ask them, if they are more difficult to create than those whom We have created? Truly We created them from sticky clay. **12.** You surely marvel as they mock, **13.** but when they are reminded, they do not remember. **14.** When they see a sign, they mock, **15.** and say, "This is nothing but clear sorcery. **16.** So if we die and turn to dust and bones, we will be resurrected **17.** along with our forefathers?" **18.** Say, "Yes, and you will be degraded." **19.** There will indeed be a single cry and then they will see. **20.** They will say, "Woe unto us! This is the Day of Judgment." **21.** This is the Day of Division that you used to deny. **22.** Gather those who did wrong jointly with their spouses and what they worshipped **23.** besides God and guide them to the path of Hellfire. **24.** Stop them! They will certainly be questioned, **25.** "What stops you from helping one another?" **26.** But they will surrender on this Day. **27.** They will turn to one another **28.** saying, "Indeed you came to us from the right." **29.** They respond, "Truly you were not believers, **30.** and we had no authority over you. You were rather a rebellious people. **31.** So the Word of our Lord is due for us. Therefore, we will indeed be tasting [blazing fire]. **32.** We seduced you and we were the seducers." **33.** Truly, on that Day, they will share in punishment. **34.** Indeed that is how We deal with the guilty. **35.** Truly when they were told, "There is no god, but God," they grew arrogant **36.** saying, "Are we to forsake our gods for an insane poet?" **37.** He has indeed come with the truth and validated the messengers. **38.** Truly you will taste the painful punishment. **39.** You will not be avenged, save for what you did, **40.** but not so for the sincere servants of God. **41.** There will be a known sustenance for them **42.** — fruits. They will be honored **43.** in the Gardens of Bliss, **44.** while on couches facing one another, **45.** and a cup circulating around them from a flowing spring— **46.** white and savoring to those who drink of it. **47.** It does not cause headaches, nor will they be intoxicated by it. **48.** For them, there will be maidens with modest gazes and bright eyes, **49.** as if they were fragile eggs. **50.** They will turn to each other and question one another. **51.** One among them will say, "I had a close companion **52.** who would say, 'Are you among those who bore truth?' **53.** So if we die and turn to dust and bones, we will be resurrected?'" **54.** He will say, "Are you looking?" **55.** So he looked and saw him in the midst of the Hellfire. **56.** He will say, "By God! You were about to destroy me! **57.** Were it not for the blessing of my Lord, I would have been among those present therein. **58.** Is it that we are not going to die **59.** except for our first death? Are we not to be punished? **60.** This is indeed the great triumph!" **61.** Because of this, let the endeavors, endeavor. **62.** Is this a better welcome than the tree of Zaqqūm? **63.** Indeed We have made it a trial for the wrongdoers. **64.** It is certainly a tree that emerges from the depths of Hellfire. **65.** Its spathes are like the heads of demons, **66.** and indeed they will eat from it and fill their bellies with it. **67.** Then on top of it, they will have a mixture of boiling liquid. **68.** Then their return will be to Hellfire. **69.** Indeed, they found their fathers astray, **70.** yet they rushed in their footsteps. **71.** Most of those before them had indeed erred, **72.** though We had truly sent warners from among them. **73.** So observe how those who were warned were reprimanded, **74.** but not so for God's sincere servants. **75.** Indeed Noah cried out to Us, and how excellent are the responders. **76.** We saved him and his people from great distress, **77.** and made his progeny endure, **78.** and left it [Our Blessing] upon him for subsequent generations. **79.** "Peace be upon Noah throughout the worlds." **80.** As such, do We reward the righteous. **81.** He was truly among Our believing servants. **82.** Then We drowned the others. **83.** Certainly among his party was Abraham, **84.** when he approached his Lord with a sound heart, **85.** and when he said to his to his father and his people, "What do you worship? **86.** Do you desire false gods instead of God? **87.** Then what do you think of the Lord of the Worlds?" **88.** He then took a glance at the stars, **89.** and said, "Truly I am sickened." **90.** They then turned their backs on him. **91.** Then he went quietly to their gods and said, "Do you not eat? **92.** Why is it that you do not speak?" **93.** Then he turned on them, striking with his right hand. **94.** Then they came rushing at him. **95.** He said, "Do you worship what you carve **96.** while God created you and that which you make?" **97.** They said, "Build a framework for him and cast him into the blazing fire!" **98.** Then they wanted to scheme against him, and so We made them among the bottommost. **99.** He said, "Truly I am going to my Lord. He will guide me. **100.** My Lord! Endow me from among the righteous." **101.** So We gave him good news of a forbearing son. **102.** When he became old enough to partake in his father's endeavors, Abraham said, "O my son! While dreaming, I saw that I am to sacrifice you. Now consider, what is your view?" He replied, "O my father! Do as you are commanded. If God so wills, you will find me to be one who practices patience." **103.** But when they had submitted and Abraham had laid him upon his forehead, **104.** We called unto him, "O Abraham! **105.** You have been true to the vision." Truly that is how We reward the righteous. **106.** Indeed this was but a clear trial. **107.** We then ransomed him with a great sacrifice, **108.** and left it [Our Blessing] upon him for subsequent generations. **109.** "Peace be upon Abraham." **110.** That is indeed how We reward the righteous. **111.** He was truly among Our believing servants. **112.** We gave him good news of Isaac, a prophet from among the righteous. **113.** We blessed him and Isaac. Among their progeny are the virtuous and those who clearly wronged themselves. **114.** We were gracious to Moses and Aaron. **115.** We saved them and their people from great distress **116.** and helped them. They were the victors. **117.** We gave both of them the Book that makes things clear, **118.** guided both of them to the straight path, **119.** and left it (Our Blessing) upon both of them for subsequent generations. **120.** "Peace be upon Moses and Aaron." **121.** That is indeed how We reward the righteous. **122.** Truly they were among Our believing servants. **123.** Indeed Elias was among the messengers **124.** when he had said to his people, "Will you not show reverence? **125.** Do you call upon Baal and forsake the Best of creators? **126.** God is your Lord and the Lord of your forefathers." **127.** But they denied him, so they will certainly be reprimanded, **128.** except God's sincere servants. **129.** We left it [Our Blessing] upon him for subsequent generations. **130.** "Peace be with Elias." **131.** That is indeed how We reward the righteous. **132.** Truly he was among Our believing servants. **133.** Indeed Lot was among the messengers. **134.** Observe! We saved him and his entire family, **135.** save for an old woman who was among those who lagged behind. **136.** Then We destroyed the others. **137.** Truly you pass by them in the morning **138.** and at night. Do you not understand? **139.** Indeed, Jonah was among the messengers. **140.** Behold! He fled to the fully loaded ship, **141.** then they drew lots, and he was among those rejected. **142.** Then the whale swallowed him, for he was blameworthy. **143.** Had he not been among those who glorify, **144.** he would have stayed in its belly until the Day they are resurrected. **145.** So We threw him out, sickened, to the barren shore. **146.** We made a gourd plant grow over him. **147.** Then We sent him to a hundred thousand or more. **148.** They believed, so We granted them enjoyment for a while. **149.** So ask them, "Does your Lord have daughters while they have sons, **150.** or did We create female angels while they were witnesses?" **151.** It is of their own distortion that they say, **152.** "God has conceived," while they are indeed, liars. **153.** Has He chosen daughters over sons? **154.** What is the matter with you? How do you judge? **155.** Do you not reflect? **156.** Or do you have a clear authority? **157.** Then bring your book if you are truthful. **158.** They have made kinship between Him and the jinn, but the jinn know that they will be in attendance. **159.** Glory to God above what they attribute. **160.** Not so for God's sincere servants. **161.** Indeed, neither you, nor what you worship **162.** can tempt any against Him, **163.** except he who is to burn in Hellfire. **164.** "There is no one among us but that he has a known station. **165.** Indeed we are those who are in ranks, **166.** and truly we are those who glorify." **167.** Indeed, they were saying, **168.** "If only we had a reminder from older generations, **169.** then we would have certainly been of God's sincere servants." **170.** However, they disbelieved in it, so soon, they will know. **171.** Our Word has already gone forth by Our messengers **172.** that they will indeed be helped, **173.** and Our host will surely be triumphant. **174.** So turn away from them for a while **175.** and watch. Soon enough, they will see. **176.** Are they trying to rush Our punishment **177.** when it lands in their very midst? Evil will be the morning of those who were warned! **178.** So turn away from them for a while, **179.** and watch. Soon enough, they will see. **180.** Glory be to your Lord, the Lord of Might, above what they attribute. **181.** Peace be upon the messengers, and **182.** praise be to God, Lord of the Worlds.

Surah 38

SĀD

Sād

In the Name of God, the Compassionate, the Merciful

1. *Sād*. By the Quran that bears remembrance, **2.** those who disbelieve are indeed in self-glory and schism. **3.** How many generations before them have We destroyed? They cried out when it was too late to escape. **4.** Now, they are astonished that a warner has come to them from among their own people. The disbelievers say, "This is a lying sorcerer. **5.** Has he made the gods one God? Truly this is an astounding thing!" **6.** The notables among them walk away, saying, "Go! Be steadfast to your gods. This is indeed something you desire! **7.** We did not hear of this from the creed of former times. Surely this is nothing but a fabrication. **8.** Has the Reminder been sent down upon him from our midst?" No! But they are in doubt regarding My Reminder! Indeed! They have not yet tasted My punishment! **9.** Or do they have the treasuries of your Lord's Mercy, the Mighty, and the Bestower? **10.** Do they hold authority over the heavens, the earth, and all that lies between them? If so, let them try to ascend by whatever means they can. **11.** A faction among them will be defeated there. **12.** The people of Noah denied before them as well as the Ād, and Pharoah, the bearer of stakes. **13.** The Thamŭd, the people of Lot, and the inhabitants of the Wood — they are the parties. **14.** Each of them did nothing but deny the messengers, so My Punishment was owed. **15.** They only await a single cry for which there will be no delay. **16.** They said, "Our Lord! Advance our sentence to us before the Day of Reckoning." **17.** Endure what they say with patience, and remember Our servant David, a possessor of might. Truly he was ever-repenting. **18.** We definitely made the mountains join him to glorify Us in the evening and at daybreak. **19.** The birds gathered, each glorifying Him. **20.** We strengthened his sovereignty, gave him wisdom and decisive speech. **21.** Has news of the dispute come to you when they scaled the sanctuary? **22.** When they entered upon David, he was frightened of them, and they said, "Do not fear! We are two disputants, one of us has wronged the other, so judge between us in truth. Do not be unjust and guide us to the right path. **23.** Truly, this, my brother has ninety-nine ewes and I have one ewe. Yet, he said, 'Put her under my care,' and he has overpowered me in speech." **24.** He said, "Indeed he has wronged you by asking that your ewe be added to his ewes. Truly many business associates wrong each other, except for those who believe and work righteousness. Yet, how few are they!" David gathered that We had tried him, so he sought forgiveness from his Lord, fell down kneeling, and repented. **25.** So We forgave him for that. Truly for him, will be closeness and a beautiful return to Us. **26.** O David! We have indeed appointed you as a vicegerent on the earth. Therefore, judge among the people in truth and do not follow impulses because it leads you astray from the way of God. For those who stray from the way of God, there will indeed be a severe punishment for having forgotten the Day of Reckoning. **27.** We did not create Heaven and earth and whatever is between them without purpose. That is what the disbelievers assume. Consequently, woe before the Fire unto those who disbelieve! **28.** Or should We treat those who believe and perform righteous deeds the same as those who do mischief on earth? Or should We treat the reverent like the reckless? **29.** We have sent down a Blessed Book upon you that they may contemplate His signs and that those endowed with insight may reflect. **30.** We bestowed Solomon on David. An outstanding servant! He was indeed ever-repenting. **31.** When well-bred steeds were presented to him in the evening, **32.** he said, "Truly, I was captivated by the love of worldly goods over the remembrance of my Lord, until it [the sun] disappeared behind the veil. **33.** Bring them back to me!" Then he began to stroke their legs and necks. **34.** We did indeed try Solomon and We threw a corpse over his throne. He was then, ever-repenting. **35.** He said, "My Lord! Forgive me and grant me a kingdom that will not befit anyone after me. You are truly the Bestower." **36.** As a result, We made the wind subservient unto him, blowing gently by his command to wherever he desired — **37.** as well as the demons, every builder, diver, **38.** and others, bound together in chains — **39.** "This is Our Gift. So either bequeath or withhold them for there will be no accountability." **40.** Truly, for him, there will be closeness and a beautiful return to Us. **41.** Remember Our servant Job when he called upon his Lord, "Truly Satan has afflicted me with distress and punishment." **42.** "Strike with your foot! This is cool water to wash with and to drink." **43.** We bestowed upon him his family and their like along with them as a mercy from Us and a reminder for those endowed with insight. **44.** "Take a bundle with your hand, strike with it, and do not break your oath." Truly We found him to be patient. The best of servants and oft yielding. **45.** Remember Our servants Abraham, Isaac, and Jacob, the possessors of strength and sight. **46.** Indeed We purified them with what is the pure remembrance of the Abode. **47.** From Our Sight, they are indeed among the elect, the worthy. **48.** Remember Ishmael, Elisha, and Dhu'l-Kifl. Each is among the worthy. **49.** This is a reminder! There will certainly be a beautiful return for the reverent. **50.** The gates of the Gardens of Eden are open for them. **51.** They will be reclining there and calling there for an abundance of fruit and drink. **52.** Theirs will be maidens of modern gaze and of like age. **53.** This is what you are promised on the Day of Reckoning. **54.** This is indeed Our provision that will never be exhausted. **55.** This will be! But for the rebellious, there will certainly be an evil return, **56.** to Hell, wherein, they will burn. What an evil resting place. **57.** So it shall be! So let them taste it—a scalding liquid and a cold, dark murky fluid, **58.** and other punishments equivalent in nature. **59.** This is a troop barging in with you, but there will be no greeting for them. Truly they will burn in the Fire! **60.** They will say, "No greeting for you! You brought this on us! What a terrible place to stay in!" **61.** They will say, "Our Lord! Whoever brought this on us, increase his punishment twofold in the Fire." **62.** They will say, "How is it that we do not see men here whom we figured would be among the evil? **63.** Did we take them in mockery? Or have all eyes veered from them?" **64.** People disputing about the Fire is indeed true. **65.** Say, "I am indeed a warner and there is no god but God, the One, the Paramount, **66.** Lord of the heavens and the earth and whatever is between them—the Mighty and the Forgiving." **67.** Say, "It is a great announcement **68.** from which you turn away. **69.** I have no knowledge of the Highest Assembly when they dispute. **70.** Nothing is revealed unto me other than I am a clear warner." **71.** Remember when your Lord said to the angels, "Behold! I am creating a human being from clay, **72.** and once I have proportioned him and breathed into him of My spirit, fall down prostrating before him." **73.** Then the angels prostrated collectively. 74. Except Iblis. He became arrogant and was among the disbelievers. **75.** God said, "O Iblīs! What stopped you from prostrating to what I created with My two Hands? Are you arrogant or are you among the glorious?" **76.** He said, "I am better than him. You have created me from fire while you have created him from clay." **77.** He said, "Then leave this place! You are indeed cursed! **78.** My curse will surely be upon you until the Day of Judgment." **79.** He said, "My Lord! Grant me respite until the Day they are resurrected." **80.** He said, "Then Truly you are among those granted respite **81.** until the Day of the Known Moment.

82. He said, "By Your might, I will surely lead them all astray except 83. for Your sincere servants among them." 84. He said, "This is the truth, and I declare it truthfully! 85. 'I will surely fill Hell with you and all those who follow you, together.'" 86. Say, "I do not ask of you any reward for it, nor am I among the pretenders. 87. It is no more than a reminder for the worlds, 88. and soon enough, you will indeed know its news."

Surah 39

THE THRONGS

al-Zumar

In the Name of God, the Compassionate, the Merciful

1. A revelation from the Book from God, the Mighty and the Wise. **2.** We have indeed sent the Book down to you in truth, so worship God by devoting religion to Him. **3.** Truly pure religion belongs only to God, but those who take protectors besides Him [say], "We only worship them to bring us closer to God." God will certainly judge between them regarding what they differed on. Truly God does not guide one who is a disbelieving liar. **4.** Had God desired to take a child, He would have chosen whomever He willed from what He created. Glory be to Him! He is the One and the Paramount. **5.** He created the heavens and the earth in truth. He rolls the night up into the day and rolls the day up into the night. He made the sun and the moon subservient, each running for an appointed term. Is He not the Mighty and the Forgiving? **6.** He created you from a single soul, then made its mate from it. He sent down eight pairs of cattle for you. He creates you in your mother's womb, creation after creation in three veils of darkness. That is God, your Lord. To Him belongs sovereignty. There is no god but Him. How then do you turn away? **7.** If you disbelieve, God can certainly manage without you. However, He does not desire disbelief for His servants. So if you show gratitude, He will be satisfied with you. No bearer of burdens will bear the burden of another. Then, to your Lord is your return wherein He will inform you of what you did. He truly knows of what lies within the breasts. **8.** When harm touches a person, he turns to his Lord in supplication. But when God bestows a blessing upon him, he forgets the One he had called upon before and assigns equals to God, leading himself astray from His path. Say, "Enjoy your disbelief for a brief time; you will surely be among the inhabitants of the Fire." **9.** What about the one who spends the night in devotion, prostrating and standing, mindful of the Hereafter and seeking the mercy of his Lord? Say, "Are those who possess knowledge equal to those who do not?" Truly, only those with understanding take heed. **10.** Say, "O My servants who believe, revere your Lord. For those who do good in this world, there is good. God's earth is wide." For indeed those who are patient will be compensated without measure. **11.** Say, "I have truly been commanded to worship God while devoting religion to Him, **12.** as I was commanded to be among the first of those who submit." **13.** Say, "For indeed should I disobey my Lord, I fear the punishment of a tremendous day." **14.** Say, "It is God Whom I worship while devoting my religion to Him. **15.** So worship whatever you want instead of Him." Say, "Truly the losers are those who lost their souls and their families on the Day of Resurrection. Ah! That is the clear loss!" **16.** They will have coverings of fire above them and coverings below them. By this, God strikes fear into His servants. O My servants! Revere Me! **17.** Those who evade worshipping false deities and turn to God will have good news. So give the good news to My servants **18.** who listen to the Word, then follow the best of it. Those are the ones whom God has guided, and those endowed with insight. **19.** What of one for whom the Word of punishment is owed, will you save one who is in the Fire? **20.** But those who revere their Lord will have lofty abodes built over lofty abodes with rivers flowing beneath. That is God's Promise. God will not neglect the meeting. **21.** Do you not consider that God sends water down from the sky, directs it to be springs running through the earth, then brings forth crops of various colors. Then they wither and you will see them yellowing, and then He turns them to chaff. Truly in that is a reminder for those endowed with insight. **22.** What of one whose breast has been expanded for submission by God? He has been enlightened by his Lord. But woe to those whose hearts have been hardened to the remembrance of God. They are in obvious error. **23.** God has revealed the finest discourse: a Book with recurring themes that resonate deeply. It causes the skin of those who revere God to shiver, and then their skin and hearts soften in devotion to the remembrance of God. This is God's guidance, which He grants to whom He wills. But for those whom God lets go astray, there is no guide. **24.** What of one who guards his face against the evil punishment on the Day of Resurrection? It will be said to the wrongdoers, "Taste what you have earned!" **25.** Those before them denied. As such, punishment came to them while they were unaware. **26.** Thus God gave them a taste of humiliation in the life of this world, but the punishment of the Hereafter is certainly greater if they only knew. **27.** Indeed, We have set forth for people in this Quran every kind of parable, that perhaps they may remember— **28.** an Arabic Quran—without crookedness that perhaps they may be reverent. **29.** God sets forth a parable: a man who is shared by quarreling partners and a man who belongs to one man. Are those two considered equal by comparison? Praise be to God, but most of them do not know. 30. Certainly you will die and indeed they will die. 31. Then on the Day of Resurrection, you will dispute before your Lord. 32. So who does more wrong than one who lies against God and denies the truth when it comes to him? Is there not in Hell an abode for the disbelievers? 33. He who comes with the truth and confirms it. It is they who are reverent. 34. They will have whatever they desire from their Lord. That is the reward of the virtuous. 35. God will exonerate them from the worst of what they have done and give them their reward for the best of what they have done. 36. Is God not enough for His servant? Yet they frighten you with those apart from Him. He, who God leads astray, has no guide. 37. Whomever God guides, no one will lead him astray. Is God not Mighty and the Possessor of Retribution? 38. Indeed if you were to ask them, "Who created the heavens and the earth?" They will certainly say, "God." Say, "Then have you considered those whom you call upon instead of God? If God desires some harm for me, would they be able to remove His Harm, or if He desired some mercy, could they withhold His Mercy?" Say, "God is enough for me. Let those who trust, trust in Him." 39. Say, "O my people! Perform whatever you can. I too, am performing. You will soon know 40. who will receive a punishment that will humiliate him and who will have earned a lasting punishment." 41. We have indeed sent the Book down to you for people in truth. Whoever is rightly guided, it is for his own soul, yet whoever goes astray, he will have wronged himself. You are not a guardian over them. 42. God takes souls at the time of their death, and those who do not die, during their sleep. He withholds those for whom He has decreed death and sends the others for a term appointed. Truly, in that are signs for a people who reflect. 43. Or do they take intercessors instead of God? Say, "Even though they do not have power and do not understand." 44. Say, "To God belongs intercession altogether. To Him belongs sovereignty over the heavens and the earth, then unto Him you will be returned." 45. When God is mentioned alone, the hearts of those who do not believe in the Hereafter are filled with disgust, but when those apart from Him are mentioned, they are surely filled with joy. 46. Say, "O God! Originator of the heavens and the earth, Knower of the Unseen and seen, it is You Who will judge between Your servants in what they differed." 47. Even if the wrongdoers had all there is on the earth and more combined, they would give it up in lieu of the horrendous punishment on the Day of Resurrection. They were not counting on what appeared to them from God. 48. The evils of what they earned will appear to them, and what they mocked will enfold them. 49. When harm touches man, he calls on Us. Then when We present him with a blessing from Us, he says, "I was only given this out of knowledge." It is truly a trial but most of them do not know. **50.** Those before them said the same, yet what they did was of no benefit to them. **51.** So the evils of what they earned will befall them and they cannot stop it. **52.** Do they not know that God extends provision for whomever He wills? In that are truly signs for a people who believe. **53.** Say, "O My servants who have transgressed against their own souls! Do not despair of God's Mercy. God truly forgives all sins. Truly He is the Forgiving and the Merciful. **54.** Turn to your Lord and submit to Him before punishment arrives at you, whereupon you will not be helped. **55.** Follow the best of what has been sent down to you from your Lord, before punishment comes upon you while you are unaware," **56.** or in case any soul would say, "Woe to me for what I neglected in my duty toward God! Truly I was among those who mocked." **57.** Or in case it would say, "If only God had guided me, I would have been among the reverent." **58.** Or once it sees the punishment, it would say, "If only I had another chance, I would certainly be among those who do good." **59.** Even when My signs did indeed come to you, you denied them, grew arrogant, and were among the disbelievers. **60.** On the Day of Resurrection, you will see those who lied against God with blackened faces. Is there not in Hell an abode for the arrogant? **61.** God saves those who were reverent through their triumph. No harm will touch them, nor will they grieve. **62.** God is the Creator of all things. He is the Guardian over all things. **63.** Unto Him belong the keys of the heavens and the earth. Those who disbelieve in the signs of God will be the losers. **64.** Say, "O ignorant ones! Do you order me to worship other than God?" **65.** It has indeed been revealed to you and to those before you that if you joined partners, your work will certainly be reduced to nothing, and you will be among the losers. **66.** Rather, worship God and be among the thankful. **67.** They did not estimate God with His true estimation. The entire earth will be but a handful to Him on the Day of Resurrection, and the heavens will be enfolded in His right Hand. Glory be to Him. Exalted is He above the partners they attribute. **68.** The trumpet will be blown and all those in the heavens and on the earth will swoon, except for those whom God wills. Then it will be blown once more, and surely, they will be standing and observing. **69.** The earth will shine with the Light of its Lord, the Book will be set down, and the prophets and the witnesses will be brought forth. Judgment will be made between them in truth, and they will not be wronged. **70.** Every soul will be paid in full for what it has done, and He knows best what they do. **71.** Those who disbelieve will be herded to Hell in groups. When they arrive, its gates will be opened, and its keepers will ask, "Did messengers not come to you from among yourselves, reciting the signs of your Lord and warning you of this Day's meeting?" They will reply, "Yes, indeed!" Yet the decree of punishment has been confirmed for the disbelievers. **72.** It will be said, "Enter the gates of Hell to abide therein."

How evil is the abode of the arrogant! **73.** Those who revere their Lord will be driven to the Garden in masses until once they reach it, its gates will be open and its keepers will say to them, "Peace be upon you. You have done well, so enter it to abide there." **74.** They will say, "Praise be to God, Who was faithful to us in His Promise, and has allowed us to inherit the land that we may settle in the Garden wherever we desire." How excellent is the reward of the workers! **75.** You will see the angels circling around the Throne, glorifying the praise of their Lord. Judgment will be made between them in truth, and it will be said, "Praise be to God, Lord of the Worlds."

Surah 40

Forgiver

Ghāfir

In the Name of God, the Compassionate, the Merciful

1. *Hā. Mīm.* **2.** The revelation of the Book from God, the Mighty, and the Knower, **3.** Forgiver of sins, Accepter of Repentance, Severe in Retribution, and the Possessor of Bounty. There is no god but He, and unto Him is the final destination. **4.** It is only the disbelievers who dispute over the signs of God. Do not be deluded by their turning about in the land. **5.** The people of Noah denied before them as did the parties after them. Every nation plotted against their messenger to seize him. They disputed by using falsehood to negate the truth. As such, I seized them. How then, was My Reprisal! **6.** By such the Word of your Lord was due to those who disbelieved. They are indeed the inhabitants of the Fire. **7.** Those who hold the Throne and those who are near it glorify the praise of their Lord, believe in Him, and beseech forgiveness for those who believe: "Our Lord! You encompass all things in Mercy and Knowledge. Forgive those who repent and follow Your way and protect them from the punishment of Hellfire. **8.** Our Lord! Admit them to the Gardens of Eden that you have promised them and the righteous among their fathers, their spouses, and their progeny. You are the Mighty and the Wise. **9.** Guard them from evil deeds. Whomever You guard from evil deeds on that Day, You, will have had mercy upon him. That is indeed the great triumph." **10.** Truly those who disbelieved will be addressed by "God's aversion that is greater than your aversion for yourselves when you were called to believe, but then, you disbelieved." **11.** They will say, "Our Lord, you have caused us to die twice and gave us life twice, so now that we have admitted to our sins, is there any way out?" **12.** That is because when God was invoked as One, you disbelieved and when partners were attributed unto Him, you believed. Judgment lies with God, the exalted, and the Great. **13.** It is He Who shows you His signs and sends provision down for you from Heaven. No one reflects, except for those who turn in repentance. **14.** So call upon God by devoting religion to Him though the disbelievers hate it. **15.** The Raiser of degrees, the Possessor of the Throne, He sends the spirit by His Command upon whomever He wills among His servants to warn of the Day of the Meeting. **16.** On the Day they come forth, not a single thing about them will be hidden from Him. To Whom is the sovereignty this Day? It is God's, the One, and the Paramount. **17.** On that Day, every soul will be compensated for what it earned. No wrong will be done on that Day. Truly God is swift in reckoning. **18.** So warn them of the approaching Day when hearts will be in throats, choking in misery. The wrongdoers will have neither a faithful friend nor an intercessor who will heed them. **19.** He knows the treachery of eyes and what hearts conceal. **20.** God will judge with truth and those who call upon what is apart from Him will not be judging by any means. Truly God is the Hearer, the Seer. **21.** Have they not traveled through the land and seen the fate of those who came before them? They were more powerful and left a greater mark on the earth, yet God seized them for their sins, and there was no one to protect them from God. **22.** That is because their messengers had brought them clear signs and they disbelieved. Thereafter, God seized them. He is indeed Strong and Severe in retribution. **23.** We indeed sent Moses with Our signs and a clear authority **24.** to Pharoah, Hāmān, and Korah. They said, "A lying sorcerer." **25.** Then when he arrived at them with the truth from Us, they said, "Slay the sons of those who believe with him and spare their women." The plotting of disbelievers was no more than delusion. **26.** Pharoah said, "Leave me to slay Moses and let him call upon his Lord. I truly fear that he will change your religion, or he will cause corruption to appear in the land." **27.** Moses said, "I have indeed sought refuge in my Lord and your Lord from everyone who is arrogant and does not believe in the Day of Reckoning." **28.** A believing man from the House of Pharoah who was hiding his faith, said, "Will you kill a man simply because he says, 'My Lord is God,' even though he has brought clear evidence from your Lord? If he is lying, his lies will be upon him, but if he is truthful, then part of what he warns you about will surely come to pass. Truly, God does not guide one who is a transgressor and a liar. **29.** O my people! Sovereignty is yours this day while you prevail over the land, but who will help us against God's Might should it come upon us?" Pharoah said, "I show you nothing but what I see, and I guide you unto nothing but the way of righteousness." **30.** He who believed said, "O my people! Truly I fear for you like the day of the clans, **31.** like the plight of the people of Noah, the Ād, the Thamŭd, and those after them. God does not desire wrong for His servants. **32.** O my people! Truly I fear for you the Day of Mutual Calling,

33. the Day you will turn back to flee while having no one to protect you from God. Whomever God leads astray will have no guide. 34. Joseph brought you clear signs before, yet you remained in doubt of what he had brought to you, so much so that when he died, you said, 'God will not send a messenger after him.' As such, God leads astray whoever is a doubtful transgressor, 35. or those who dispute God's signs without any authority having come to them, is grievous and odious from God's perspective and the perspective of those who believe. Thus does God place a seal over the heart of every arrogant tyrant." 36. Pharoah said, "O Hāmān, construct for me a tower so that I might reach the means— 37. the means to ascend to the heavens and look upon the God of Moses. I believe he is truly a liar." Pharaoh's actions were made to appear enticing to him, leading him astray from the right path. His schemes only resulted in destruction. 38. He who believed said, "O my people! Follow me. I will guide you to the way of rectitude. 39. O my people! The life of this world is but amusement, whereas the Hereafter is truly the permanent abode. 40. Whoever commits an evil deed will not be requited, except with a similar deed, but whether male or female, whoever performs a righteous deed and is a believer, will enter the Garden without reckoning, and will be provided for therein. 41. O my people! How is it that I call you to salvation while you call me to the Fire? 42. You call on me to disbelieve in God and to attribute a partner to Him of which I have no knowledge. It is I who calls you unto the Mighty and the Forgiving. 43. Indeed, there is no doubt that what you are calling me to, has no call in this world or in the Hereafter and that our return will be to God and that the transgressors will be the inhabitants of the Fire. 44. You will soon remember what I have said to you, and I entrust my affair to God. Truly God is observant over His servants." 45. Therefore, God protected him from the evils of what they had plotted, and evil punishment befell the House of Pharaoh, 46. exposure to the Fire morning and evening. On the Day when the Hour arrives, "Admit the House of Pharoah to the most severe punishment." 47. While they argue with one another in the Fire, the weak will say to those who were arrogant, "Truly we were your followers, so can you save us from any portion of the Fire?" 48. Those who were arrogant will say, "Indeed, we are all in it. God has certainly judged between His servants." 49. Those who are in the Fire will say to the keepers of Hell, "Call upon your Lord to relieve us from punishment for a day." 50. They will respond, "Did your messengers bring you clear signs?" They will say, "Yes, indeed." They will say, "Then supplicate!" But the supplication of disbelievers will be in vain. 51. Indeed, We will help Our messengers and those who believe during the life of this world and on the Day when the witnesses stand forth, 52. and the Day when excuses by the wrongdoers will not benefit them. Damnation and the evil abode

will be theirs. **53.** We have indeed given Moses guidance, and We bequeathed the Book unto the Children of Israel 54. as a guidance and a reminder for those endowed with insight. **55.** So be patient. God's Promise is indeed true. Ask forgiveness for your sin and glorify the praise of your Lord in the evening and at dawn. **56.** Indeed those who dispute God's signs without having been given the authority have nothing in their hearts but a sense of greatness that they will never attain. So seek refuge in God. He is indeed the Hearer and the Seer. **57.** Indeed the creation of the heavens and the earth is greater than the creation of people, but most people do not know. **58.** One who is blind and one who can see are not equal, nor are those who perform righteous deeds and the evildoer. Little do you reflect. **59.** The Hour is certainly coming. There is no doubt about it, but most people do not believe. **60.** Your Lord has said, "Call upon Me, and I will respond to you. Those who are too arrogant to worship Me will indeed enter Hell humiliated." **61.** It is God Who has made the night for you that you may rest therein and the day by which to see. God is indeed Possessed of Bounty for people, but most people do not offer gratitude. **62.** That is God, your Lord, Creator of all things. There is no god, but He. How then are you deluded? **63.** That is how those who rejected the signs of God will be deluded. **64.** It is God Who made the earth a dwelling place for you and the sky a canopy. He formed you, made your forms beautiful, and provided you with good things. That is God, your Lord. So blessed is God, Lord of the Worlds. **65.** He is the Living and there is no god but He. Therefore, call upon Him while devoting religion unto Him. Praise be to God, Lord of the Worlds. **66.** Say, "I have been forbidden to worship those who you call upon besides God through the clear signs that have come to me from my Lord, and I am commanded to submit to the Lord of the Worlds." **67.** It is He who created you from dust, then from a drop of semen, then from a blood clot. Then He brings you forth as infants that you may then reach maturity, and that you may then grow old—though some of you die earlier—that you may reach a term appointed, and that perhaps you may understand. **68.** It is He Who gives life and death. Then when He decrees a thing, He only says to it, "Be!" and it is. **69.** Have you not observed those who disputed the signs of God and how they were turned away, **70.** and those who rejected the Book and what We sent with Our messengers? But soon they will know **71.** since they will be dragged by shackles and chains around their necks **72.** into boiling liquid, then set to flames in the Fire. **73.** Then they will be asked, "Where are those you used to associate as partners **74.** with God?" They will reply, "They have abandoned us. In fact, we were not truly worshiping anything." This is how God leads the disbelievers astray. **75.** "This is because you celebrated on earth without a viable reason and acted brazenly." **76.** Enter the gates of Hell to abide there."

How evil is the abode of the arrogant! **77.** So be patient. God's Promise is absolutely true. Whether We show you some of what We promised them, or if We take you, unto Us they will be returned. **78.** Indeed, We sent messengers before you; some of them We have told you about, while others We have not. No messenger could bring a sign except by God's permission. When God's command comes, judgment will be rendered in truth, and those who fabricated lies will be the losers. **79.** It is God Who made cattle for you that some of them you may ride and that some of them you may eat. **80.** There are benefits for you in that respect to fulfill anything your hearts may desire. You are carried upon them and upon ships. **81.** He has shown you His signs, so which of God's signs do you reject? **82.** Have they not travelled the earth and observed what punishment was like for those before them? They were greater than them in strength and impression on the earth, yet all of what they accomplished was of no benefit to them. **83.** When their messengers brought them clear signs, they exulted in the knowledge they possessed and what they used to mock hemmed them in. **84.** Then when they saw Our Might, they said, "We believe in God alone, and we disbelieve in what we ascribed as partners unto Him." **85.** But professing their faith did not benefit them after they saw Our Punishment. Such is God's way of dealing with His servants wherewith the disbelievers were then lost.

Surah 41

EXPOUNDED

Fussilat

In the Name of God, the Compassionate, the Merciful

1. *Hā. Mīm.* 2. A revelation from the Compassionate and the Merciful, 3. a Book with signs that have been expounded in detail. It is an Arabic Quran for people who understand. 4. It offers good news and serves as a warning, yet most have turned away and do not listen. 5. They say, "Our hearts are closed to what you are calling us to; there is deafness in our ears, and a barrier between us and you. So continue! We too will continue!" 6. Say, "I am only a human being like you, but it has been revealed to me that your God is One God. So turn to Him with sincerity and seek His forgiveness. Woe to those who associate partners with God." 7. those who do not give alms, and who disbelieve in the Hereafter. 8. Indeed those who believe and perform righteous deeds, will have a never-ending reward." 9. Say, "Do you truly disbelieve in the One Who created the earth in two days? Do you set up equals unto Him? That is the Lord of the Worlds!" 10. There, He placed firm mountains to rise above it, blessed it, and apportioned its means of sustenance there in four days in accordance with those who ask. 11. He then turned to Heaven while it was smoke and said to it and to the earth, "Come together willingly or unwillingly!" They said, "We come willingly!" 12. Then He decreed they be seven heavens in two days and revealed to each heaven its command. We adorned and guarded the lowest heaven with lanterns. That is the decree of the Mighty and the Knowing. 13. So then, if they turn away, say, "I warned you of a thunderbolt similar to the thunderbolt of the Ãd and the Thamŭd. 14. When the messengers had come to them from before them and behind them—'Worship none but God,'—they said, 'Had our Lord willed, He would have sent angels down. So we truly disbelieve in what has been sent to you.'" 15. As for the Ãd, they grew arrogant on the earth without merit and said,

"Who is greater than us in strength?" Have they not observed that God Who created them is greater than them in strength? Yet, they denied Our signs. **16.** So We sent a furious wind against them during days of ill fortune that We may give them a taste of disgrace in the life of this world, though the punishment of the Hereafter is more disgraceful, and they will not be helped. **17.** As for the Thamŭd, We guided them, but they preferred blindness over guidance, so the thunderbolt of humiliating punishment seized them for what they had earned. **18.** We salvaged those who believed and were reverent. **19.** That day, the enemies of God will be marshalled to the Fire, **20.** but when they reach it, their ears, eyes, and skins will bear witness against them for what they did. **21.** They will say to their skins, "Why do you bear witness against us?" and they will respond, "God Who makes all things speak, made us speak. He created you the first time and to Him you will be returned. **22.** You did not seek to hide in case your hearing, your sight, and your skins bear witness against you. You assumed that God would not know much about what you did. **23.** But your skepticism that led you to be skeptical of your Lord has destroyed you, so you have become among the losers!" **24.** Then if they are patient, the Fire will be a home for them, and indeed if they seek for a favor, they will not be among those given favors. **25.** We assigned companions to them, but they made what is before them and what is behind them seem appealing to them. So the Word among the nations of jinn and people that had passed before them was owed to them. They were indeed lost. **26.** The disbelievers will say, "Do not listen to this Quran, but speak nonsense of it that perhaps you might prevail." **27.** We will indeed make those who disbelieve taste a severe punishment, and We will certainly requite them for what is worse than what they did. **28.** The Fire! That is the requital of the enemies of God. The everlasting Abode will be theirs therein, as a reward for having rejected Our signs. **29.** Those who disbelieve will say, "Our Lord, show us those who led us astray among the jinn and the people so we can place them under our feet that they may be among the lowest." **30.** Truly, those who say, "Our Lord is God," then stand firm, the angels will descend upon them— "Do not fear, nor grieve and celebrate the Garden you have been promised." **31.** We are your protectors in the life of this world and in the Hereafter. There, you will have whatever your souls desire, and there, you will have whatever you call for, **32.** a hospitality from One Forgiving and Merciful. **33.** Who is better in speech than one who calls unto God, performs righteousness, and says, "Indeed I am among those who submit?" **34.** A good deed and an evil deed are not equal. Take charge with what is better, and then if there is enmity between you and him, it will be as though he is a loyal and protective friend. **35.** Yet only those who are patient will receive it. No one will receive it, save those who are extremely fortunate. **36.** But if a temptation by Satan provokes you, seek refuge in God. He is indeed the Hearing and the Knowing. **37.** Among His signs are the night and the day, and the sun and the moon. Do not prostate to the sun, nor to the moon. Prostrate to God Who created them, if it is He Whom you worship. **38.** For if they grow arrogant, then those who are with your Lord glorify Him night and day and they never tire. **39.** Among His signs, you will indeed see the earth barren. Then when We send water down upon it, it quivers and yields. He Who gives it life is certainly the One Who gives life to the dead. He is truly powerful over all things. **40.** Truly, those who deviate from Our signs are not hidden from Us. Is one who is thrown into the Fire better or one who arrives in safety on the Day of Resurrection? Do what you desire, for indeed, He Sees whatever you do. **41.** Truly those who disbelieve in the Remembrance when it arrives to them—it is truly a powerful Book. **42.** Falsehood does not come upon it from before it or behind it—a revelation by One Who is Wise and Praised. **43.** Nothing has been said to you, except what has been said to the messengers before you. Truly your Lord is possessed of Forgiveness and possessed of a Painful Retribution. **44.** Had We made it a non-Arabic Quran, they would have said, "If only its signs were explained. What! A foreign tongue and an Arab?" Say, "It is a guidance and a healing for those who believe. Those who do not believe have deafness in their ears. It is blindness for them as though they are called from a distant place." **45.** Truly We gave Moses the Book, but disputes arose concerning it. Were it not for a Word that had already gone forth from your Lord, judgment would have been made between them. Yet, they certainly remained skeptical and in doubt of it. **46.** Whoever performs righteousness, it will be for his own soul, and whoever performs evil, it will be for his own soul. Your Lord is never unjust to His servants. **47.** The knowledge of the Hour is referred unto Him. No fruits may leave their sheaths, nor does a female bear or deliver but by His knowledge. On the Day when He will call unto them, "Where are my partners?" they will say, "We admit to You that no one among us can bear witness." **48.** What they used to call upon will abandon them and they will surely know that they have no escape. **49.** Man does not get tired from supplicating for good, and if evil touches him, he is hopeless and in despair. **50.** After hardship has touched him, and We grant him a taste of Our mercy, he will certainly say, "This is my due. I don't believe the Hour will come. But if I am returned to my Lord, I will surely have the best with Him." Yet, We will make the disbelievers aware of their deeds and let them taste a severe punishment. **51.** When We bless man, he withdraws and turns sideways, yet when evil touches him, he is full of prolonged supplication. **52.** Say, "Did you see that it was from God, and yet, you disbelieved in it? Who is more astray than one who is in extreme schism?" **53.** We will show them Our signs upon the horizons and within themselves until it becomes clear to them that it is the truth. Is it not enough that your Lord is Witness over all things? **54.** Truly they are in doubt about the meeting with their Lord, and truly, He encompasses all things.

Surah 42

Counsel

al-Shūrā

In the Name of God, the Compassionate, the Merciful

1. *Hā. Mīm.* **2.** *Ayn. Sīn. Qāf.* **3.** Thus does He reveal to you and to those before you. God is the Mighty and the Wise, and **4.** to Him belongs whatever is in the heavens and whatever is on the earth. He is the Exalted and the Magnificent. **5.** The heavens are almost riven asunder from above while the angels glorify the praise of their Lord and pray for forgiveness for those on earth. Behold! God is truly the Forgiving and the Merciful. **6.** As for those who take protectors apart from Him, God is Guardian over them. You are not a guardian over them. **7.** Thus We have revealed to you an Arabic Quran that you may warn the Mother of Cities and those around it and warn of the Day of Gathering in which there is no doubt. A group will be in the Garden and a group will be in the Inferno. **8.** Had God willed, He would have made them one nation, but He admits whomever He wills into His Mercy. The wrongdoers will have no protector, nor helper. **9.** Or have they taken protectors apart from Him? But He, God is the protector. He gives life to the dead and He is powerful over all things. **10.** Whatever you disagree upon, its ruling lies with God. That is God, my Lord. In Him I trust and unto Him I turn, **11.** the Originator of the heavens and the earth. He has appointed mates for you from among yourselves and has also appointed mates from among the cattle. He multiplies you from within. Nothing is comparable to Him. He is the Hearer and the Seer. **12.** To Him belong the keys of the heavens and the earth. He provides and withholds sustenance for whomever He wills. He truly has knowledge of all things. **13.** He has prescribed for you as a religion what He had ordained for Noah, and what We revealed unto you, and what We ordained for Abraham, Moses, and Jesus, that you uphold religion and not become divided in that respect. What you are calling the idolaters is difficult for them. God chooses for Himself whomever

He wills and guides unto Himself whomever turns in repentance. **14.** They only became divided after knowledge had reached them out of envy among themselves. Were it not for a Word that had previously gone forth from your Lord to an appointed term, judgment would have been made between them. Yet those who were given the Book after them are in perplexing doubt of it. **15.** So call upon them and remain steadfast as you have been commanded. Do not follow their whims, and say, "I believe in the Book that God has revealed, and I have been commanded to establish justice among you. God is our Lord and your Lord. We are accountable for our deeds, and you are accountable for yours. There is no dispute between us and you. God will gather us all together, and to Him is our final return." **16.** As for those who argue about God after having had acknowledged Him, from God's perspective, their pretext is baseless. Wrath will be upon them, and a severe punishment will be theirs. **17.** It is God Who sent the Book down in truth, and in the Balance, so what do you know? The Hour may be soon. **18.** Those who do not believe in it seek to expedite it, but those who believe are wary of it and know that it is the truth. Those who dispute the Hour are indeed, distantly astray. **19.** God is kind to His servants. He provides for whomever He wills. He is the Strong and the Mighty. **20.** Whoever desires the tilth of the Hereafter, We will add to his tilth, but whoever desires the tilth of this world, We will give him some, but he will have no share in the Hereafter. **21.** Or do they have partners who have prescribed for them a religion that God did not warrant? Were it not for the Word of Judgment, the matter would have been decreed between them. Truly the wrongdoers will have a painful punishment. **22.** You will see the wrongdoers wary of what they have earned, and it will fall upon them. Those who believe and perform righteous deeds will be in the blooming meadows of the Gardens. They will have whatever they desire with their Lord. That is the Great Bounty! **23.** That is how God gives good news to His servants who believe and perform righteous deeds. Say, "I do not ask of you to be rewarded for it, save for the goodwill of those near in kin." Whoever accomplishes a good deed, We will add to his goodness. Truly God is Forgiving and Grateful. **24.** Or do they say, "He has forged a lie against God?" Had God willed, He would have placed a seal over your heart. God erases falsehood and justifies the truth through His Words for truly, He is well aware of what lies within hearts. **25.** It is He Who accepts repentance from His servants and pardons evil deeds. He knows of whatever you do. **26.** He responds to those who believe and perform righteous deeds and will add to them from His Bounty. However, there will be a severe punishment for the disbelievers. **27.** Had God increased His sustenance for His servants, they would have behaved repressively on the earth, but He sends down whatever He wills in due measure. He is truly Aware and Observant of His servants. He sends down whatever He wills according to a measure. **28.** It is He Who extends His mercy and sends down the rain after they despair. He is the Protector and the Praised. **29.** Among His signs is the creation of the heavens and the earth and all moving creatures that He has scattered there. He is capable of gathering them together whenever He wills. **30.** Whatever misfortune happens to you is because of what your hands have accomplished, yet He forgives abundantly. **31.** You do not interfere on the earth, nor do you have a helper or protector besides God. **32.** Among His signs are the sailing ships similar to mountains on the sea. **33.** If He wills, He could still the wind and they would be at a standstill at its surface. Truly in that are signs for the patient and grateful. **34.** Or He may cause them to perish for what they have earned, but He forgives abundantly. **35.** Those who dispute His signs will have no refuge. **36.** Whatever you have been given is for amusement in the life of this world, but what lies with God is better and more lasting for those who believe and trust in their Lord, **37.** who avoid major sins and immoralities, who when angry, forgive, **38.** who respond to their Lord, who perform prayer, who consult in their affairs with mutual accord, who spend from what We have provided them, **39.** and who, when inflicted by oppression, defend themselves. **40.** The retribution for an evil act is a corresponding evil act, but whoever pardons and reconciliates, his reward is with God for indeed, He does not like wrongdoers. **41.** Whoever defends himself after having been wronged, will have no course against them. **42.** The blame is only against those who wrong people and behave repressively on the earth without merit. For them, there will be a painful punishment. **43.** But whoever is patient and forgives, that is indeed a commendable solution. **44.** Whomever God leads astray has no protector beyond Him. After they see the punishment, you will see the wrongdoers saying, "Is there a way of return?" **45.** You will see them exposed to it, humbled by disgrace, and observing stealthily. Those who believe will say, "Indeed the losers are those who lost themselves and their families on the Day of Resurrection." Behold! Truly the wrongdoers are in lasting punishment. **46.** They have no protectors to help them besides God. Whomever God leads astray, will have no course. **47.** Respond to your Lord before there comes a day from God that no one can repel. You will have no refuge on that Day, nor will you have the right to denial. **48.** If they turn away, We did not send you as a keeper over them. Nothing is incumbent upon you save the proclamation for indeed, when We give man a taste of Mercy from Us, he delights in it. Yet, when evil happens to them because of what their hands had accomplished, man is truly, ungrateful. **49.** Unto God belongs sovereignty over the heavens and the earth. He creates whatever He wills, bestowing females upon whomever He wills, and bestowing males upon whomever He wills, **50.** or He pairs them to be males and females and causes whomever He wills to be barren. He is Knowing and Powerful. **51.** It is not for any human being that God should speak to him, except through revelation, from behind a veil, or by sending a messenger to reveal what He wills by His Leave. He is, indeed, Exalted and Wise. **52.** Thus We have revealed unto you a Spirit from Our Command. You did not know what scripture was, nor faith, but We made it a light by which We guide whomever We will among Our servants. For truly, you guide to a straight path, **53.** the path of God unto Whom belongs whatever is in the heavens and whatever is on the earth. Behold! All matters are trending toward God.

Surah 43

GOLD ORNAMENTS

al-Zukhruf

In the Name of God, the Compassionate, the Merciful

1. Hā. Mīm. **2.** By the clear Book. **3.** We truly have made it an Arabic Quran that perhaps you may understand. **4.** It is indeed with us in the Mother Book, the Sublime, and the Wise. **5.** Should We withdraw the reminder by disregarding all of you for having been a reckless people? **6.** How many a prophet did We send to those of former times? **7.** Never did a prophet approach them but that they mocked him. **8.** We destroyed those of greater competence than them, and the parable of those of former times has passed. **9.** Were you to ask them, "Who created the heavens and the earth?" they would certainly say, "The Mighty and the Knowing created them." **10.** It is He Who expanded the earth and made pathways for you there, that perhaps you may be guided; **11.** and Who sent water down from the sky in due measure, and in accordance, We revived a land that was lifeless. As such, you will be brought forth. **12.** He Who has created the pairs, all of them, and made ships and cattle for you to ride, **13.** that you may mount their backs. Then, remember the blessing of your Lord once you are settled upon them, and say, "Glory be to God, Who made this subservient to us, something we could not have accomplished ourselves. **14.** Truly to our Lord, do we turn." **15.** Yet, they attributed a portion of some of His servants to Him. Truly man is ungrateful. **16.** Or has He taken daughters from what He created and favored you with sons? **17.** When one of them receives good news from what He has set forth as a description of the Compassionate, his face blackens, and he is filled with anguish. **18.** One who is reared amid ornaments cannot be rational in a dispute. **19.** They make into females the angels that are servants of the Compassionate! Did they witness their creation? Their witnessing will be recorded, and they will be questioned. **20.** They say, "Had the Compassionate willed, we would not have worshipped them." They do not know anything about that. They do nothing but guess. **21.** Or did We give them a book earlier and they are clutching it? **22.** Truly they said, "We found our forefathers following a certain way, and we are indeed guided by their footsteps." **23.** Similarly, We did not send a warner to a town before you, but its affluent there would say, "We found our fathers following a path and we are indeed guided by their footsteps." **24.** He replied, "Even though I brought you better guidance than what you found your fathers following?" They said, "We are indeed disbelievers in what you have been sent." **25.** So We took vengeance upon them and observe what the end of rejectors was like. **26.** Remember when Abraham said to his father, "Truly I am acquitted from what you worship, **27.** except for He who originated me. Indeed, He will guide me." **28.** He made it an enduring word among his descendants that perhaps they may return. **29.** Indeed I have provided for these and their fathers until the Truth and a clear messenger had come to them. **30.** When the Truth came to them, they said, "This is nothing but magic, and we do not believe in it." **31.** They said, "Why was this Quran not sent down to a great person from one of the two towns?" **32.** Is it they who apportion the Mercy of your Lord? We have apportioned their livelihood among them in the life of this world and have raised some above others in ranks, that some may take the service of others, but your Lord's Mercy is better than what they amass. **33.** If not, people would have been under one nation. We would have made for those who disbelieve in the Compassionate homes with silver roofs, staircases to ascend, **34.** doors to their homes, couches to recline upon, **35.** and gold ornaments. Indeed, all of that would be but enjoyment in the life of this world, but from your Lord's perspective, the Hereafter is for the reverent. **36.** For whoever deters from the remembrance of the Compassionate, We will assign to him a demon that will then become a companion unto him. **37.** They will turn them from the way, but they will assume that they are rightly guided, **38.** until when he comes to Us, he will say, "Would that there was between you and me the distance of the two easts! What an evil companion!" **39.** That Day will not benefit you if you did wrong. Indeed, you will partake in the punishment. **40.** Can you then, make the deaf hear, guide the blind and those in obvious error? **41.** We will either take you away and then retaliate against them, **42.** or We will show you what We have promised them. For indeed, We have power over them. **43.** So hold fast to what We have revealed unto you. Indeed, you are on a straight path. **44.** It is truly a reminder to you and your people, and you will be questioned. **45.** Ask those whom We have sent before you, "Have We appointed gods to be worshipped other than the Compassionate?" **46.** Truly We have sent Moses with Our signs to Pharoah and his notables. He said, "I am a messenger of the Lord of the Worlds." **47.** But when he brought them Our signs, observe, they laughed at them. **48.** Not a sign did We show them, but that it was greater than its sister. We seized them with punishment that perhaps they may return. **49.** They said, "O sorcerer, call upon your Lord for us by what He has promised you. Then, we will certainly be guided." **50.** Yet when We removed the punishment from them, sure enough, they reneged. **51.** Pharoah called out to his people, "O my people! Is not the sovereignty of Egypt mine, and do these streams not flow beneath me? Then do you not see? **52.** Am I not better than this one who is contemptuous and can hardly express himself? **53.** Why then has he not been bequeathed armlets of gold, or has he not been accompanied by angels in procession?" **54.** So he bluffed his people, and they obeyed him. Indeed, they were a sinful people. **55.** So when they roused Our Anger, We retaliated against them and drowned them all together. **56.** We made them a precedent and an example for others. **57.** When the son of Mary was held up as an example, observe, your people turned away. **58.** They say, "Are our gods better, or is he?" They do not bring him up to you except to argue. Truly they are a contentious people. **59.** He was no more than a servant Whom We had blessed and Whom We set as an example for the Children of Israel. **60.** Had We willed, We would have had angels among you, succeeding one another upon the earth. **61.** He is indeed a sign of the Hour, so do not be in doubt of it, and follow Me. This is a straight path. **62.** Do not let Satan turn you away. He is indeed a clear enemy to you. **63.** When Jesus brought clear signs, he said, "I have come to you with wisdom and to clarify some of what you disagree upon. So revere God and obey me. **64.** Indeed God is my Lord and your Lord, so worship Him. This is a straight path." **65.** But then, the parties differed among themselves. Woe unto those who did wrong from the punishment of a painful Day. **66.** Are they only waiting for the Hour to come upon them suddenly while they are unaware? **67.** On that Day, friends will be enemies of one another, except for the reverent. **68.** O My servants! No fear will be upon you this Day, nor will you grieve. **69.** You who believed in Our signs and who were Muslims, **70.** enter the Garden, you, and your spouses, and rejoice. **71.** Round trays and goblets of gold will be brought to them. There will be whatever souls desire and eyes find pleasing, and you will abide there. **72.** This is the Garden you inherited for what you did. **73.** You will have an abundance of fruit to eat from there. **74.** The guilty will indeed abide in the punishment of Hell. **75.** It will not be lightened for them. There, they will despair. **76.** We did not wrong them, rather, it is they who were the wrongdoers. **77.** They will yell, "O Mālik, let your Lord put an end to us." He will reply, "You will surely stay. **78.** Indeed We brought you the truth, but most of you were averse to the truth." **79.** Or have the devised anything? Truly it is We Who devise. **80.** Or do they assume We do not hear their secret and their private conversations? Our messengers are indeed present with them, recording. **81.** Say, "Truly if the Compassionate has a child, then, I would be the first of worshippers." **82.** Glory be to the Lord of the heavens and the earth, the Lord of the Throne, above what they attribute. **83.** So leave them to converse vainly and amuse themselves until they meet the Day that they are promised. **84.** It is He Who is God in Heaven and God on earth. He is the Wise and the Knowing. **85.** Blessed is He unto Whom belongs sovereignty of the heavens and the earth and whatever is between them, and with Whom lies knowledge of the Hour, and unto Whom you will be returned. **86.** Those whom they invoke instead of Him have no interceding power, save those who bear witness to the truth, and have knowledge. **87.** Were you to ask them, "Who created you?" they would certainly say, "God." How then are they deluded? **88.** As for his saying, "O my Lord, indeed these are a people who do not believe," **89.** bear with them and say, "Peace," for soon they will know.

Surah 44

SMOKE

al-Dukhān

In the Name of God, the Compassionate, the Merciful

1. Hā. Mīm. 2. By the clear Book, 3. We have sent it down on a blessed night for We were indeed ever warning. 4. In it, every wise command is made clear 5. as a command from Us. We are truly ever conveying, 6. as a mercy from your Lord. Truly He is the Hearing and the Knowing, 7. Lord of the heavens and the earth and whatever is between them, would you be assured. 8. There is no god but He who gives life and gives death — your Lord — the Lord of your forefathers. 9. Yet, they are indeed playing around in doubt. 10. So watch out for the day when the sky comes forth with clear smoke, 11. enveloping people. This is a painful punishment. 12. "Our Lord! Remove the punishment from us. We are truly believers." 13. How can there be a reminder for them when a clear messenger had come to them? 14. They had then turned away from him and said, "He was taught and is insane." 15. We will indeed remove the punishment a little, but surely you will revert. 16. On the Day when We strike with the great striking, We will certainly be vengeful. 17. Truly We tried the people of Pharoah before them. A noble messenger had come to them, 18. "Deliver God's servants to me! I am truly a trustworthy messenger to you. 19. Do not rise against God. I have indeed come to you with clear authority. 20. In case you stone me, I will indeed seek refuge in my Lord and your Lord. 21. If you do not believe me, then stay away from me." 22. Then he called unto his Lord, "These are sinful people." 23. "Go forth with My servants by night, and you will indeed be pursued. 24. Leave the sea at rest. They will certainly be a drowned host." 25. How many gardens and springs did they leave behind, 26. sown fields, a noble dwelling, 27. and fortunes in which they took delight? 28. By such, We bequeathed it unto another people. 29. Neither heaven nor earth wept over them, nor were they granted respite. 30. We have delivered the Children of Israel from a humiliating

punishment **31.** from Pharoah. Truly he was among the highest of transgressors. **32.** We had knowingly chosen them above all others in the worlds. **33.** We gave them signs wherein was a clear trial. **34.** Indeed these say, **35.** "There is nothing besides our first death and we will not be resurrected. **36.** Bring us our fathers if you are truthful." **37.** Are they better or the people of Tubba and those before them? They were truly sinful, and We destroyed them. **38.** We did not create the heavens and the earth and whatever is between them in play. **39.** We did not create them, save in truth, but most of them do not know. **40.** Indeed the Day of Division is their meeting, all together. **41.** It will be a Day when no friend will benefit a friend by any means, nor will they be helped, **42.** except he unto whom God has been merciful for indeed, He is the Mighty and the Merciful. **43.** Truly the tree of Zaqqūm **44.** is food for the sinner, **45.** like the molten lead boiling in their bellies, **46.** like the boiling of scalding liquid. **47.** "Seize him and drag him into the midst of the Hellfire! **48.** Then pour the punishment of boiling liquid on his head." **49.** "Taste! You are indeed the mighty and the noble! **50.** This is what you doubted." **51.** Truly the reverent are in a secure place **52.** amid gardens and springs, **53.** wearing fine silk and rich brocade while facing one another. **54.** So it is. We will wed them to lustrous-eyed maidens. **55.** They will call for every fruit therein while feeling secure. **56.** They will not taste death there, save for the first death. He will shield them from the punishment of the Hellfire **57.** as a Bounty from your Lord. That is the great triumph. **58.** We have made this easy on your tongue that perhaps they may remember. **59.** So stay alert for they are watching as well.

Surah 45

The Kneeling

al-Jāthiyah

In the Name of God, the Compassionate, the Merciful

1. Ḥā. Mīm. **2.** The revelation of the Book is from God, the Mighty and the Wise. **3.** Truly in the heavens and the earth are signs for believers. **4.** In your creation and in what He has scattered of animals are signs for a people who firmly believe. **5.** In the variation of night and day, and in what God has sent down from the sky as sustenance to revive the earth after its death, and the shifting of winds are signs for a people who understand. **6.** These are the signs of God that We recite unto you in truth. So in what discourse beyond God and His signs do they believe? **7.** Woe unto every sinful liar! **8.** He hears the sign of God recited unto him, then remains arrogant as though he did not hear it. So announce to him of a painful punishment. **9.** When he learns of any of Our signs, he takes them in mockery. For them will be a humiliating punishment. **10.** Beyond them awaits Hell, where their accumulated deeds and the guardians they chose besides God will offer no benefit; a severe punishment is destined for them. **11.** This is guidance. There will be a painful punishment for those who disbelieve in the punishment of their Lord. **12.** It is God Who made the sea subservient that the ships may sail upon it by His Command, and for you to seek of His Bounty that perhaps you may be grateful. **13.** He made whatever is in the heavens and on the earth, entirely subservient unto you. Truly in that are signs for a people who reflect. **14.** Tell those who believe to forgive those who do not look forward to the days of God that He might reward people for what they earned. **15.** Whoever does a righteous deed, it will be for his own soul and whoever commits evil, it will be on them. Then unto your Lord you will be returned. **16.** Indeed We gave the Children of Israel the Book, judgment, and prophethood. We provided them with good things and favored them above the worlds. **17.** We had given them clear signs from the Command. They only differed after knowledge had come to them and out of envy among themselves. Your Lord will certainly judge between them on the Day of Resurrection over what they differed upon. **18.** Then We placed you on an ordained path from the Command, so follow it and do not follow the impulses of those who do not know. **19.** Indeed they will not benefit you by any means against God. The wrongdoers are strictly the protectors of one another while God is the Protector of the reverent. **20.** These are insights for people, and guidance and mercy for a people who firmly believe. **21.** Or do those who commit evil deeds assume We will treat them like those who believe and perform righteous deeds equally in their life and in their death? The judgment they make is indeed, evil. **22.** God created the heavens and the earth in truth so that every soul will be rewarded for what it earned. They will not be wronged. **23.** Have you considered one who takes his own fancy to be his god? God knowingly led him astray. He sealed his hearing and heart and placed a cover over his sight. Who, then, will guide him after God? Will you then, not remember? **24.** They say, "There is nothing but our life in this world. We die and we live, and nothing can destroy us but time." But they have no knowledge of that. They do no more than speculate. **25.** When Our signs are recited unto them as clear signs, their argument is nothing but to say, "Bring us our fathers if you are truthful." **26.** Say, "God revives you, then causes you to die. He then gathers you on the Day of Resurrection in which there is no doubt, but most people do not know." **27.** To God belongs sovereignty over the heavens and the earth. The Day when the Hour arrives, on that Day, the falsifiers will lose, **28.** and you will see every nation on its knees. Every nation will be called to its book. "Today you will be rewarded for what you did. **29.** This, Our Book, speaks against you in truth. Truly We were recording all that you did." **30.** As for those who believed and performed righteous deeds, the Lord will admit them unto His Mercy. That is the clear triumph. **31.** As for those who disbelieve, were My signs not revealed unto you, yet you acted arrogant? You were a sinful people. **32.** "When it was said, 'Indeed, God's promise is true, and there is no doubt about the Hour,' you replied, 'We do not know what the Hour is. We only speculate and are not convinced with certainty.'" **33.** The evils of what they had done will become clear to them, and they will be enclosed by what they used to mock. **34.** It will be said, "We will forget you today just as you forgot the meeting of this Day of yours. Your abode is the Fire, and you will have no helpers. **35.** That is because you took the signs of God in mockery, and you were deceived by the life of this world." So today they will not be removed from it, nor can they seek restitution. **36.** Thus praise be to God, Lord of the heavens and the earth, Lord of the Worlds. **37.** To Him belongs the Grandeur in the heavens and the earth. He is the Mighty and the Wise.

Surah 46

THE SAND DUNES
al-Ahqāf

In the Name of God, the Compassionate, the Merciful

1. *Hā. Mīm.* 2. The revelation of the Book is from God, the Mighty and the Wise. 3. We did not create the heavens and the earth and whatever is between them except in truth, and for an appointed term. Yet those who disbelieve turn away from what they were warned. 4. Say, "Do you perceive what you call upon instead of God? Show me what they have created on the earth. Or do they have a share in the heavens? Bring me a book before this or some trace of knowledge if you are truthful." 5. Who is more astray than one who calls on something besides God that will not respond to him and will be heedless of their calling until the Day of Resurrection? 6. When people are gathered, they will be enemies to them and will renounce their worship. 7. Yet when Our signs are recited to them as clear proofs, those who disbelieve say to the truth when it comes to them, "This is clearly sorcery." 8. Or do they say, "He has made it up?" Say, "Had I made it up, you have nothing that will benefit me against God. He knows best about what you devise. He is enough of a witness between me and you. He is the Forgiving and the Merciful." 9. Say, "I am no novelty among the messengers, and I do not know what will be done with me or you. I only follow what has been revealed unto me. I am no more than a clear warner." 10. Say, "Have you considered that if this is from God and you have disbelieved in it, while a witness from the Children of Israel testified to its truth and believed in it, yet you remained arrogant? Surely, God does not guide those who are unjust." 11. The disbelievers say about the believers, "If it were any good, they would not have embraced it before us." And since they refuse to be guided by it, they say, "This is nothing but an old myth." 12. Before this, there was the Book of Moses. This is an authenticated Book in an Arabic tongue to warn wrongdoers and to be good news for the righteous. 13. Indeed, those who say, "Our Lord is God," then stand firm, no fear will come upon

them, nor will they grieve. **14.** They will be inhabitants of the Garden, abiding therein, as a reward for what they did. **15.** We have commanded man to be kind to his parents. His mother carried him with difficulty and gave birth to him in hardship. His period of gestation and weaning lasts thirty months. When he reaches maturity and turns forty, he says, "My Lord, inspire me to be grateful for the blessings You have bestowed upon me and my parents. Help me to do righteous deeds that please You and make my descendants righteous as well. Truly, I repent to You, and I am among those who submit." **16.** Those are the ones from whom We accept the best of what they have done, overlooking their ill deeds that they may be among the inhabitants of the Garden, the promise of truth that they were promised. **17.** But as for the one who says to his parents, "Fie on you both! Do you promise me that I will be resurrected, even though generations before me have already passed away?" while they plead to God for help, saying, "Woe to you! Believe! God's promise is undoubtedly true." Yet he replies, "This is nothing but old myths!" **18.** It is they and those among nations of jinn and people that passed before them on whom the Word came due. Truly they were lost. **19.** For each, there are degrees for what they had done. He will fully compensate them for their deeds, and they will not be wronged. **20.** The day when those who disbelieve are exposed to the Fire: "You exhausted your pleasures during your worldly life, and you indulged in them. So today, you will be awarded with the punishment of disgrace for having been arrogant upon the earth without justification and for having transgressed." **21.** Mention the brother of the Ãd when he warned his people by the sand dunes. Warners had passed away before him and after him, "Worship none but God. I truly fear for you the punishment of a tremendous day." **22.** They said, "Have you come to us to deter us from our gods? Then, bring us what you have threatened us with if you are among the truthful." **23.** He said, "Knowledge lies only with God. I deliver to you what has been sent to me, but I see that you are an ignorant people." **24.** When they saw a cloud approaching their valleys, they said, "This is but a cloud bringing us rain." No! It was what you sought to hasten, a wind that carries a painful punishment, **25.** destroying everything by the Command of its Lord. By morning, they saw nothing but their homes. As such, do We reward a guilty people? **26.** Indeed, We gave them a level of establishment that We did not grant to you. We provided them with hearing, sight, and hearts, yet their hearing, sight, and hearts were of no benefit to them because they rejected God's signs. Ultimately, they were overwhelmed by the very things they used to mock. **27.** We have indeed destroyed the towns around you, and We varied the signs that perhaps they may return. **28.** Why then, did no help come to them from those they had taken as gods instead of God, that they be drawn closer? Indeed, they abandoned them. That was their falsification and what they made up. **29.** Remember when We directed a party of jinn toward you. They were listening to the Quran and while in its presence, they said, "Be quiet!" Then when it came to an end, they went back to their people as warners. **30.** They said, "O our people! We have indeed listened to a Book sent down after Moses, confirming what had come before it, guiding to the truth, and to a straight path. **31.** O our people! Respond to God's caller and believe in him, He will then forgive you for some of your sins and protect you from a painful punishment. **32.** Whoever does not respond to God's caller cannot escape on earth and will have no protector besides Him. They are in obvious error." **33.** Do they not see that God, Who created the heavens and the earth, did not weary in their creation and is able to give life to the dead? Truly He is powerful over all things. **34.** On the day when those who disbelieve are exposed to the Fire, "Is this not with justification?" They will say, "Absolutely! By our Lord!" He will reply, "Taste the punishment for having disbelieved." **35.** So remain patient, just as the resolute messengers before you were patient, and do not hasten concerning them. On the day they witness what they were promised, it will seem as though they had stayed no more than an hour of a single day. Announce: Will anyone be destroyed except the sinful people?

Surah 47

MUHAMMAD

Muhammad

In the Name of God, the Compassionate, the Merciful

1. For those who disbelieve and turn from the way of God, He renders their deeds astray. 2. For those who believe, perform righteous deeds, and believe that what was sent down to Muhammad is the truth from their Lord, He has pardoned their evil deeds and placed their mind at ease. 3. That is because those who disbelieve follow untruthfulness and those who believe follow the truth from their Lord. God thus sets forth examples for people from those who were like them. 4. When you encounter those who disbelieve in battle, strike their necks. Once you have subdued them, secure their captivity firmly. Then, afterward, release them graciously or hold them for ransom until the war comes to an end. So it is! If God had willed, He could have exacted retribution upon them Himself, but He chooses to test you through one another. As for those who are killed in the cause of God, He will not let their deeds go to waste. 5. He will guide them by placing their mind at ease 6. and admitting them to the Garden, having made it known to them. 7. O you who believe! If you help God, He will help you and ground your footsteps. 8. But those who disbelieve, will be wretched and their deeds will go astray. 9. This is because they were averse to what God had sent down, so He made their deeds fruitless. 10. Have they not traveled upon the earth and observed the destiny of those before them? God destroyed them, and the disbelievers will have the same outcome. 11. That is because God is the Master of those who believe, and the disbelievers have no master. 12. Indeed God causes those who believe and perform righteous deeds to enter Gardens with rivers running beneath while those who disbelieve entertain themselves and feed as cattle feed. The Fire will be their abode. 13. How many a town with more power than your town — that had driven you out — have We destroyed, while they had

no one to help them? **14.** So is one who holds clear proof from his Lord the same as he whose evil deeds are made to seem fair to him while they follow their caprices? **15.** This is a parable of the Garden promised to the God-conscious. It contains rivers of unspoiled water, rivers of milk whose taste never changes, rivers of delightful wine for those who drink it, and rivers of pure honey. They will enjoy every kind of fruit and receive forgiveness from their Lord. Can this be compared to someone who dwells in the Fire, forced to drink scalding water that tears apart their insides? **16.** Then, when they leave your presence, they ask those with knowledge, "What did he say?" They are the ones who follow their desires, and whose hearts God has sealed. **17.** But those who are guided, He will add to their guidance and grant them their piety. **18.** Do they but wait for the Hour to come upon them unexpectedly? But its indications have already come. Therefore, what will their reminder do for them when it comes? **19.** Know that there is no god but God and ask for forgiveness for your sin, and for the believing men and the believing women. God knows of your whereabouts and your living quarters. **20.** Those who believe say, "If only a sūrah were revealed." But when a decisive sūrah is sent down mentioning fighting, you see those with sickness in their hearts looking at you as if overcome by the shadow of death. Yet, what is more appropriate for them **21.** is obedience to God and speaking respectfully. Then, once the matter is settled, it would be better for them to remain true to God. **22.** Were you to turn away, would you possibly perform corruption upon the earth and sever your family ties? **23.** They are those whom God has cursed. He made them deaf and blinded their sight. **24.** Do they not reflect upon the Quran or have hearts that lock themselves up? **25.** Truly those who turn their backs after guidance has been made clear to them—Satan has seduced them and brought their hopes up. **26.** That is because they say to those who are averse to what God has sent down, "We will obey you in some matters." But God knows their secrets. **27.** Then how will it be when the angels seize them while striking their faces and their backs? **28.** That is because they followed what angers God and were averse to His pleasure, so He nullified their deeds. **29.** Or do those in whose hearts is a disease assume that God will not uncover their hatred? **30.** Had We willed, We would have shown them to you that you would know them by their mark, but you will certainly know them by their tone of speech. God is Aware of your deeds. **31.** We will test you until We know those among you who strive and those who are patient, and We will test your assertions. **32.** Indeed those who disbelieve and turn from the way of God and oppose the Messenger of God after guidance has been made clear to them will not harm God in the least. He will make their deeds plummet. **33.** O you who believe! Obey God and obey the Messenger and do not let your deeds be worthless. **34.** Indeed, those who disbelieve and turn from the way of God, then die while they are disbelievers, God will not forgive them. **35.** So do not be weak and call for peace while you have the upper hand. God is with you and will not deprive you of your deeds. **36.** The life of this world is but entertainment and diversion. If you believe and are reverent, He will give you your rewards and not ask you for your wealth. **37.** Were He to ask you for it, then appeal to you, you would be miserly, and He would expose your hatred. **38.** Behold! You are the ones called to spend in the cause of God, but some of you are tightfisted. Whoever is miserly is only being miserly toward himself. God is Rich, while you are the needy. If you turn away, He will replace you with another people who will not be like you.

Surah 48

VICTORY

al-Fath

In the Name of God, the Compassionate, the Merciful

1. Indeed, We have granted you a clear victory **2.** that God may forgive your prior and oncoming sins, complete His Blessing upon you, guide you on a straight path, **3.** and that God may help you with immense help. **4.** He is the One who sends down tranquility into the hearts of the believers, so they may add to their faith. To God belong the forces of the heavens and the earth. God is All-Knowing and Wise. **5.** He will admit believing men and women into Gardens beneath which rivers flow, where they will dwell forever, and He will forgive their sins. That is a great triumph from God's perspective, **6.** He may punish hypocritical men and hypocritical women, and the idolatrous men and idolatrous women who have evil thoughts about God. They are surrounded by evil. God is rages at them, curses them, and prepares Hell for them. What an evil final destination! **7.** To God belong the forces of the heavens and the earth. God is Mighty and Wise. **8.** We have indeed sent you as a witness, as a bearer of good news, and as warner, **9.** that you may believe in God and His Messenger and support Him, honor Him, and glorify Him morning and evening. **10.** Indeed, those who pledge allegiance to you, pledge allegiance only to God. The Hand of God is over their hands. Whoever reneges, reneges only upon his soul. Whoever fulfills what he has pledged unto God, He will grant him a great reward. **11.** The Bedouin who stayed behind will say to you, "We were busy with our properties and families, so ask forgiveness for us." They say with their tongues what is not in their hearts. Say, "Who can benefit you with anything from God should He desire to harm you, or should He desire to benefit you? But indeed, God is Aware of whatever you do. **12.** Truly you thought the Messenger and the believers would never return to their families and this seemed pleasing to your hearts. You postulated an evil postulation, and you are a wasted people.

13. For whoever does not believe in God and His Messenger, We have indeed prepared an Inferno for the disbelievers. **14.** To God belongs sovereignty over the heavens and the earth. He forgives whoever He wills and punishes whomever He wills. God is Forgiving and Merciful. **15.** Those who stayed behind will say when you head out to acquire spoils, "Allow us to follow you." They desire to change the Word of God. Say, "You will not follow us. Thus has God had said previously." Then they will say, "You are rather jealous of us." However, little do they understand. **16.** Say to the Bedouin who stayed behind, "You will be summoned against a people possessed of great might. You should fight them, or they should *submit*. Therefore, if you obey, God will grant you a goodly reward, but if you turn away as you had previously turned away, He will punish you with a painful punishment." **17.** There is no blame upon the blind, nor is there blame upon the lame, nor is there blame upon the sick. Whoever obeys God and His Messenger, He will admit him to Gardens with rivers running beneath, and whoever turns away, He will punish him with a painful punishment. **18.** God was satisfied with the believers when they pledged allegiance beneath the tree. He knew what was in their hearts and sent Tranquility down upon them and rewarded them with ensuing victory **19.** and the abundant spoils that they would capture. God is Mighty and Wise. **20.** God has promised that you will capture abundant spoils. He then advanced this for you and restrained people's hands from you that it may be a sign for the believers, and that He may guide you upon a straight path. **21.** Others that you were not capable of, God had them surrounded. God is Powerful over all things. **22.** If those who disbelieve had fought you, they would have redressed and found neither protector, nor helper — **23.** the practice of God that came to pass before — and you will not find change in the practice of God. **24.** It is He Who restrained their hands from you and your hands from them in the valley of Makkah after He made you victorious over them. God sees whatever you do. **25.** They are the ones who disbelieved and prevented you from entering the Sacred Mosque, blocking the offerings from reaching their place of sacrifice. Had it not been for believing men and women — whom you did not know — who might have been harmed unknowingly, causing you guilt, God held back His punishment to admit whomever He wills into His mercy. If they had been clearly separated, We would have surely inflicted a painful punishment on the disbelievers. **26.** When those who disbelieve had set fanaticism in their hearts, fanaticism of the Age of Ignorance, God sent His Tranquility down upon His Messenger and upon the believers and commanded the Word of reverence upon them since they were more worthy and deserving of it. God has knowledge of all things. **27.** God has indeed fulfilled the vision of truth for His Messenger. You will enter the Sacred Mosque in security, if God wills, with your heads shaven or hair shortened. Do not fear, for He knew what you did not know, and besides, He has arranged for an ensuing victory. **28.** It is He Who sent His Messenger with guidance and the Religion of Truth to be manifest over all religions. God is enough of a Witness. **29.** Muhammad is the Messenger of God, and those with him are firm against the disbelievers but kind and compassionate toward one another. You see them bowing and prostrating, seeking God's bounty and His pleasure. The mark of their prostration is visible on their foreheads. This is their description in the Torah. Their likeness in the Gospel is like a seed that sprouts its shoot, strengthens it, and grows sturdy, standing upright on its stalk, delighting the farmers. Through them, God intends to enrage the disbelievers. God has promised forgiveness and a great reward to those among them who believe and do righteous deeds.

Surah 49

The Chambers
al-Hujurāt

In the Name of God, the Compassionate, the Merciful

1. O you who believe! Do not set yourselves ahead of God and His Messenger. Revere God. Truly God is Hearing and Knowing. **2.** O you who believe! Do not raise your voices above the voice of the Prophet, nor speak loudly to him as you would speak loudly with one another lest your deeds be in vain while you are unaware. **3.** Truly those who lower their voices before the Messenger of God are the ones whose hearts God has tested for reverence. Forgiveness and a great reward will be for them. **4.** Truly most of those who call out to you from behind the chambers do not understand. **5.** It would have been better for them had they been patient until you came out to them. God is Forgiving and Merciful. **6.** O you who believe! If a sinful person comes to you with news, then be judicious to avoid harming people out of ignorance and regret what you have done. **7.** Know that the Messenger of God is among you and if he were to obey you in many matters, you would suffer hardship. But God has caused you to love faith and has made it pleasing to your hearts. He made you despise disbelief, sinfulness, and disobedience. Truly such are those who are righteous, **8.** a grace from God and a blessing. God is Knowing and Wise. **9.** If two parties among the believers fall into dispute, make peace between them. If one of them oppresses the other, fight those who oppress until they return to God's Command. If they return, make peace between them with justice and impartiality. Truly God loves the just. **10.** Truly believers are but brothers, so make peace between your brethren and revere God that perhaps you may receive mercy. **11.** O you who believe! Do not let some people ridicule another people, for it may be that the ridiculed are better than those who mock. Nor should women deride other women; perhaps those being mocked are superior to those mocking. Do not defame one another, nor insult each other with offensive nicknames. Evil is the act of calling someone by a bad name after having faith. And those who do not repent—it is they who are the wrongdoers. **12.** O you who believe! Avoid most speculation for some speculation is a sin. Do not spy on one another, nor gossip maliciously about one another. Would any of you like to eat the flesh of his dead brother? You would detest it. Revere God. Truly God is Relenting and Merciful. **13.** O people! Truly We created you from a male and a female and We made you peoples and tribes that you may come to know one another. Truly the most noble of you before God are the most reverent of you. Truly God is Knowing and Aware. **14.** The Bedouin say, "We believe." Say, "You do not believe. Rather say, 'We have submitted,' for belief has not yet entered your hearts. Yet if you obey God and His Messenger, He will not diminish your deeds. Truly God is Forgiving and Merciful." **15.** Believers are only those who believe in God and His Messenger, are not skeptical, and strive with their wealth and their persons in the way of God. It is they who are truthful. **16.** Say, "Would you teach God about your religion when God knows of whatever is in the heavens and the whatever is on the earth?" God has knowledge of all things. **17.** They consider it a favor to you that they have submitted. Say, "Do not consider your submission to be a favor to me. Rather, God truly confers a favor upon you by guiding you to belief if you are truthful. **18.** Truly God knows the Unseen of the heavens and the earth, and God sees whatever you do."

Surah 50

QĀF
Qāf

In the Name of God, the Compassionate, the Merciful

1. *Qāf*: By the glorious Quran, **2.** they were truly confounded that a warner had come to them from among their own, so the disbelievers say, "This is a strange thing! **3.** What! When we are dead and have become dust — that is a far-fetched return!" **4.** We already know what the earth takes of them, and We have the preserved Book. **5.** But they denied the truth when it came to them. So now, they are in a confused state of mind. **6.** Have they not seen the sky above them, how We constructed it and adorned it, without any flaws? **7.** We spread out the earth, placed sturdy mountains upon it, and brought forth pairs of every beautiful type to grow, **8.** as a means of reflection and a reminder for every servant who turns in repentance. **9.** We sent down blessed water from the sky and brought forth gardens and crops of grain, **10.** as well as tall date palms with layered clusters, **11.** as provision for His servants. We gave life to a barren land — and just like that will be the resurrection. **12.** Before them, the people of Noah, the Companions of al-Rass, and the Thamŭds had denied **13.** as did the Ād, Pharoah, the brethren of Lot, **14.** the inhabitants of the thicket, and the people of Tubba, by which each denied the messengers. Consequently, My Warning came due. **15.** Did We then tire in the first creation? No, but they are undeniably in doubt of a new creation. **16.** We truly created man and We know what His soul whispers to him. We are closer to him than his jugular vein. **17.** When the two recorders take note, one seated on the right and the other on the left, **18.** not a single word does he speak without an observer present and prepared. **19.** The throes of death bring the reality — that is what you sought to escape. **20.** The trumpet is blown. That is the Day of Warning. **21.** Then every soul arrives with a driver and a witness. **22.** "You were indeed heedless of this. So now, We have removed your veil from you. So today your vision is sharp." **23.** His companion says, "This is what I already have."

24. "Toss into Hell every stubborn disbeliever, 25. every inhibitor of good, every transgressor, every doubter 26. who has set up another god along with God. Toss him into the severe punishment." 27. His companion will say, "Our Lord, I did not make him rebel. He was quite far astray." 28. He will say, "Do not dispute before Me since I have already presented you with the Warning. 29. The Word does not change with Me, and I do not wrong My servants." 30. That Day, We will say to Hell, "Have you been filled?" and it will say, "Is there more?" 31. The Garden will be brought close to the reverent, not distant. 32. "This is what has been promised to every mindful, repentant person— 33. one who reveres the Compassionate Unseen and approaches with a humble, penitent heart. 34. Enter in peace. This is the day of abiding." 35. There they will have whatever they desire and with Us there is more. 36. How many a generation before them have We destroyed who were of even greater fortitude than them? Then they searched about in the lands: "Is there any refuge?" 37. Truly in that is a reminder for whoever has a heart or lends an ear as a witness. 38. Indeed, We created the heavens and the earth and whatever is between them in six days. No weariness has touched Us. 39. So bear patiently with what they say and glorify the praise of your Lord before the rising of the sun and before the setting. 40. Glorify Him at night and after prostrations. 41. Listen on the Day when the caller calls from a nearby place, 42. on the Day when they hear the Cry of Truth. That is the Day of Resurrection. 43. Indeed it is We Who give life and death and unto Us is the final destiny. 44. On that Day, the earth will break open around them as they hurry forth. Gathering them is easy for Us. 45. We are fully aware of what they say, and it is not your task to force them. So use the Quran as a reminder for those who fear My Warning.

Surah 51

THE SCATTERERS

al-Dhāriyāt

In the Name of God, the Compassionate, the Merciful

1. By the scatterers as they scatter, 2. and by those who bear a burden, 3. by those who drift with ease, 4. and by those who apportion by Command, 5. indeed what you are promised is true, 6. and indeed judgment will come to pass. 7. By Heaven with its pathways, 8. for indeed you are of differing assertions. 9. Whoever turns away from it, will be turned away. 10. Accursed be the deniers 11. by those who are immersed in confusion 12. asking, "When is the Day of Judgment?" 13. A day when they are tried over the Fire. 14. Taste your trial! This is what you sought to expedite. 15. Truly the reverent will be amidst gardens and springs, 16. partaking in what their Lord has given them, for indeed, they were previously virtuous. 17. They would barely sleep at night, 18. would seek forgiveness before dawn, 19. and the beggar and the deprived were given what was owed to them in wealth. 20. On the earth there are signs for those who firmly believe, 21. and within your souls. Do you not see? 22. In Heaven is your provision and what you were promised. 23. By the Lord of the Heaven and the earth, it is as certain as your own ability to speak. 24. Has the story of Abraham's honored guests reached you? 25. They had entered upon him and said, "Peace!" He said, "Peace—unfamiliar people." 26. Then he veered toward his family and came back with a fattened calf. 27. He placed it close to them saying, "Will you not eat?" 28. Then he was apprehensive of them. They said, "Do not fear!" They gave him good news of a son endowed with knowledge. 29. Then his wife came forward with a loud cry. She struck her face and said, "A barren woman!" 30. They said, "Thus has your Lord pronounced. He is indeed, the Wise and the Knowing." 31. He said, "What is your charge, O messengers?" 32. They said, "We have been sent to a guilty people 33. to hurl upon them stones of clay 34. marked by your Lord for the reckless." 35. As a result, We evacuated those among them who were believers, 36. Though

We only found therein, one house of submitters. **37.** We left a sign there for those who fear the painful punishment. **38.** And in Moses when We sent him to the Pharoah with clear authority, **39.** but he turned away with his chieftains and said, "A sorcerer or one insane." **40.** Therefore, We seized him and his forces and threw them into the sea. He was blameworthy. **41.** And in the Ād people when We sent them the harsh wind. **42.** Anything it came upon was left as decayed bones. **43.** And in the Thamŭd when it was said to them, "Enjoy yourselves for a while." **44.** They then, insolently defied the Command of their Lord, and the thunderbolt seized them while they were looking on. **45.** Afterward, they were unable to rise or assist one another. **46.** And before that, the people of Noah were indeed a sinful people. **47.** We established the sky with might; truly we make it vast. **48.** We laid out the earth—what excellent Expanders! **49.** We created pairs of all things that perhaps you may remember. **50.** So flee to God. I am truly a clear warner to you from Him. **51.** Do not set up another god along with God. I am truly a clear warner to you from Him. **52.** Similarly, no messenger was sent to those before them but said, "A sorcerer or one insane." **53.** Do they bequeath it to one another? No, they are rather a rebellious people. **54.** So turn away from them for you will not be blamed. **55.** So remind, for indeed the Reminder benefits the believers. **56.** I did not create jinn and people, except to worship Me. **57.** I do not want sustenance, nor do I want them to feed Me. **58.** Truly God is the Provider, Possessor of Strength, and the Firm. **59.** Certainly for those who did wrong, is a portion, like the portion of their companions. So do not let them try and rush. **60.** Woe to those who disbelieve on account of the Day of theirs that they were promised!

Surah 52

The Mount

al-Tūr

In the Name of God, the Compassionate, the Merciful

1. By the Mount, 2. and by a Book inscribed, 3. on a parchment unfolded, 4. by the occupied house, 5. by the raised canopy, 6. and by the inflated sea. 7. Indeed your Lord's punishment will come to pass. 8. No one can avert it 9. on the Day the sky churns with a great churning, 10. and the mountains move in great motion. 11. Woe on that Day to the deniers 12. who amuse themselves with vain talk, 13. a Day when they are violently thrust into the Fire of Hell, 14. (and told) "This is the Fire that you denied. 15. Is this sorcery or do you not see? 16. Burn in it! Be patient or not be patient, it will be the same for you. Truly you will only be rewarded for what you did." 17. Truly the reverent will be cheerful in Gardens, 18. enjoying what their Lord had given them. Their Lord safeguarded them from the punishment of Hellfire, 19. [and told them] "Eat and drink in good health (as a reward) for what you have done." 20. They will be reclining on aligned couches, and We will wed them to lustrous-eyed maidens. 21. For those who believed and whose progeny followed them in faith, We will arrange for their progeny to be with them. We will not deprive them from any of their deeds. Every person will earn what he pledged to. 22. We will provide them with an abundance of fruits and meats of their choice. 23. They will pass goblets around to one another where there be no vain talk or provocation to sin. 24. Youth who are like hidden pearls will circle around, waiting on them. 25. They will approach one another and question each other 26. saying, "Truly when we were among our families before, we were anxious, 27. but God was gracious to us and safeguarded us from the punishment of the scorching wind. 28. We indeed called upon Him before. He is truly the Righteous and the Merciful." 29. So remind them that through the blessing of your Lord, you are neither insane nor a fortuneteller. 30. Or do they say, "A

poet—let us await for a misfortune to happen for him." **31.** Say, "Wait! For truly I am waiting along with you." **32.** Do their reveries command them to this or are they just a transgressing people? **33.** Or do they say, "He has forged it?" Truly they have no faith. **34.** Let them produce a similar account to it if they are truthful. **35.** Were they created from nothing or are they the creators, **36.** or did they create the heavens and the earth? Yet, they are truly not convinced. **37.** Are the Treasures of your Lord with them or are they the controllers? **38.** Do they have a ladder whereby they listen? Then let their listener produce a clear warrant. **39.** Does He have daughters while you have sons, **40.** or do you ask a reward of them that will overburden them with debt? **41.** Do they possess the Unseen and write it down, **42.** or do they want to devise a scheme? Those who disbelieve are themselves schemers. **43.** Or do they have a god other than God? Glory be to God above the partners they attribute. **44.** Were they to see a fragment falling from the sky, they would say, "A heap of clouds." **45.** So leave them until they meet the Day when they will be shell-shocked, **46.** a Day when their scheming will not benefit them, and they will not be helped. **47.** For indeed those who do wrong will have a punishment beyond that, but most of them do not know. **48.** Be patient with your Lord's decree, for you are under Our watch. Praise your Lord when you rise, **49.** and glorify Him during parts of the night and as the stars fade away.

Surah 53

THE STAR

al-Najm

In the Name of God, the Compassionate, the Merciful

1. By the star when it sets, 2. your companion has neither gone astray nor misled, 3. nor does he speak impulsively. 4. It is no more than a revelation revealed, 5. taught by the Mighty and Powerful. 6. Possessed of soundness, he stood upright 7. when he was at the highest horizon. 8. Then he approached and came close 9. until he was within two bows' length or closer. 10. Then He revealed to His servant what He meant to reveal. 11. The heart did not lie in what it saw. 12. Do you dispute with him about what he saw? 13. For indeed, he saw him during another time 14. at the boundary of the lote tree 15. situated by the Garden of the Abode. 16. Then the lote tree enveloped in mystery — 17. where sight neither wavered nor exceeded its bounds. 18. Indeed he saw the greatest of his Lord's signs. 19. Have you observed *al-Lāt* and *al-Uzzā*, 20. and the other third one, *Manāt*? 21. Unto you males and unto Him females? 22. Then this would be an unfair division. 23. These are nothing but names you and your ancestors have invented, for which God has given no authority. They follow only assumptions and the desires of their own souls, even though guidance had surely come to them from their Lord. 24. Or does man have whatever he yearns for? 25. To God belongs the beginning and the end. 26. How many an angel is there in the heavens whose intercession will benefit no one except after God gives permission to whomever He wills and to whomever He is satisfied with? 27. Indeed, those who do not believe in the Hereafter name the angels with female names. 28. Yet they have no knowledge thereof. Truly they only follow conjecture, and surely, conjecture avails nothing against the Truth. 29. So avoid whoever turns away from Our Reminder and desires nothing more than the life of this world. 30. That is the extent of their knowledge. Your Lord certainly knows best those who stray from His way, and He knows best those who are rightly guided.

31. Unto God belongs whatever is in the heavens and on the earth, that He may reward those who commit evil for what they have done, and that He may reward those who are virtuous with what is best. **32.** Indeed, your Lord is boundless in forgiveness for those who steer clear of major sins and immoral acts, except for minor lapses. He knows you best from when He brought you forth from the earth and when you were concealed within your mothers' bellies. So do not declare yourselves pure — He knows best who is truly reverent. **33.** Have you seen the one who turned away, **34.** gave little and then hardened? **35.** Does he have knowledge of the Unseen such that he can see it? **36.** Or has he not been informed of what is in the scriptures of Moses **37.** and Abraham fulfilled: **38.** that no one will bear the burden of another, **39.** that man will have nothing more than what he strives for, **40.** and that his striving will be observed. **41.** As such, he will be rewarded for it with the fullest reward, **42.** and unto your Lord is the ultimate end. **43.** That it is He who grants laughter and tears; **44.** that it is He who grants life and death; **45.** that He creates the two, male and female **46.** from a drop of semen when emitted; **47.** that with Him lies the second genesis; **48.** that it is He who enriches and appropriates; **49.** that He is the Lord of Sirius; **50.** that He destroyed the former Ãd **51.** and the Thamŭd, sparing no one, **52.** including the people of Noah in time past. They were indeed most sinful and most rebellious. **53.** He destroyed and overthrew cities **54.** such that it covered what it covered. **55.** So which of your Lord's blessings do you dispute? **56.** This is a warning from warners of former times, **57.** the imminent is near. **58.** No one can unveil it besides God. **59.** Does this discourse then surprise you? **60.** Do you laugh and not weep, **61.** while you stand proudly with your head held high? **62.** So prostrate unto God and worship!

Surah 54

THE MOON

al-Qamar

In the Name of God, the Compassionate, the Merciful

1. The Hour has drawn near, and the moon is riven asunder. **2.** Truly if they see a sign, they turn away and say, "Unceasing sorcery!" **3.** They rejected the truth and followed their desires, but every matter is resolved to last. **4.** Indeed, they have received reports that served as a warning, **5.** established wisdom, but the warnings did not benefit. **6.** So turn away from them on the Day when the Caller will call to a terrible thing. **7.** With downcast eyes, they will rise from their graves, resembling swarming locusts, **8.** rushing toward the Caller. The disbelievers will say, "This is an arduous Day." **9.** The people of Noah denied before them. They denied Our servant and said, "Insane!" and he was berated. **10.** Then he called upon his Lord, "Truly I am overcome. Help!" **11.** So We opened the floodgates of heaven with water pouring forth. **12.** We caused the earth to burst into springs, that waters amass for a matter decreed. **13.** Then We carried him over what was made of planks and nails, **14.** coursing under Our eyes as a reward for one who was rejected. **15.** We indeed left it as a sign, so are there any who remember? **16.** How then, were My punishment and My warnings? **17.** We have indeed made the Quran easy to remember, so are there any who remember? **18.** The Ād denied. How then, were My punishment and My warnings? **19.** On a day of relentless calamity, We sent a fierce wind upon them, **20.** uprooting people as though they were fallen palm trunks. **21.** How then, were My punishment and My warnings? **22.** We have indeed made the Quran easy to remember, so are there any who remember? **23.** The Thamŭd denied the warnings. **24.** They said, "Should we follow a single human being from among us? Then we would truly be mad and astray! **25.** Is it that the reminder been sent to him from among us? Truly he is but an insolent liar." **26.** Tomorrow they will find out who the insolent liar is. **27.** We are indeed sending the she-camel as a trial for them. So watch them and be patient. **28.** Inform them that water is to be divided among them and that each drink will be accounted for. **29.** Then they called their companions, seized, and hamstrung her. **30.** How then, were My punishment and My warnings? **31.** We truly sent a single thunderbolt, and they became like the debris around a fence maker. **32.** We have indeed made the Quran easy to remember, so are there any who remember? **33.** The people of Lot denied the warnings. **34.** We truly sent a storm of stones upon them except for the family of Lot whom We delivered at dawn **35.** as a blessing from Us. Thus, do We reward whoever offers gratitude. **36.** He had indeed warned them of Our assault, but they disputed the warnings. **37.** They had sought to snatch him away from his guests, so We blurred their eyes. So taste of My punishment and My warnings! **38.** Indeed an abiding punishment greeted them early in the morning. **39.** So taste of My punishment and My warnings! **40.** We have indeed made the Quran easy to remember, so are there any who remember? **41.** The warnings had indeed come to the House of Pharoah. **42.** They denied all of Our signs, so We seized them with the seizing of One Powerful, Omnipotent. **43.** Are your disbelievers better than they, or are you exonerated in the Sacred Scriptures? **44.** Or do they say, "We are all victorious?" **45.** They will soon be defeated and will turn [their] backs. **46.** Indeed the Hour is their meeting, and the Hour is more grievous and more bitter. **47.** Indeed the guilty are astray and mad. **48.** On the Day they are dragged on their faces into the Fire, "Taste the touch of *Saqar*!" **49.** Truly We have created everything in due proportion. **50.** Our Command is but one—like the blinking of an eye. **51.** We have indeed destroyed the likes of you, so are there any who remember? **52.** Everything that they have done is in the scriptures. **53.** Everything small and great is inscribed. **54.** Truly the reverent are amidst Gardens and a stream, **55.** upon a seat of Truth before an Omnipotent Sovereign.

Surah 55

THE COMPASSIONATE

al-Rahmān

In the Name of God, the Compassionate, the Merciful

1. The Compassionate **2.** taught the Quran, **3.** created man, **4.** taught him to speak. **5.** The sun and the moon follow a precise course, **6.** and the stars and the trees prostrate. **7.** He has raised Heaven and set the balance, **8.** so you do not transgress in the balance. **9.** So set the weight accurately and do not fall short on the scale. **10.** He set the earth for living beings **11.** with fruits and covered palm trees, **12.** husked grains, and fragrant plants. **13.** So which of your Lord's blessings do you both deny? **14.** He created man from dried clay like earthenware, **15.** and He created jinn from smokeless fire. **16.** So which of your Lord's blessings do you both deny? **17.** (He is) Lord of the two easts and the two wests. **18.** So which of your Lord's blessings do you both deny? **19.** He let the two seas flow to meet, **20.** yet between them is a barrier they cannot cross. **21.** So which of your Lord's blessings do you both deny? **22.** Out of them come pearls and coral stones. **23.** So which of your Lord's blessings do you both deny? **24.** His are the ships that rise high on the sea, like noble banners. **25.** So which of your Lord's blessings do you both deny? **26.** Everything on it will cease, **27.** but the Countenance of your Lord Possessed of Majesty and Bounty will remain. **28.** So which of your Lord's blessings do you both deny? **29.** All in the heavens and the earth turn to Him in need. Each day, He is engaged in new affairs. **30.** So which of your Lord's blessings do you both deny? **31.** We will dedicate attention to you, O weighty ones. **32.** So which of your Lord's blessings do you both deny? **33.** O company of jinn and humans, if you are able to pass beyond the regions of the heavens and the earth, then pass, however, you will not pass, save by an authority. **34.** So which of your Lord's blessings do you both deny? **35.** A sear of fire and molten brass will be sent against you, and you will not prevail. **36.** So which of your Lord's blessings do you both deny? **37.** When the sky is riven asunder and turns crimson like tanned leather, **38.** which of your Lord's blessings do you both deny? **39.** No jinn or human will be questioned about his sin on that Day. **40.** So which of your Lord's blessings do you both deny? **41.** The guilty will be known by their marks. They will be seized by the forelocks and by the feet. **42.** So which of your Lord's blessings do you both deny? **43.** This is Hell that the guilty deny; **44.** they will rotate back and forth between it and boiling waters. **45.** So which of your Lord's blessings do you both deny? **46.** For one who fears standing before his Lord, there are two Gardens— **47.** So which of your Lord's favors do you both deny? **48.** —Each flourishing with an abundance of green branches. **49.** So which of your Lord's blessings do you both deny? **50.** There are two flowing streams in each. **51.** So which of your Lord's blessings do you both deny? **52.** There are two kinds of every fruit in each. **53.** So which of your Lord's blessings do you both deny? **54.** They will rest on couches adorned with exquisite brocade, where the fruits of both gardens will be within easy reach. **55.** So which of your Lord's blessings do you both deny? **56.** There will be maidens never touched by man or jinn, restraining their glances— **57.** So which of your Lord's blessings do you both deny? **58.** —as if made of rubies and coral. **59.** So which of your Lord's blessings do you both deny? **60.** Is the reward of goodness, nothing but goodness? **61.** So which of your Lord's blessings do you both deny? **62.** Beyond them are two gardens— **63.** So which of your Lord's blessings do you both deny? **64.** —of deepest green. **65.** So which of your Lord's blessings do you both deny? **66.** In each are two springs gushing forth. **67.** So which of your Lord's blessings do you both deny? **68.** In each are fruits, date palms, and pomegranates. **69.** So which of your Lord's blessings do you both deny? **70.** Therein are good and beautiful ones— **71.** So which of your Lord's blessings do you both deny? **72.** —maidens reserved in pavilions— **73.** So which of your Lord's blessings do you both deny? **74.** —never touched by man or jinn; **75.** so which of your Lord's blessings do you both deny? **76.** —they recline on green cushions and beautiful carpets. **77.** So which of your Lord's blessings do you both deny? **78.** Blessed is the name of your Lord, Possessed of Majesty and Honor.

Surah 56

The Inevitable

al-Wāqiah

In the Name of God, the Compassionate, the Merciful

1. When the Inevitable takes place, 2. no one can deny its occurrence 3. bringing down some and elevating others. 4. When the earth trembles violently, 5. and the mountains crumble 6. turning to scattered dust, 7. you will be in categories of three. 8. The companions of the right—what of the companions of the right? 9. The companions of the left—what of the companions of the left? 10. And the foremost will be the foremost. 11. They are the ones brought near 12. in the Gardens of Bliss. 13. Many from those of earlier times 14. and many from those of later times 15. upon embroidered couches 16. reclining upon them while facing one another. 17. Immortal youths will wait upon them 18. with goblets, jugs, and a cup from a flowing spring. 19. where they will not suffer from a headache nor intoxication. 20. There will be fruits from whatever they desire, 21. poultry from whatever they desire, 22. and lustrous-eyed maidens 23. in the likeness of concealed pearls 24. as a reward for what they did. 25. Therein, they will not hear idle talk, nor incitement to sin, 26. besides the utterance of "Peace! Peace!" 27. The companions of the right— what of the companions of the right? 28. Among thornless lote trees, 29. clustered plantains, 30. extended shade, 31. gushing water, 32. and abundant fruit, 33.—neither limited, nor forbidden— 34. on raised couches. 35. We indeed fashioned them as a new creation, 36. then made virgins for them, 37. as kind-hearted companions. 38. "As for the companions of the right— 39. many will be from the earlier generations, 40. and many from the later generations. 41. But the companions of the left— who are the companions of the left? 42. They will be amidst scorching winds and boiling water, 43. and under the shadow of black smoke, 44. neither cool nor comforting." 45. Indeed, prior to that, they lived in luxury, 46. persisted in great sin, 47. and would say, "What! When we are dead and have become dust and bones,

we are to be resurrected? **48.** What! And our forefathers?" **49.** Say, "Truly those of earlier and those of later times **50.** are gathered for the meeting of a day appointed." **51.** Then indeed you, O straying deniers, **52.** will eat from the tree of Zaqqūm, **53.** and fill your bellies therewith. **54.** Then you will drink from boiling liquid, **55.** drinking as do parched camels. **56.** This will be their welcoming on the Day of Judgment. **57.** We created you, so why will you not bear the truth. **58.** Do you observe what you emit? **59.** Is it you who created it or are We the creators? **60.** We have decreed death among you, and We cannot be outraced **61.** from replacing of your likeness and bringing you into existence again in what you do not know. **62.** You have indeed known the first genesis, so why then do you not reflect? **63.** Have you observed what you have sown? **64.** Is it you sowing it or are We the Sowers? **65.** Had We willed, We would have turned it into debris, and you would have remained in wonder: **66.** "Indeed we have suffered loss. **67.** We are truly deprived." **68.** Have you observed the water that you drink? **69.** Is it you who sent it down from the clouds, or is it We Who send down? **70.** Had We willed, We would have made it bitter. Will you not then offer gratitude? **71.** Have you observed the fire that you kindle? **72.** Is it you who brought the tree into existence or are We the originators? **73.** We made it a reminder and comfort for desert dwellers. **74.** So glorify the name of your Lord, the Magnificent! **75.** I swear by the places where the stars descend! **76.** Indeed it is a magnificent oath, if you only knew. **77.** Truly it is a Noble Quran **78.** in a Book concealed. **79.** None touch it except those who are pure— **80.** a revelation from the Lord of the Worlds. **81.** Do you then scorn this discourse, **82.** and make the denial thereof your livelihood? **83.** Why then, when it reaches the throat, **84.** are you looking on? **85.** We are closer to him than you, though you do not see. **86.** Why then, if you are unconstrained, **87.** do you not return it if you are truthful? **88.** So if one is among those brought near **89.** then comfort, bounty, and a Garden of bliss. **90.** If one is among the companions of the right, **91.** then peace unto you from the companions of the right. **92.** But if one is among the deniers who are astray, **93.** then a welcome of boiling liquid, **94.** and burning in Hellfire. **95.** Indeed this is the truth and the certitude, **96.** so glorify the name of your Lord the Magnificent!

Surah 57

IRON

al-Hadīd

In the Name of God, the Compassionate, the Merciful

1. Whatever is in the heavens and the earth glorifies God. He is the Mighty and the Wise. 2. To Him belongs sovereignty over the heavens and the earth. He gives life and death, and He is powerful over all things. 3. He is the First and the Last, and the Evident and the Imminent. He has knowledge of all things. 4. It is He Who created the heavens and the earth in six days, then ascended the Throne. He knows what goes into the earth and what emerges from it, what comes down from Heaven and what rises up to it. He is with you wherever you are, and God observes all that you do. 5. To Him belongs sovereignty over the heavens and the earth and to God all matters are returned. 6. He fuses night into day, and He fuses day into night, and He knows what lies within hearts. 7. Believe in God and His Messenger and spend from what He has entrusted you with. There will be a great reward for those of you who believe and spend. 8. How is it that you do not believe in God when the Messenger calls you to believe in your Lord? If you are believers, He has indeed made a covenant with you. 9. It is He Who sends down clear signs upon His servant to take you from darkness into light. Truly God is Kind and Merciful unto you. 10. Why do you not give for the cause of God when the inheritance of the heavens and the earth belongs to Him? Those who gave and fought before the victory are not equal to you; they are higher in rank than those who give and fight later. Yet God has promised the best to all. God is fully aware of all that you do. 11. Who is it that will lend God a goodly loan? He will double it for him. He will have a generous reward. 12. On the Day when you see the believing men and the believing women with their light spreading before them on their right, "Good news for you on this Day: Gardens with rivers running beneath to abide there, and that is the great triumph." 13. On the Day when the hypocritical men and women will say to the believers, "Wait for us so we may borrow

some of your light," it will be said to them, "Go back and seek your own light!" Then a wall with a gate will be set up between them. On the inside will be mercy, while on the outside, there will be punishment. **14.** They will call unto them, "Were we not with you?" They will say, "Indeed! But you tempted yourselves, awaited, and doubted. False hopes deluded you until the Command of God arrived. The deluder deluded you regarding God. **15.** So this day, no ransom will be taken from you or from those who disbelieved. Your refuge will be the Fire. It will be your master. What a wretched final destination!" **16.** Is it not time for believers to humble their hearts in remembrance of God and the Truth that has been revealed, and not follow the example of those who were given the Book before them? Over time, their hearts grew hard, and many among them became sinful. **17.** Know that God revives the earth after its death. We have indeed made the signs clear for you that perhaps you may understand. **18.** Indeed men who give in charity and women who give in charity and lend to God a goodly loan, it will be doubled for them, and they will have a generous reward. **19.** It is those who believe in God and His messengers who are truthful and are witnesses before their Lord. They have their reward and their light. The inhabitants of Hellfire are those who disbelieve and deny Our signs. **20.** Know that the life of this world is nothing more than play, amusement, adornment, boasting among yourselves, and rivalry in wealth and children. It is like rain that produces vegetation which delights the farmers, but then it dries up, turns yellow, and crumbles into dust. In the Hereafter, there is severe punishment as well as forgiveness and approval from God. The worldly life is nothing but a fleeting enjoyment of deception. **21.** Race to forgiveness from your Lord and to a Garden whose breadth is as the breadth of Heaven and earth prepared for those who believe in God and His messengers. That is the Bounty of God that He gives to whomever He wills. God is Possessed of Tremendous Bounty. **22.** No misfortune can happen on the earth or to yourselves except that it is in a Book before We bring it forth—for truly that is easy for God— **23.** that you do not despair over what has passed you by and not exult in what God has provided you with. God does not love every vainglorious boaster. **24.** Those who are miserly and order people to be miserly, and those who turn away, know that He, God, is certainly the Self-Sufficient and the Praised. **25.** We have indeed sent Our messengers with clear signs, and We sent down the Book and the Balance so that people may uphold justice. We also sent down iron, which holds great strength and benefits for humanity, to reveal those who, unseen, support God and His messengers. Truly God is Strong and Mighty. **26.** We have truly sent Noah and Abraham and established among their progenies the Book and prophethood. Some of them are rightly guided and many of them are transgressors. **27.** Then We sent Our messengers to follow in their footsteps, and We sent Jesus, son of Mary, giving him the Gospel. We instilled compassion and mercy in the hearts of those who followed him. However, they introduced monasticism, which We had not prescribed for them, seeking only to please God. Yet, they did not observe it as should have been observed. So We granted the believers among them their reward, but many of them remain sinful. **28.** O you who believe! Revere God and believe in His Messenger. He will bestow on you a double portion of His mercy. He will provide a light for you to walk with and He will forgive you — God is Forgiving and Merciful — **29.** such that the People of the Book may realize that they have no control over any part of God's Bounty. Indeed, all Bounty is in God's Hands, and He grants it to whomever He wills. God is the Possessor of Immense Bounty.

Surah 58

SHE WHO DISPUTES
al-Mujādilah

In the Name of God, the Compassionate, the Merciful

1. God has certainly heard the statement of she who disputes with you about her spouse and complains to God. God hears your conversation. Truly God is Hearing and Seeing. 2. Those among you who commit *zihār* (pre-Islamic pagan form of divorce) against their wives, they are not their mothers. Their mothers are only those who gave birth to them. They say words that are iniquitous and false. Truly God is Pardoning and Forgiving. 3. Those who declare *zihār* against their wives and then take back what they said must free a slave before they can be intimate again. This is what We command you to do, and God is fully aware of all that you do. 4. Whoever cannot do so must fast for two consecutive months before they come together. If unable to fast, they must feed sixty needy people. This is to help you affirm your belief in God and His Messenger. These are the boundaries set by God, and those who disbelieve will face a painful punishment. 5. Indeed those who oppose God and His Messenger will be disgraced just as those before them were disgraced. We have truly sent clear signs down, and the disbelievers will have a humiliating punishment. 6. On the Day when God resurrects them all together, He will then inform them of what they did. God has kept record of it while they have forgotten it. God is Witness over all things. 7. Can you not see that God knows whatever is in the heavens and whatever is on the earth? There is no private conversation among three, but that He is their fourth, nor among five, but that He is their sixth, no less than that, nor more, but that He is with them wherever they are. Then on the Day of Resurrection, He will inform them of what they did. God indeed has knowledge of all things. 8. Have you not seen those who were forbidden from secret conversations, yet they return to what they were prohibited from, whispering about sin, hostility, and defiance of the Messenger? When they come to you, they greet you in a way

that God has not ordained and say to themselves, "Why does God not punish us for what we say?" Hell is enough for them—they will burn in it. What an awful destination! **9.** O you who believe! If you converse privately, then do not converse in private about sinning and enmity, and disobeying the Messenger, converse in private about piety and reverence. Revere God unto Whom you will be gathered. **10.** Private conversations are only from Satan that those who believe may grieve though he does not harm them in the least, save by God's Leave. In God let the believers keep their trust. **11.** O you who believe! When it is said to you, "Make room for another in the assemblies," then make room and God will make room for you. When it is said, "Rise," then rise, and God will raise in degrees those among you who believe and those who have been given knowledge. God is Aware of whatever you do. **12.** O you who believe! When you converse in private with the Messenger, offer charity before your private conversation. That is better and purer for you. But if you cannot, indeed God is Forgiving and Merciful. **13.** Are you worried about giving in charity prior to your private conversation? If you do not do so and God relents unto you, then perform prayer, give alms, and obey God and His Messenger. God is Aware of whatever you do. **14.** Have you not seen those who befriend a people with whom God has been angry? They are not of you, and you are not of them. They knowingly swear upon falsehood. **15.** God has prepared a severe punishment for them. What they did is truly evil. **16.** They took their oaths as armor and so deviated from the way of God. As a result, their punishment will be humiliating. **17.** Neither their wealth nor their children will be of any benefit to them against God. They are the inhabitants of the Fire, abiding there. **18.** On the Day when God resurrects them all, they will swear to Him just as they swear to you under the assumption that they have some standing. But indeed, they are but liars! **19.** Satan acquired the best of them and made them forget the remembrance of God. Those are from the party of Satan. But indeed, the party of Satan are losers! **20.** Truly those who oppose God and His Messenger, will be among the humiliated. **21.** God has decreed, "I will certainly prevail, I and My messengers!" Truly God is Strong and Mighty. **22.** You will not find people who believe in God and the Last Day forming close bonds with those who oppose God and His Messenger, even if they are their fathers, sons, brothers, or close relatives. God has planted faith in their hearts and strengthened them with a spirit from Him. He will admit them into Gardens beneath which rivers flow, where they will live forever. God is pleased with them, and they are pleased with Him. They are the party of God, and truly, the party of God will be successful.

Surah 59

THE GATHERING

al-Hashr

In the Name of God, the Compassionate, the Merciful

1. Whatever is in the heavens and whatever is on the earth glorifies God. He is the Mighty and the Wise. 2. It is He who, at the first gathering, expelled from their homes those among the People of the Book who disbelieved. You did not think they would depart, and they believed their fortresses would shield them from God. But God came upon them unexpectedly, instilling terror in their hearts. They destroyed their homes with their own hands and with the hands of the believers. So take a lesson, O you who have eyes to perceive. 3. Had God not ordained their banishment He would have punished them in this world. In the Hereafter, they will face the torment of the Fire. 4. That is because they defied God and His Messenger. Truly God is severe in retribution on whoever defies God and His Messenger. 5. Whether you cut down the palm trees or left them standing upon their roots, it was by God's Leave that He might disgrace the transgressors. 6. As for the spoils that God has granted to the Messenger from them, you did not march with cavalry or camels to obtain them. Rather, God grants His messengers authority over whomever He wills. Indeed, God is Powerful over all things. 7. What God has given to His Messenger from the people of the towns is for God, His Messenger, the kinfolk, the orphans, the indigent, and the traveler that it may not circulate among your wealthy. Whatever the Messenger gives you, take it, and forgo whatever he forbids you, and revere God. Truly God is severe in retribution. 8. For the poor emigrants who were expelled from their homes and their property, seeking bounty and satisfaction from God and who help God and His Messenger, it is they who are truthful. 9. Those with true faith who had already established themselves in the land and in belief before them hold love for those who emigrated to join them. They feel no envy in their hearts for what the emigrants have been given and prioritize

others over themselves, even when they are in need. Whoever is protected from the selfishness of their soul—such people are the ones who will succeed. **10.** Those who came after them say, "Our Lord! Forgive us and our brothers who preceded us in faith and do not place rancor in our hearts toward those who have believed. Our Lord! Truly You are Kind and Merciful." **11.** Have you not seen those who act hypocritically, saying to their brothers who disbelieve among the People of the Book, "If you are expelled, we will certainly go with you. We will never obey anyone against you, and if you fight, we will surely help you?" But God bears witness that they are truly liars. **12.** Were they expelled, they would not leave with them, and were they fought, they would not help them. Were they to help them, they would certainly turn their backs. Then they will not be helped. **13.** You surely incite more severe fear in their hearts than God. That is because they are a people who do not understand. **14.** They will not fight you together except from within fortified towns or behind walls. Their hostility is intense among themselves. You may think they are united, but their hearts are divided. This is because they are a people who do not comprehend. **15.** They are like those who came before them, who tasted the consequences of their actions, and for them is a painful punishment. **16.** And like Satan when he says to man, "Disbelieve!" Then, when he disbelieves, he says, "I am indeed acquitted of you. I certainly fear God, Lord of the Worlds." **17.** However, the reprimand for both is that they will be in the Fire, abiding there forever. That is the reward of the wrongdoers. **18.** O you who believe! Revere God, and let every soul reflect on what it has prepared for the future. Truly God is Aware of whatever you do. **19.** Do not be like those who forgot about God such that He made them forget their souls. It is they who are the transgressors. **20.** The inhabitants of the Fire and the inhabitants of the Garden are not equal. They, the inhabitants of the Garden, are the triumphant. **21.** Had We sent down this Quran upon a mountain, you would have seen it humbled and shattered out of awe for God. These are the examples We present to people so they may reflect. **22.** He is God, on Whom there is no other god than He, the Knower of the Unseen and the Seen. He is the Compassionate and the Merciful. **23.** He is God, upon Whom there is no other god than He, the Sovereign, the Holy Peace, the Faithful, the Protector, the Mighty, the Compeller, and the Proud. Glory be to Him above the partners they attribute. **24.** He is God, the Creator, the Maker, and the Fashioner, and to Him belong the Most Beautiful Names. Whatever is in the heavens and on the earth glorifies Him. He is the Mighty and the Wise.

Surah 60

SHE WHO IS TESTED

al-Mumtahenah

In the Name of God, the Compassionate, the Merciful

1. O you who believe! Do not take My enemies and your enemies as allies. You extend affection to them even though they have rejected the truth that has come to you. They drive you and the Messenger out simply because you believe in God, your Lord, and because you strive in My cause, seeking My pleasure. You secretly show them affection, but I am fully aware of what you conceal and what you reveal. Whoever among you does this has surely strayed from the straight path. **2.** Were they to get the better of you, they would be your enemies and would stretch their hands and their tongues forth against you in evil. They hope that you will disbelieve. **3.** Your family relations and your children will not benefit you on the Day of Resurrection. He will distinguish between you, and God sees whatever you do. **4.** Indeed, there is a worthy example for you in Abraham and those with him when they said to their people, "We certainly disassociate ourselves from you and all that you worship besides God. "We have disowned you, and hostility and hatred have arisen between us and you until you worship God alone." This excludes Abraham's statement to his father: "I will surely ask forgiveness for you, though I have no power to protect you from God." They also said, "Our Lord, in You we place our trust, to You we turn in repentance, and to You is the final return." **5.** Our Lord! Do not make us a trial for those who disbelieve and forgive us. Our Lord! Truly You are the Mighty and the Wise." **6.** You have a good example in them for whoever hopes for God and the Last Day. Whoever turns away, truly God is the Self-Sufficient, and the Praised. **7.** It may be that God will grant affection between you and those of them with whom you are enemies. God is powerful. God is Forgiving and Merciful. **8.** God does not forbid you from treating righteously and justly those who did not fight you because of religion and did not expel you from your homes. Truly God loves the just. **9.** God only forbids you from befriending those who fought you because of religion and expelled you from your homes and supported your expulsion. Whoever befriends them are the wrongdoers. **10.** O you who believe! When believing women come to you as emigrants, examine them. God knows best their faith. If you determine that they are believers, do not return them to the disbelievers. These women are not lawful for them, nor are they lawful for these women. Return to the disbelievers what they had spent. There is no blame on you if you marry them, provided you give them their dowries. Do not maintain ties with disbelieving women. Request what you have spent and let them request what they have spent. That is the Judgment of God. He judges between you for God is Knowing, and Wise. **11.** If any of your wives should go over to the disbelievers, then you will have your turn. Give those wives who have gone, the like of what they have spent. Revere God in Whom you are believers. **12.** O Prophet! When believing women come to you pledging to you that they will not attribute anything to God, nor steal, nor fornicate, nor slay their children, nor bring a slanderous lie that they had made up between their hands and feet, nor disobey you in anything honorable, then accept their pledge and seek God's forgiveness for them. Truly God is Forgiving, Merciful. **13.** O you who believe! Do not befriend a people on whom is the wrath of God. They have despaired of the Hereafter just as the disbelievers have despaired of the occupants of graves.

Surah 61

THE RANK

al-Saff

In the Name of God, the Compassionate, the Merciful

1. Whatever is in the heavens and whatever is on the earth glorifies God. He is the Mighty and the Wise. **2.** O you who believe! Why do you say what you do not do? **3.** From God's Perspective, it is grievously odious that you say what you do not do. **4.** Indeed God loves those who fight in His way in ranks as if they were a solid structure. **5.** Remember when Moses said to his people, "O my people! Why do you hurt me though you know well that I am the Messenger of God to you?" Then when they swerved, God had their hearts swerve. God does not guide a sinful people. **6.** Remember when Jesus, son of Mary said, "O Children of Israel! Truly I am the Messenger of God unto you confirming what came before me in the Torah and bearing the good news of a messenger to come after me whose name is Ahmad." When he went to them with clear signs, they said, "This is clear sorcery." **7.** Who does greater wrong than one who invents lies against God while he is being called to submission? God does not guide a wrongdoing people. **8.** They want to extinguish the Light of God with their mouths, but God completes His Light even though the disbelievers are opposed. **9.** It is He Who sent His Messenger with guidance and the Religion of Truth to make it prevail over all religion, though the idolaters are opposed. **10.** O you who believe! Should I direct you to a trade that will save you from a painful punishment **11.** that you will believe in God and His Messenger and strive in God's way with your wealth and your souls? That is better for you if you only knew. **12.** He will forgive you your sins and admit you to Gardens with rivers running beneath along with goodly dwellings in the Garden of Eden. That is the great triumph. **13.** Another thing that you love is help from God and a soon to be victory. So give good news to the believers. **14.** O you who believe! Be supporters of God, just as Jesus, the son of Mary, said to the apostles, "Who will be my helpers in the cause of God?" The apostles replied, "We are helpers in the cause of God." Then a group among the Children of Israel believed, while another group disbelieved. Consequently, We strengthened those who believed against their enemies, and they prevailed.

Surah 62

CONGREGATIONAL PRAYER

al-Jumu'ah

In the Name of God, the Compassionate, the Merciful

1. Whatever is in the heavens and whatever is on the earth glorifies God the Sovereign, the Holy, the Mighty, and the Wise. 2. It is He Who sent an unlettered Messenger from among themselves, reciting His signs to them, purifying them, and teaching them the Book and Wisdom, though previously they were in obvious error, 3. along with others among them who had not yet joined him. He is the Mighty and the Wise. 4. That is the Bounty of God which He gives to whomever He wills. God is Possessed of Tremendous Bounty. 5. The simile of those who carried the Torah, then did not carry it, is like that of a donkey carrying books. How evil is the parable of a people who denied God's signs! God does not guide a wrongdoing people. 6. Say, "O you who stand on Judaism! If you claim that you are friends unto God to the exclusion of others, then long for death if you are truthful." 7. But they will never long for it because of what their hands have sent forth. God knows the wrongdoers. 8. Say, "Truly the death from which you flee will certainly catch up with you. You will then be returned to the Knower of the Unseen and the Seen. He will inform you of what you did." 9. "O you who believe! When you are called to congregational prayer, rush to the remembrance of God, and leave off trade. That is better for you if you only knew. 10. When prayer is completed, diffuse throughout the land, and seek the Bounty of God and remember God abundantly that perhaps you may prosper." 11. When they see a trade opportunity or entertainment, they rush toward it and leave you standing. Say, "What is with God is far better than entertainment or trade, for God is the Best of Providers."

Surah 63

THE HYPOCRITES

al-Munāfiqūn

In the Name of God, the Compassionate, the Merciful

1. When the hypocrites come to you, they say, "We bear witness that you are indeed the Messenger of God." But God truly knows that you are His Messenger. God bears witness that the hypocrites are absolute liars. 2. They used their oath as armor and thus deterred from the way of God. What they did was definitely evil. 3. That is because they believed and then disbelieved. So a seal was set upon their hearts. Subsequently, they do not understand. 4. When you see them, their physiques impress you, and if they speak, you listen to their speech, yet they are like blocks of wood. They assume that every cry is against them. They are the enemy, so beware of them. May God curse them! How are they so deluded? 5. When it is said to them, "Come! The Messenger of God will ask forgiveness for you," they twist their heads, and you see them turning away in arrogance. 6. It is the same for them whether you ask forgiveness for them or you do not ask forgiveness for them, for God will never forgive them. Truly God does not guide a sinful people. 7. They are the ones who say, "Do not spend on those who are with the Messenger of God that they may disband." Yet to God belongs, but the hypocrites do not understand the treasures of the heavens and the earth. 8. They say, "If we return to Madinah, the mightier will certainly expel the weaker therefrom." Yet might belongs to God, to His Messenger, and to the believers, but the hypocrites do not know. 9. O you who believe! Do not let your wealth or your children divert you from the remembrance of God. For whoever does so, it is they who are the losers. 10. Give from what We have provided you before death overtakes any of you, and he says, "Lord, if only You would delay me for a little while, I would give in charity and be among the righteous." 11. But God will not grant any soul respite when its term has come. God is Aware of whatever you do.

Surah 64

MUTUAL LOSS AND GAIN

al-Taghābun

In the Name of God, the Compassionate, the Merciful

1. Whatever is in the heavens and whatever is on the earth glorifies God. He is the Sovereignty, and the Praise is His. He is Powerful over all things. 2. It is He Who created you. Among you are disbelievers and among you are believers. God sees whatever you do. 3. He created the heavens and the earth in truth and formed you, then, made your forms beautiful. Unto to Him is the final destiny. 4. He knows of whatever is in the heavens and on the earth. He knows what you reveal and what you disclose. God knows what lies within breasts. 5. Has the story of those who disbelieved in times past come to you? They had tasted the evil consequences of their affair, and their punishment will be painful. 6. That is because their messengers brought them clear signs, but they said, "Will a human being guide us?" So they disbelieved and turned away. But God is beyond need. God is Self-Sufficient and Praised. 7. Those who disbelieve claim that they will not be resurrected. Say, "Indeed! By my Lord! You will certainly be resurrected. Then you will be informed of what you did. That is easy for God." 8. So believe in God and His Messenger and the light We have sent down. God is Aware of whatever you do. 9. The Day that He gathers you on the Day of Gathering will be the Day of Mutual Loss and Gain. Whoever believes in God and works righteousness, He will absolve him of his evil deeds and admit him to Gardens with rivers running below to abide forever therein. That is the great triumph. 10. Those who disbelieve and deny Our signs will be the inhabitants of Fire abiding therein. What a wretched destination! 11. No misfortune can occur save by God's Leave. Whoever believes in God, He guides his heart. God has knowledge of all things. 12. Obey God and obey the Messenger, then, if you turn away, it was only incumbent upon Our Messenger to proclaim the clear message.

13. For God, there is no god but He, and in God, believers must trust. 14. O you who believe! Truly from among your spouses and your children is an enemy unto you, so beware of them. Yet if you pardon and forgive, God is indeed Forgiving and Merciful. 15. Your wealth and your children are only a trial, but with Him, God, is the great reward. 16. So revere God as much as you can. Listen, obey, and spend. That is better for your souls. Whoever is saved from the greediness of his soul, it is they who will prosper. 17. If you lend to God a goodly loan, He will multiply it for you and forgive you. God is Thankful, Clement, 18. Knower of the Unseen and the Seen, and the Mighty and the Wise.

Surah 65

DIVORCE

al-Talāq

In the Name of God, the Compassionate, the Merciful

1. O Prophet! When you divorce your wives, divorce them after the waiting period, be accurate with the waiting period, and revere your Lord. Do not remove them from their homes, nor should they leave unless they commit a flagrant indecency. These are the limits set by God, and whoever transgresses the limits set by God has truly wronged himself. You never know, maybe God will bring about some new situation thereafter. **2.** So when they have fulfilled their term, take them back in an amicable way or part with them in an amicable way. Call two just persons among yourselves to witness and uphold testimony for God. Such is the admonition given to him, who believes in God and the Last Day. Whoever reveres God, He will prepare a way out for him, **3.** and will provide for him when he is not counting on it. Whoever trusts in God, He is enough for him. Truly God fulfills His Command. God has certainly set a measure for all things. **4.** As for your women who no longer menstruate, and you are in doubt, their waiting period is three months — the same applies to those who have not yet menstruated. For those who are pregnant, their term is when they deliver. Whoever reveres God, He will ease their affairs. **5.** That is the Command of God that He has sent down to you. Whoever reveres God, He will exonerate him of his evil deeds and will expand his reward. **6.** Let them reside where you reside, according to your means. Do not mistreat them in a way that causes them hardship. If they are pregnant, provide for them until they give birth. Then if they are breastfeeding for you, compensate them and consult together amicably. However, if you face difficulty with one another, then someone else can breastfeed for him (the father.) **7.** Let one who has abundant wealth spend from his abundance. Let one who rations his provision, spend from what God has given him. God does not burden a soul with more than what He has given it. God will grant ease after hardship. **8.** How many towns arrogantly defied the command of their Lord and His messengers? We held them accountable with a strict reckoning, and their punishment was dreadful. **9.** As a result, it tasted the evil consequences of its affair, and the end of its affair was failure. **10.** God prepared a severe punishment for them. Therefore, 'O possessors of insight' who have believed, revere God. God has certainly sent down a reminder unto you, **11.** a Messenger reciting unto you the clear signs of God to bring those who believe and perform righteous deeds out of darkness and into light. Whoever believes in God and works righteousness, He will admit him to Gardens with rivers running below to abide forever therein. Truly God has prepared for him a goodly provision. **12.** It is God Who created the seven heavens, and similarly, of the earth. His command descends upon them so that you may recognize that God is capable of all things and that His knowledge encompasses everything.

Surah 66

FORBIDDANCE

al-Tahrīm

In the Name of God, the Compassionate, the Merciful

1. O Prophet! Why do you forbid what God has made lawful to you? You are seeking to please your wives. God is Forgiving and Merciful. 2. God has already provided a way for you to absolve your oaths. God is your Master. He is the Knower and the Wise. 3. When the Prophet confided a matter to one of his wives, and she disclosed it, God made it known to him. He revealed part of it and withheld part. When he informed her about it, she asked, "Who told you this?" He replied, "The Knower and the Aware informed me." 4. If you both repent unto God, your hearts are truly inclined to do so, but if you back each other up against him, God is indeed his Protector, as are Gabriel and the righteous among the believers. Furthermore, the angels support him. 5. If he divorces you, it is possible that his Lord will replace you with better spouses—ones who are devoted, faithful, obedient, repentant, worshipful, traveling for the cause of faith, some previously married and virgins. 6. O you who believe! Protect yourselves and your families from a Fire whose fuel is of men and stones. Over it are stern and severe angels who never disobey God in what He commands of them and who act on what they are commanded. 7. O you who disbelieve! Make no excuses on this Day since you will indeed be requitted for what you did. 8. O you who believe! Turn to God in sincere repentance, so that your Lord may forgive your sins and admit you into Gardens beneath which rivers flow. This will be on the Day when God will not disgrace the Prophet and those who have believed with him. Their light will shine before them, and in their faith, they will say, "Our Lord, perfect our light for us and forgive us. You are truly Powerful over all things." 9. O Prophet! Strive against the disbelievers and the hypocrites. Be harsh with them. Their refuge is Hell. What a wretched final destination! 10. God presents the wife of Noah and the wife of Lot as an example

for those who disbelieve. They were married to two of Our righteous servants, yet they betrayed them. Their husbands could not protect them at all from God, and it was said to them, "Enter the Fire along with those who enter." **11.** God also presents the wife of Pharaoh as an example for those who believe. She said, "My Lord, build for me a house near You in Paradise, save me from Pharaoh and his actions, and save me from the wrongdoing people." **12.** And then Mary, the daughter of Imran, guarded her chastity. So We breathed therein of Our Spirit and she testified to the truth of the Words of her Lord and His Scriptures and she was among the devout.

Surah 67

SOVEREIGNTY

al-Mulk

In the Name of God, the Compassionate, the Merciful

1. Blessed is He in Whose Hand lies dominion and He is Powerful over all things, **2.** Who created death and life that He may test which of you is the best in performance. He is the Mighty and the Forgiving **3.** Who created seven heavens, one upon the other. You will not see any disproportion in the creation of the Merciful. Take another look. Do you see any flaw? **4.** Then take a double look and your sight will return to you, humbled, and fatigued. **5.** We have indeed adorned the lowest heaven with lamps and made them missiles to drive away the demons. We have prepared for them the punishment of the Inferno. **6.** For those who disbelieve in their Lord is the punishment of Hell. What a wretched final destination! **7.** When they are thrown therein, they will hear it blaring as it blazes over, **8.** nearly bursting in fury. Whenever a group is thrown therein, its keepers ask them, "Did a warner not come to you?" **9.** They say, "Indeed a warner came to us, but we denied him and said, 'God did not send anything down. You are no more than a great delusion.'" **10.** They say, "Had we listened, or had we understood, we would not be among the companions of the Inferno." **11.** By such, they admit to their sin. So away with the companions of the Inferno! **12.** Indeed for those who fear their Lord unseen, there will be forgiveness and a great reward. **13.** If you keep your speech a secret or declare it, He certainly knows what lies within hearts. **14.** Does He Who created not know? He is the Subtle and the Aware. **15.** He is the One Who made the earth manageable for you. So walk through its tracts and eat of His provision. To Him is the Resurrection. **16.** Do you feel secure that He Who is in Heaven will not cause the earth to engulf you while it churns? **17.** Do you feel secure that He Who is in the Heaven will not send a storm of stones upon you? You will soon know what My warning is like

18. Indeed those before them denied. How terrible was My rejection! 19. Have they observed the birds above them spreading outward and folding inward? Nothing holds them, except the Compassionate. He truly sees all things. 20. Who is it that will be a host for you and might help you besides the Compassionate? The disbelievers are in no more than a delusion. 21. Who is it that will provide for you if He withholds His provisions? Truly they persist in egotism and repulsiveness. 22. Is one who walks with his face bent downward more guided, or one who walks upright on a straight path? 23. Say, "It is He Who brought you into being and endowed you with hearing, sight, and hearts. Little do you show gratitude." 24. Say, "It is He who multiplied you on the earth and unto Him you will be gathered." 25. They say, "When will this promise come to pass, if you are truthful?" 26. Say, "Indeed knowledge lies with God alone. I am only a clear warner." 27. When they see it nearby, the faces of those who disbelieved will be stricken and it will be said, "This is what you called for." 28. Say, "Have you observed whether God destroys me or those with me or has mercy on us? Who will protect the disbelievers from a painful punishment?" 29. Say, "He is the Compassionate. We believe in Him and trust in Him. You will soon know who is in obvious error." 30. Say, "Do you see? If your water were to sink into the ground, who would bring you flowing water?"

Surah 68

THE PEN

al-Qalam

In the Name of God, the Compassionate, the Merciful

1. *Nūn.* By the pen and what they inscribe, **2.** you are not, by the blessing of your Lord, insane. **3.** Indeed your reward will be never-ending. **4.** You are truly of an exalted character. **5.** So you will see, and they will see **6.** which of you is afflicted. **7.** Your Lord truly knows best those who stray from His way, and He knows best those who are rightly guided. **8.** So do not obey the deniers. **9.** They hope that you might compromise and that they might compromise. **10.** So do not follow every contemptible swearer, **11.** backbiter, and spreader of slander, **12.** one who prevents good, transgresses, and sins, **13.** harsh in character, and furthermore, utterly corrupt — **14.** merely because he has wealth and children. **15.** When Our signs are recited to him, he says, "Tales of the ancient." **16.** We will brand him on the snout. **17.** Indeed We tried them just as We tried the owners of the garden who vowed they would harvest its fruit in the morning **18.** without reservation. **19.** Then a visit by your Lord visited it while they were sleeping, **20.** such that it appeared harvested. **21.** Then they called out to one another in the morning, **22.** "Go early to your tillage if you would harvest." **23.** Therefore, they took off while whispering to one another, **24.** "Indeed, no indigent will come in upon you today." **25.** They took off early and strongly determined. **26.** Then when they saw it, they said, "We are indeed astray," **27.** and "We are certainly deprived!" **28.** The most reasonable among them said, "Did I not tell you, why do you not glorify?" **29.** They said, "Glory be to our Lord! We certainly transgressed." **30.** Then they turned to one another reproaching each other, **31.** saying, "Oh woe unto us! We are truly rebellious. **32.** Perhaps our Lord will give us something better in exchange. To our Lord, we turn in repentance." **33.** Such is the punishment, but the punishment of the Hereafter is certainly greater if they only knew. **34.** Indeed for the reverent there will be Gardens of Bliss in the presence of their Lord. **35.** Are We then, to treat Muslims like the guilty? **36.** What bothers you? How do you judge? **37.** Or do you have a book from which you are learning **38.** that you will have of whatever you choose in it? **39.** Or do you have oaths binding upon Us until the Day of Resurrection that you will have whatever you demand? **40.** Ask them who among them will stand confidently, **41.** or do they have partners? Let them bring their partners if they are truthful. **42.** On the Day when the shin is uncovered, they will be called to prostrate but will not be able to. **43.** Their eyes cast downward, overwhelmed by humiliation, because they were once invited to prostrate while they were able but chose to refuse. **44.** So leave Me to deal with those who reject this message. We will lead them on step by step, and they will not even be aware. **45.** I will grant them respite. Truly My scheme is firm. **46.** Or do you ask a reward of them that they become burdened with debt? **47.** Or do they hold the Unseen, so that they can write it down? **48.** So be patient with your Lord's Judgment and do not be like the companion of the fish who cried out in agony. **49.** Had grace from his Lord not reached him, he would have certainly been thrown offshore bare and reprehensible. **50.** But his Lord chose him and made him among the righteous. **51.** Truly those who disbelieve would almost strike you down with their glances when they hear the Remembrance, saying, "He is certainly insane." **52.** It is nothing but a reminder for all creation.

Surah 69

THE UNDENIABLE REALITY

al-Hāqqah

In the Name of God, the Compassionate, the Merciful

1. The Undeniable Reality! **2.** What is the Undeniable Reality? **3.** What do you know of the Undeniable Reality? **4.** The Thamŭd and the Ād denied the calamity. **5.** As for the Thamŭd, they were destroyed by the disaster. **6.** As for the Ād, they were annihilated by a howling, furious wind. **7.** He imposed it upon them for seven nights and eight days consecutively that they might see the people collapse as if they were hollowed palm trunks. **8.** So do you see any remnant of them? **9.** And the Pharaoh and those before him, and the subverted in sinfulness, **10.** disobeyed the messenger of their Lord. He seized them with an overpowering grip. **11.** Indeed, when the waters overflowed, We carried you on the Ark, **12.** that We might make it a reminder for you, and that attentive ears will pay attention. **13.** When a single blast is blown by the trumpet, **14.** and the earth and mountains are carried away and crushed by a single crush, **15.** the event will take place on that Day. **16.** The sky will be riven asunder for it will be weak on that Day. **17.** The angels will be at its sides on that Day and eight will carry the Throne of your Lord above them. **18.** That Day you will be exposed, and no secret of yours will be hidden. **19.** As for one who is given his book in his right hand, he will say, "Here, read my book. **20.** I knew for sure that I would be meeting my reckoning." **21.** Therefore, he will live a satisfactory life **22.** in a lofty Garden **23.** with fruit in low-hanging bunches. **24.** Eat and drink in enjoyment for what you sent ahead of you in days passed. **25.** As for one who is given his book in his left hand, he will say, "I wish I were not given my book. **26.** I did not predict my reckoning. **27.** I wish this were the final end! **28.** My wealth did not benefit me. **29.** My power has perished from me." **30.** Seize him and shackle him. **31.** Then throw him into Hellfire. **32.** Then put him in a chain seventy cubits in length.

33. Indeed he did not believe in God the Magnificent, 34. and did not yearn to feed the indigent. 35. So today he has no loyal friend here, 36. nor food, except for rubbish 37. that no one will eat except the sinful. 38. So I swear by what you see 39. and by what you do not see, 40. for truly it is the speech of an honorable messenger, 41. and not the speech of a poet. Little do you believe! 42. Nor is it the speech of a soothsayer. Little do you reflect! 43. It is a revelation from the Lord of the Worlds. 44. Had He attributed any sayings unto Us, 45. We would have taken him by the right hand. 46. Then We would have severed his life vein, 47. and no one among you could have protected him from it. 48. Indeed it is a reminder for the reverent. 49. We certainly know that among you are those who deny. 50. It is truly a source of regret for the disbelievers. 51. It is indeed the truth of certitude. 52. So glorify the Name of your Lord, the Magnificent.

Surah 70

THE ASCENDING WAYS

al-Ma'ārij

In the Name of God, the Compassionate, the Merciful

1. A questioner asked about punishment to ensue **2.** the disbelievers, after which he will have no defense **3.** from God, Lord of the ascending ways. **4.** Unto Him ascend the angels and the Spirit on a day measured to be fifty thousand years. **5.** So be patient with beautiful patience. **6.** They truly see it as far off, **7.** but We see it as nearby. **8.** On a day when the sky is like molten lead, **9.** and the mountains are like carded wool, **10.** and no close friend will ask of a close friend, **11.** though they can see each other. The guilty would wish to trade himself off from the punishment of that Day with his children, **12.** his spouse, and his brother, **13.** his kin who had sheltered him, **14.** and all on the earth that he may be delivered. **15.** Indeed it is but a churning fire, **16.** ripping away the scalp, **17.** calling on to those who turned their backs and fled, **18.** and who accumulated and stashed away. **19.** Indeed man was created hasty, **20.** fretful when evil touches him, **21.** and indignant when good touches him, **22.** except for those who perform prayer, **23.** who remain steadfast to their prayers, **24.** in whose wealth is an acknowledged right **25.** for the beggar and the deprived, **26.** those who attest to the Day of Judgment, **27.** and who are wary of the punishment of their Lord. **28.** Truly there is no escape from the punishment of their Lord. **29.** Those who guard their chastity, **30.** save from their spouses or those whom their right hands possess will not be blamed, **31.** but whoever seeks beyond that are transgressors. **32.** Those who safeguard their trusts and their pact, **33.** who uphold their testimony, **34.** and who are dedicated to their prayers, **35.** will be honored in the Garden. **36.** So how is it that those who disbelieve scramble toward you **37.** from the right and from the left in hordes? **38.** Does every man among them desire to be admitted into a Garden of bliss? **39.** Indeed! For truly We created them from what they are familiar with. **40.** So I swear by the Lord of the easts and the wests that We are certainly able **41.** to replace them with what is better, and no one can outrace Us. **42.** So leave them to indulge in futile talk and amusement until they meet the Day that they are promised, **43.** a day when they emerge from their graves, hurrying as if racing toward a marker, **44.** their eyes cast down, overwhelmed by humiliation. That is the Day they have been promised.

Surah 71

NOAH

Nūh

In the Name of God, the Compassionate, the Merciful

1. Indeed, We sent Noah to his people—"Warn your people before a painful punishment comes upon them." 2. He said, "O my people! I am a clear warner to you 3. that you may worship God, revere Him, and obey me, 4. that He may forgive you for some of your sins and grant you reprieve until a term appointed. For indeed, when God's term approaches, it will not be delayed, if you only knew." 5. He said, "My Lord! I have called on my people day and night, 6. but my calling has only caused them to distance themselves even more. 7. Indeed whenever I call them so that You may forgive them, they plug their ears, cover themselves with their garments, persist in their denial, and become increasingly arrogant. 8. Then I called upon them openly. 9. I revealed it to them and confided to them in secret." 10. I said, "Seek forgiveness of your Lord! Truly He is Forgiving. 11. He will send the sky upon you with abundant rains, 12. increase you in wealth and sons, and make gardens and rivers for you. 13. What is it with you that you do not hope for God with dignity 14. seeing that He has created you in stages? 15. Have you not seen how God created the seven heavens, one above the other, 16. and placed the moon as a light within them and the sun as a radiant lamp 17. God brought you forth from the earth like plants, 18. and He will return you to it, then withdraw you from it withdrawingly. 19. God made the earth an open expanse for you 20. that you may travel the spacious paths therein." 21. Noah said, "My Lord! They disobeyed me and followed those whose wealth and children will accumulate to nothing but loss." 22. They devised a mighty plot, 23. saying "Do not leave your gods. Do not leave *Wadd* or *Suwā*, *Yagūth*, *Ya'ūq*, or *Nasr*." 24. They have indeed led many astray. It increases the wrongdoers in nothing but deviation. 25. They were drowned because of their sins, then made

to enter a Fire. They then, found no helpers for themselves besides God. **26.** Noah said, "Do not leave a single disbeliever to dwell on the earth. **27.** For indeed if you leave them, they will mislead Your servants and will beget nothing but disbelieving insurgents. **28.** My Lord, forgive me, my parents, anyone who enters my house as a believer, and all believing men and women. Do not grant the wrongdoers anything but further destruction."

Surah 72

The Jinn

al-Jinn

In the Name of God, the Compassionate, the Merciful

1. Say, "It was revealed to me that a group of jinn listened and said, 'Indeed we have heard a wondrous Quran 2. that guides to sound judgment, so we believe in it and will attribute nothing as a partner unto our Lord. 3. Indeed the Majesty of our Lord is exalted, and He has neither consort nor child. 4. Truly the fool among us has uttered defamations against God, 5. though we had thought that mankind and jinn would not utter lies about God. 6. Truly some men from among humans sought refuge with some men from among the jinn, but they only increased them in oppression. 7. Just as you did, they thought that God would not resurrect anyone. 8. We reached out to Heaven and found it filled with mighty guards and flaming stars. 9. We used to sit in seating areas there to listen, but whoever listens now will find a flaming star lying for him in ambush. 10. We do not know whether evil is desired for those upon the earth, or whether their Lord desires guidance for them. 11. Some among us are righteous, and some among us are otherwise. We are on split paths. 12. We thought we could never elude God on earth, nor could we escape Him by fleeing. 13. When we heard the guidance, we believed in it. For whoever believes in his Lord will fear neither detraction nor burden. 14. Some among us *submit* and some among us swerve from justice. Those who submit, seek guidance, 15. but as far as the unjust, they are the firewood for Hell.'" 16. And "If they hold firm to the path, We will give them abundant water 17. that We may try them in addition to that, and whoever turns away from the remembrance of his Lord, He will lead him to a grievous punishment. 18. Places of worship are for God, so do not call upon another along with God. 19. When the servant of God rises to call upon Him, they will almost swarm over him." 20. Say, "I call only upon my Lord, and I

attribute none as partner unto Him." **21.** Say, "I have no power over what harm or guidance may come to you." **22.** Say, "No one will protect me from God, and I will never find refuge besides Him **23.** unless I proclaim what is received from God and His messages. Whoever disobeys God and His Messenger, the Fire of Hell will be his to abide forever therein, **24.** such that when they see what they are promised, they will know who is weaker in helpers and fewer in number." **25.** Say, "I do not know whether what you are promised is close or whether my Lord has appointed a term — **26.** the Knower of the Unseen. He does not disclose His Unseen to anyone, **27.** except to the one He approves of as a messenger. Then He dispatches a guard before him and behind him **28.** that He may know that they have indeed conveyed the messages of their Lord. He encompasses whatever is with them and takes every single thing numerically, into account."

Surah 73

FOLDED IN GARMENTS

al-Muzzammil

In the Name of God, the Compassionate, the Merciful

1. O you, folded in garments! 2. Stand vigil at night, save a little, 3. half of it or slightly reduce it, 4. or add to it, and recite the Quran rhythmically. 5. Indeed We will soon launch upon you a weighty Word. 6. Truly the vigil of the night is strongest in pace and most fitting in speech. 7. Indeed, by day you have prolonged occupations, 8. so remember the name of your Lord and devote yourself to Him with utter devotion — 9. the Lord of the East and the West. There is no god but He, so take Him as a guardian. 10. Be patient with what they say and abandon them politely. 11. Tolerate them for a while but leave the deniers that are living in luxury to Me. 12. Truly with Us are fetters and Hellfire, 13. food that chokes and a painful punishment. 14. On a day when the earth and the mountains shake, the mountains will be like heaps of shifting sand. 15. We have indeed sent you a messenger to be witness over you just as we sent a messenger to Pharoah. 16. However, Pharoah disobeyed the messenger, so We seized him with a terrible seizing. 17. So if you disbelieve, how will you guard against a day that would make children gray-haired? 18. Whereupon the sky will be riven asunder, His Promise will be fulfilled. 19. Indeed this is a reminder, so let whoever wills, take the path to his Lord. 20. Your Lord knows that you stand in prayer for nearly two-thirds of the night, or half of it, or a third, along with a group of those with you. God determines the length of the night and the day. He knows you cannot keep an exact count, so He has lightened the burden for you. Recite from the Quran whatever is within your capacity. He knows that some of you may be ill, others traveling the land in pursuit of His bounty, and others fighting in His cause. So recite what is manageable, establish prayer, give in charity, and offer God a goodly loan. Whatever good you send forth for

yourselves, you will find it with God, far better and greater in reward. Seek God's forgiveness, for He is indeed Forgiving and Merciful.

Surah 74

THE ENWRAPPED ONE

al-Mudda'thir

In the Name of God, the Compassionate, the Merciful

1. O you who are enwrapped, **2.** arise and warn! **3.** Magnify your Lord! **4.** Purify your garments! **5.** Shun defilement! **6.** Do not grant favor seeking gain! **7.** Be patient for the sake of your Lord. **8.** For when the trumpet is blown, **9.** that Day will be a difficult day, **10.** not easy for the disbelievers. **11.** Let Me be with the one whom I created, **12.** and to whom I gave wealth in abundance, **13.** sons at his side, **14.** and made the path smooth for him. **15.** Then he becomes greedy and wants Me to give more. **16.** But no! He truly remained headstrong against Our signs. **17.** I will force him to a mount of misfortunes. **18.** Indeed he reflected and rendered. **19.** May he perish for what he rendered. **20.** Then may he perish for what he rendered. **21.** Then he observed. **22.** Then he frowned and scowled. **23.** Then he turned his back, grew arrogant, **24.** and said, "This is no more than sorcery passed down. **25.** This is no more than the speech of a human being." **26.** I will throw him into *Saqar*. **27.** What do you know about *Saqar*? **28.** It does not spare, nor leave behind. **29.** It scorches the human being. **30.** There are Nineteen over it. **31.** We have only commissioned angels as guardians of the Fire. We arranged their number merely as a trial over those who disbelieve, to grant assurance to those who have been given the Book, and to increase in faith those who believe. Those in whose hearts is a disease and the disbelievers will say, "What does God want to achieve by this example?" So does God lead astray whomever He wills and guides whomever He wills. No one knows your Lord's hosts but Him. It is but a reminder for mankind. **32.** By the moon, **33.** and by the night as it fades, **34.** and by the morning as it brightens, **35.** is truly one of the greatest **36.** of warners to mankind. **37.** For those of you who wish to move forward or lag behind, **38.** every soul will be held in pledge for its deeds,

39. except for the companions of the right 40. in Gardens questioning one another 41. about the guilty – 42. "What led you into *Saqar*?" 43. They say, "We were not among those who prayed, 44. nor did we care for the needy, 45. and we indulged in idle talk along with those who engage in it, 46. and we denied the Day of Judgment 47. until certainty came to us." 48. Therefore, the intercession of the intercessors will not benefit them. 49. So what is with them that they turn away from the Reminder 50. as if they were frightened donkeys 51. fleeing from a lion? 52. Rather every man among them wants to be given unrolled scriptures. 53. But no! They do not fear the Hereafter. 54. For of course! It is truly a reminder. 55. So let whoever will, remember it. 56. But they will not remember save as God wills. He is the most worthy of reverence and the most worthy of granting forgiveness.

Surah 75

THE RESURRECTION

al-Qiyāmah

In the Name of God, the Compassionate, the Merciful

1. I swear by the Day of Resurrection. 2. I swear by the self-reproaching soul. 3. Does man assume that We will not gather his bones? 4. Indeed We are able to fashion even his fingers and toes. 5. But man would like to corrupt what lies in front of him, 6. asking, "When is the Day of Resurrection?" 7. Then when the eyes are dazzled, 8. the moon is eclipsed, 9. and the sun and the moon are brought together— 10. that Day—man will say, "Where is the way out?" 11. Indeed! There will be no refuge. 12. Your abode that Day will be before your Lord. 13. Man will be informed that Day of what he has sent forth and what he has left behind. 14. Indeed man will be a testimony against himself, 15. though he prefers his excuses. 16. Do not move your tongue to expedite it. 17. It is truly for Us to gather it and recite it. 18. So when We recite it, follow its recitation. 19. Then it is certainly on Us to explain it. 20. But truly you love the fleeting 21. and forsake the Hereafter. 22. That Day, faces will be beaming, 23. gazing upon their Lord, 24. and faces that Day will be scowling, 25. knowing of the back-breaking calamity that will befall them. 26. Indeed! But when it reached the collarbones, 27. and it was said, "Who will ascend?" 28. He believed that it is the parting, 29. and one leg is entwined with the other. 30. To your Lord that Day is the driving. 31. For he neither attested to the truth, nor prayed, 32. but he denied and turned away, 33. and then went boastfully to his people. 34. So nearer to you and nearer! 35. Then nearer to you and nearer! 36. Does man assume that he will be left uncontrolled? 37. Was he not a drop of semen emitted? 38. Then he was a blood clot that He created and fashioned, 39. and He made from him the two genders, male and female. 40. Is He not able, after all this, to revive the dead?

Surah 76

THE HUMAN BEING

al-Insān

In the Name of God, the Compassionate, the Merciful

1. Was there an era in time that had come upon man where he was nothing to be mentioned? **2.** Indeed, We created man from a drop of mingled semen that We may test him, and We endowed him with hearing and seeing. **3.** We have indeed guided him upon the way, whether he is grateful or ungrateful. **4.** We have indeed prepared chains, shackles, and a blazing flame for the disbelievers. **5.** The pious will certainly drink of a cup mixed with *Kāphur,* **6.** a fountain upon which the servants of God drink while they make it gush forth abundantly. **7.** They fulfill their vows and fear a day whose evil is widespread, **8.** and out of love for Him, they feed the indigent, the orphan, and the captive. **9.** "We feed you for the Countenance of God alone. We do not want any reward or thanks from you. **10.** We fear a grim, distressful day from our Lord." **11.** Therefore, God has delivered them from the evil of that Day, conferred upon them radiance and joy, **12.** and rewarded them with a Garden and with silk for having been patient. **13.** They recline upon couches therein and see no sun or excessive cold. **14.** Its shade will be close above them, and its bunches will be made to hang low. **15.** Vessels of silver and goblets of crystal are passed around for them, **16.** silvern crystal that they have measured with due measure. **17.** They will drink from a cup of gingered mixture therein, **18.** a spring therein, named *Salsabil.* **19.** Immortal youth wait upon them and when you see them, you would assume they were scattered pearls. **20.** When you look, you will see bliss and a great kingdom. **21.** They are dressed in garments of fine green silk and rich brocade. They are adorned with silver bracelets and their Lord will give them to drink of a very pure drink. **22.** This is truly a reward for you, and your endeavoring is held in gratitude. **23.** We have indeed sent the Quran down to you as a revelation.

24. So be patient with your Lord's judgment and do not obey the sinner or the disbeliever among them. **25.** Mention the Name of your Lord morning and evening, **26.** prostrate to Him during the night and glorify Him for extended periods in the night. **27.** They indeed love the fleeting and place a weighty day behind them. **28.** We created them and made their frameworks firm and whenever We desire; We will exchange them for others like them. **29.** This is indeed a reminder, so let whoever wills, take the path toward his Lord, **30.** for you do not will, only God wills. Truly God is the Knowing and the Wise. **31.** He admits whomever He wills into His Mercy. As for the wrongdoers, He has prepared a painful punishment for them.

Surah 77

THOSE SENT FORTH

al-Mursalāt

In the Name of God, the Compassionate, the Merciful

1. By those driven forth in succession! 2. By the stormy tempests! 3. Scattering far and wide! 4. By those who distinguish with clarity! 5. By those who bring forth the Reminder, 6. to excuse or to warn, 7. for indeed what you are promised will take place. 8. So when the stars are faded out, 9. when the sky is riven asunder, 10. when the mountains are scattered, 11. when the messengers are scheduled, 12. for which day was it deferred? 13. —For the Day of the Division. 14. What do you know of the Day of the Division? 15. Woe that Day to the deniers! 16. Did We not destroy those of former times, 17. then make those who came later follow them? 18. That is how We deal with the guilty. 19. Woe that Day to the deniers! 20. Did We not create you from an insignificant fluid, 21. then affix it in a secure dwelling place 22. for a determined period? 23. So We determine, and We are the best of determiners! 24. Woe that Day to the deniers! 25. Did We not make the earth a receptacle 26. for the living and for the dead? 27. We placed firm soaring mountains therein and provided you with sweet water to drink. 28. Woe that Day to the deniers! 29. Head out to what you denied! 30. Head out to a threefold shadow 31. that provides no shade, nor avails against the flame. 32. Indeed it throws up sparks like huge fortresses, 33. as if they were yellow camels. 34. Woe that Day to the deniers! 35. That is the Day in which they do not speak, 36. nor is permission granted to them, for they will offer excuses. 37. Woe that Day to the deniers! 38. This is the Day of Division, "We have gathered you and those of former times." 39. So if you have a scheme, then scheme against Me! 40. Woe that Day to the deniers! 41. Indeed, the God-conscious will dwell in shade and springs, 42. enjoying fruits of their choice. 43. "Eat and drink with delight for what you have done." 44. This is how

We reward those who do good. **45.** But woe on that Day to the deniers! **46.** "Eat and enjoy yourselves briefly, for you are guilty." **47.** Woe on that Day to the deniers! **48.** And when they are told, "Bow down," they do not bow. **49.** Woe on that Day to the deniers! **50.** So in what message after this will they believe?

Surah 78

THE GOOD NEWS

al-Naba

In the Name of God, the Compassionate, the Merciful

1. What are they questioning one another about? 2. About the Good News 3. that they disagree over? 4. Indeed, they will know! 5. Then indeed, they will know. 6. Did We not make the earth a resting place, 7. the mountains pegs, 8. created you in pairs, 9. made your sleep for rest, 10. made the night a shelter, 11. and the day for livelihood. 12. We built seven firmaments over you, 13. made a radiant lantern, 14. and sent water down from the clouds, pouring abundantly, 15. that We might thereby, produce grain, plants, 16. and luxurious gardens? 17. Indeed the Day of Division is a fixed time, 18. a day when the trumpet is blown, and you come forth in mass. 19. The sky will be opened as if it were doors, 20. and the mountains will be set in motion as if they were a mirage. 21. Indeed Hell lies in ambush, 22. a place unto which the rebellious return 23. to live therein, for ages. 24. Therein, they will taste neither coolness, nor drink, 25. except for boiling liquid and cold murky fluid, 26. a suitable reward. 27. Indeed they did not anticipate the reckoning, 28. and denied Our signs utterly. 29. We have recorded everything in a book. 30. So taste! For We will not increase you in anything but punishment! 31. Indeed, for the reverent there will be triumph. 32. There will be gardens and vineyards, 33. full-bosomed maidens of similar age, 34. and an overflowing goblet. 35. They will neither hear vanity, nor falsehood there, 36. a reward from your Lord, a plentiful gift 37. from the Lord of the heavens and the earth and whatever is between them, the most Compassionate Whom they will have no power to address. 38. That Day, the Spirit and the angels will stand in rows, and no one will speak except whom the Compassionate authorizes and who speaks righteously. 39. That is the True Day. So let whoever will, take a path of return unto his Lord

40. Indeed, We have warned you of a nearby punishment on a day when man perceives what his hands have sent forth and the disbeliever says, "Oh! I wish I were dust!"

Surah 79

THE WRESTERS

al-Nāzi'āt

In the Name of God, the Compassionate, the Merciful

1. By those who wrest with force, 2. by those who draw out swiftly, 3. by those who glide smoothly, 4. by those who speed ahead, 5. and by those who manage affairs, 6. on the Day when the quake quakes violently, 7. and is followed by another quake, 8. hearts will be filled with fear that Day, 9. and eyes will be cast down in humility. 10. They will say, "Are we to be restored as we were before, 11. after we have become decayed bones?" 12. They say, "Then, this will be a lost return!" 13. Yet it will be but a single cry, 14. then, behold, they will be in a wide awakening. 15. Has the story of Moses reached you 16. when his Lord called out to him in the Holy Valley of Tuwā? 17. "Go to Pharoah! He has truly rebelled!" 18. Say, "Do you wish to be purified 19. and that I guide you to your Lord that you might be fearful?" 20. He then showed him the greatest sign, 21. but he denied and disobeyed, 22. and then, he turned his back moving swiftly. 23. He then gathered and declared, 24. and he said, "I am your highest lord." 25. So God seized him and made him an example in the Hereafter and in this world. 26. Indeed in that is a lesson for whoever fears. 27. Are you more difficult to create or the sky that He has built? 28. He raised its canopy high and fashioned it, 29. darkened its night, and brought about its day. 30. In turn, He spread out the earth. 31. From it He brought forth its water and its pastures, 32. and the mountains He set firm 33. as fulfillment for you and your flocks. 34. So when the Great Calamity takes place, 35. a day when a person will remember what he strove for, 36. Hellfire will be made visible to one who sees. 37. But as for one who rebels 38. and prefers the life of this world, 39. indeed Hellfire is the refuge. 40. But the one who stands in awe of his Lord and restrains his soul from desires, 41. truly, the Garden is the refuge. 42. They ask you about the Hour, "When will

its arrival be?" **43.** What do you have to do with mentioning it? **44.** Unto your Lord is its ending. **45.** You are but a warner for whoever fears it. **46.** The Day they see it; it will be as if they had tarried but an evening or its looming morning.

Surah 80

HE FROWNED

'Abasa

In the Name of God, the Compassionate, the Merciful

1. He frowned, and he turned away 2. because the blind man came to him. 3. What do you know? He might purify himself, 4. or be reminded such that the Remembrance might benefit him. 5. As for one who considers himself self-sufficient, 6. you should attend to him, 7. though it is not on you if he does not become purified. 8. As for he who came to you striving earnestly 9. while fearful, 10. you were unmindful of him. 11. But no! It is truly a remembrance. 12. So let whoever will, remember it 13. on honored pages, 14. exalted and purified 15. in the hands of scribes, 16. who are noble and pious. 17. May man be eliminated! How ungrateful he is! 18. From what thing did He create him? 19. He created him from a drop of semen, then proportioned him, 20. then He made the way easy for him. 21. Then He caused him to die and buried him. 22. Then when He willed, He resurrected him. 23. No way did he fulfill what God had commanded him. 24. So let man consider his food, 25. for indeed, We pour water down in abundance. 26. Then We split the earth in fissures 27. and caused grains to grow there, 28. and vines and herbs, 29. and olives and date palms, 30. and gardens of thick foliage, 31. and fruit and pastures, 32. as fulfillment for you and your flocks. 33. For when the Piercing Cry arrives, 34. that Day, when a man will flee from his brother, 35. his mother and his father, 36. and his spouse and his children. 37. For every man that Day, his affair will be enough for him. 38. On that Day, faces will be beaming, 39. laughing and rejoicing. 40. On that Day, faces will be covered with dust, 41. and overspread with darkness. 42. Those will be the disbelievers and the wicked.

Surah 81

THE ENFOLDING

al-Takwīr

In the Name of God, the Compassionate, the Merciful

1. When the sun is enfolded, 2. and when the stars fade away, 3. and when the mountains are set in motion, 4. and when expecting camels are unattended to, 5. and when wild beasts are gathered, 6. and when the seas overflow, 7. and when souls are paired, 8. and when the female infant who was buried alive was questioned 9. about the sin for which she was killed, 10. and when the records are unrolled, 11. and when the Heaven has its veil removed, 12. and when Hellfire is set ablaze, 13. and when the Garden is brought near, 14. each soul will know what it has prepared. 15. So I swear by the retractors, 16. by the stars that rise and set, 17. by the night as it closes in, 18. and by the morning as it breathes! 19. Indeed it is the speech of a noble messenger, 20. possessed with strength before the Possessor of the Throne, of high rank, 21. compliant and henceforth, trustworthy. 22. Your companion is not insane. 23. He certainly saw him upon the clear horizon. 24. He does not withhold the Unseen grudgingly, 25. nor is it the speech of an accursed demon. 26. So where are you going? 27. It is nothing but a remembrance for the worlds, 28. for those of you who are willing to go straight. 29. You do not will, unless God, Lord of the Worlds, wills.

Surah 82

THE RIVEN ASUNDER

al-Infitār

In the Name of God, the Compassionate, the Merciful

1. When the sky is riven asunder, 2. and when the stars are scattered, 3. and when the seas are burst forth, 4. and when graves are overturned 5. then, each soul will know what it has sent forth and what it has left behind. 6. O mankind! What has seduced you from your noble Lord, 7. Who created you, then fashioned you, then proportioned you 8. and put you together in any form He willed? 9. But no! You denied religion. 10. Yet truly there are guardians over you, 11. who are honorable, writing down, 12. knowing what you do. 13. Indeed the pious will be in bliss, 14. and indeed the wicked will be in Hellfire 15. arriving at it on the Day of Judgment. 16. They will not be absent from it. 17. What do you know about the Day of Judgment? 18. Then what do you know about the Day of Judgment, 19. a Day when no soul will have power over another soul in any way? The Command on that Day is with God.

Surah 83

THOSE WHO DEFRAUD

al-Mutaffifīn

In the Name of God, the Compassionate, the Merciful

1. Woe unto the defrauders 2. who when they take measure, they receive it in full, 3. but when they measure for them, or weigh for them, they make them lose. 4. Do they not think they will be resurrected 5. unto a great day, 6. a day when mankind will stand before the Lord of the Worlds? 7. Never! Truly the book of the wicked is in the *Sijjīn* (lowliest). 8. What do you know about the *Sijjīn*? 9. A book inscribed. 10. Woe that Day to the deniers 11. who deny the Day of Judgment 12. that no one will deny, except for every sinful transgressor. 13. When Our signs are recited unto him, he says, "Ancient tales!" 14. No doubt! What they earned has covered their hearts with rust. 15. No doubt! On that Day, they will be veiled from their Lord. 16. They will then burn in Hellfire. 17. Then it is said to them, "This is what you used to deny." 18. Truly the book of the pious is in the *Alliyyūn* (highest). 19. What do you know about the *Alliyyūn*? 20. A book inscribed, 21. witnessed by those brought close. 22. Indeed the pious will be in bliss, 23. upon couches observing. 24. You will recognize in their faces the brilliance of bliss. 25. They are given to drink of pure sealed wine, 26. whose seal is of musk. So for that, let the pursuers pursue. 27. Its mixture is of *Tasnīm* 28. a spring that those nearest to God will drink from. 29. Indeed those who sinned laughed at those who believed. 30. When they passed them by, they would wink at one another. 31. When they returned to their people, they would return jesting. 32. Whenever they saw them, they would say, "Indeed these are astray!" 33. But they were not sent as guardians over them. 34. That Day, those who believe will laugh at those who disbelieve, 35. while upon couches observing. 36. Have the disbelievers been repaid for their deeds?

Surah 84

THE SUNDERING

al-Inshiqāq

In the Name of God, the Compassionate, the Merciful

1. When the sky is riven asunder, 2. and listens to its Lord, as it must, dutifully. 3. When the earth is flattened out, 4. and casts forth what is in it, emptying itself, 5. and listens to its Lord, as it must dutifully. 6. O mankind! Truly you are laboring unto your Lord laboriously and will meet Him! 7. As for one who is given his book in his right hand, 8. his account will be reckoned easily 9. and he will return to his people rejoicing. 10. But as for one who is given his book from behind his back, 11. he will cry out for obliteration, 12. and will enter an Inferno. 13. Verily among his people he was joyful. 14. He truly thought that he would never return. 15. But undeniably, His Lord was certainly watchful of him! 16. So I swear by the twilight, 17. by the night and what it covers, 18. and by the moon when full, 19. you will surely travel from stage to stage. 20. So what is it with them that they do not believe 21. and that when the Quran is recited to them, they do not prostrate? 22. Instead, those who disbelieve deny, 23. but God knows best what they conceal. 24. So inform them of a painful punishment, 25. save those who believe and perform righteous deeds. They will have a never-ending reward.

Surah 85

THE CONSTELLATIONS
al-Burūj

In the Name of God, the Compassionate, the Merciful

1. By the sky possessed of constellations, **2.** by the Day promised, **3.** and by the witness and the witnessed. **4.** May the inhabitants of the pit perish. **5.** The fire was supplied with fuel **6.** when they sat by it **7.** and were witness to what they did to the believers **8.** as they took vengeance upon them for nothing, but that they believed in God, the Mighty, and the Praised, **9.** unto Whom belong sovereignty over the heavens and the earth. God is witness over all things. **10.** Indeed, those who persecute believing men and believing women, then do not repent, will have the punishment of Hell, and will have the punishment of the burning. **11.** Truly those who believe and perform righteous deeds, will have Gardens with rivers running beneath. That is the supreme triumph. **12.** Indeed the Lord's assault is severe. **13.** Truly, it is He Who originates and restores. **14.** He is the Forgiving and the Loving, **15.** Possessor of the Throne, the Glorious, **16.** and the Doer of whatever He wills. **17.** Has the story of the armies reached you? **18.** The Pharoah and the Thamŭd? **19.** Yet those who disbelieve are in denial. **20.** God, the All-Encompassing is behind them. **21.** Indeed it is a glorious Quran **22.** upon a Preserved Tablet.

Surah 86

THE NIGHTLY STAR

al-Tāriq

In the Name of God, the Compassionate, the Merciful

1. By the sky and that which comes by night. 2. What do you know about that which comes by night? 3. It is the piercing Star. 4. Over every soul there is a guardian. 5. So let man consider what he was created from. 6. He was created from a propelled fluid 7. emerging from between the loins and the pelvic arch. 8. Indeed, He is able to bring him back 9. on the Day when secrets are tested, 10. upon which man has neither strength nor helper. 11. By the resurgent sky, 12. and by the fissured earth, 13. for indeed, it is certainly a decisive Word. 14. It is not for amusement. 15. They are genuinely planning a scheme. 16. I too, am planning a scheme. 17. So be gentle with the disbelievers. Grant them respite for a while.

Surah 87

THE MOST HIGH

al-A'lā

In the Name of God, the Compassionate, the Merciful

1. Glorify the name of your Lord, the Most High, **2.** Who created, then fashioned, **3.** Who predetermined, then guided, **4.** Who brought forth pasture, **5.** then made it as blackened stubble. **6.** We will teach you to recite, so you will not forget, **7.** except for what God wills. Truly He knows what is declared and what is hidden. **8.** We will ease the way unto ease. **9.** Therefore, remind if the reminder is beneficial. **10.** He who fears will remember, **11.** but the most unfortunate will avoid it. **12.** He who enters into the greatest Fire, **13.** neither dies nor lives in it. **14.** He who is purified prospers, **15.** remembers the name of his Lord and prays. **16.** But you undeniably prefer the life of this world, **17.** while the Hereafter is better and more enduring. **18.** This is genuinely ancient scriptures, **19.** the scriptures of Abraham and Moses.

Surah 88

THE OVERWHELMING EVENT

al-Ghāshiyah

In the Name of God, the Compassionate, the Merciful

1. Has the story of the overwhelming event reached you? 2. Faces on that Day will be humbled, 3. endeavoring and weary, 4. entering a scorching Fire, 5. given drink from a boiling spring. 6. They will have no food except from the poisonous thorn 7. that neither nourishes, nor helps against hunger. 8. Faces that Day will be blessed, 9. satisfied with their endeavoring 10. in a lofty Garden 11. wherein, they will not hear futile talk. 12. A flowing spring lies in it, 13. raised couches are in it, 14. goblets set in place, 15. cushions set in rows, 16. and carpets spread out. 17. Do they not observe camels and how they are created, 18. the sky, how it is raised 19. the mountains, how they are established, 20. and the earth, how it is spread? 21. So remember! You are no more than a reminder. 22. You are not a warder over them. 23. But whoever turns away and disbelieves, 24. God will punish him with the greatest punishment. 25. Indeed to Us is their return, 26. and then, truly with Us lies their reckoning.

Surah 89

THE DAWN

al-Fajr

In the Name of God, the Compassionate, the Merciful

1. By the dawn, 2. by the ten nights, 3. by the even and the odd, 4. and by the night when it departs. 5. Is there an oath in it for one who is heedful? 6. Have you not seen how your Lord dealt with the Ãd, 7. Iram, the pillared, 8. upon which nothing like it was ever created in all the land, 9. the Thamŭd who cut out rocks in the valley, 10. and the Pharoah of the tent poles 11. who tyrannized the land 12. and increased corruption in it? 13. So your Lord poured upon them the curse of punishment. 14. Truly your Lord lies in ambush. 15. Now as for man, when his Lord tries him, then honors him and blesses him, he says, "My Lord has honored me." 16. However, when He tries him and restricts his sustenance, he says, "My Lord has humiliated me." 17. Not at all, but you do not honor the orphan, 18. nor encourage the feeding of the indigent. 19. You devour inheritance with greedy devouring, 20. and love wealth with abundant love. 21. Indeed when the earth is pulverized, leveled, and crushed, 22. your Lord comes with the angels, row upon row, 23. and Hell is brought forth that Day. That Day, man will remember, but how will that reminder benefit him? 24. He will say, "Ah! I wish I would have sent forth for my life!" 25. That Day, none will punish as He punishes, 26. and none will bind as He binds. 27. O soul at peace! 28. Return unto your Lord satisfied and satisfying. 29. Enter among My servants. 30. Enter My Garden.

Surah 90

THE CITY

al-Balad

In the Name of God, the Compassionate, the Merciful

1. Indeed I swear by this land 2. as you are free in this land, 3. — the giver of life and what he gave life to, 4. We have truly created man in hardship. 5. Does he assume that no one will ever have power over him? 6. He says, "I have wasted the abundant wealth I have." 7. Does he assume that no one sees him? 8. Did We not make two eyes for him, 9. a tongue, and two lips, 10. and guide him upon the two highways? 11. But he has not broken through the steep pass. 12. What do you know about the steep pass? 13. The freeing of a slave, 14. or the giving of food at a time of famine 15. to an orphan near of kin, 16. or the dusty indigent. 17. Then he will be of those who believe and urge patience while urging each other to compassion. 18. Those are the companions of the right. 19. Those who disbelieve in Our signs, are the companions of the left. 20. A Fire will be bounded over them.

Surah 91

THE SUN

al-Shams

In the Name of God, the Compassionate, the Merciful

1. By the sun and its rising brightness, **2.** by the moon when it follows it, **3.** by the day when it displays it, **4.** by the night when it discloses it, **5.** by the sky and the One Who developed it, **6.** by the earth and the One Who spread it, **7.** by the soul and the One Who proportioned it, **8.** and inspired it to be sinful or reverent. **9.** Indeed, he who purifies it, will have prospered, **10.** and truly, he who obscures it, will have failed. **11.** The Thamŭd denied in their rebelliousness **12.** when the most wicked of them was sent out. **13.** So the messenger of God said to them, "The she-camel of God—with what she must drink!" **14.** But they denied him, then hamstrung her. Therefore, their Lord equally destroyed them for their sin, **15.** since He does not fear the consequences.

Surah 92

THE NIGHT
al-Layl

In the Name of God, the Compassionate, the Merciful

1. By the night as it veils, 2. by the day as it unveils, 3. and by Him Who created the male and the female. 4. Truly your efforts are diverse, 5. but for one who gives and is reverent, 6. and testifies to the best, 7. We will smooth his way to ease. 8. As for one who is miserly and considers himself free of need, 9. and denies what is best, 10. We will ease his way to hardship. 11. His wealth will not benefit him when he perishes. 12. Truly, on Us is to give guidance, 13. and truly unto Us belongs the ending and the beginning. 14. Consequently, I have warned you of a raging Fire, 15. that no one will enter except for the most unfortunate, 16. and who rejects and turns away. 17. The most reverent will be removed from it. 18. He who spends of his wealth to purify 19. without expecting a favor in return, 20. save to seek the Countenance of his Lord, the Most High, 21. will certainly be satisfied.

Surah 93

THE MORNING BRIGHTNESS

al-Duhā

In the Name of God, the Compassionate, the Merciful

1. By the morning brightness, **2.** and by the night when still, **3.** your Lord has not forsaken you, nor does He scrutinize. **4.** The Hereafter will be better for you than this life. **5.** Your Lord will certainly give you, and you will be satisfied. **6.** Did He not find you an orphan and then shelter, **7.** find you astray and then guide, **8.** and find you in need, and then enrich? **9.** Therefore, do not scorn the orphan, **10.** and accordingly, do not chide the asker; **11.** however, proclaim the blessing of your Lord!

Surah 94

THE EXPANSION

al-Sharh

In the Name of God, the Compassionate, the Merciful

1. Did We not open your breast for you **2.** and relieve you of your burden **3.** that weighed heavily upon your back? **4.** Did We not hold you high in recognition? **5.** For indeed, with hardship comes relief. **6.** Indeed, with hardship comes relief. **7.** So when you are free, work hard, **8.** and turn your desire to your Lord.

Surah 95

THE FIG

al-Tīn

In the Name of God, the Compassionate, the Merciful

1. By the fig and the olive, 2. by Mount Sinai, 3. and by this land made safe, 4. We truly created man in the best of statures, 5. and then, We returned him to the lowest of the low, 6. except for those who believe and perform righteous deeds. They will have a never-ending reward. 7. What then will make you deny religion? 8. Is God not the most just of judges?

Surah 96

THE BLOOD CLOT

al-'Alaq

In the Name of God, the Compassionate, the Merciful

1. Recite in the name of your Lord Who created, 2. created man from a blood clot. 3. Recite! Your Lord is most Bountiful, 4. Who taught by the Pen, 5. and taught man what he did not know. 6. But no! Man is truly rebellious 7. and he sees himself beyond need. 8. Indeed, to your Lord is the return. 9. Have you seen him who prohibits 10. a slave when he prays? 11. Have you seen if he acts upon guidance, 12. or commands reverence? 13. Have you seen if he denied and turned away? 14. Does he not know that God sees? 15. But no! If he does not stop, We will certainly seize him by the forelock, 16. a lying, sinful forelock. 17. So let him call his advisors. 18. We will call the guards of Hell. 19. So no! Do not obey him! Prostrate and draw near.

Surah 97

POWER

al-Qadr

In the Name of God, the Compassionate, the Merciful

1. Truly We sent it down during the Night of Power. **2.** What do you know about the Night of Power? **3.** The Night of Power is better than a thousand months. **4.** The angels and the Spirit descend therein, by the Leave of their Lord upon every command. **5.** It is peace until the break of dawn.

Surah 98

THE CLEAR PROOF
al-Bayyinah

In the Name of God, the Compassionate, the Merciful

1. Those who disbelieve among the People of the Book and the idolaters will not give in until clear proof comes to them, **2.** a messenger from God reciting purified scriptures, **3.** containing upright righteous books. **4.** Those who were given the Book did not become divided until after clear proof had come to them. **5.** They were commanded to worship only God, dedicating their faith sincerely to Him as uprights, to establish prayer, and to give alms. This is the true and upright way of religion. **6.** Truly the disbelievers among the People of the Book and the idolaters will be in the Fire of Hell abiding there. They are the worst of creation. **7.** Truly those who believe and perform righteous deeds are the best of creation. **8.** Their reward is with their Lord, Gardens of Eden with rivers running beneath, abiding there forever. God is pleased with them, and they are pleased with Him. That is for whoever fears his Lord.

Surah 99

THE EARTHQUAKE

al-Zalzalah

In the Name of God, the Compassionate, the Merciful

1. When the earth is shaken with her utmost convulsion, **2.** and the earth yields up her burdens, **3.** man will say, "What is with her?" **4.** That Day she will report her news, **5.** for your Lord has truly inspired her. **6.** That Day mankind will go forth in scattered groups to witness their deeds. **7.** So whoever does a mote's weight of good, will see it, **8.** and whoever does a mote's weight of evil, will see it.

Surah 100

The Chargers

al-'Ādiyāt

In the Name of God, the Compassionate, the Merciful

1. By the panting chargers, 2. by the strikers of sparks, 3. by the chargers at dawn, 4. raising thereby a trail of dust, 5. arriving at its midst collectively, 6. for indeed mankind is ungrateful to his Lord. 7. He truly bears witness to that, 8. and he is certainly fierce in his love for good things. 9. Does he not know that what lies within graves is overturned, 10. and what lies within hearts is made known? 11. Indeed on that Day, their Lord will be aware of them!

Surah 101

THE CALAMITY

al-Qāri'ah

In the Name of God, the Compassionate, the Merciful

1. The calamity. **2.** What is the calamity? **3.** What do you know about the calamity? **4.** A Day wherein mankind will be like scattered moths, **5.** and the mountains will be like carded wool. **6.** As for one whose scales are heavy, **7.** he will have a life of contentment, **8.** but as for one whose scales are light, **9.** a boundless abyss will be his mother. **10.** Do you have any notion of what it could be? **11.** It will be a blazing fire.

Surah 102

Vying for More

al-Takāthur

In the Name of God, the Compassionate, the Merciful

1. Vying for more distracts you, **2.** until you visit the graves. **3.** But indeed! You will soon know. **4.** Indeed! You will soon know. **5.** Indeed, if you knew with the knowledge of certainty, **6.** you would surely see Hellfire. **7.** Then you would surely see it with the eye of certainty. **8.** Then indeed, on that Day, you will be questioned about the blessing.

Surah 103

OVER TIME

al-'Asr

In the Name of God, the Compassionate, the Merciful

1. Over time 2. mankind will truly be at loss, 3. except for those who believe, perform righteous deeds, press one another to truth, and press one another to patience.

Surah 104

THE SLANDERER

al-Humazah

In the Name of God, the Compassionate, the Merciful

1. Woe unto every slanderer and backbiter **2.** who amasses wealth and counts it, **3.** assuming that his wealth makes him immortal. **4.** Not so! He will certainly be thrown into the demolishing Fire. **5.** What do you know about the demolishing Fire? **6.** The Fire of God ignited **7.** that engulfs hearts. **8.** It is truly enclosed upon them **9.** in extended columns.

Surah 105

THE ELEPHANT

al-Fīl

In the Name of God, the Compassionate, the Merciful

1. Have you seen how the Lord dealt with the leaders of the elephant? 2. Did he not make their scheming go astray 3. and send birds against them in swarms, 4. shelling them with stones of dried clay 5. and then, He made them like consumed stalks of grain.

Surah 106

Quraysh

Quraysh

In the Name of God, the Compassionate, the Merciful

1. For the secure passage of the Quraysh, **2.** their secure passage in the journey of winter and of summer. **3.** So let them worship the Lord of this house **4.** Who provided them with sustenance in times of hunger and protected them from fear.

Surah 107

ACTS OF KINDNESS

al-Mā'ūn

In the Name of God, the Compassionate, the Merciful

1. Have you seen the one who rejects religion? **2.** That is the one who scorns the orphan, **3.** and does not encourage the feeding of the indigent. **4.** So woe unto the praying **5.** who are mindless of their prayers, **6.** those who want to be seen, **7.** yet refrain from acts of kindness.

Surah 108

Abundant Good

al-Kawthar

In the Name of God, the Compassionate, the Merciful

1. We have indeed granted you abundant good. 2. So pray to your Lord and sacrifice. 3. Indeed, your adversary will be the one without posterity.

Surah 109

THE DISBELIEVERS

al-Kāfirūn

In the Name of God, the Compassionate, the Merciful

1. Say, "O disbelievers! 2. I do not worship what you worship, 3. nor are you worshippers of what I worship. 4. I will not worship what you worship, 5. nor will you worship what I worship. 6. Unto you, your religion, and unto me, my religion."

Surah 110

HELP

al-Nasr

In the Name of God, the Compassionate, the Merciful

1. When God's help and victory arrive, 2. and you see mankind entering God's religion in mass, 3. glorify the praises of your Lord and seek forgiveness from Him. For indeed, He is Ever-Relenting.

Surah 111

THE PALM-FIBER

al-Masad

In the Name of God, the Compassionate, the Merciful

1. May the hands of Abu Lahab perish, and may he perish! **2.** His wealth will not benefit him, nor what he has earned. **3.** He will enter a blazing Fire **4.** and his wife will be the wood carrier. **5.** A cord of palm-fiber will be around her neck.

Surah 112

SINCERITY

al-Ikhlās

In the Name of God, the Compassionate, the Merciful

1. Say, "He, God, is One, 2. God, the Eternal-Absolute. 3. He does not beget, nor was He begotten, 4. and no one is comparable to Him."

Surah 113

THE DAYBREAK

al-Falaq

In the Name of God, the Compassionate, the Merciful

1. Say, "I seek refuge in the Lord of the Daybreak, **2.** from the harm of all that He has created, **3.** from the harm of darkness as it spreads, **4.** from the harm of those who (cast spells) by blowing on knots, **5.** and from the harm of the envious when he envies."

Surah 114

Mankind

al-Nās

In the Name of God, the Compassionate, the Merciful

1. Say, "I seek refuge in the Lord of mankind, 2. the King of mankind, 3. the God of mankind, 4. from the evil of the stealthy whisperer 5. who whispers into the breasts of mankind, 6. — from the jinn and mankind."

THE STORY OF PROPHET MUHAMMAD

The Quran is the only living document considered to be the direct Word of God. It was revealed to Prophet Muhammad that he might seal God's final words and warn mankind to believe in God's Oneness and that he may correct any distortions or misinterpretations of previous religious scriptures and revelations: *"Muhammad is not the father of any man among you, rather he is the Messenger of God and the Seal of the prophets. God is the Knower of all things"* (Quran, 33:40).

Prophet Muhammad was born in Mecca (Makkah), Saudi Arabia, in 570 CE. The name Muhammad, meaning "the praised one," was given to him by his grandfather, Abd al-Muttalib, who believed his grandson was destined for greatness and deserved praise. His mother, Amina, was the daughter of Wahab, and his father, Abdallah, was the son of Abd al-Muttalib of the Banu Hashim clan, part of the Quraish tribe. The family traced its lineage directly to the Prophet Abraham and his son, the Prophet Ismail.

Before Prophet Muhammad was born, his father, Abdallah, fell ill and passed away in Medina (then known as Yathrib), while traveling with a trade caravan to Syria. His mother, Amina, died when he was about six years old, leaving him in the care of his grandfather, Abd al-Muttalib, and his governess, Halima Al-Saadya. However, his grandfather passed away a few years later, after which Muhammad came under the care and guidance of his paternal uncle, Abu Talib. Abu Talib, the new leader of the Hashim clan of the Quraish tribe, provided him with love and protection as he grew up within the most powerful tribe in Mecca.

At around the age of twelve, Prophet Muhammad joined his uncle Abu Talib on a business trip to Damascus, Syria. During this caravan journey, they stopped in Busra, where a Nestorian monk named Bahira observed the group. He noticed a cloud shading young Muhammad from the sun and was intrigued. Inviting Abu Talib and his company to dinner, Bahira carefully observed the boy and based on his knowledge of sacred scriptures, predicted that Muhammad could be the foretold and final prophet.

According to the Quran, Jesus, the son of Mary, foretold the arrival of a prophet named Ahmad, a name that is closely linked to Muhammad: *"Remember when Jesus, son of Mary said, "O comm! Truly I am the Messenger of God unto you, confirming what came before me in the Torah and bearing the good news of a messenger to come after me whose name is Ahmad." When he went to them with clear signs, they said, "This is clear sorcery"* (Quran, 61:6). Note that in Arabic, the words Ahmad and Muhammad are derivatives of the same verb.

Over the years, Prophet Muhammad earned a reputation as an honest and trustworthy young man. When his uncle Abu Talib grew old and financially strained, he encouraged Muhammad to work for Khadija bint Khuwaylid, a twice-widowed woman who was among the wealthiest of the Quraish. Khadija, having heard of Muhammad's integrity and reliability, hired him to take her goods to Syria and sell them on her behalf. Upon his successful return, she was impressed by his results and sent him on another journey.

Although Khadija had received many proposals from other suitors, after Muhammad's second return, she became convinced that he was the man with whom she wanted to share her life. Despite being approximately fifteen years his senior, they married in 595 CE and formed a loving and supportive partnership.

Prophet Muhammad was born into Arabia's Age of Ignorance (*Jahiliya*) and spent much of his adult life retreating to the cave of Hira to meditate and reflect on the world around him. He was deeply troubled by the beliefs of those who rejected the existence of a higher power or considered life to be the result of mere chance: *"They say, There is nothing but our life in this world. We die and we live, and nothing can destroy us but time. But they have no knowledge of that. They do no more than speculate."* (Quran, 45:24). At the age of forty, while contemplating in the cave, Prophet Muhammad was visited by the Archangel Gabriel (*Jibril*). The Archangel directed him to recite from the Sura of al-Alaq: *"Recite in the name of your Lord Who created, created man from a blood clot. Recite! Your Lord is most Bountiful, Who taught by the Pen, and taught man what he did not know . . ."* (Quran, 96:1-5). In Arabic, the word "*Iqra*" means "to read;" however, Prophet Muhammad was illiterate. Hence, when the Prophet heard the word "*Iqra*," he was shaken and terrified by the power and weight of his mission and shared his experience with his wife Khadija. She believed his account and encouraged him to consider that he was indeed chosen by God to lift Arabs from the Age of Ignorance.

The Prophet began his mission cautiously but faced strong opposition, particularly from Abu Sufyan and his paternal uncle, Abu Lahab, who viewed him as a threat. These men controlled the Ka, which had been transformed over the years into a sanctuary filled with hundreds of idols, symbolizing the Meccans' political and economic dominance. To protect Prophet Muhammad from Abu

Lahab's hostility, his uncle Abu Talib advised him to sleep in a different place each night for safety.

Among the Prophet's foes was Abu Jahl, who placed a bounty of one hundred camels or one thousand ounces of gold on the Prophet's life. Tempted by the reward, Omar ibn Khattab set out to kill him. However, upon reaching Prophet Muhammad's doorstep, Omar encountered Hamzah, the Prophet's paternal uncle, who had recently embraced Islam. Hamzah invited Omar to meet the Prophet. As soon as Omar stood before him and gazed at his face, he began to tremble. Prophet Muhammad, fully aware of Omar's previous intentions, welcomed him and invited him to accept Islam.

Throughout this time, Abu Talib remained a steadfast protector and shield for Prophet Muhammad against their own tribe, the Quraish. The Quraish, seeing Muhammad as a threat to their polytheistic beliefs and authority, tried to negotiate with Abu Talib, even suggesting a trade of the Prophet for another wise young man. Abu Talib refused. In 616 CE, the Quraish and allied tribes imposed a social and economic boycott on the Hashim and Muttalib clans, hoping to isolate and starve them into submission. This boycott lasted three years, placing immense hardship on Prophet Muhammad and his followers (Ummah). During this time, Prophet Muhammad endured constant verbal abuse and mistreatment from his enemies.

Abu Lahab, the Prophet's uncle, openly expressed his hatred and refused to shield him from the persecution he faced in the streets of Mecca. To escape this abuse, Prophet Muhammad and his followers gradually emigrated to Medina (then Yathrib), a city about 250 miles away. The migration was carried out in stages to avoid suspicion. Prophet Muhammad, his cousin Ali (Abu Talib's son), and his close companion Abu Bakr were among the last to leave Mecca.

One night, Prophet Muhammad learned of a plot by the Quraish to assassinate him. To outwit his enemies, he had his cousin Ali sleep in his bed while he and Abu Bakr fled. The Quraish, enraged upon discovering Ali in the Prophet's place, announced a significant reward for his capture. Prophet Muhammad and Abu Bakr took refuge in a cave near Mecca, where Abu Bakr expressed fear. The Prophet reassured him, saying that God would protect them: *"If you do not help him, God has certainly helped Him. Remember when the disbelievers expelled him and while in the cave, the second of the two, said to his companion, "Do not grieve, God is truly with us." Then God sent down His Serenity upon him and supported him with combatants that you could not see. He made the word of those who disbelieve to be bottommost and the Word of God to be the uppermost. Do not grieve . . . God is Mighty and Wise."* (Quran, 9:40). Miraculously, immediately after Prophet Muhammad had entered the cave, a spider wove a web, and a pair of pigeons built their nest at the cave's entrance. This helped to divert his enemies from the cave. Prophet Muhammad, who was then fifty-three years of age, entered Medina and laid the foundations of the first mosque, namely the Quba Mosque, also referred to as the mosque of piety (*Masjid al-Taqwa*). Thus, the year 622 CE became known as the first calendar year of Islam, the year of *Hijra* or Emigration.

During the Age of Ignorance, the only way to become a member of an *Ummah* was to be born into it, but this was not so in Islam. By submitting one's will to God and uttering the words "there is no God but God, and Prophet Muhammad is God's messenger" (*la illaha ila Allah wa Muhammad rasoul Allah*) one becomes a member of the *Ummah*. The news that Islam was growing in Medina inflamed the *Quraish*, and they prepared to fight the Prophet. They gathered a large army and marched toward Medina in 624 CE. The Prophet was prepared and defeated the *Quraish* in what is known historically as the Battle of Badr. A year later, the *Quraish* prepared once more to avenge the Prophet. They attacked him and his followers at the Battle of *Uhud*. After the battle, the Jews and the *Quraish* were frightened and vowed to persistently fight the Prophet. Once again, the Prophet and his followers faced and defeated their enemies at the Battle of Khandaq in 627 CE and the Battle of Khaybar in 628 CE.

Shortly after his victory, the Prophet signed a peace treaty, the treaty of *Hudaybiyya*, with the Meccans. Thereafter, the Prophet visited Mecca, accompanied by two thousand Muslims. This was Prophet's way to build people's trust. A year later, the Meccans breached the treaty, and the Prophet conquered Mecca. The Meccans surrendered, with the exception of Abu Sofian, who remained doubtful of Muhammad's prophethood and chose not to greet him. The Prophet then made his way to the Ka'ba and broke over 360 idols that were fixed to its walls. Therefore, by 630 CE, Islam was embraced by multitudes of Meccans and their surrounding tribes. Thereafter, all pagans were forbidden from entering the Ka'ba. In 632 CE, the Prophet performed his last pilgrimage while in Mecca, then returned to Medina and passed away at the age of sixty-three. His death devastated believers, who thought it was inconceivable for the Messenger of God to die. However, his supporters claimed, "O men, if anyone worships Prophet Muhammad, Prophet Muhammad is dead; if anyone worships God, God is alive, immortal!"

According to the Quran, the word *Muslim*, as mentioned earlier, is "one who has submitted his will to God." Thus, those who believe that there is Only one God, and that the Prophet Muhammad was His final messenger, are Muslims in faith. God welcomes and protects all those who join Islam. However, Muslims who change their faith and follow a religion other than Islam will no longer find protection from God. *"How will God guide a people who have disbelieved after having believed, having borne witness that the messenger was true, and clear signs had come to them? God does not guide people who are wrongdoers. For them, recompense is the curse of God, the angels, and all people"* (Quran, 3: 86-87).

It was Prophet Muhammad's duty to inform people that he and his followers have submitted their wills to God and that the Quran is merely the completing chapter of the Old and New Testaments. To strengthen the faith of the Prophet and his followers, Prophet Muhammad was marvelously transported from the Sacred Mosque of Mecca to the Farthest Mosque of Jerusalem—the Temple of the Prophet Suleiman on the hill of *Moriah* at or near the Dome of the Rock in Jerusalem—in a special night and shown signs of the Divine. Prophet Muhammad was first transported to Jerusalem and then taken to the seven Heavens. The Ascension of Prophet Muhammad is presumed to have taken place on the twenty-seventh night of *Rajab*, the year before the *Hijra*. *"Glory to Him Who carried His servant by night from the Sacred Mosque to the Farthest Mosque. We blessed its precincts that We might show him some of Our signs. Truly He is the Hearer and the Seer"* (Quran, 17:1). To minimize doubt of the ascension, more details of its occurrence were introduced: *"By the star when it sets, your companion has neither gone astray, nor misled, nor does he speak impulsively. It is no more than a revelation revealed, taught by the Mighty and Powerful. Possessed of soundness, he stood upright when he was at the highest horizon. Then he approached and came close until he was within two bows' length or closer. Then He revealed to His servant what He revealed. The heart did not lie in what it saw. Do you dispute with him about what he saw? For indeed, he saw him during another decent at the boundary of the lote tree situated by the Garden of the Abode. Then the lote tree covered what it covered – sight did not swerve – not did it transgress. Indeed, he saw the greatest of his Lord's signs"* (Quran, 53:2-18). Therefore, Prophet Muhammad was not astray, nor did he lack intelligence as alleged by non-believers. His revelations revealed beauty, power, and wisdom, and they were undoubtedly a direct inspiration from God.

Prophet Muhammad was God's final messenger and the ultimate embodiment of peace and mercy for mankind. His words, actions, and interactions with others exemplify the purity and excellence of his character. God encourages Muslims to study and understand the Quran as revealed through Prophet Muhammad, along with the divine message it conveys. This process may require multiple readings and a thorough analysis of each verse, supported by Quranic exegesis as documented by countless researchers and religious scholars.

For those who wish to study the Quran, I strongly encourage an enthusiastic and independent approach. The pursuit of knowledge will help dispel any doubts about

God as the absolute Creator and ultimate possessor of mankind.

In the end, when those who are doubtful rise above the internal struggle between the mind and spirit, devote themselves entirely to God, and believe in the Day of Judgment, they may become among those who are granted the privilege of joining Him in His eternal Dominion: *"For those who believed and whose progeny followed them in faith, We will arrange for their progeny to be with them. We will not deprive them from any of their deeds. Every person will earn what he pledged to"* (Quran, 52:21). Prophet Muhammad was notably in favor of peace and did everything to protect his people and Islam. His message is clear, and Islam has been established for those who completely believe in God and the Prophet's message.

Today, the majority of Muslims strive for peace in every moment of their lives. The Prophet taught his followers to emulate his ways and to turn to God for solutions to their challenges and hardships. He instilled patience and endurance in the face of adversity and guided his followers with wisdom to perfect human relationships through peace and negotiation.

Throughout history, peace has never been fully achieved without negotiation, and war has never been the objective of any prophet. Prophet Muhammad did not build the *Ummah* or the Islamic world overnight, nor did those who followed him. Yet today, over a billion Muslims by birth and millions of converts have submitted themselves to Islam, seeking atonement and divine reward in the afterlife.

The Quran itself is a miracle, and its contents serve as living proof that God is the ultimate power above all powers. Believing in God's prophets is the first step toward embracing the possibility of eternal peace and deliverance. Ultimately, believers play a crucial role in proclaiming Islam as a religion of love and peace. Prophet Muhammad lived his life according to Islamic principles, and it is the responsibility of every Muslim to emulate him spiritually and faithfully in order to attain liberation in this life and in the Hereafter.

Timeline

Sixth Century (500–599) C.E.

545 – Birth of Abdullah bin Abd al-Muttalib, the Holy Prophet's father.

571 – Birth of the Holy Prophet Muhammad.

577 – Death of the Holy Prophet's mother, Amina bint Wahab.

580 – Death of Abd al-Muttalib, the grandfather of the Holy Prophet.

583 – The Holy Prophet's journey to Syria in the company of his uncle, Abu Talib.

594 – The Holy Prophet becomes the business manager for Lady Khadija, and leads her trade caravan to Syria and back.

595 – The Holy Prophet marries Lady Khadija.

Seventh Century (600–699) C.E.

610 – The first revelation in the cave at Mt. Hira (Jabal al Hira). The Holy Prophet is commissioned as the Messenger of God.

613 – Declaration at Mt. Safa inviting the general public to Islam.

614 – Invitation to the Hashemites to accept Islam.

615 – Persecution of the Muslims by the Quraish. A party of Muslims leaves for Abyssinia.

616 – Second Hijrah to Abyssinia.

619 – Deaths of Abu Talib (the uncle of the Holy Prophet) and Lady Khadija.

620 – Journey to Taif. The Holy Prophet's ascension to the heavens.

621 – First pledge at Aqaba.

622 – Second pledge at Aqaba. The Holy Prophet and the Muslims migrate to Yathrib (Medinah).

624 – Battle of Badr.

625 – Battle of Uhud. Massacre of 70 Muslims at Bir Mauna. Second expedition of Badr.

627 – Battle of the Trench.

629 – The Holy Prophet performs the pilgrimage at Mecca. Expedition to Muta.

630 – The Holy Prophet conquers Mecca.

632 – Farewell pilgrimage at Mecca.

632 – Death of the Holy Prophet.

Resources

Ali, Abdullah Yusuf. *The Meaning of the Holy Quran:* Beltsville, MD: Amana Publications, 2001.

Al-Makhtum, Ar-Raheeq: *The Sealed Nectar: Biography of the Noble Prophet.* Riyad, Darussalam, 2021.

Almaany English Arabic Dictionary. Accessed October 7, 2023. www.almaany.com

Gimson, A.C. *An Introduction to the Pronunciation of English*. London: Arnold, 1980.

Hazelton, Lesley. *The First Muslim: The Story of Muhammad*. New York: Riverhead Books, 2014.

Kramsch, Claire. *Language and Culture*. Oxford: Oxford University Press, 2021.

Lings, Martin. *Muhammad: His Life Based on Earliest Sources*. London: Islamic Texts Society, 1983.

Nasr, Raja T. *The Essentials of Linguistic Science: Selected and Simplified Reading*. Harlow, UK: Longman, 1984.

Nasr, Raja T. and Ahmed Khatib. *Al Mufid: Learner's English-Arabic Dictionary*. Beirut: Librairie du Liban, 1985.

Nasr, Seyyed Hossein. *The Study Quran: A New Translation and Commentary*. New York: HarperOne, 2015.

Sarwar, Sheikh Muhammad. *The Holy Qu'ran*. New York: Tahrike Tarsile Qur'an, Inc., 2015.

Wehr, Hans, and J. Milton Cowan (Editor). *A Dictionary of Modern Written Arabic*. Hawthorne, CA: BN Publishing, 2020.

Index

A

Aaron (Prophet Harun), 157, 201
    brother of Moses, 83–84, 108, 160, 162
    Criterion granted, 167
    God's kindness toward, 235
    House of, 26
    Egypt, 176, 188–89, 201
    lineage of revelations, 53, 70
adornment
    physical and spiritual covering, 78, 180
Age of Ignorance (Jahiliya), 38, 59, 220, 274, 374, 376
Ark of the Covenant, 26
Abraham (Prophet Ibrāhīm), 27, 32–37, 39–41, 51, 53, 69–70, 81–82, 114–15, 118, 131–32, 142, 156–57 167, 171–72, 174, 190, 206, 234, 239, 255, 260, 269–70, 280, 285, 293, 373
    continuity of prophets, 218, 343
    covenant with, 17–18,
    creed of, 17, 35, 51, 75, 142
    dream of Isaac's sacrifice, 235
    House of, 32, 46
    lineage of Muhammad, 373
    people of, 99, 172
    plea of, 114
    statement of, 299
    station of, 17, 35
Abd al-Muttalib, 379
Abdullah bin Abd al-Muttalib, 379
Abu Jahl (Amr ibn Hisham), 373
Abu Lahab, 367, 374–75
Abu Talib (Abu Talib ibn Abd al-Muttalib), 373, 379
Ãd (Ãdites)
    denied messengers, 172, 190, 237, 278
    given clear signs, 99, 129

(Ãd continued)
    punishment of, 185, 247, 251, 281, 285-86 315, 345
    response to Prophet Hud, 114, 268
Adam (Prophet Adam), 1, 12 , 32–33, 37, 57, 152
    Children of, 78–79, 87, 232
    covenant with, 163
    forbidden tree, 1
    progeny of, 87, 157
    prostrate before, 11, 77, 146, 152, 163, 90, 167, 175
    removal from the Garden, 1
    temptation by Satan, 163
    vice-regent on Earth, 11
adultery, 144
advisors, sincere, 82, 200
Al-Kitab. *See* Book (the); Heavenly Book; Heavenly Tablet
Al Masjid Al Haram (Ka'ba). *See* Ka'ba; mosques
alms (almsgiving), 56, 172, 181, 211, 156-57
    avoid vain speech, 175
    believe in God, 96, 194
    be reverent, 86
    dedicate faith, 354
    establish prayer, 172, 174
    forbid wrong, 99
    obey the messenger, 182
    perform prayer, 12, 14, 16, 20, 28, 47, 53, 56, 59, 96, 213, 220, 296
    perform good deeds and give, 167
    repent and give, 95
    those who do not give, 251, 354
Amina bint Wahab, 379
Ancient House. *See* Ka'ba; Sacred Mosque

angels, 19–20, 22, 34–37, 51, 71–72, 75, 77–78, 90, 93, 126, 145, 146, 152, 163, 169, 174, 252, 261, 309, 373
   as messengers, 147, 227
   at Babylon, 15 bless, 220–21
   Ark of the Covenant, and 26
   contact Zachariah, 32
   Day of Judgment (The Day), 185, 225, 315, 317, 325, 332, 345
   endowed with insight, 31
   glorify praise, 245, 255
   guardians, 325
   Messenger believes in, 29
   Night of Power, 353
   prostrate to Adam, 11, 134, 146, 152, 163, 239
   prostrate to God, 138, 253
   send (sent) down, 53, 133, 136, 147, 175, 185, 251,
   take souls 49, 137, 271
Arabs, 374
Arabic, 1, 3, 6–7, 127, 141, 161, 192, 267, 374
Arabic Quran, 118, 121, 136, 163, 242, 251, 255, 259
   verbatim, 1
Ark (of the Covenant), 26
Ark (of Noah), 81, 108, 113, 176, 190, 231, 315

B

Baal, 235
Badr
   God assisted at, 36
   battle of, 376, 380
baptism of God, 18
Bayt al-Atiq (Ancient House).
See also Ka'ba; mosque(s): Sacred Mosque
bee, 138
birds, 172, 194, 237, 361
   Abraham and, 27
   communities 167
   divine control, 140, 312, 361
   glorify God, 168, 181, 223, 237
   hoopoe, 195
   Joseph and, 120
   messengers, 194

(birds, continued)
   quail, 12, 86, 161
blood clot, 170, 175, 249, 327, 352, 374. *See also* semen.
Book (the), 22–24, 39–40, 45–46, 208, 55, 60–62, 66–67, 70, 72, 75, 79, 87–88, 94, 97, 104, 106, 109, 112, 117, 128, 139, 143, 145, 150–51, 155–57, 176, 185, 195, 201–02, 204, 207, 216–19, 235, 242, 244, 246, 249, 253, 293, 303, 305, 323, 339, 354
   clearly in, 68, 223
   covenant of, 87
   God sent down, 20, 30, 50, 59, 149, 241, 243, 256
   grant assurance, 325
   guidance, of, 10
   hidden from, 56
   hypocrites distort, 12
   increase faith,
   inscribed, 218
   knowledge of, 128, 195
   messengers, 15
   Mother of, 127
   People of the Book, 16–19, 31, 33–36, 41, 50, 52–53, 57, 60–61, 207, 219, 294, 297–98, 394
   portion of, 31, 45–46
   recite, 12, 16, 228
   remember, 156–57
   revealed, 30, 140 246, 265, 267
   signs of, 104, 125, 133
   teach, 33, 63
   threw, 15
   validating, 59
   write, 14
Book (the) and Wisdom, 17, 19, 24, 34, 39, 46, 303
bracelets, 174, 229
   gold, 151
   gold and pearls, 171, 229
   pearl, 197
   silver, 328
breastfeeding, 307

C

camels, 74, 297, 344, 375
   expecting, 337

(camels, continued)
   hundred, 421
   parched, 291
   sacrificial, 172
   she-camel, 95, 132, 167, 221, 393
   yellow, 330
Cave of Hira, 374, 379
charity. *See* wealth
chastity, 44, 168, 175, 180, 220, 310, 317
Children of Israel (Banu Israel), 25, 35, 57, 61, 192, 197, 217, 261, 263
   (the) Book, and, 143, 249, 265
   clear signs, 22, 33, 63, 148
   covenant with, 14, 56, 60
   belivers–disbelievers, 61, 302
   Egypt, 83–84, 109, 160–162, 188–89
   God's blessing, 12, 17
   Jesus–Messiah, 61, 301–02
   Companions of the Cave, 149–50
   corruption, 203
   angels doubt God, 11
   Egypt, 84, 199, 247
   generations past, 117
   hypocrites, 271
   God prohibits, 22, 57–58, 60, 80–82
   learning by consequence, 211
   punishment for, 58, 115, 126, 140, 191, 196, 345
   result of disunity, 94
   warning Children of Israel, 143
   do not trade, 141
   fulfill, 140
   people of Madyan, 83
clear signs
   disbelievers, 15, 22–23, 61, 75, 81–83, 99, 105, 112, 114, 129, 295
   conceal, 19
   God guides with, 171, 249,
   God sends(t) down, 179, 181–82, 265, 292–293
   messengers–prophets brought, 14, 15, 26, 35, 40, 52, 58, 63, 108, 148, 161, 201, 207, 209, 211, 247–48, 250, 261, 301, 305, 308, 374, 377
   Remembrance, the, 138
   scriptures, and, 228–29, 265–66, 292–93, 295
   Covenant, God's, 11, 17, 26, 40–41

(clear signs continued)
   Adam forgot, 163
   believers, 34, 55–56, 100, 175, 292
   breaking God's covenant, 11, 34, 40, 87, 93, 126
   Children of Israel and 12–15, 17, 52, 60, 84
   disbelievers, 93, 93–94
   with prophets, 218–19
   creation, 2
   Day of Judgment and 169, 175
   doubt and disbelief, 216
   God's signs, 19, 40, 104, 209–10, 232, 257, 265
   resurrection, 125, 145, 147, 206, 223, 228, 270, 279
   Satan defaces, 50
   sole creator and guide, 152, 160, 213–14, 315
   to God belongs, 80, 130
   ultimate creator, 106, 126, 197, 241, 249, 312
Creator, 1, 2, 244, 249, 284, 298
   absolute, 377–378
   criterion, 91
   guardian over all, 71, 126,
   supreme, 232
   sole and ultimate, 227, 235, 249, 299
Criterion, 12, 21, 30, 167, 184

D

David (Prophet Dāwud)
   Children of Israel, 61
   devotion to God, 237
   God bestows grace upon, 223-24
   David and Solomon, 194-95, 238
   God's guidance of prophets, 70
   judgment of David, 168, 238
   Psalms, 53, 145, 169
   slew Goliath 26,
Day of Adornment, 160. *See also* Day of Resurrection.
Day of Discrimination, 92
Day of Division, 233, 264, 330, 332. *See also* Hell
Day of Hunain (Battle of Hunayn), 96
Day of Gathering, 255, 305

Day of Judgment, 9, 134, 190, 233, 239, 280, 291, 317, 326, 338–39, 377
Day of Mutual Calling, 247
Day of Reckoning, 237–39, 247
Day of Regret, 156
Day of Resurrection
   God's covenant, 87, 140–41
   God's judgment, 14, 48, 52, 56, 60, 107, 109, 142, 143–44, 167, 170–71, 173, 175, 253, 257, 266–67, 279, 295, 314
   believers, 33, 41, 187, 211–12, 299
   certainty of, 327
   clarify signs on, 78
   consequences on, 50, 52, 65–66, 137, 145–47, 162–63, 242–44
   denial upon, 228
   disbelievers, 14, 20, 34, 58, 114, 137
   miserliness, 40
   People of the Book, 53, 217
   reverent, 34, 158
   those who defraud, 39
Day of the Moment Known, 134
Day of Victory (Yawm al-Furqan), 217
death
   acceptance of, 2–3
   Angel of, 216
   decreed, 224, 243, 291
   disbelivers say, 11, 178, 184
   every soul, 166, 208
   evildoers, 266
   fear of, 11,
   first death, 234, 264
   God causes, 27, 37, 134
   God's challenge to hypocrites, 39
   God created, 311
   God gives, 38, 86, 102, 107, 177, 249, 263, 279, 292
   God grants, 285
   God resurrects, 25, 111, 170
   God takes souls, 243
   innocents, 5
   Israelites, 12, 15,
   martyrs, 37
   no one can prevent, 2
   revive earth after, 208, 227, 265
   shadow of, 271
   throes of, 278
   triumph of Paradise, 43

(death, continued)
   unavoidable reality, 40, 43, 47
Dhu'l-Kifl. *See* Ezekiel
Dhu'l Qar'nayn, 153, 154
divorce, 24–25, 218, 221, 307
dowry, 25, 42, 56
drunk, 45, 170
drunkenness, 135

E

earthquake, 81–82, 85, 207, 334, 355
Elijah (Prophet Elias), 70, 235
Elisha (Prophet Al-Yasa), 70, 239
emigrants, 101–02, 218, 297, 300
emígrate, 41, 96, 138, 141, 173, 180, 221, 297
   Prophet emigrates, 375
Emigration (Hijra), 376
Enoch (Prophet Idris), 157, 168
evil, 61, 67, 97, 104, 111, 114, 116–17, 119, 121, 125–26, 139, 141–45, 152, 156–57, 166–68, 174, 178–79, 185–186, 191–92, 196–98, 219, 236, 239, 243–44, 250, 252, 296, 299, 303–04, 321, 328, 355, 370
   abode of, 38, 41, 127, 131, 248
   act, 257, 277
   against oneself, 76
   cause, 48
   change in fortune, 101
   combined with good, 101
   commit to, 14, 265, 285
   companion of, 45, 171, 260
   consequences, 50, 62, 75, 106, 305, 308
   deed(s), 43–44, 56, 60, 75, 85, 106, 115, 137–38, 167, 187, 203, 205, 209, 227, 245–46, 256, 266, 270–71, 305, 307
   evildoers, 249
   final destination, 50, 273
   hypocrisy, 10
   man supplicates for, 143
   miserly, 40
   omen, 230
   overtakes, 36,
   pardon of, 20, 29, 38, 40, 44, 52, 56, 91, 99, 256–57, 270, 295, 306
   perform(s), 32, 68, 85, 253
   plotting, 229

(evil continued)
　postulation, 273
　punishment of, 82–83, 242, 248
　repel, 126, 128, 202
　rejecting signs, 87–88
　repentance of at death, 43
　resting place, 22, 30, 41, 126, 151, 239
　reward, 106
　Satan commands, 20, 22
　Satan incited, 123
　spirits, 234
　thoughts, 273
　touches, 147, 253, 317
　trade soul for, 15
　transgressors, 95,
　upon disbelievers, 130
Ezekiel (Dhu'l-Kifl), 168, 239

F

faith, 10, 15–16, 18, 20, 34, 39–40, 44, 56, 59, 63, 90, 99, 103–104, 141, 243, 217–19
　reject, 22, 65
　true, 249, 338
faithful, 247, 249, 298, 309, 378
Farthest Mosque (Al-Aqsa Mosque), 143, 377. *See also* mosque(s)
fast(ing), 20-22, 48, 62, 220, 295
fiqh. *See* Islamic jurisprudence.
forbidden
　consuming what is, 60–61
　disbelivers' true nature, 66
　falsely consume wealth, 97
　food, 20, 55, 62, 72, 142 hunting during
　grave sins, 44
　only what God forbids, 142
　pagan practices, 74
　turn away from, 58
　usury, 28, 53
　pilgrimage, 55
　misled by caprice, 72,
　worship, to, 68, 248–49
forgiveness, 23, 28, 50, 56, 180, 325, 367
　advance evil before good, 196
　angels pray for, 255
　ask forgiveness, 249
　believers, for 29, 90, 183, 220, 230, 238, 246, 273, 276–77, 301

(forgiveness continued)
　believing women, for 301
　despite wrongdoing, 125
　disbelievers, for, 61, 100–102, 274
　exchange for punishment, 20
　faithful, for the, 31, 230
　follow hajj, 22
　God-fearing, for the, 312
　God's grace, 327
　God grants, 367
　hypocrites, for, 305
　kind words and, 27
　223, 227, 281
　martyrs, for, 38
　nothing prevents, 152
　obedience to messengers, 46
　repentance, after, 111, 114, 116, 246
　righteous, reward for, 37, 88, 111, 173, 281, 286
　seek, 91, 251
　strive for, 49, 94

G

Gabriel (Archangel), 1, 15, 309, 374. *See also* Jibril (Archangel Gabriel)
gambling, 23, 62
Gardens (Heaven/Eternity), 175, 184, 191, 196, 290
　believers, 11, 46, 50, 56, 61, 130, 171, 217, 256, 271, 302, 309, 342
　believing men and women, 99, 274, 293
　emigrants, 41, 96, 101
　faithful, 297
　forgiven, 37, 320
　obedient, 41, 43, 275
　perform patience, 126
　pray and give alms, 56
　reverent, 41, 264, 281, 283, 288
　repentant, righteous, for the 46, 61, 50, 104, 134, 254, 256, 306, 327
　those who strive, 100 truthful, , 15–16, 20, 31, 40, 47, 61, 64, 7, 63–64, 88, 103, 106, 112–113, 217
Gardens of Bliss (Jannah), 60, 104, 173, 190, 213, 234, 291, 314, 315

Garden(s) of Eden, 126, 137, 151, 157, 161, 229, 239, 246, 354
Gardens of Paradise, 154
God (Allah)
  created, 1, 5, 71, 130, 139, 182, 207, 227, 235, 256, 266, 319
  curse of, 15, 19, 33, 35, 79, 112, 179, 376
  devote religion to, 105, 241, 242, 247, 249
  earth glorifies, 292, 297–98, 301, 303, 305
  enemy of, 15, 93, 102
  fear of, 25, 67, 107, 180, 210, 260, 338
  forgiving and merciful, 32, 50, 101,137, 142, 187, 222, 252, 276
  gives or grants life and death, 27, 38, 86, 102, 107, 177, 249, 279, 285, 292
  goodly loan to, 56, 292–293, 306, 323
  guidance, 10, 12, 20–21, 28, 69–70,
  guided by, 10, 71, 141, 213, 260, 267
  guides, 23, 28, 56, 87, 106, 147, 150, 181–182, 202, 243
  honor God's rituals, 172
  Knower of Unseen and the Seen, 69,
  leads astray, 52, 88, 127, 129, 227, 243, 248, 257
  limits set by, 21, 24, 43, 102, 307
  messenger of, 52–53, 99–100, 219–221, 271, 275–76, 301, 304
  obey, 32, 37, 46, 62, 90–92, 182, 220, 271, 277, 296, 305, 309
  revere, 24, 33, 41, 56, 62, 91, 93, 276, 296
  retribution, 19–22, 30, 55, 59, 76, 87, 91–93, 125, 132, 194, 211, 243, 246–47, 253, 257, 270, 297
  rope of God, 35
  severe in punishment, 19, 48, 101–02, 125, 178, 216, 298, 303, 306
  sustenance, 11,13, 31, 111, 206, 255, 362
  wills, 13, 58, 72– 73, 88, 107, 123, 150–52, 197, 244, 275, 326, 329
God and His Messenger(s),
  believe(s) in, 40, 51–53, 86, 183, 219–20, 222, 273–74, 276–77, 292–93, 295, 301, 305
  defy, 297
  disbelieve in, 52, 97–98, 100, 274

(God and his messengers continued)
  disobey(s), 43, 220, 322
  emigrating to (with), 49, 297
  obey(s), 43, 90–92, 99, 182, 274, 296
  offend, 221
  oppose, 295–96
  priotize devotion to, 96
  protector is, 59
  repudiation from, 95
  repent to, 100
  revere, 28
  sincere toward, 102
  wage war against, 58
God and the Last Day, 36, 101, 179
  believers, 13, 17, 20, 24, 46, 53, 60, 96, 98, 296, 307
  hope for, 219, 299
  hypocrites, 10
  unbelievers, 45, 97, 98
God's will, 15, 26, 58. *See also* God: wills.
Gog and Magog (Yājūj and Mājūj), 154, 168
gold, 31, 35, 97
gold ornaments, 147, 260
golden calf, 12, 15, 52, 85, 115, 162
Goliath, 26
good deeds, 18, 117, 193, 229
  combined with evil, 101
  perform, 158, 167–68, 187
  quick to do, 36, 177
  soul review, 32
Gospel, 294
  believers' likeness in, 275
  God taught, 63
  guidance, 59
  People of, 59
  practice, 60
  promise binding in, 102
  prophet inscribed in, 86
  sent down, 30, 33
gratitude (to God)
  does not show, 77, 107, 216
  offer, 91, 224,
  ingratitude, 131, 168
  show(s), 36, 62, 129, 136, 140, 195
Great City. *See* Mecca (Makkah)

H

hajj, 19, 21–22, 171. *See also* pilgrimage
ḥanīf, 17, 33, 35, 51, 76, 110, 142
hardship, 37, 67, 82, 276
    created man in, 346
    grant ease, relief after, 308, 348, 35
    patience in, 20
Heavenly Book (Al-Kitab), 1.
    See also Book (the)
Heavenly Tablet (Lawh Mahfouz), 1.
    See also Book (the)
Heaven(s)
    seven heavens, 11, 145, 177, 251, 308, 311, 319, 377
    heavens and earth, 11
    dominion over, 16
    forces of, 273
    keys of, 244, 255
    Lord of, 126, 148–49, 157, 167, 188, 233, 239, 262–63, 266, 332
    Originator of, 16, 66, 71, 123, 129, 227, 243, 255
    sovereignty over, 40, 57–58, 64, 86, 102, 181, 184, 243, 257, 266, 274, 292, 341
    to God belongs, 29, 36–37, 40, 51, 53, 57–58, 107, 140, 181, 183, 214, 266, 274, 285, 304
    Unseen of, 11, 140, 150, 277
Hell, 186, 345
    abode for the arrogant, 244, 249, 265
    created for men and jinn, 87, 117, 216
    evil resting place, 22, 39, 87, 126
    deniers, 291, 293,
    deny (disobey) the Messenger, 185, 296, 315, 322–323
    disbelievers, 38, 41, 46, 52, 92, 98, 130, 143, 154, 185, 208, 244, 259, 311, 354
    fire (hellfire) 97, 99, 102, 190, 229, 234, 236, 334, 337–39, 358
    follow Satan, 50, 146, 173, 232,
    gates of, 134, 137, 234, 249
    guilty, 261, 289
    hypocrites, 52, 99–101
    God protects from hellfire, 246, 264, 282

    inferno, 46
(Hell continued)
    ingratitude, 131
    inhabitants/inmates of, 56, 61, 248
    on Day of Division, 233
    on Day of Reckoning, 239
    penalty of fire, 49, 88
    persecution of believers, 341
    rebellion, 352
    Saqar, 287, 325–26
    set up god with God, 145, 166
    Sijjin, 339
    sinner, 264,
    unjust, 321
    wrongdoers, 157, 178
helpers, 33, 101–102, 210, 302, 322
    deniers have no, 138
    disbelievers have no, 31, 33, 35
    idolators have no, 206
    those astray have no, 210
    wrongdoers have no, 28, 40, 61, 174, 229
Holy Quran, 6–7, 428
Holy Spirit, 14, 26, 63, 141
homes, 33
    covenant concerning, 14
    place of rest, 140
    proper entry, 14, 21
    those who emigrated, of 41
Home of Peace (Dar al-Salaam), 106. *See also* Paradise; straight path.
Hour (the), 67, 88, 124, 135, 140, 150–51, 158, 167, 170, 173, 184, 209, 211, 215, 222, 223, 248, 249, 253, 256, 261–62, 266, 271, 286–87, 334. *See also* Day of Judgment
Hŭd (Prophet)
    Ādites disobey messenger, 114, 116
    God's mercy extended to, 114
humanity, 1–2, 22, 26, 43, 55, 201, 333
humiliate, 99, 109, 156, 278
humiliation, 14, 85, 158, 170, 278, 356, 361
humility, 158, 165, 170, 217, 227, 378
    complete, 158
husbands, 24, 180, 310
hypocrisy, 116–17
hypocrites, 45, 56, 60, 107, 114–15, 117, 234, 248–49, 251–52, 346, 351–352

I

Iblīs (Shayṭān)
  God allows to test faith, 190, 224, 239
  refuses to prostrate, 11, 77, 134, 146, 152, 163, 239
Iddat 251. *See* divorce
idolaters, 39, 41, 77, 109, 207, 342, 400
idols, 31, 53, 72, 81, 98, 150, 182, 192, 198, 235, 421, 423
Idrīs, 181, 193
Imrān, 37
indecency, 140, 180, 220, 307
  commit, 196, 206
  brazen, 250
  flagrant, 51, 349
inheritance, 40, 292, 345
intoxicants, 62
Isaac (Prophet Ishaq), 115, 131, 157, 167, 206, 235
Ishmael (Prophet Ismael), 70
  Abraham's gratitude for, 131
  belief in all prophets, 34, 53, 70, 239
  God's covenant with, 17–18
Islam (submission), 2, 3, 5, 7–8, 375–76, 378. *See also* Islām
Islām, 31, 35, 55
Islamic jurisprudence, 6
Islamic principles, 378

J

Jabal al-Hira (Mount Hira). *See* Cave of Hira
Jacob (Prophet Ya'qūb), 17–18. *See also* Tribes
  continuity of prophets, 20, 53, 70, 239
  divine knowledge of, 122
  House of Jacob, 118
  prophecy to Sarah, 115
  reward to Abraham, 157, 167, 206
  submit unto God, 17, 34, 120
Jahiliya. *See* Age of Ignorance
Jannah. *See* Gardens of Bliss
Jesus (Prophet Isā)
  angels reveal Unseen to Mary, 32–33
  Children of Israel, disbelievers 61, 302
  disavows divinity and sonship, 64
  emphasizes faith, 63–64

(Jesus continued)
  faith in all prophets, 255
  given clear signs, 14, 26, 261
  God affirms Jesus as prophet, 156
  God bestows blessings upon, 63
  God gave Gospel to, 59, 264
  Islam recognizes all prophets, 17, 34, 53, 70
  Islam refutes crucifixion, 53
  reveals future messenger, 301, 373
Jethro (Prophet Shu'ayb), 82, 99, 115-16, 192, 207
Jews, 13
Jibril (Archangel Gabriel), 1. *See* Gabriel
jinn, 71–73, 79, 87, 117, 134, 147, 152, 195, 216, 224–225, 236, 252, 268–69, 281, 288–89, 321, 370
  ifrit (rebel jinn), 195
Job (Prophet Ayūb), 53, 70, 168, 238
John the Baptist (Prophet Yahya), 32, 70, 155
Jonah (Prophet Yūnus), 53, 70, 109, 235
Joseph (ProphetYusuf), 82, 118–123, 136–38, 138–42, 283
Judaism, 303
judgment. *See also* Day of Judgment
  messenger for every nation, 107
  ultimate judge, 72, 82, 110, 127–28, 150, 190, 197, 204, 246–47, 256, 300, 351
justice
  fate of commiting injustice, 193
  God commands justice, 140, 256, 293
  judgment with justice, 46, 58, 107, 169
  settling believer conflicts, 276
  truth and, 72, 87,
  ultimate insight, 31, 167
  uphold justice, 51

K

Ka'ba (Bayt al-Atiq–Ancient House), 35, 62, 78, 376, 394. *See also* mosque: Sacred House; mosque: Al Masjid Al Haram
kerchiefs (khimar), 180, 209
Khadija (bint Khuwaylid), 374
Khattab, Omar ibn. *See* Prophet Muhammad
kindness, 23, 28, 49, 51, 58, 236, 409

kinsfolk, 16, 23, 26, 49, 52, 60, 106, 160, 208
kinship, 109–10, 205, 271
knowledge
  dispute without, 170, 214
  God's knowledge (of all things), 11, 29, 62, 102, 181, 221, 305
  pursuit of, 377
  those rooted in, 30, 53

L

Last Day, 1
  believers and the, 13, 17, 20, 36, 46, 53, 60, 96, 98, 101, 219, 296, 299, 307
  disbelievers and the, 10, 17, 27, 45, 51, 97, 98, 179, 207, 296
Lawful (halal), 51, 64, 19, 24, 35, 43–44, 53, 55, 61, 62, 86, 107, 141-2, 93, 97, 221, 300, 309
Lawh Mahfouz (Heavenly Tablet), 1.
livelihood, 152, 296, 329, 376
livestock, 36, 59, 86, 102, 122, 155–56, 159, 198, 202
losers
  breaking God's covenant, 11
  deny signs, 109
  disbelievers, 13, 35, 56, 112, 207
  fabricate lies, 250
  greatest, 154
love
  giving, 35
  of believers by God, 21, 32, 37, 38, 39, 56, 58, 59, 62, 95, 102, 158, 276, 300, 301
  of God by believers, 19, 20, 32, 34, 59
  of disbelievers, 36
  of worldly pleasures, 31
Lot (Prophet Lūt), 70, 115, 134, 167, 172, 191, 196, 206, 235, 237, 278, 287, 309
lump of flesh, 170, 175. *See also* blood clot; semen, drop of
Luqmān, 213

M

Makkah (Mecca), 274. *See* Mecca
mankind
  creation of, 1, 197,
  guide to, 30
  Lord of, 370

(mankind continued)
  reminder for, 325
manna, 12, 86, 161
Mary (Maryam), 32, 52–53, 155–156, 176, 310
  son of Mary, 14, 26, 32, 53, 56–57, 59, 61, 63–64, 97, 156, 176, 261, 294, 301–02, 373
marriage, 25, 44, 186
married women, 51, 65
marry, 23, 43–44, 51, 179, 181, 221, 300
  remarry 24, 43
mates, 5, 49, 139, 210, 255
menstruation, 23, 24
Mecca (Makkah), 373–377, 380
men
  believing, 179, 273–74, 320
  bewitched, 184
  good, 180
  hypocritical, 222, 273, 292
  wicked, 180
Messiah, 32, 53, 56–57, 61, 97l. *See also* Jesus (Prophet Isā)
Michael (Archangel), 15
Middle (prayer), 25
Midian, 99, 172
  Jethro (Shu'ayb,) 82, 115–16, 207
  Moses (Prophet Musa), 160, 172, 200–01
milk-mother(s), 44
milk-sisters, 44,
miserly, 40, 45, 100, 272, 293, 348
monasticism, 294
Moses (Prophet Musa), 12–17
  Book of Moses, 112, 117, 267, 269. *See also* Book (the), People of the Book.
  Children of Israel, and 25–26, 57, 301
  clear signs, 116, 129
  confrontation with Pharoah, 108–09, 334
  consequence of rejecting messengers, 281
  divine guidance of tablets, 85
  God addresses directly, 53
  People of the Book, and 52
  scriptures of Abraham and Moses, 285, 343
  tablets, 85
mosque(s), 16, 21, 96, 172
  Al Masjid Al Haram (Ka'ba), 35

(mosque(s) continued)
    Farthest Mosque (Al-Aqsa), 143, 377
    First Mosque (Masjid al-Taqwa), 378
    Grand Mosque (Masjid al-Haram), 35.
    Ka'ba (Sacred Mosque), 18, 21–22, 23, 35, 55, 62, 78, 95, 96, 143, 171, 274, 377
    Quba Mosque (Masjid al-Taqwa), 376
Most Beautiful Names, 87, 148. 159, 298
Mother of Cities (Makkah), 70, 255
Mother of the Book, 147
mothers, 24, 44, 140, 183, 199, 218, 285, 295
Mount Sinai, 175, 351
Muhammad (Prophet Ahmad), 1–3, 6, 37, 373–78
    boycott of, 375
    characteristics of, 275
    faith and deeds, 270
    family of, 373
    Jesus (Isā) prophecy of, 373–74
    illiteracy of, 374
    marriage to Khadija bint Khuwaylid, 374
    mortality of messengers, 37
    Quraish assassination plot, 375
    true status of, 220
murder
    retribution for, 20
    value of single life, 57
Muslim, 17, 33, 63, 202, 211, 220, 376, 378
Muslims, 1, 6, 63, 109, 112, 133, 169, 174, 196, 197, 261, 314, 376–78, 379–80

N

Night of Power (Laylat al-Qadr), 353. *See also* Ramadan
Noah (Prophet Nūh), 80–81, 108, 112–13, 116, 129, 190,
    continuity of Divine covenant, 32, 53, 70, 157, 218, 255, 293
    divine justice for deniers, 144, 172, 185, 237, 246–47, 278, 281, 285, 286, 319–20
    God's response to distress, 168, 234
    gratitude to God, 143
    messengers' clear signs to, 99, 175,
    perseverance of, 205 wife of, 309

O

oath(s)
    broken, 59
    contradicting piety, 24
    disbelievers, 138
    fulfill pledges, 140–41
    guided by warner, 182
    God's ultimate judgment, 229, 314
    God's signs, 71–72
    honest testimony, 63
    hypocrisy in, 296, 304
    lawful breaking of, 309
    objectives of, 95–96
    Quran as divine oath, 291
    reflect upon, 345
    true righteousness, 20
    unintentional, 62
    solemn, 72, 157, 210, 260
Omar ibn Khattab, 375. *See also* Muhammad: Quraish assassination plot
orphans
    deal justly with, 42
    distribution of wealth to, 92, 297
    kindness to, 45
    property of, 42, 75
    uphold justice for, 51

P

pairs
    fruit and crops, 125, 278
    God created humans in, 227, 258
    heavens and earth, 165
    night and day, 19, 40, 104, 131, 136, 166, 177, 203
    pairs of all things, 281, 332
    sun and moon, 125, 166
parables, 114, 118, 126, 130, 131, 139, 181, 185, 207
Paradise, 178, 202, 352. *See also* Home of Peace
parents
    be good (kind) to, 51, 75, 205, 268
    gratitude to God for, 268
    give thanks to, 213
    inheritance from, 44

(parents continued)
   share wealth with, 32, 42–43,14, 20, 23
   42–45, 78, 123, 131, 144, 153, 155, 135,
   213, 268, 320
partners (with God)
   attribute partners to God (Shirk), 45–
   46, 61, 88
   attribute what is not known, 79
   consequences of attributing partners
   to God, 38, 50, 106
   rejection of false gods, 106, 108
   God exalted above all, 88, 97, 136, 178,
   197
   oneness of God, 66
   paradox of distress, 67
   return solely to God, 71
   ultimate judge and witness, 68-69
peace, 1, 22, 377
   abode of the reverent, 137,
   everlasting, 157
   forgiveness, 262
   God guides to, 24, 56, 93, 104, 160, 202,
   232, 298
   invoke upon prophets, 221, 236
   making peace or war, 48–49, 276
   on Day of Resurrection, 79, 245, 279,
   290-91, 345
   on Night of Power (Laylat al-Qadr),
   353
   repentance for, 68
   reward for faith, 126–27, 130, 141, 220
   safety and security of, 134
   steadfast in, 272
   true servants of, 186–87
   victory from God, as, 90
People of the Book, 18, 36, 39–40, 41–42,
   48, 59, 61–62, 66, 70–71, 236, 250, 333,
   337–38, 400
People of the House, 132, 250
Pharaoh, 84, 93, 116, 199, 201, 247–48, 310,
   315
pilgrimage, 22, 35, 41
Pilgrimage (hajj), 19, 22, 35, 95
prayer
   congregational, 303
   establish prayer, 172, 174, 354,
   disbelievers and hypocrites, 92, 98, 363
   distractions from, 60

(prayer continued)
   for God, 75
   guard, 25
   how to recite, 49, 148, 182, 207, 323
   humble in, 175
   keep vigil in, 147
   maintain, 28
   mindful of, 70
   practice/perform, 10, 12, 14, 20, 52–53,
   69, 87, 96, 99, 117, 126, 131, 147, 172,
   181, 194, 210, 213, 220, 257, 317
   protectors of, 59–60,
   purification before, 56
   repent and practice prayer, 95, 101,
   sanctity of, 45,
   seek help in, 12, 16, 19
   shortening prayers, 45,
   station of Abraham in, 17, 35
Prophet Muhammad (Ahmad). *See*
   Muhammad (Prophet Ahmad)
prostrate
   before the Compassionate, 186, 288
   bow, worship and, 17, 32, 174
   good news to those who, 102
   recite revelations and, 36.
   to God, 89, 126, 138, 171, 253, 285, 329
prostrations, 49, 279
Psalms, *see* David (Prophet Dāwud)
purify, 228
   before Day of Resurrection, 325
   before prayer, 56
   Book and Wisdom, 17
   for Hajj, 171
   God loves those who, 102
   God will not purify wrongdoers, 20,
   34, 37, 58,
   repent and purify self, 24
   through generosity, 348
   truth transforms, 336

Q

Qarūn, 203, 207
qiblah, 18
Quran, 1–8
   clear, 265
   Divine Tablet, 341
   glorious, 316, 387

(Quran continued)
   Mighty, 154
   Noble, 329
   non-Arabic, 289
   sent down, 21
   Wise Book, 213
Quranic exegesis, 2, 3, 6, 377
Quraysh, 362

R

Ramadan, 21
ransom, 12, 14, 17, 20, 21, 58, 69, 99, 107, 126, 235, 270, 293
remembrance,
   divert from, 304
   forget, 296
   of God, 22, 52, 62, 127, 150, 154, 181, 207, 242, 293, 303
   of God's signs, 108,
   of reverence, 69
reverence,
   oaths of, 24
   best of provisions, 22,
   God tests for, 276
   help one another toward,
   revere God, 35, 56, 296, 326, 352
righteousness, 211
   affirming, 36
   believers work, 60, 141, 153, 178, 195, 216, 220, 223, 225, 227, 238, 305, 308
   command righteousness, 88
   disbelievers stray from, 56,
   God guides toward, 150
   perform(s), 13, 157, 161, 176, 252
   speak only, 145
rituals, 19, 172
riven asunder, 185
   when heavens are, 255,
   when moon is, 286–87
   when sky is, 315, 323, 330, 338, 340

S

Saba (Sheba), 223–24
Sabbath, 13, 45, 52, 86, 142
   Sabbath breakers, 45
   Sabbath do not transgress, 61
   sacred months, 109

(Sabbath continued)
   salvation, 283
Samaritan, 187
sanctuary, 17, 202, 208, 374
Satan
   betrays, 130
   clear enemy, 20, 74, 227, 261
   causes forgetfulness, 69, 152
   clear enemy, 118, 145, 200
   confounds, 28
   cunning is weak, 47
   deceives, 185, 296
   desires enmity and hatred, 62
   disbelievers' companion, 45, 48
   disobedient, 156
   divining arrows, 62
   enjoins indecency, 180
   fight allies of, 47
   God removes influence of, 90, 173
   hardens hearts, 67
   in Garden of Eden, 78
   instills fear, 39
   leads astray, 50, 87, 139, 195, 207, 214
   party of, 296
   promises delusion, 50
   provokes dissent, 145
   seduces, 271
   seek protection from, 141
   seek refuge in God from, 253
   tempts, 88, 92, 253
   threatens, 28
   turns from straight path, 261
   turned back believers at Uhud, 38
   ungrateful to God, 144
Saqar, 287, 325–26. *See also* hell
Saul, 29–30
schism, 18, 20, 90, 173, 237, 254
scribes, 336
scriptures,
   Abraham and Moses, 343
   messengers and believers, 29
   clear signs from, 40, 138, 164, 228
   challenge disbelievers, 51
   everything small and great inscribed, 287
   in clear Arabic, 192
   Muhammad's knowledge of, 373
   purified, 354

security, 44, 56, 82, 104, 117, 153–54, 313
semen, drop of, 136, 151, 170, 175, 227, 232, 249, 285, 327, 328, 336
Shu'ayb (Prophet Shuaib), 82, 115–16, 192, 207. *See also* Jethro (Prophet Shu'ayb).
Sijjīn, 339. *See also* hell.
sins, 12, 14, 30–32, 37–38, 41, 44, 57, 59, 65, 244, 246–247, 269, 273, 301, 309, 313, 319
   clear, 51, 252
   grave, 52
   great, 27, 49, 166, 329
   oncoming, 311
   practiced, 101
   renounce, 85
   unjustifiable, 92
Solomon (Prophet Suleiman), 15, 53, 70, 168, 194–96, 223, 238
sorcerers, 83, 108, 161, 189
sorcery, 15, 63, 65, 83, 108, 111, 160–61, 165, 189, 194, 201, 225, 233, 267, 282, 286, 301, 325, 374
sovereignty
   God grants, 31, 40
   God seizes, 31
   granted to David, 26, 237
   granted to Abraham, 27
   no partner in sovereignity, 148
   on all occasions, 69, 173, 247
   over heaven and earth, 57, 58, 64, 102, 181, 184–85, 241, 257, 262, 266, 274, 292
   powerful over all things, 305
   sign of God's, 26,
   to God belongs, 40, 57, 228, 237
speech
   avoid false, 172
   avoid vain, 175
   conveying truth, 252
   complaisant, 220
   disbelievers' words, 108, 232, 325
   focused, 323,
   God knows all, 311
   hypocritical, 22, 271, 304
   of messenger, 316, 337
   pure, 171
   sinful, 60
   well-founded, 130–31
spider, 207, 375

straight path
   God guides on, 9, 18, 23, 35, 45, 54, 56, 67, 70, 75, 106, 114, 142, 164, 173, 177, 182, 235, 258, 273–74
   revere God and obey, 33
   parable of two men, 139
   Satan lies in ambush on, 77
   strayed from, 299
   walks upright on, 312
sūrah, 11, 99, 100, 103, 106, 112, 179, 271

T

Tablet, Preserved, 341
Tablets (Moses), 85
temptation, 103, 112, 205, 289
testimony, 20, 33, 73–74, 77, 207, 349, 359, 370
Thamūd, 95, 114, 199, 215, 220, 225, 236, 272, 283, 288, 319, 323–24, 357, 387–91, 393
Torah, 35, 38, 39, 41, 68, 70, 74, 100, 117, 313, 342–44, 420
torment, 14, 100, 217, 254, 337
transgressors
   disobedience, 13,
   final retribution, 194
   forget God, 298,
   God does not like/love, 21, 61, 80,
   God knows best, 72,
   hypocrisy, 105
   inventing lies against God, 35,
   lament of, 165-168
   no respect for faith, 95
   penalty of fire, 91, 248,
   renounce sin, 72
   seal on hearts, 108,
   skepticism toward messenger, 184,
   unlawful sexual relations, 175
   uphold moral boundaries, 317
tree(s)
   date palm, 28, 7, 74, 125, 146, 139, 147, 151, 156, 175, 191, 231, 278, 289,
   forbidden, 1, 11, 78
   green, 232
   lote, 224
   Lote (Sidrat al-Muntaha), 284, 377
   olive, 181

(tree(s) continued)
    336 tamarisk, 224
Tree of Eternity, 163
Tribes, the (descent from Jacob), 17, 18, 34, 53
triumph, 210, 279, 376
    great, 43, 47, 64, 222, 234, 246, 264 273, 292, 301, 305
    supreme, 341
trumpet
    Day of Division, 332
    Day of Judgment, 69, 197
    Day of Resurrection, 154, 162, 178, 278
    difficult day for disbelievers, 325
    initial blast, 244, 315
    second blast, 231, 244
Truth, 69, 110, 117, 214, 218, 284, 287, 293
    Manifest Truth, 180
    Religion of Truth, 97, 275, 301
Tuwā, sacred valley of, 184

U

Uhud, Battle of, 376, 380
Ummah, 375–76, 378
Umrah, 19. *See also* pilgrimage
Unseen
    believers in, 10
    unto God belongs, 140, 150
    knower of, 178, 197, 216, 223, 226, 229
    Unseen Lord, 228
upright, 17, 26, 36, 70, 75, 97, 120, 142, 143, 149, 153, 167, 172
    religion, 210
    Muslim, 20
usury, 28, 37, 53, 211. *See also* forbidden

V

victory, 59, 66, 91, 273–275, 292. *See also* Day of Victory
    with God's forgiveness, 273
    with God's help, 90, 99–102, 108, 366
    for believers, 274–75, 292, 301
    over disbelivers–hypocrites, 14, 52, 96, 130
    virtuous
    consequence of denial, disbelief, or evil, 143, 154, 280

(victory continued)
    God created for, 111
    God's blessing for, 16, 39, 56, 101, 106, 117, 142, 243, 285
    obey (submit), 47, 51, 126
    with parents, 144

W

war, 378
    against believers 48
    against God, 58, 102
    God extinguishes flame of, 60
    with disbelievers, 270
warners
    messengers sent as, 68, 285
    Muhammad sent as, 192
    reminder of divine justice, 192
    warnings. *See also* warners.
    sent prophets and, 16, 23, 53, 57, 152
    to disbelievers, 109, 286–87
wasteful, 74, 78, 144
wealth
    allocation of, 297
    believers tried with, 19, 40, 177, 272
    danger of arrogance, 151, 225
    distraction of, 304, 319
    do not consume another's, 24
    futility of, 367
    influence by corrupt people, 313
    God's metaphorical transaction, 102
    God saves from greediness, 319
    holds no value with God, 190, 315
    hypocritical spending, 45, 100, 346
    leadership not determined by, 26
    manage properly, 42
    migrate and strive with, 94, 96, 98, 301
    of disbelievers, 30, 36, 92, 158, 296
    pious give of, 20,
    prohibition of usury, 28, 53, 211
    provide according to means, 307
    purify through charity, 23, 317
    role within marriage, 44
    spend and strive in way of God, 27, 277
    spend to purify, 348
    transitory nature of, 151, 293

(wealth continued)
   warning against excessive accumulation, 348, 360
   warning against hoarding and corruption, 97, 348
   warning against worldly desire, 99
   will not benefit at death, 348
widows, 28
wives, 21, 24, 25, 44, 74, 127, 218-222, 295, 300, 307, 309
woman, 6, 27, 50, 160
   nursing, 196
   old, 132, 221, 270
   religious equals of men, 5
   pregnant, 196
   woman ruling, 224
women
   abstain from during menses, 23–24, 307
   believing, 5, 44, 99, 180, 221–22, 271, 300, 341
   bridewealth, 221
   charitable, 250
   chaste, 55–56, 179–80
   commit indecency, 43
   concealing ornament, 180–81, 183, 222
   devout, 250
   disbelieving, 300, 340
   divorce, 221, 307
   divorced, 24–25
   dowry, 42
   emigrants, 300
   engagement to, 25
   free, 51
   good, 208
   humble, 250
   hypocritical, 253, 311
   idolatrous, 222, 253, 311
   paramours, 44, 56
   polygamy, 42, 51

(women, continued)
   prohibited for marriage, 43–44
   religious equals, 5
   righteous, 44, 52
   ten virtues, 220
   tilth, 24
   truthful, 250
   unbelieving women, 23
   wicked, 180, 208
   witnesses in trade transaction, 29
   women deriding other women, 276, 315
   women standing, 229
   women's rights, 6
work, 41, 106, 108, 154, 350
   Satan's work, 62, 200
   work corruption, 115, 126–27, 196
   work(s) righteousness, 60, 113, 153, 195, 200, 202, 211, 216, 220, 223, 225, 227, 238, 305, 308
   Work of God, 198
worship, 1, 9, 11, 362, 365, 376
   worship God, 14, 20, 22, 45, 61, 64, 80–82, 109, 114–15, 127, 138, 175–76, 241–42, 244, 299, 319
   faltering in belief, 170–71, wrongdoers
   regarding quiblah, 18
   transgression of God's limits, 24
   worshipping equals to God, 19

Z

Zachariah (Prophet Zakariyyā), 70, 155
   God entrusts care of Maryam to, 32
   humility and faith of, 168
Zaqqūm, tree of, 234, 264, 291
   accursed tree, 146
zihār, 218, 295. *See also* divorce

Northville, Michigan